How to Create Champions
The Theory and Methodology of Training Top-Class Gymnasts

L. I. Arkaev & N. G. Suchilin

How to Create Champions

The Theory and Methodology of Training Top-Class Gymnasts

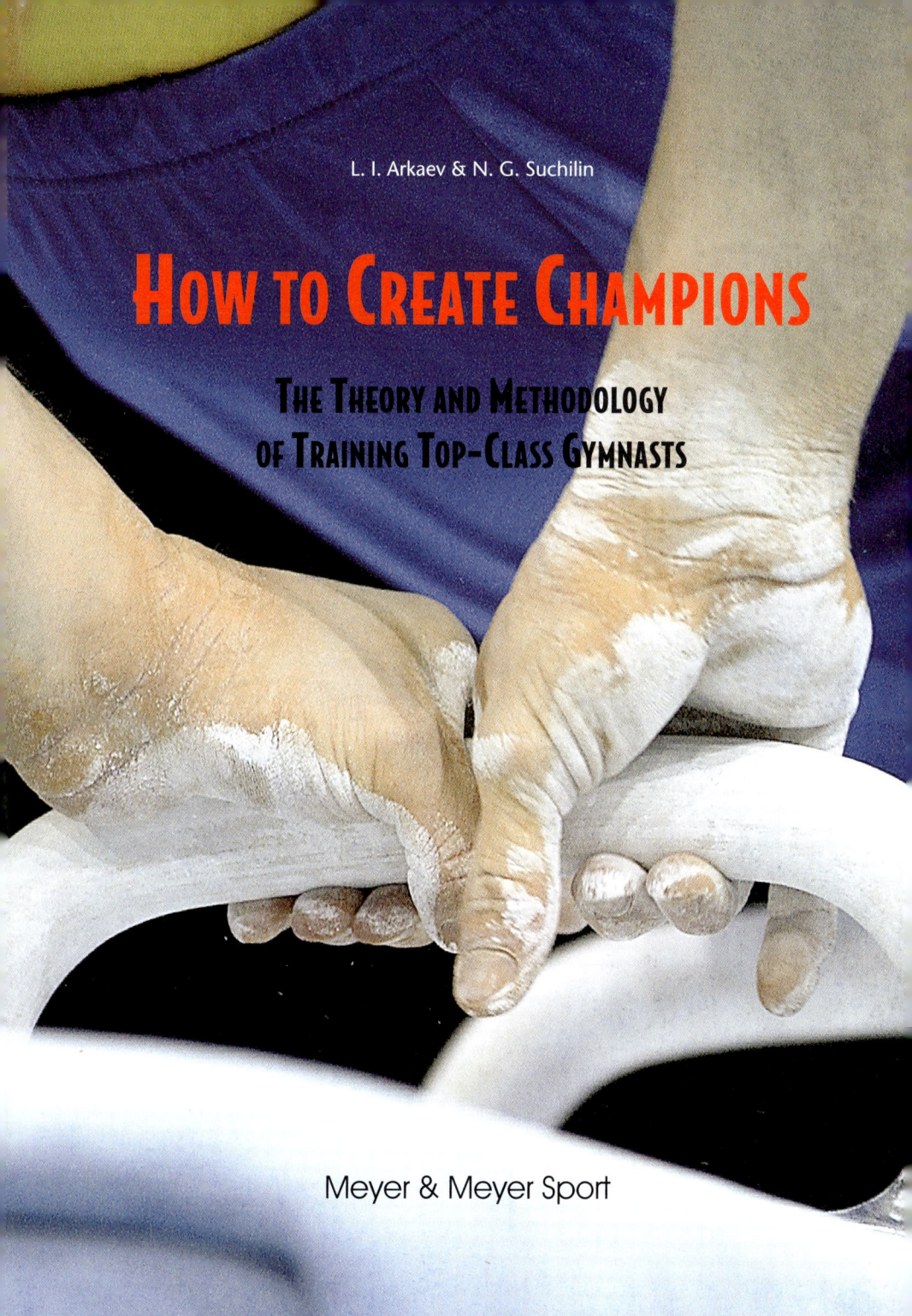

Meyer & Meyer Sport

Original title:

Kak gotovit chempionov
Teoria i technologia podgotovki
gimnastov vysshey kwalifikacii
©Fizkultura i Sport, Moscow, 2003

Translated by James Riorden
Technical Translation: Vera Atkinson

British Library Cataloguing in Publication Data
A catalogue record for this book is available from the British Library

L. I. Arkaev & N. G. Suchilin:
How to Create Champions
The Theory and Methodology of Training Top-Class Gymnasts
Oxford: Meyer & Meyer Sport (UK) Ltd., 2004
ISBN 1-84126-141-6

All rights reserved, especially the right to copy and distribute,
including the translation rights. No part of this work may be reproduced –
including by photocopy, microfilm or any other means –
processed, stored electronically, copied or distributed in any form whatsoever
without the written permission of the publisher.

© 2004 by Meyer & Meyer Sport (UK) Ltd.
Aachen, Adelaide, Auckland, Budapest, Graz, Johannesburg,
Miami, Olten (CH), Oxford, Singapore, Toronto
Member of the World
Sports Publishers' Association (WSPA)
www.w-s-p-a.org
Printed and bound by: FINIDR, s. r. o., Český Těšín
ISBN 1-84126-141-6
E-Mail: verlag@m-m-sports.com
www.m-m-sports.com

Contents

Introduction 11

Chapter 1 **Characteristics of Gymnastics** 15
    1.1   A Short History 15
    1.2   Characteristics of Gymnastics 30
    1.3   Specifics of the Contemporary Stage 36
    1.4   Trends 38
    1.5   Forecasts and Prospects 42
    1.6   Rules of Competition 47

Chapter 2 **Methodological Basis of Preparation Technique** 55
    2.1   Methodological Basis 55
    2.2   The Concept of Preparation 67
    2.3   Methodological Principles of Preparation 79
    2.4   Similarities and Differences in Preparing
           Men and Women Gymnasts 81

Chapter 3 **Preparation Modelling** 85
    3.1   Models and Model Characteristics 85
    3.2   Modelling Competitive Activity 91
    3.3   Sports-Goal Prospective-Forecasting Models 97
           3.3.1   Normative Forecasting Model 97
           3.3.2   Model Characteristics of Competitive Activity ... 99
           3.3.3   Model Characteristics of Olympic Champions .. 100
                 3.3.3.1   Winning Team Model 100
                 3.3.3.2   Model of Absolute Olympic Champion .. 101
                 3.3.3.3   Model of Olympic Champion
                             in the Multi-events 101
           3.3.4   Forecast Model of Sporting-technical
                 Achievements 101
           3.3.5   Technical Preparedness Model 109
           3.3.6   Model of Special Physical Preparedness (SPP) .. 109
           3.3.7   Functional Preparedness Model 112
           3.3.8   Psychological Preparedness Model 113
           3.3.9   Selection Model for the National Team 114

		3.3.10	Pre-competition Preparation Stage Model..... 115
		3.3.11	Competition Preparation Model 117
		3.3.12	Competition Micro-cycles Model............ 119
		3.3.13	Goal Exercise Models 120
		3.3.14	Model for Elaborating and Directing the Preparation Programme................. 122

Chapter 4 Integrated Preparation System 123

- 4.1 Ways and Means of Preparation 123
  - 4.1.1 Ways of Preparation 123
  - 4.1.2 Means of Preparation 124
- 4.2 Technical Preparation 125
  - 4.2.1 Sports Technique and Technical Skill 125
  - 4.2.2 Conception of Technical Preparation......... 130
  - 4.2.3 Basic Technical Preparation 134
- 4.3 Physical Training 138
  - 4.3.1 Physical Qualities 138
  - 4.3.2 Physical Preparation Conception 145
  - 4.3.3 Special Physical Preparation................ 148
    - 4.3.3.1 Morning SPP Training Session 148
    - 4.3.3.2 SPP at the End of the Training Session 148
    - 4.3.3.3 Circuit SPP Training 149
- 4.4 Tactical Preparation............................. 152
- 4.5 Psychological Preparation........................ 153
- 4.6 Functional Preparation 155
- 4.7 Theoretical Preparation.......................... 156
- 4.8 Various Forms of Preparation 157
  - 4.8.1 Basic Preparation 157
  - 4.8.2 Rotational Preparation 158
  - 4.8.3 Combined Preparation..................... 159
    - 4.8.3.1 Basic Combined Technical-physical Preparation..................... 159
    - 4.8.3.2 Basic Combined Functional-rotational Preparation..................... 162
  - 4.8.4 Jump Preparation 162
  - 4.8.5 Acrobatic Preparation..................... 163
  - 4.8.6 Choreographic Preparation 164

		4.8.7	Centralised Preparation 165
		4.8.8	Altitude Preparation 166
		4.8.9	Pharmacological Preparation 167
		4.8.10	Pre-competition Preparation 167
		4.8.11	Competition Preparation 167

Chapter 5 Planning and Projecting Preparation 171

5.1 Methodics Basis 171
5.2 Training Load Structure 172
    5.2.1 Training Load Indicators. 173
    5.2.2 Basic Training load Parameters. 174
5.3 Structure of Olympic Cycle of Training. 175
5.4 Structure of Macro- and Mezzo-cycles 176
5.5 Structure of Training Micro-cycles 177
5.6 Structure of Training Day 181
5.7 Structure of Training Sessions. 182
    5.7.1 First Training Session 183
    5.7.2 Second Training Session 192
    5.7.3 Third Training Session. 192
    5.7.4 Characteristic Features of the
           Preparatory Part 193
           5.7.4.1 Main Tasks 193
           5.7.4.2 Warming up before Basic Training . . . 194
           5.7.4.3 Warm up before Auxiliary
                    Training Sessions. 207
5.8 Structure of the Pre-competition Training Stage 208

Chapter 6 Biomechanical Basis of Technique 219

6.1 Main Concepts and Terms 219
6.2 Movements in Support Position 234
    6.2.1 General Laws 234
    6.2.2 Exercises on the Parallel Bars 252
    6.2.3 Exercises on the Rings. 257
    6.2.4 Exercises on the Asymmetric Bars. 261
    6.2.5 Exercises on the Beam 261
6.3 Movement in Flight 262
    6.3.1 Basic Parameters of Flight. 262
    6.3.2 Projectile Movement 263

		6.3.3	Rotating Movement 264
			6.3.3.1 Simple Rotating Movement 265
			6.3.3.2 Complex Rotating Movement 269
			6.3.3.2.1 First Means of Forming a Complex Rotation 270
			6.3.3.2.2 Second Means of Forming a Complex Rotation 274
			6.3.3.2.3 Third Means of Forming a Complex Rotation 279
	6.4	Landing.. 283
	6.5	Complexity and Difficulty of Gymnastic Exercises 290
	6.6	Laws of Growth in Complexity.................... 291

Chapter 7 — Structure of Gymnastics Exercises 297

7.1	Methods of Technique Analysis 297
7.2	Technical Structure of Exercises 298
7.3	Structure of Technical Faults...................... 307
7.4	Control and Evaluation of Technique 312
7.5	Methods of Pedagogical-biomechanical Analysis of Technique 318
7.6	Structure of Self-control 321

Chapter 8 — Basic and Strategic High Level Elements 327

8.1	Universal Basic Habits of General Designation 327
8.2	General Premises 327
8.3	Men 330
	8.3.1 Floor Exercise 330
	8.3.2 Pommel Horse 333
	8.3.3 Rings................................... 336
	8.3.4 Vault 340
	8.3.5 Parallel Bars............................. 343
	8.3.6 Horizontal Bar........................... 350
8.4	Women 366
	8.4.1 Support Vault 366
	8.4.2 Asymmetric Bars......................... 366
	8.4.3 Beam................................... 367
	8.4.4 Floor Exercises........................... 368

Chapter 9	**Sports-science and Sports-medicine Back-up to Training** **371**
	9.1 Basic Principles and Tasks 371
	9.2 Comprehensive Control System....................... 372
	9.3 Assessing Level of Preparation 374
	9.3.1 Assessing Specific Physical Fitness (SPP) 374
	9.3.2 Assessing Technical Preparedness............. 375
	9.4 Observing Competition Activity...................... 375
	9.5 Pharmacological Preparation 377
	9.6 Diet.. 379

Chapter 10	**Material-technical Provision of Training** **381**
	10.1 Basic Equipment 381
	10.2 Additional Equipment 382
	10.2.1 Mechanical Training Devices for Developing Strength 382
	10.2.2 Training Aid for Warm up and Strengthening Muscle-ligament Leg Apparatus 382
	10.2.3 The 'Wave' Training Aid 383
	10.2.4 Training Aid for Twisting and Turning 384
	10.2.5 Parallel Bars Training Aid 385
	10.2.6 The 'Horse' Training Device 386
	10.2.7 The 'Vault' Device 387
	10.2.8 Pneumatic Training Apparatus 388
	10.2.9 Biomechanical Mount 390
	10.2.10 Electro-stimulation of the Muscles 390
	10.2.11 Biomechanical Massage 392
	10.2.12 Video-analysis 394
	10.2.13 Teaching Machine 396

Conclusion 399

Bibliography 400

Photo & Illustration Credits 408

Acknowledgements 408

How to Create Champions

Introduction

'O Sport, You are Peace!' exclaimed the founder of the modern Olympic Games, Pierre de Coubertin, at the outset to his famous Olympic ode. And the French baron hit the nail on the head, providing one of the widest definitions of sport. Gymnastics is one of the most respected Olympic sports, as well as being a wonderful, beautiful and severe discipline. It is not accessible to everyone, only talented and hard-working athletes, as is, incidentally, any worthwhile pursuit.

One may take up gymnastics for one's own satisfaction without aiming for high sporting results and even without taking part in competitions. One may love and enjoy high level gymnastics also as a fan, but one cannot experience anything comparable to the acute, all-embracing joy that one gets from this wonderful sport. This comes from experiencing the extremely complicated exercises, maybe of the type that no one in the world has yet tried, and the fantastic feeling of complete control of one's body in supreme condition, and the joy of taking part in world level tournaments, and the excitement of competitive struggle at the level of top sporting achievements, and the happiness of victory over the strongest world gymnasts, and much besides.

If you are young, proud and in love with gymnastics, you have the right to sense the magical smell of gymnastics within you and fully lose yourself in its enchanting atmosphere as a gymnast or coach. This book describes those feelings: what, how, when and why it has to be done. It is the first in a series of books, whose principal aim is to generalise in popular form the best experience, theory and practice of preparing gymnasts from novices to Olympic champions.

Why does the book series begin with the theory and techniques of preparing top class gymnasts and with the preparation of champions? Would it not be better to learn from the beginning, ie from initial preparation? At first glance, this approach would seem more logical. But only at first glance.

If you stand in the foothills and look up at the mountain peak, you may simply adore the view. But for a person with a sporting bent it is natural to want to try to climb the mountain and find out what is at the top. So it is with coaches and gymnasts. A good coach, like a good gymnast, is bound to want to run ahead and scale the heights of the gymnast's art. He is always focusing on the mountain top of the Olympic podium, even working in its foothills.

A clear presentation of the technique of preparing top-class gymnasts, at the height of the gymnast's ability, its structure and gymnastic trends enables the coach to create the most harmonious, organic and flexible system to develop gymnasts from novice to international class. It is important here to stress that one must create the system and refine it, not from the bottom up, but from the top down, bearing in mind that gymnastics is constantly evolving and that its highest level at the given moment is not the limit. Therefore, any honest coach instinctively strives to obtain information of a higher level and to rely on that, so as to know where to go further and to know prospects for the future. What is more, this approach enables him/her to avoid dead ends and pitfalls.

This approach is typical of preparing top-class specialists in any field. If we know precisely the requirements for highly qualified specialists in any area, we may gradually descend from the top to the bottom of the qualifications ladder, and form a more adequate basis for learning, for acquiring skills and habits that future specialists will master at various stages of preparation. Following this methodology we can construct a more economic, non-contradictory system of training such specialists, obviating unnecessary energy on acquiring knowledge and habits that will be needed at the top level.

That is why we have decided to begin this series with a book on the theory and technique of preparing men and women gymnasts at the top level. Its objective is to raise the level of professional preparation of coaches and specialists in gymnastics, deepening their professional education. The major problems of the book comprise what to teach, why to teach and how to teach so as to attain best results in modern gymnastics.

The authors have endeavoured to make their book understandable and accessible for practical use. We set out in popular form our many years of practical experience in training the men's and women's USSR and Russian national gymnastics teams taking into account our world of experience of preparing top-class gymnasts. The successes of USSR and Russian gymnasts internationally is well known and needs no further commentary.

Introduction

The concepts and techniques of top class gymnast preparation are set out in the seven most recent Olympic cycles of training the national team (men's, women's and junior), starting in 1972. The book is based on wide factual material, personal coaching experience and the results of scientific research, most of which the authors have made themselves. The book is also for the most part based on specific information on techniques of training the national team which has not previously been published.

It is worth noting that all the basic material and specific data relating to the techniques of training the national team belong to the Russian Gymnastics Federation and may be published only with their permission.

Gymnastics is a broad family to which a group of complicated coordination sports being connected with the art of movement. We range over the surface here depending on what and how an athlete does in competition. The subject of evaluation of sporting activity in this group is the form and content of competitive exercises, and the principal object of learning and improvement of technical mastery are technical actions and movements of progressive difficulty. This group includes artistic gymnastics, rhythmic gymnastics, sports acrobatics, trampolining, diving, synchronised swimming, figure skating, free style and sports aerobics.

Inasmuch as gymnastics is the unchallenged leader of the gymnastics family in the methodology and technology of training, this book will be useful to coaches and specialists in all related gymnastics sports. The major ideas and propositions of the book retain their actuality for all top attainment sport.

The book is addressed to athletes, coaches, and experts in training top-class athletes, to students and researchers specialising in gymnastics and related sports, as well as to scientific specialists.

How to Create Champions

CHAPTER ONE
Characteristics of Gymnastics
A Short History

Since World War II, USSR gymnasts attained outstanding success internationally. We shall take a short excursion into the history of Russian and USSR gymnastics, to better understand why this happened.

In the year when the International Gymnastics Federation (FIG) was founded, Moscow witnessed the opening of the first hall for gymnastics on the basis of which the 'Russian Gymnastics Society' was founded on 2nd of May 1881. On 15 April 1887, the first all-Russia gymnastics contests took place at the level of Russian championships, in Saint Petersburg. About twenty people took part. The first Russian gymnastics champion was Lieutenant F. Kreps. From 1897 to 1915, Russian gymnastics championships took place almost every year under the patronage of His Imperial Highness Prince Vladimir Romanov, the brother of the last Russian Emperor, Nicholas II.

In 1912, Russian gymnasts participated in the Olympic Games. They also took part in other international competitions, but with no notable success. One should note, however, that the difficulty and originality of the exercises performed by Russian gymnasts (especially on the parallel bars) at displays in France and Czechoslovakia in 1914 produced quite an impression on foreign gymnastics experts.

After the October Revolution of 1917, the new government ignored gymnastics for a time as a 'bourgeois' sport. But shortly after, it was rehabilitated and occupied a worthy place among other sports cultivated in the USSR. Gymnastics sections began to be set up in sports societies and clubs all over the country. It became one of three major sports on which the USSR physical training system was built (gymnastics, athletics and swimming). Departments of gymnastics were gradually formed in physical culture institutes.

How to Create Champions

National championships were renewed in 1928. From 1931 up to the present time they have been taking place almost annually (apart from 1935, 1941 and 1942). Up until 1949, USSR gymnastics developed in isolation from the world gymnastic movement. In 1949, however, the USSR Gymnastics Federation joined FIG.

The debut of USSR gymnastics at the 1952 Olympic Games came as a shock to world gymnastics. USSR gymnasts won the absolute all around and team championships for both men and women, and won at five disciplines (the horse, rings, men's vault and the beam, and women's vault). Out of the 14 sets of Olympic prizes they won 9 gold, 11 silver and two bronze medals. The first USSR absolute Olympic champions in gymnastics were Victor Chukarin and Maria Gorokhovskaya. Since all members of the men's and women's teams were rewarded with gold medals in the team championship, the actual number of gold medals won at the Olympics was much higher.

The USSR team included 11 Russians (5 men and 6 women), and they took home 12 gold medals from Helsinki. The USSR gymnastics school had its national characteristics and differed from the then dominant Swiss school of men's gymnastics. Thanks to that victory, the USSR attained the status of a great gymnastics power and it maintained its leadership right up to the fall of the USSR.

Valentine Muratov
World Champion 1954

Galina Shamrai
World Champion 1954

From 1952 up to 2000, as many as 76 Russian gymnasts took part in the Olympic Games, of whom 49 won the title of Olympic champion, some of whom won it more than once. All in all, Russian gymnasts won 89 Olympic gold medals (45 men, 44 women). These medal figures for Russian gymnasts at the Olympics, World and European championships refer up to

Characteristics of Gymnastics

December 1, 2001 without taking into account the results of members of the USSR team from other Republics. Data for medals won by the USSR team referring to the 1952-92 period include the results of Russian gymnasts. In our calculation we have included all medals won by gymnasts for victory in the team championship.

Seven Russians bear the top gymnastics title of absolute Olympic champion: Turishcheva, Andrianov, Davydova, Dityatin, Shushunova, Artemov and Nemov. Nikolai Andrianov won the most Olympic gold medals among Russian gymnasts.

Mikaail Voronin
World Champion

As many as 96 Russian gymnasts took part in world championships, winning a total of 133 gold medals (67 medals for the men and 66 medals for the women). 49 Russian gymnasts carry the title of World Champion, including some who have won it more than once. The title of absolute World Champion has been awarded to 14 Russian, men and women gymnasts, 18 times. Two times Absolute World Champions are: Ludmilla Turishcheva (1970, 1974), Yury Korolev (1981, 1985), Dmitri Bilozerchev (1983, 1987), Svetlana Khorkina (1997, 2001)*. Yuri Korolev (9) holds the record for gold medals won by Russians at the world championships. He is one ahead of Bilozerchev (8). Ludmilla Turishcheva, Alexander Dityatin and Svetlana Khorkina have 7 gold medals each.

At 24 men's and 22 women's European championships, 54 Russian gymnasts have taken part, winning a total of 112 gold medals (72 men's and 40 women's). 36 Russians hold the title of absolute European champion, including some more than once. The title of absolute European champion has

---

* Khorkina – at the time of writing has achieved two titles, but in 2003 she became absolute all-around champion for the third time.

been won by 10 Russians a total of 18 times (7 men and 3 women). Mikhail Voronin, Ludmilla Turishcheva, Victor Klimenko, Dmitri Bilozerchev and Svetlana Khorkina have won this title twice. Dmitri Bilozerchev (10) has won the European championship gold more than anyone else. He is also a record-holder among Russians, in total number of gold medals won at the Olympic, World and European championships (21).

The number of gold medals won by Russian gymnasts at the Olympic Games, World and European championships is shown in Tables 1 and 2.

Altogether, Russian gymnasts have won 768 medals (334 gold, 287 silver and 155 bronze) at the Olympic Games, World and European championships. Of those 208 (89 gold, 76 silver and 43 bronze) were at the Olympics; 297 (133 gold, 108 silver and 56 bronze) were at the World Championships; and 272 (112 gold, 104 silver and 56 bronze) were at the European Championships.

Nikolai Andrianov
Olympic Champion 1976
World Champion 1978

The attainments of Soviet gymnasts are even more impressive. They won a total of 1037 medals (516 gold, 344 silver and 177 bronze): of which 316 were won at ten Olympics (158 men: 72+67+19, and 158 women: 88+37+33), 419 at World Championships (220 men: 108+79+33, and 199 women: 107+61+31), and 302 at European Championships (190 men: 91+64+35, and 112 women: 50+36+26). However it is specifically Russian gymnasts who have contributed the most to the overall number.

The successes of Russian gymnasts are a result of the coordinated efforts of highly-qualified specialists – coaches, sports officials, scientists, doctors. The success of Russian gymnast champions has been due to the efforts of merited coaches of the USSR and Russia; B.N.

CHARACTERISTICS OF GYMNASTICS

Astafiev, M.V. Levin, V.G. Andreyev, V.A. Korolkov, N.N. Merkulov, K.S. Karakashyants, S.S. Litvinov, Y.E. Shtukman, A.A. Zhirov, A.M. Polezhayev, I.S. Zhuravlyov, A.I. Alexandrov, N.G. Tolkachov, M.Y. Klimenko, V.S. Rastvorotsky, V.F. Aksenov, V.A. Shevchuk, V.A. Belyaev, L.Y. Arkaev, A.G. Yarmovsky, P.F. Korchagin, M.A. Genkin, M.Y. Voronin, B. Orlov, A. Vfedorov, A.S. Alexandrov, V.G. Gavryuchenkov, V.N. Firsov, V.V. Lomtev, D.N. Derzhavin, Y.A. Dokhov, G.A. Gribanov, Y.G. Nikolko, B.V. Pilkin, A.M. Genkin, A.V. Kudimov, V.A. Somsikov, V.P. Alfosov, N.V. Maslinnikova, and many others.

Alexandre Detiatin
World Champion 1979
Olympic Champion 1980

Over many years the following Russian senior coaches of the national team have provided high-quality training for the main and junior squads: Popov, Lavrushenko, Muratov, Alexandrov (A.I.), Demidenko, Latynina, Ivanova, Smolevsky, Arkayev, Shaniyazov, Rodionenko, Alexandrov (A.S.), Kozeyev, Andrianov, Kolchev, Bulashenko, as well as the specialist coaches Safronov, Khaldushkin, Suchilin, Maslov, Goverdovsky, Rozin, Savarina, Sokolova, Kapitonova. L.Y. Arkaev set a unique record for long service, having been in charge of the national team for 30 years (from 1972 the men, and from 1992 up until today both men and women).

Under the leadership of Ukran, Smolevsky and later Cheburayev, researchers working at the All-Russian Research Institute for Physical Culture (VNIIFC); Moscow and St. Petersburg Institutes of Physical Culture (GTSOLIFC) and (GDOIFC) have provided top-class scientific and medical-biological service to the national teams.

Thanks to the efforts, above all of Russian experts, we have formed a unique national gymnastics school and Russian system of preparing gymnasts that has no parallel in the world community. Russian professors Orlov, Ukran,

Gaverdovsky, Smolevsky and Suchilin have made a fundamental contribution to the theory and methodology of gymnastics. Russian gymnastics possesses the strongest scientific potential in the World; Russians have defended more than 300 PhD dissertations on gymnastics.

USSR and Russian gymnastics has never been localised in capital centres. Gymnastics has always had a broad geography. Russian physical culture and research institutions have played a decisive role in preparing highly-qualified gymnastics personnel and promoting gymnastic science. It is worth highlighting the Russian (formerly GCOLIFC), the Saint Petersburg (formerly GDOIFC) and the Moscow state physical culture academies, as well as the All-Union Research Physical Culture Institute.

Yuri Korolev
World Champion 1981 and 1985

In analysing the path covered by USSR and Russian gymnastics since World War II we cannot say it has been smooth or free of obstacles. There have been ups and downs, conflicts and crises. For example, after eight years of dominance in the World, at the 1960 Rome Olympics the men's team for the first time conceded the team championship to Japanese gymnasts and then it had to spend 19 years trying to catch up.

This was certainly an ideological, methodological crisis which beset Russian gymnastics; but it took place behind the scenes, inasmuch as the personal achievements of Soviet gymnasts like Shakhlin, Titov, Stolbov, Lisitsky, Voronin, Diomidov, Klimenko and Andrianov camouflaged the crisis.

The crisis manifested itself more obviously in 1970 at the world championship in Lubliana, where the USSR men's team won two silver, three bronze and only one gold medal. For other sports these results might have been

CHARACTERISTICS OF GYMNASTICS

fully acceptable, but for men's gymnastics this was very serious. This was due to a large degree to the long-term discussion, the theme of what is more important: complexity or quality? How long and exactly how should we train? One side of USSR gymnasts took the path of increasing the load and complexity of exercises with a certain loss of quality; the other took the path of enhancing quality of performance with a loss of complexity. At the same time, Japanese gymnasts continued to increase the complexity and quality of performance of their competitive programmes, training at extreme intensities.

**Vladimir Artiomov
Olympic Champion 1988**

What to some extent hampered the growth in skill of Soviet gymnasts in the 1970s was the mentality of still being the second best team in the world, and the ideology of permanently trying to catch up with the Japanese. The slogan 'mass sport is the basis of proficiency' also did harm to high level gymnastics. An increase in the number of gymnasts in the country was not directly connected to growth in results of the national team internationally.

After a change of leadership in the USSR men's team in 1972 (Arkaev became senior coach) there was a change in the national gymnastics paradigm (the theory or model of posing problems taken as template for resolving tasks in scientific and practical activity. According to the concept of the American scientific historian T. Kuhn, a change in paradigm is presented as a scientific revolution which is followed by a technical revolution) and we elaborated a new concept of preparing top-class gymnasts. The slogan was 'high quality, super-complexity', and the 'catch the Japanese' slogan was replaced by 'overtake everyone!' At the base of the training system for the national team and reserves were the principles of 'outstripping' development and optimal surplus that had their theoretical grounding in our work, [60,63, 9].

How to Create Champions

The new national doctrine required a radical improvement in the entire system of training, which ultimately led to the creation of a national technique of training top-class gymnasts. The methodological and organisational innovations bore fruit and the men's national team emerged from its crisis. The battle between the Soviet and Japanese men's teams in the 1970s was extremely acute and dramatic.

Dimitri Biloserchev
World Champion 1983 and 1987

In 1974, at the Varna World Championships, a sensation occurred: after a 16-year interval the Russians once again overtook the Japanese in the free programme, but the team championship went to the Japanese. At the 1976 Olympics in Montreal the youngest ever Soviet team (average age was 19.8) overtook the Japanese team (average age 26.5) in the compulsory programme and lost to its rival by only 0.4 points in the team championship. This was the smallest difference in scores in the history of the Olympics.

At the Strasbourg World Championships in 1978, the Soviet team lost to the Japanese by some three points in the compulsories, but beat them in the free programme by more than two points. And, finally, at the 1979 World Championships in Fort Worth, after more than a twenty-year gap, the Soviet team again conquered the Japanese, beating them in the compulsory and free programme by a total of 3.8 points. Since then USSR gymnasts have firmly held on to the leading position, not losing an Olympics in the team and individual championships.

A comparable crisis occurred in the Soviet women's team, although it did not take such an acute form and was more hidden. This was aided by the individual successes

CHARACTERISTICS OF GYMNASTICS

of the gymnasts (Latynina, Astakhova, Manina, Kuchinskaya, Turischeva, Korbut, etc.), and that, since its debut in 1952, the USSR women's team had never lost the team championship at any Olympic Games. The crisis in women's gymnastics was overcome in the same manner as in the men's.

After the disintegration of the Soviet Union, Russian gymnastics found itself in a difficult position. Only two Russians (Voropayev and Grudneva) were part of the united team of independent states (the former USSR) at the Barcelona Olympics of 1992. After the Games, Russian gymnasts were not invited for a time to any international tournaments, at the same time as Russia was ignored as a world gymnastics power.

Serious problems arose with the majority of all aspects of ensuring training of Russian gymnasts (financial, material, scientific, medical, personnel and informational). The Russian team lost its top training camps at Lower Esher in Sukhumi (Georgia) and Tsakhkadzor in Armenia. The main training camp for the Russian team at Lake Krugloye near Moscow no longer met international standards. Our main rivals at the time continued to train in the best conditions and had a more quality-based training system.

Nikolai Kriukov
Olympic Champion 1999

Moreover, a mass exodus abroad began of the top Russian coaches and gymnasts. Because of Russia's economic problems, the volume and intensity of research into gymnastics substantially diminished. So too did the number of top-class scientific personnel in gymnastics being trained as postgraduates and

How to Create Champions

Ljudmilla Turischeva
Olympic Champion 1972
World Champion 1970 and 1974

researchers writing dissertations on gymnastics. Another problem was the drastic fall in popularity of gymnastics, whereas its popularity in other countries continued to grow. For example, according to a public opinion survey by American TV companies at the 1996 Atlanta Games, women's gymnastics was the most popular Olympic sport.

In Western countries the number of gymnastics clubs increased, while gymnastics sections in many junior clubs in Russia began to close down or find themselves with hardly any gymnasts. The USSR had made high-quality gymnastics equipment that had met the requirements of gymnastics. Today we cannot compete with the top Western firms making gymnastics equipment.

Despite all these setbacks Russian gymnastics is successfully coming to grips with its problems. After 1992, the Russian national team managed to attain and firm up its leading position in the gymnastics world and maintain the reputation of the national gymnastics school and national gymnastics traditions.

At the Atlanta Olympics Russian gymnasts won three gold, two silver and three bronze medals. The men's team became Olympic champions as well as Alexei Nemov and Svetlana Khorkina. Considering the sharply increased competition the debut of Russian gymnasts as an independent national team was extremely successful.

In the following year, at the Lausanne World Championships, Russian gymnasts again won three gold, but now five silver and three bronze medals. Svetlana Khorkina became absolute World Champion and World asymmetric bars champion, and Alexei Nemov was World Champion in the floor exercises.

Elena Moukhina
World Champion 1978

CHARACTERISTICS OF GYMNASTICS

At the 1999 World Championships in Tianijn (China), the Russians made a significant step forward, winning five gold, three silver and three bronze medals. Nemov (free exercises and horse), Khorkina (parallel bars) and Yelena Zamolodchikova (vault) all became World Champions. Nikolai Kryukov became the seventeenth Russian absolute World Champion. In the medal table at the championships, the Russians came first, overtaking the very strong Chinese gymnasts on their own territory encouraged by strong support from their fans and mass media.

Jelena Davidova
Olympic Champion 1980

At the 2000 Sydney Olympics the Russian gymnastics squad again made big steps forward, despite losing the men's and women's championships. They gained 15 medals, including five gold, five silver and five bronze medals. That beat gymnasts of all other participating nations in the Games, and more than any other Russian team. The outstanding Alexei Nemov became absolute Olympic champion, as well as Olympic champion on the horizontal bar. Yelena Zamolodchikova became twice Olympic champion, having won the floor exercises and the vault, while Svetlana Khorkina won the asymmetric bars.

Thus the dynamics of the Russian team's results at the World Championships and the Olympic Games in the 1996 – 2000 cycle was clearly positive. It is worth mentioning, however, because of the economic difficulties of 1992-95, a considerable fall in basic statistical indicators reflecting the level of development of gymnastics in the country. Then, in 1996, they substantially improved, as witnessed by the change in trends and emergence from the crisis.

How to Create Champions

Olga Bicherova
World Champion

According to statistics, on 1 December 2000, some 61,662 (47,189 in 1995) of these 30,039 (24,232 in 1995) did gymnastics in the whole of Russia. Of these 30,458 did so in initial training groups, 15,916 (11,041 in 1995) in training groups, 854 (629 in 1995) in sports proficiency groups and 174 (142 in 1995) in top skill groups.

As many as 21,040 gymnasts were ranked in 2000 (15,306 in 1995). On 1 December 2000, 1,221 (1,035 in 1997) held the first ranking, 691 (550 in 1995) were candidate masters of sport, 267 gymnasts were masters of sport (107 in 1995), and 43 (29 in 1995) were masters of sport international class.

As many as 2,280 coaches (1,870 in 1995) worked with gymnasts at this time, of whom 420 (218 in 1995) have the highest category, and 521 the first category (412 in 1995). 32 Russian cities were represented in the men's and women's national team.

Thus, the statistics show a considerable rise in the number of coaches over the last five years. In the last Olympic Cycle 1997-2000, the figures had been relatively stable. The growth in results over this period took place as a result of improved quality of training.

Natalia Yurchenko
World Champion 1983

CHARACTERISTICS OF GYMNASTICS

Comparative analysis shows the basic statistical indicators have remained relatively stable in the 1997-2000 period. We see that we have ensured a stable trend in growth of results for the Russian national team at the major championships (Olympics and World Championships). We conclude that this has happened as a result of an improved quality of training.

At present, we have created the pre-requisites for further successful development of gymnastics in Russia and achievements by Russian gymnastics in terms of top international results.

Elena Shushunova
Olympic Champion 1988
World Champion 1985

How to Create Champions

Table 1 – **Men** *Russian gymnasts with gold medals at the Olympics, World and European championships*

OC = Olympic Champion
AOC = Absolute Olympic Champion
WC = World Champion
AWC = Absolute World Champion
EC = European Champion
AEC = Absolute European Champion

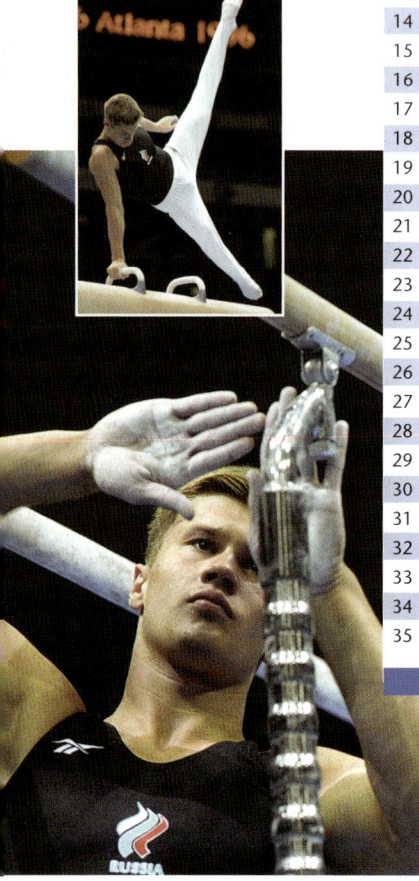

No.	Name DOB	DOB	OC	AOC	WC	AWC	EC	AEC
1	Aleshin Maxim	1979	1					
2	Andrianov Nikolai	1952	7	1	4	1	9	1
3	Artemov Vladimir	1964	4	1	6			
4	Belyakov Vladimir	1926	1					
5	Berdiev Josef	1924	1					
6	Bilozerchev Dimitri	1966	3		8	2	10	2
7	Bondarenko Alexei	1978					3	1
8	Vasilenko Dimitri	1975	1				1	
9	Voronin Mihail	1945	2		2	1	8	2
10	Voropayev Alexei	1973	2		2		2	
11	Vostrikov Ivan	1924			1			
12	Diamidov Sergei	1943			1			
13	Dityatin Alexander	1957	2	1	7	1	2	
14	Karbanenko Dimitri	1973					1	
15	Klimenko Victor	1949	1				6	2
16	Korolev Yuri	1962			9	2		
17	Korolkov Evgeny	1930	1		1			
18	Kryukov Nikolai	1978	1		1	1		
19	Leonkin Dimitri	1928	1					
20	Lipatov Valentin	1929			1			
21	Lisitsky Victor	1940					7	1
22	Marinich Vitali	1970			1			
23	Markelov Vladimir	1957	1		1		2	1
24	Mogilny Valentin	1965			5		6	1
25	Muratov Valentin	1928	4		5	1	1	1
26	Nemov Alexei	1976	4	1	5		3	
27	Perelman Michail	1923	1					
28	Podgorny Evgeny	1977	1				2	
29	Stolbov Pavel	1929	1		1		1	
30	Tikhanovsky Yuri	1977					1	
31	Tikhonov Vladimir	1958					1	
32	Tikhonkikh Alexei	1961			2			
33	Tkachev Alexander	1957	2		3		4	
34	Trush Dimitri	1973	1					
35	Kharkov Sergei	1970	3		1		1	
	Total		45	4	67	9	72	12

Alexei Nemov
Olympic Champion 2000

1 CHARACTERISTICS OF GYMNASTICS

Table 2 – Women

No.	Name	DOB	OC	AOC	WC	AWC	EC	AEC
1	Agapova Svetlana	1964			1			
2	Andrianova-Burda Lubov	1953	2		1			
3	Bicherova Olga	1967			2	1	3	1
4	Varonina Zinaida	1947	1		1			
5	Galiyeva Rosalia	1977					1	
6	Gromova Ludmila	1942	1					
7	Grudneva Elena	1974	1					
8	Grozdova Svetlana	1959	1					
9	Davydova Elena	1961	2	1	1			
10	Danilova Pelageya	1918	1		1			
11	Dolgopolova Elena	1980					1	
12	Yegorova Ludmila	1931	1					
13	Zhaleyeva Tamara	1932			1			
14	Ivanova Lidia	1937	2		2			
15	Zamolodchikova Elena	1982	2		1		1	
16	Kalinchuk Ekaterina	1922	2					
17	Karaceva Olga	1949	1		1		1	
18	Kolesnikova Vera	1968					1	
19	Kochetkova Dina	1977			2			
20	Kuznetsova Evgenia	1980					2	
21	Kuchinskaya Natalia	1949	2		3			
22	Lobaznyuk Ekaterina	1983					1	
23	Lyukhina Tamara	1939	2					
24	Manina Tamara	1934	2		6			
25	Minaicheva Galina	1929	1		1			
26	Mostepanova Olga	1968			3			
27	Muratova Sofia	1929	2		3			
28	Mukhina Elena	1960			3	1	4	
29	Naimushina Elena	1964	1					
30	Pervushina Irina	1942			2			
31	Produnova Elena	1980					1	
32	Saadi Elvira	1952	2		1			
33	Turishcheva Ludmila	1952	4	1	7	2	8	2
34	Urbanovich Galina	1917	1					
35	Filatova Maria	1961	2		2		1	
36	Frolova Tatiana	1967			1			
37	* Khorkina Svetlana	1979	2		7	2	9	2
38	Shamrai Galina	1931	1		2	1		
39	Shaposhnikova Natalia	1961	2		1		1	
40	Shevchenko Elena	1971	1					
41	Shishova Albina	1959			1			
42	Shushunova Elena	1969	2	1	5	1	5	1
43	Yurchenko Natalia	1965			3	1		
	Total		44	3	65	9	40	6
	M & W		89	7	132	18	112	18

Svetlana Khorkina
World Champion 1997, 2001 and 2003
Two times Olympic Champion and five times World Champion on Assymetric bars.

29

1.2 Characteristics of Gymnastics

Gymnastics is one of the oldest Olympic sports. The FIG was formed in Liege, Belgium on 23 July 1881 eleven years before the federations for speed skating and rowing. The other international sports federations are the offspring of the twentieth century.

Over the past hundred years gymnastics has made colossal strides. If we compare the exercises of champions at the first and last Olympic Games, we can only say 'what fantastic progress!'. It considerably accelerated after the introduction into training of foam rubber mats, pits and training equipment, as well as new methods, means and techniques of learning and training.

In a relatively short time the difficulty of exercises has increased immeasurably, the quality of performance and training loads has also increased. Gymnastics techniques are changed beyond all measure. We have created a huge structural variety of movements which along with a great variety of technical actions and contrasting motor regimes has no analogy in contemporary sport.

At the same time, the principal criteria of gymnastics have remained traditional since the moment of its formation as a sport. This is the difficulty of exercises, their composition and quality of execution. The object of evaluation in all this time is what the gymnast does and how he or she does it.

Gymnastics belongs to a group of sports with a stabilised kinematic structure of complicated coordination actions performed in relatively constant conditions without direct contact with opponents. By contrast with other sports the self-regulating actions are relatively simple. They are bending-straightening movements mainly in the shoulders and hips, since in many exercises the arms and legs are prescribed as being straight.

But these relatively simple governing movements must be very precise and carefully coordinated in time and space. They must be performed in time and precisely within very different support and unaided conditions, moreover in most cases with a very complicated, rapidly changing orientation of the body in space given an acute shortage of time. For singular exercises we need motor actions that are strictly set in space and time and in strength parameters, while for performing other exercises we need maximum impulse of strength; others

CHARACTERISTICS OF GYMNASTICS

require optimal application of efforts of varying strength; others need extreme skill; yet others require highly developed sense of balance. And all this often applies to one and the same exercise.

Modern gymnastics is multifaceted and multi-logical. Top gymnastics is biologically energy-sapping and is complex in terms of coordination, which makes high demands on the level of technique, physical, functional and psychological preparation of top-class athletes. Modern gymnasts must possess highly developed physical qualities, such as strength, speed, skill, flexibility, special endurance, a high degree and love of hard work.

The gymnast's weight is the major objective obstacle to performing exercises. To move one's weight it is necessary to apply strength and perform mechanical work of a certain power. What is of cardinal importance here is not absolute, but relative indicators of muscle strength and speed-strength indicators which depend on calculation per one kilogram of the gymnast's own weight. Owing to the constant increase in complexity of exercises modern-day gymnastics is progressively acquiring a marked speed-strength nature, without losing its difficult coordination status.

One cannot perform gymnastics without a high level of development of the muscles of the upper and lower back, of the trunk and jumping ability ('springiness'). The trunk is amazing in construction and a very important tool for mastering the technique of performing modern gymnastics exercises. But modern gymnasts for the moment pay scant attention to developing and improving the necessary qualities of the trunk.

Loads on the support-motor apparatus in gymnastics are sufficiently well balanced. When performing exercises in various gymnastics events, the compressed loads in compact form alternate with loads in stretching the muscular-ligament apparatus and spinal column. On some equipment exercises are performed only in support (horse, beam), on others there is a mixed regime highlighting hanging or support (horizontal bar, parallel bars), while with a third type we have a dominant regime of shock interactions with support (vaults, floor exercises).

From the viewpoint of physiological motor activity gymnastics exercises apply to physical work of moderate and high power. This work is done mainly in anaerobic or aerobic-anaerobic conditions, moreover often holding one's breath. The energy provision of gymnastic exercises is not from oxygen taken from the surrounding air by the athlete's lungs when breathing and delivered to the organism tissues directly when performing the exercise (as, for example, in aerobics or cyclical sports), but through energy formed as a result of chemical reactions taking place in the muscles. Thus, the energy supply regime of muscular activity in gymnastics is normally an-aerobic.

Pulse rate (PR) during training with top-class gymnasts varies from 120 to 200 beats a minute (bpm). In recent years, owing to a substantial rise in the difficulty of exercises, there has been a considerable increase in both the volume and intensity of training and competitive loads. Members of the Russian gymnastics team train three times a day during centralised preparation. A large part of training and competitive loads is performed in an anaerobic regime. For example, immediately after performance of floor exercises the PR can attain more than 200 bpm. A high PR may be maintained up to 1.5 minutes. In the pauses between approaches it comprises around 120 bpm.

Before performing routines the PR of top-class gymnasts varies within 138-156 bpm. Before performing on the horizontal bar it is at its maximum, while before the support vault is it at its minimum – 137 bpm (on the horse – 154 bpm, on the parallel bars 152 bpm, floor exercises – 150 bpm, on the rings – 148 bpm).

Immediately after floor exercises and horizontal bar the PR is at its maximum – 201 bpm, on the parallel bars – 194 bpm, on the horse – 193 bpm, on the rings – 189 bpm. The pulse value of vaults is minimal: 168 bpm [6, 7, 32].

The characteristics of top gymnastics presuppose a need for constant control of the state of top-class gymnasts, the level of their technical, physical and functional preparation, as well as training loads, diet and restoration.

With the present-day exercises of a strength and speed-strength nature the best results are normally attained by relatively light and strong gymnasts of relatively short height and small weight: 160-170 cm and 56-70 kg for men, and 150-160 cm and 38-50 kg for women. However, one comes across real 'Gullivers' among the champions. Alexander Dityatin (height 178 cm, weight 72 kg), Eberhard Ginger (176 cm, 70 kg), Alexei Nemov (174 cm and 74 kg), Elvira Saadi (166 cm, 52.5 kg) and Svetlana Khorkina (165 cm, 47 kg).

CHARACTERISTICS OF GYMNASTICS

Typical of both men and women modern gymnasts, is the 'ectomorph' and 'ecti-mesomorph' type of body composition or constitution, moderately wide shoulders (wide with women), narrow hips, long arms, relatively long legs and a short trunk. Given the considerable differences in height and weight, the body proportions of top-class gymnasts are relatively constant. Thus, arm length is 42-47% in relation to body length, while legs are correspondingly 52-56%.

The age of gymnastic participants in the Olympic Games has a clear-cut tendency to fall. While at the 1964 Tokyo Games the average age for men was 25.6 +/- 2.9, and for women 22.2 +/- 2.8, at the 1976 Montreal Games it was 23.7 +/- 5.5 and 18.3 respectively [56].

The trend in declining average age of national teams is evident today. The average age of the Russian men's team at the 1996 Atlanta Games was 21 (from 18 to 26), and the women's 17 (from 16 to 18). At the Sydney 2000 Games the average age of Russian team members increased slightly. For men it was 21.7 (from 18 to 24), and for women it was 18 (from 16 to 20). Thus in 26 years, members of the men's and women's national teams had grown younger by approximately four years on average. The difference in average age between men's and women's national team members remained more or less the same over that period: 3.4 in 1964, 4 in 1996, and 3.7 in 2000.

The youngest absolute Olympic champion was the Romanian gymnast Nadya Comeneci (14 years 250 days) in 1976, while the youngest absolute men's World champion was, in 1983, the sixteen-year old Russian gymnast Dmitri Biolzerchev (16 years 10 months). The sharp decline in age began in the second half of the 1960s. It is associated with the names of Larissa Petrik and Natalia Kuchinskaya. In 1965, these young girls with pigtails created a sensation at the Soviet championships, pushing aside a galaxy of multiple Olympic, World and European champions headed by Larissa Latynina, absolute World record-holder in Olympic medals (in three Olympics – 1956, 1960 and 1964 – she won 18 medals: nine gold, four silver and five bronze).

Being a biologically determined phenomenon, the rejuvenation of women gymnasts began a long time ago and ended a long time ago. Despite the mass media information that gymnastics is harmful to children, that it maintains and even diminishes natural growth, that coaches artificially reduce a gymnast's age, all this has no serious foundation. It is equally claimed that an active basketball career increases athlete's growth. In their pursuit of sensation the mass media highly exaggerate harm from doing gymnastics to the female organism and, especially, to reproductive functions. Medical research testifies to the fact that almost all outstanding women gymnasts give birth to healthy children after leaving their sporting career. For example, the three times World champion Olga Mostepanova, is the mother of five children.

The results of investigation into genetics also show that height, body proportions and other major anthropometric parameters of humans are genetically conditioned and set at birth. Owing to the specifics of modern gymnastics advantages are held by athletes whose anthropometric indicators fall within the above-mentioned limits. The advantages of individuals with a set anthropometric system is a result of natural and sporting selection. One may say the same about tall athletes who dominate basketball.

The advantages in gymnastics of relatively light, small athletes may also be shown from biomechanics on the basis of the relationship between absolute and relative strength, height and weight. We know that in people with roughly the same amount of training, but different weight, absolute strength increases with an increase in weight, while relative strength falls. If body length increases, say, by 1.5 times, the area of basic body sections (including also physiological muscle diameters) increases by 2.25 times, while body weight grows by 3.4 times. Thus, between these indicators there is a correspondingly square and cubic dependence [22].

If we take two athletes, identically trained and similar in body composition but of different weights (for example, the second is 1.5 times heavier than the first), the second athlete in absolute strength will be 2.25 times stronger than the first. This is because the athlete's strength of muscle pull (all things being equal) is determined by their physiological diameter. But if the athletes will not lift a heavy bar, but their own weight when performing exercises in gymnastics, the advantage will lie with the first athlete – ie he is roughly 3.4 times lighter, and his relative strength is higher. And since the essential in gymnastics is how the gymnast copes with his own weight, and not with barbells or weights in general, this therefore explains the advantage of light, relatively small gymnasts at international tournaments.

It is a given fact that when sexual maturation occurs (puberty), people are

CHARACTERISTICS OF GYMNASTICS

divided into accelerators (early sexual maturation), normal juvenile and retardants (late sexual maturation). It is the retardants that have the advantage in gymnastics. High training loads in one degree or another enhance retardation of sexual maturation.

The peak of development of relative strength and speed-strength qualities for most juveniles occurs during the pre-puberty period. During puberty these indicators fall because of the rapid rise in body length and bone levers, growth in muscle mass and body weight. This creates serious problems for gymnastics: it leads to a fall in sporting results and even to an end to active life in high level gymnastics. But this is far from being a general rule. For example, Dityatin grew by 12 cm and increased in weight by at least ten kilos in one year of puberty. However, a careful selection of optimal training loads and the coach's good sense enabled him in the pubertal period, not to decrease, but to increase his results: at 16 he became the absolute Soviet champion.

In contrast with young men, the process of the decline of relative indicators with young women normally takes place more intensively. A series of absolute indicators in terms of physical attributes may increase. But this makes no difference to female gymnasts. After reaching the period of sexual maturation, relative indicators of speed-strength preparation again reach the pre-puberty level only with some girls. But with boys they usually surpass this level subsequently. So male gymnasts generally compete longer in high level sport.

Statistics show that the path from the first strides in the gymnastics hall to reaching the master of sport category takes 5-7 years with girls, and 8-10 years to achieving top results. The puberty period begins late: at 15-18. According to current rules, gymnasts can only take part in the Olympic Games from the age of 16. In order to optimally use their biological chances and successfully compete in their first (and, probably, their last) Olympics, girls from the age of 14 must have mastered the arsenal of world level exercises in gymnastics so that, over two years, they can basically 'catch up' at competitions and training sessions, and meet the puberty period fully equipped. Hence the simple arithmetical calculation that the optimal age for starting gymnastics for girls is 5-6.

With boys the path to the pinnacle of the gymnastics Olympus is even longer: it takes 10-12 years to reach Olympic standard and 7-9 years to reach Master of Sport level. Thus, taking into account the differences in biological development of men and women the optimal age for beginning gymnastics for boys falls within the same spectrum as with girls.

Optimal attributes of gymnastics are expressiveness, theatricality, figurativeness, plasticity and rhythm of movement, striving to create an artistic form in specifically gymnastic motor actions.

It is worth noting that in a state of top form and after submaximal physical loads top-class gymnasts reduce their immune reactions. In this state they are highly vulnerable to illness, especially colds. In like fashion this applies to all top-class athletes. This phenomenon was discovered and demonstrated by Russian sports physiologists [49].

1.3 Specifics of the Contemporary Stage

Today gymnastics is at a crossroads. The competition rules have radically changed. Replacement of the compulsory programme and other innovations in the competition rules have created a number of problems. The main one is where is present-day gymnastics going? Will it develop as a form of athletics, where the decathlon exists side by side with individual events, or will it retain its gymnastics traditions?

Gymnastics at the present stage is developing in width and depth. 'In depth' means a further complexity of competition programmes and a growth in technical proficiency. This is one of the most stable trends in gymnastics. By the term 'in width' we understand a widening of the geography of gymnastics and increase in its forms and varieties. More and more countries in one structure or another are beginning to cultivate this wonderful sport. Top-class gymnasts are appearing in those countries which had previously been white spots on the gymnastics map. Thanks to new rules this process is intensifying. If competition rules do not change, we may expect specialist gymnasts at various events who become champions with non-standard anthropometric parameters.

Contemporary gymnastics is actively being commercialised and becoming more professional. Within the training process we see an increasing role and share of special physical training. We see an increase in volume of competitive preparation in the annual cycle and, correspondingly, the number and scope of competitions. We see a wider use of various additional means, we see the creation of a special gymnastics environment that is lightening the process of learning gymnastics exercises and making it safer. A gymnastics infrastructure is developing.

At the same time the lack of a compulsory programme with special activity poses the question of programmes with basic preparation. How often can we see young gymnasts who, barely able to perform a somersault, begin to boldly try a double somersault? Even if they are not prepared for it, they even want to master a complex routine and as fast as possible. This is understandable: the new and complex, even more so if it carries some risk, is always interesting. However, an early and unprepared attempt at complexity is a dangerous pursuit.

Just as it is impossible to write words and sentences immediately, without having mastered the alphabet, just as it is impossible straightaway to learn to play the piano without knowing the notes, so it is immediately impossible in gymnastics to master complex movements. At best the gymnast will very indirectly master this notorious tuck double somersault. But later he will come to serious grief. More complex exercises (such as triple somersault) will become a stumbling block. His progress in gymnastics will be slowed down, if not come to a complete standstill.

If the same gymnast carries through a timely realistic basic preparation and forms an optimal motor foundation, then, having lost a certain time on this not always interesting work, he will in the final analysis not only master the element more quickly, he will set up the necessary conditions for a rapid and successful mastery of its more complex modifications. Learning through many years of technical training in this case will be more effective according to such criteria as speed, quality and reliability of mastering elements and routines of progressive complexity. The difference between the first and second approaches to mastering complex elements is figuratively shown in Figure 1.

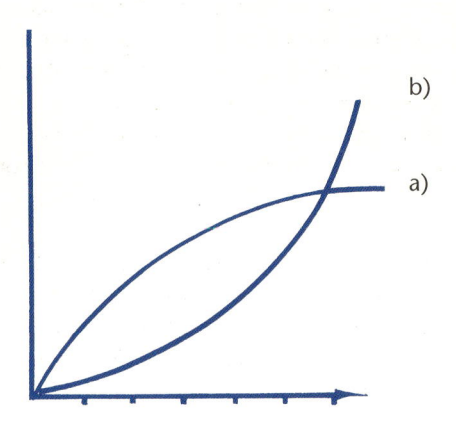

Figure 1 – *The development of results in the case of a) basic preparation b) early attack on complexity*

In gymnastics it is important to be able to see and do the complex in the simple, and the simple in the complex. One must see the difference between very close elements and the similarity between elements which at first glance seem completely different (for example, the Kovacs on the horizontal bar and the Tsukahara in the vault). One of the most important tenets of a coach and gymnast lies in the ability to see and do the complex in the simple and the simple in the complex.

1.4   Trends

Constant analysis of gymnastics trends is a necessary condition of elaborating and improving an effective system of preparing top-class gymnasts and the techniques of their 'conveyor' production. To comprehend where modern gymnastics is heading we must know the trends in world sport. Basic among them is the following:

- rise in motivation and prestige of supreme sports achievements;
- growth in sporting technical results;
- tougher competition for the top sports titles.

CHARACTERISTICS OF GYMNASTICS

The attraction of finance into sport is a system-forming factor ensuring the development of these trends. The rise in popularity of the Olympic Games, World Championships and other international tournaments has become the reason for serious sponsorship and funding coming into sport to advertise products. But the scope of sponsorship in various sports differs greatly. Although the popularity of gymnastics is growing in the world, it cannot compare in terms of funding and sponsorship with football, ice hockey or tennis.

The interaction of the above-mentioned trends is determined by the appearance and development of often more expressed trends-consequences. The result of their mutual action is the acceleration of competitive and training activity in high level sport with the replacement of simple work by complexity in all spheres of training top-class athletes.

Gymnastics is developing in accordance with trends in international sport, but it has its own specifics. As a result of research we see the following trends in contemporary gymnastics:

- growth in skill;
- broadening of the geography of medals and of gymnastics, as a result of the general rise in level of preparation in countries with a tradition of high level gymnastics and the appearance internationally of successful gymnasts from 'traditionally non-gymnastic states';
- growth and concentration of complexity in competitive programmes;
- search for new complex exercises;
- rise in the role and share of special physical preparation in the training process;
- taking technical skill to the level of virtuosity;
- intensification of the learning-training process with an increasing share of training in zones of high and top intensity;
- acceleration of the preparation process as a result of constant improvement in learning methods with swift devaluation of the uniqueness of very complex elements and connections;
- unification of techniques of training top-class gymnasts as a result of rapid diffusion throughout the gymnastics world of progressive methods and technical innovations;
- routine of general and individual approaches in planning and programming the preparation of national teams;

- personalisation of individual preparation within the bounds of stabilised parameters of training loads over time, number of training sessions and training days;
- increase in number of competitive starts in the annual macro-cycle;
- bringing top-class gymnasts up to the level of permanent preparation for competition;
- erosion of boundaries between preparation periods and reduction of the transitional period to a minimum in the annual cycle (2-4 weeks);
- intensification of research in elaborating and substantiating the basic components of top-class gymnast technical preparation, training equipment and technical means of control enabling one to improve the effectiveness of learning complex exercises and development of the necessary physical attributes;
- improving all aspects of ensuring top-class gymnast preparation (finance, personnel, material-technical, scientific-methodological, medical-biological, psychological, information, motivation);
- centralisation of training national teams;
- professionalisation and commercialisation of gymnastics;
- advancing the FIG competition rules as a major instrument of controlling the development of world gymnastics.

These are the general and fairly stable trends which have been operating for many years. We should especially stress that a forecast from which any elaboration of any gymnastic training programmes should start may be made only on the basis of a careful analysis of trends and prospects of gymnastic development. Without that it is impossible to set adequate aims, while the efforts of coaches and specialists connected with the planning, programming and forecasting of the learning-training process will resemble a journey down an unfamiliar road leading nowhere.

We should make special mention of the fact that trends and prospects for gymnastic development should be specified and subjected to comparative analysis before the commencement of each Olympic cycle. This analysis has enabled us to extract the following basic trends in the Olympic cycle of 1997-2000:

- growth in popularity of gymnastics, heightened interest from the mass media (women's gymnastics at the 1996 Atlanta Olympics were called the most popular sport, while at the Sydney Olympics gymnastics was also named as one of the most popular sports, where Russians won the largest number of medals: 15 = 5+ 5 + 5);
- increase in the number of countries taking part in large international competitions;
- sharp growth in difficulty of competitive exercises (as a result of a substantial change in competition rules);
- more acute competition and broadening of the medal geography (of 8 sets of medals competed for in the men's competition at the Atlanta Olympics , representatives of seven countries won gold medals, while 15 countries received points. Four years later at the Sydney Olympics 6 and 18 countries respectively won gold medals and points. The gymnasts from Spain and Latvia became Olympic champions for the first time;
- wide-scale copying and swift introduction of advanced techniques into the system of gymnast training by most developed countries (to a significant degree this is a consequence of the export of qualified coaches from the former Soviet Union and, above all, Russia);
- development of a system of integral training of top-class gymnasts along the lines of multiple enlistment of various types of preparation, primarily physical and technical (physical-technical routine);
- a substantial improvement in material-technical and scientific-methodological provision for preparing the principal components (gymnastic halls, equipment and means of instant information, special training apparatus, technical aids, means of rehabilitation and restoration, methodological aids);
- acceleration of the rate of commercialisation of gymnastics (through attracting financial funding from major sponsors for marketing their products);
- growth in the authority of Russian gymnastics and interest in it from foreign organisations (this is evident in the growing number of invitations to Russian team members to competitions, displays and joint training);
- growing number of large international competitions and volume of competitive preparation during the annual cycle.

1.5 Forecasts and Prospects

So where is gymnastics going and what will happen to it? Forecasting, as we know, is an invidious occupation. Nonetheless, virtually all experts put themselves on the line. We too will give way to the tradition.

The FIG Competition Rules are the main instrument of gymnastics development in the world. They are created and confirmed by the men's and women's technical committees, answerable only to the FIG Congress which elects them. So the personnel composition of the technical committees, and their vision of prospects and paths of gymnastic development are decisive for world gymnastics.

At the present time a number of problems connected with judging have arisen in gymnastics. They are examined in some detail in the final section of this Chapter (1.6). Let us merely remark that subjectivity and the voluntary nature of the FIG technical committees, given their isolation and lack of control, could well cause serious harm to gymnastic development.

All the same, there are grounds for optimism, since the history of gymnastics shows that, despite everything, gymnastics as a whole has developed and will develop in accordance with its integral stable and natural development trends (see Chapter 1.4).

The main feature of this is the growth in complexity of competitive programmes and improvement in technical performance, bringing it up to the level of virtuosity in accord with the Olympic slogan 'Citius, Altius, Fortius!' However, within the framework of these trends, there are great possibilities for manipulation. Subjectivity, incompetence, lack of feedback and accountability pose a serious threat to progress.

In our opinion, one of the most fundamental principles of gymnastics remains unshakeable – determining the result from the external picture of exercises performed on the basis of a visual assessment of movements according to the given rules. However, there may also be additional quantitative approaches.

With the help of programming we can, for example, automatically determine conformity to the competition rules of geometric parameters of movements

Characteristics of Gymnastics

(length and height of flight, side deviations, etc.), lines, angles, poses and positions of the gymnast's body. Here the corresponding deductions will occur automatically by computer and be seen on the tableau. Technically this is not very difficult and may be done today, for example, in support vaults, on the rings, parallel bars and horizontal bar. We can work out powerful versions of programmes guaranteeing objective judging.

Elaboration and introduction of judging by such technical means seem to us to be extremely expedient. This would substantially ease the process of judging, enhance its objectivity, enable us to make it more transparent for the public and mass media and, finally, would present to specialists, the audience and press valuable additional information.

The main problems of judging, however, will not alter: what the gymnast does, and how he does it. Therefore the key instrument of evaluation of competitive activity will for a long time to come remain the eyes, ears and brains of a qualified judge, his knowledge of the competition rules and experience.

Accumulated gymnastic mentality will not undergo any substantial changes. For gymnasts of the future there will remain the need and urge to consistently master new complex exercises, new forms of movement and to seek new ways of raising the quality of their performance. Gymnastics in all its facets will remain a vividly expressive and creative form of sport close to art. And here each gymnast can and must possess his or her own inimitable personality for which a huge multiplicity of elements and routines exist, as well as styles and nuances in manner of execution.

Poor gymnastics equipment is dangerous. This cannot be ignored. To turn head over heels, all other things being equal, is always more risky than to walk or run fast round a stadium. But this potential danger can be minimised through the broad introduction of quality equipment, safety precautions and learning programmes into world gymnastics.

These programmes must embrace the whole process of preparation from novice to master, all the main forms of preparation and supervision. They should be created for specific elements, routines and whole structural groups. They should be constructed on the principle of continuity and class didactic principles (gradualness, accessibility, systemisation, awareness, simplicity). These programmes may exist in the form of hard copies or in electronic form (for example, as a CD-Rom prepared by FIG). They should be the accumulation of advanced practical experience and scientific attainments. Being accessible through the internet to coaches, gymnasts, experts and any other users interested in gymnastics, these programmes may become powerful anti-monopoly factors in gymnastics of the future.

One of the principal conditions of progressive development in gymnastics is growth in its world popularity. The gymnastics public ought to be activated through efforts to involve gymnastics into the school curriculum in all countries where this does not so far exist. This would give a powerful stimulus to gymnastics development, the gymnastics industry and infrastructure. We should also stress that a quality gymnastics set of equipment, together with good methods of instruction and technical preparation, are necessary for enhancing the accessibility of complex gymnastics exercises, for raising the mass nature of the sport and top skills, as well as reducing injuries.

Another prerequisite of growth in popularity is the creation of a widespread system of stimulation for doing gymnastics at all ages. We must accept that objective anti-stimuli also exist that hamper active involvement in gymnastics. This includes insufficient and poor quality equipment in gymnastics halls (and, indeed, the halls themselves), expensive equipment, the high work load of teaching, the inaccessibility of complex exercises for the mass of gymnasts, the long period of preparation of top-class gymnasts (by comparison with other sports), the poor competition schedule, the lack of objective judging and accidents.

In terms of gymnastics injuries we should stress that the paramount reasons are the following:

- insufficient amount of high quality equipment;
- unsatisfactory safety technique;
- lack of necessary training aids and safety structures;
- inadequate methods of teaching and preparation techniques;
- inability of the coach to conduct the preparatory part of the lesson, wrong or inadequate warming up (general and on the equipment);
- insufficient knowledge by coaches of the principles of technique and basic preparation, their inadequate qualifications;

- exaggeration by coaches and athletes of their real potential;
- too early attempts at complex exercises;
- insufficient information about the learning-training process.

Injuries may be reduced and even removed altogether through removing the above-listed reasons. An important condition of further development is the creation of real stimuli for investing in the preparation of top-class gymnastics, in gymnastics education and science, in the preparation of personnel and in improving the training of coaches.

A real possibility for raising the popularity of gymnastics is the development of more accessible forms and introduction of new gymnastics competitions. For these purposes we should widely encourage mass competitions, on a regional, national and international scale, in general and team-group gymnastics (General Gymnastics and Eurogym), as well as competitions in fitness-gymnastics of a testing nature.

Mass gymnastics competitions in a maximum number of circles on the horse, longswings on the horizontal bar, on the spot somersaults, pull ups, press ups, angle retention, rope climbing (incidentally, rope climbing was included in the first modern Olympics as an independent form of gymnastics multi-events) could be extremely popular. In these competitions one should ensure the award of prizes for victory in both individual events and as a whole. Contests for the most complex and original element or routine could be of interest to gymnastics, the audience and the press.

An increase in the number of gymnastics clubs, schools and gymnastics boarding schools is important to promote gymnastics and its popularity. To stimulate this process we might introduce into the FIG calendar continental and world championships or cups among gymnastics clubs and schools. We might also work out a more intensive and qualitative international calendar of special junior tournaments.

To ensure the progressive development of gymnastics we must increase the number of international tournaments. This would provide additional stimulus for raising skill levels and the world ratings of gymnasts and coaches from different countries. A full and stable calendar of international competitions is a pre-requisite for the successful development of high achievement gymnastics.

In concluding this section we would enumerate the conditions on which depends the successful development of gymnastics on a national and world basis and the attainment of high sporting results:

- the existence of bases for preparation equipped with up-to-date gymnastics equipment and means of supervision;
- the existence of a sufficient number of qualified coaches;
- a system for preparation and raising coach qualifications;
- a scientifically grounded system of preparing a reserve of budding gymnasts and its constant improvement;
- coach knowledge of the basic laws of biomechanics, physiology, sports psychology and sports education with account for gymnastics specifics;
- systematic publication of good quality literature and method aids for gymnastics (including drawings and photo albums, colourful posters, videofilms, computer programmes, CDs, etc.);
- modernisation of equipment in the sense of increasing their 'elasticity', which will enable coaches to increase the volume and intensity of the training load and reduce injuries;
- elaboration and mass production of training aids and additional gymnastics equipment;
- automation of the learning and training process with use of computers for the purpose of learning and supervision;
- lengthy centralised preparation;
- widescale utilisation of restorative means in the learning and training process;
- full and varied calendar for all ages and forms of gymnastics;
- increasing the number and forms of competition that require multiple preparation;
- simplification of competitions for children and juniors;
- improving the rules of competition;
- help to countries starting to cultivate gymnastics;
- commercialisation of gymnastics.

As far as the techniques for preparing top-class gymnasts elaborated in this book are concerned, we do not see them as a finished closed system. We set them out not as dogma, but as an open, progressively developing system that is swiftly adapting itself to new trends, scientific progress, and methodological and organisational innovations. We believe that Russian gymnastic ideology and methodology, as well as technology and experience of training Russian top-class gymnasts, will be valuable to gymnasts and coaches the world over. And not only to gymnasts.

We look to the future of Russian and world gymnastics with optimism and we believe that gymnastics has real prospects of becoming an elite, self-ensuring sport.

1.6 Rules of Competition

As already mentioned in the previous Chapter, the rules of FIG international competitions are one of the most powerful tools for promoting gymnastics. And this tool is completely in the hands of the FIG men's and women's technical committees which are virtually unaccountable to anyone.

In 1996, the FIG ratified new rules of international competition drawn up by the technical committees [81]. They made the most radical changes for the past fifty years. Along with many positive features we believe that the rules were not totally adequate – for the following reasons.

They artificially simplify competition for countries with an insufficiently high level of gymnastics development. Having raised the factor of chance outcome of competitive struggle, they have confused the sense of one of the fundamental principles of any sport – 'May the best man win!'. Instead, they raise the less able to the level of the top gymnasts, the rules have turned this principle on its head.

This is due to a number of factors. Above all, it has retained the earlier introduced rule of selecting participants in the final competitions according to the results of qualifying contests (no more than three gymnasts per country in the final full events and no more than two in the individual finals). As a result of this discriminatory limit, the objectively best athletes do not compete in the finals, while the weaker do only because they are from another country.

By encouraging the trend to reduce the numerical composition of national teams at the World and Olympic Championships, as well as the possibility of varying this composition in the multiple events during the team competitions, they have created artificial rewarding conditions for the weakly prepared teams and countries where gymnastics is for the moment less developed. To a certain extent this has devalued the team medals.

Certainly, we must acknowledge that in a short period the new rules have actually ensured a sharp growth in the difficulty of competitive programmes of the world gymnastics elite. But this growth has occurred at the expense of a change in ideas about the difficulty of gymnastics exercises canonised by the technical committees at their own whim. As a result of this artificial devaluation the difficulty of exercises has grown in an unbalanced way and only in a single direction. Exercises of the world gymnastics elite have become similar to the compulsory programme comprising a very limited number of elements and routines.

We believe that the FIG 1996 Rules go against one of the main trends in world gymnastics, expressed in the athletic rise in complexity of exercises. We must explain this further; it is a fact that two key directions exist in the growth of difficulty and complexity: *athletic* and *coordinated*.

The athletic direction in growth of complexity is evident in the following consecutive actions: somersault, double somersault, triple somersault, etc. Here each somersault can be done from the start in simple form, then in tuck, then finally with twist. In all cases the growth in complexity is ensured by an increase in basic parameters of flight given to the gymnast from support, which requires a higher level of special physical preparation and more complex coordination of technical actions (see Chapter 6).

A growth in complexity in the coordinated direction is evidenced by that in a single unit of time gymnasts perform more varied complex elements or more complex technical actions. Here the phase of culminating actions of a single complex element becomes simultaneously the phase of preparatory actions of another, often more complex element or routine. Complex elements are closely intertwined and as it were, bind into each other. All simple connecting elements are removed from complex routines. What happens is a concentration of complexity of movements in time and space.

The FIG 1996 Rules have stimulated a growth in complexity precisely in the coordinated direction, thereby hampering an athletic growth in complexity. With regret we have to say that the system predetermined by these rules is an addition to the basic evaluation that has operated in the 1997-2000 Olympic cycle, and it has not encouraged the acquisition of new super-complex elements of an athletic nature which objectively are more complex than the routines. As practising coaches we maintain that the routines being rewarded by the judges can in practice be mastered much more easily and quickly. And the gymnast, having exerted less work and psychological energy, has received greater addition to the basic evaluation.

Thus, to perform a triple somersault in the free exercises the gymnast through powerful explosive muscle effort must create a very large impulse of strength at the outset. He must coordinate very precisely his efforts and actions in time and space in conditions of an acute shortage of time. He needs an extremely high level of speed-strength qualities, precise coordination, excellent technique, extraordinary courage and a lot of hard work.

Insufficient preparation or a technical error in performing the triple somersault may be very costly. In order to master the triple somersault, even a very talented, well-prepared gymnast needs to spend a great deal of time, he needs strong nerves and strength under the leadership of a top-class coach. This exercise is therefore objectively very difficult, complex and risky.

The triple somersault in free exercises was a rare element; only a few were able to execute it. However, at the 1988 Seoul Olympics two Soviet gymnasts (Ljukin and Gogoladze) successfully performed this most complex and spectacular element in their free exercises. After the introduction by FIG of new rules in 1997, it disappeared from the top international and national competitions. At the Sydney Olympics no single gymnast performed the triple somersault in the multiple events.

This sad phenomenon is due to the fact that a routine, like a handspring, a straight forward somersault, a straight forward somersault with 360 turn and a forward somersault with a turn of 540° are all quicker and easier to master, all other things being equal, than a triple somersault. But the addition to this routine by the 1996 FIG Rules has constituted 0.5 points, while the triple somersault has only 0.3. The gymnast may well lose 0.2 for spreading his legs in tuck position during flight, without which a successful triple somersault is very problematic. Another one or two tenths will probably be lost on landing. Thus, real deductions are higher than potential additions to the score. One wonders which coach and gymnast would risk it.

Not surprisingly, most gymnasts in the world elite have gone down the road of least resistance. As a result of insufficiently thought-out actions by the technical committees the triple somersault in both the free exercises and on the horizontal bar and rings has practically vanished. At the same time a number of other very complex and spectacular elements have also disappeared.

Personal understanding of techniques and prospects for gymnastics development, as well as subjective aesthetic views on individual members of the technical committees have led to the introduction of unfounded deductions to biomechanically expedient elements of technique without which a successful performance of several very complex elements is becoming practically impossible.

This primarily applies to spreading the knees during the triple somersault (without which the injury potential of the element is acutely increased), as well as the requirement for full straightening of the body before landing in performing such super-complex support vaults as the 2.5 forward somersault. Thus, at the 1999 world championships in China, Yelena Produnova was the first woman to execute this vault, yet received a relatively low mark because of the deductions laid out in the above-mentioned requirements.

One may gain the impression that technical committee experts, by introducing these and similar requirements, bans and deductions for execution technique, have never worked as coaches, let alone with a squad of top-class gymnasts. That is why at best they are just realistically out of touch. At worst they are simply giving in to lobbying by those countries whose gymnasts have not risen to the level of complexity and technique of top-class gymnasts.

Therefore, the main flaw in the 1996 FIG rules is that they go against the natural trend of direct athletic growth in complexity of elements inherent in gymnastics. These rules have largely stimulated a coordinated growth in complexity of routines for the mastering of which we require a lower level of physical and technical preparation. What is more, the value of the routines in the rules have been artificially raised, while the value of athletic elements has been lowered.

Of course, the growth in complexity of routines has to be welcomed. But for the harmonious development of gymnastics we need it organically to be

CHARACTERISTICS OF GYMNASTICS

related to the growth in athletic complexity of these elements. If not, the development of world gymnastics will contradict the Olympic motto of 'Citius, Fortius, Altius!' After all, to perform a triple somersault one must run up faster, push off more strongly and fly higher than when executing any element of the above-mentioned routine.

As we know, the way to hell is paved with good intentions, but what is important is the result, not the intention. As we say, 'Don't count your chickens until they are hatched'. Unfortunately, the good intentions of the FIG technical committees have led to an artificial judgement on the opportunities for creative self-expression of gymnasts, which has caused harm to the harmonious development of gymnastics. It has substantially narrowed the selection of elements and routines performed at the top international and national competitions.

In the 1997-2000 Olympic cycle the exercises of the world gymnastics elite have become more monotonous in structure, less spectacular and less individual. This is apparent in the results of a comparative analysis of the content of exercises by finalists in all the recent major international competitions, starting with the 1987 World Championships [9]. True, the exercises have become more complex, but their difficulty has risen at the expense of an artificial devaluation of some elements and the rise in value of others, without sufficient biomechanical grounds for this.

After the Sydney 2000 Olympics the newly-selected FIG men's and women's technical committees drew up and ratified new versions of the rules for international men's and women's competition [82]. These rules made considerable strides forward. They reviewed the table of difficulty of elements in the various disciplines, they reviewed the value of routines, they changed the basic assessment. Many of the above-mentioned remarks were taken into consideration in this new version of the rules, but far from all. As before (though in less degree) they continue predominantly to reward coordinated growth in complexity of exercise and actually hold back the athlete.

We do not understand the criteria governing the men's technical committee in assessing the difficulty of lateral crosses (Azarian) and banning the crossing of the ropes when executing elements of longswings on the rings. These beautiful and complex elements are actually forbidden and totally devalued. In their place the rules now reward monotonous (in terms of limited selection) direct routines of complex power elements – ie sheer strength, but not complex technique.

This will lead (and has already led) to a compositional distortion, a lack of balance and disharmony in exercises on the rings by top-class gymnasts. They are becoming even more primitive, monotonous and based purely on strength. This is encouraged also by the inexplicable classification principle of determining certain structural groups of elements in this and other events. The rules also practically devalue longswings on one arm on the horizontal bar and a number of other beautiful and complex elements.

Analysis of the new rules has shown they continue to be replete with special explanations or exceptions repeated in various versions which, instead of making requirements more transparent, understandable and unambiguous, confuse the sense of what is being explained. On reading them there arises the possibility of multiple interpretation of certain points, which diminishes objective judging. This naturally provokes subjectivity, which enables some judges to judge incorrectly and relatively to get away with 'murder'. One would like to think this is not done deliberately.

It is worth adding that an important condition of the successful growth in gymnastic popularity is accessibility and transparency of the competition rules and, above all, judging for spectators and the mass media. The current rules, as in the previous 1997-2000 Olympic cycle, are too complex for mass perception.

One of the important conditions for the successful preparation of gymnasts is that the competition rules should operate for a fairly long time without amendment; at least for a single Olympic cycle. Unfortunately, almost immediately after ratification of the last rules and, especially, the previous version of the rules, the technical committees began to send amendments, additions and explanations to national federations. This indicates an insufficiently thought through set of ratified rules.

We believe the new versions of rules for international competition drawn up by the technical committees ought to be ratified only after sufficiently broad, competent and qualified discussion by specialists, particularly leading coaches and biomechanics experts. Hopefully the renewed structure of FIG as a result of reforms will ensure this, as long as the technical committee experts will be prepared to concede an iota of their independence.

How to Create Champions

CHAPTER TWO

Methodological Basis of Preparation Technique

2.1 Methodological Basis

The many years required to prepare gymnasts represents a complicated dynamic system which consists of interconnected elements which together function as an integral whole. The preparation system is composed of elements or forms of preparation. The means of interaction and the interrelationships between the elements of the preparation system define its structure.

The concept of system plays an important role in modern science and technology. Even in antiquity, Aristotle formulated a thesis about the whole being greater than the sum of its parts. This thesis even today is one of the cornerstones of the systems approach, A system has qualities different from those which its elements possess. For example, a chair may be seen as a system with a certain structure. The chair possesses qualities which not one of its elements possesses (legs, back, seat). You can sit comfortably on it higher than floor level, but not on its separate parts.

The system of gymnast preparation also possesses special integrative attributes which are different from those which its elements possess. For example, it enables you to attain a level of preparation which cannot be achieved by any of the forms of preparation by themselves. The highest level of this system is the technique of preparing top-class gymnasts that represents a complicated developing object.

As a result of development a new qualitative state of the preparation system arises which is expressed in a change in its composition and structure. In accordance with changes in the competition rules and new information, the preparation technique also changes form. These changes are inevitable over time. But they can be reversible too. Development of the preparation system, like any other complex dynamic system can be progressive and regressive.

Progressive development represents an irreversible, directed, law-governed change in the composition and structure of the system that is characterised by transition from lower to higher, from less refined to more refined. Progressive development in any system is connected with its complication, intensive structuring and growth, integration and differentiation of its elements, an increase in the scope of expedient functions in the attainment of the required result [70]. All these signs are integral to gymnastics today which is constantly becoming more complex and consequently, is developing progressively.

The motor activity of gymnasts (like all athletes) over many years of preparation depends on the action of many factors (sociological, historical, pedagogical, psychological, physiological, medical-biological, genetic, biomechanical, biophysical, etc.). Therefore these different aspects are studied by different sciences. They develop into new scientific directions reflecting the processes of differentiation and specialisation of scientific sports disciplines, as well as general methodological trends towards the integration of knowledge about sport in general and about gymnastics in particular. The leading edge of sports science gradually results in the evolution of border and interdisciplinary areas.

One of the major trends in the methodology of modern sciences is the investigation of complex phenomena, processes, events of phenomena and any complex functioning systems in the direction not from the start to the end, but on the contrary – from the end (peak or exit) to the beginning (foundation or entry). This trend by its very roots goes into the work of the great Russian physiologist Ivan Sechenov whose words were: 'from the end to the beginning – that is indeed materialism' [54].

This methodology received its theoretical grounding in the general systems theory [12], in the theory of functional systems [2,3], in the physiology of activity [11], and other theoretical conceptions of contemporary natural science. It has been shown theoretically and experimentally that this approach is more productive than the path from beginning to end, not only when studying complex functional systems and processes, but also when planning practically any purposive activity, especially scientific research, as well as when working out and projecting complex systems and high techniques. We consistently use this methodology in our work.

We view the activity of gymnasts in preparation and the preparation itself as functional systems with a purposive outcome in the form of the sporting-technical result. If we analyse the gymnast's activity in the direction of end to start – ie from the viewpoint of the accessible result – we obtain the following picture.

The specific sporting-technical result is a direct consequence of certain gymnastic movements which represent a *biomechanical process*. This process arises and takes place owing to the regulated work of muscles guided by the central nervous system, which represents a *physiological process*. The gymnast's higher nervous activity to some extent is conditioned by *psychological processes*. For them to develop in the required direction, the coach uses various educational means, thereby carrying out a *pedagogical process* (Figure 2).

As a result of the coach's pedagogical impact on the gymnast, certain psychological processes arise and set into motion neuro-physiological mechanisms. Their working ensures certain movements in the gymnast's body and/or links in time and space, which in the final event leads to a specific sporting-technical result. The latter in turn is a direct result of technical actions which, from outside, once again, are expressed in the gymnast's movements representing the same biomechanical process.

How to Create Champions

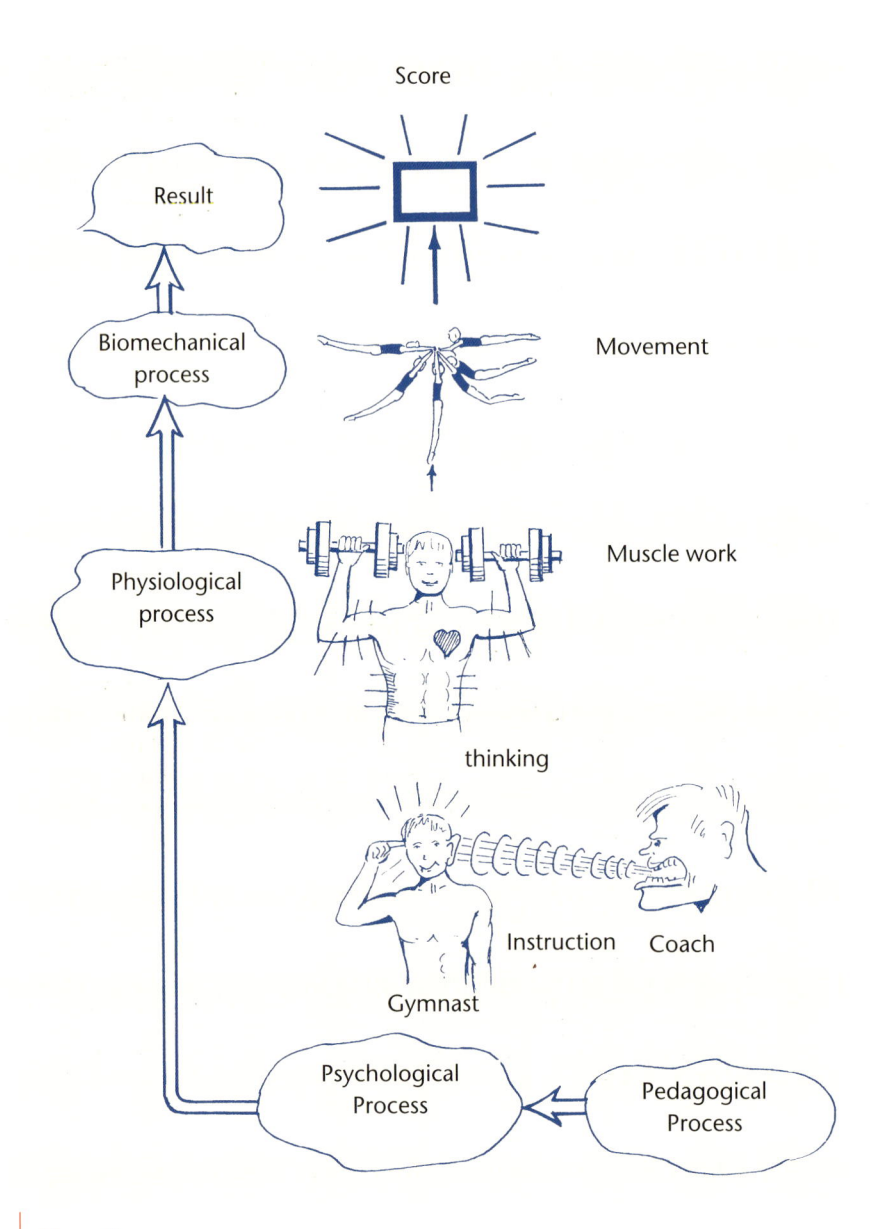

Figure 2 – *Structure of Gymnast's Activity*

All of the above-mentioned processes in principle should be directed at a precise realisation of an optimal biomechanical programme [1]. The fact that the purpose itself, the process of its attainment and the result, ultimately and objectively are manifested at the level of biomechanical characteristics predetermines the special role and place of biomechanics in the structure of sports science. This is a unique outcome of sporting-motor activity (Figure 3).

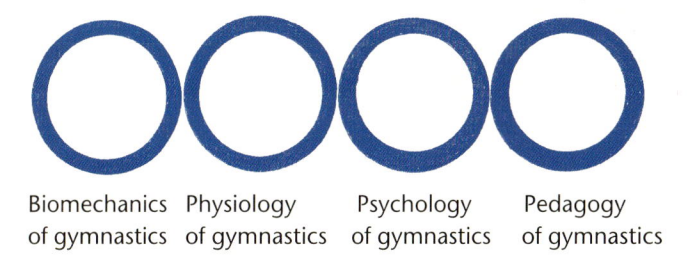

Biomechanics of gymnastics   Physiology of gymnastics   Psychology of gymnastics   Pedagogy of gymnastics

Figure 3 – *Structure of Gymnastic Science*

In the light of what has gone before, a model of sporting-motor activity, for example, the gymnast (athlete) may be presented in the form of a three-sector 'black box' with semi- permeable internal partitions (figure 4), where each sector reflects corresponding biomechanical, physiological and psychological aspects of the gymnast's motor activity. *Entry* into this black box is the gymnast's psyche, while the *exit* is the biomechanical characteristics of his movements. If necessary the lid over each sector may be mentally raised and one can make a biomechanical, physiological, psychological or pedagogical analysis of the gymnast's actions.

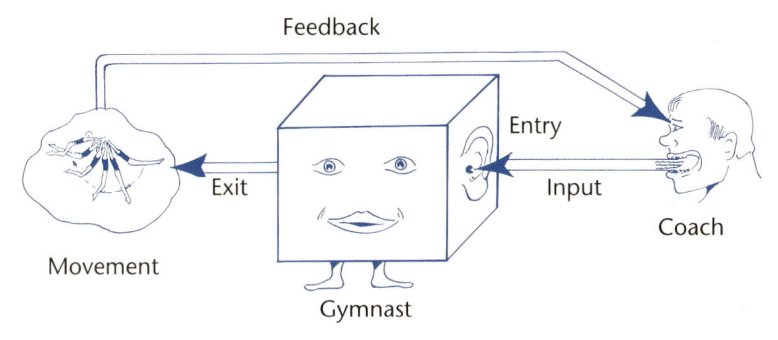

Feedback
Entry
Exit   Input
Movement   Coach
Gymnast

Figure 4 – *The "black box" model*

The gymnast's activity, like any activity, is bound to be purposive. It must always be preceded by some ideal model or aim – global or concrete. So before the gymnast begins to perform whatever actions, the coach must set him an understandable and attainable goal. In other words, the aim of the actions before their commencement must be explicitly formulated and set as a psychological entry to the 'black box', as some ideal model of what has to be received as a result of these actions. This integral model is usually rapidly transformed in one degree or another into a developed 'tree of aims'. In general it should be formulated at a conscious level and be reinforced by kinetic sensations. As a result, a large part of its branches will move to the subconscious level controlled in the automated psycho-physiological regime.

Thus, as a result of psycho-pedagogical actions on the gymnast before the start of specific actions an ideal picture must be created of what has to happen as a result of the gymnast's actions (the *aim*) and what concretely is necessary for this to happen (*tasks*). Physiologists call this an *action acceptor* [3], or a *model of required future* [11], while psychologists call it an *image* [40].

After the aim is formulated and understood, the gymnast performs purposive actions and operations which lead to a certain outcome. Information about the result of the gymnast's actions along channels of feed-back must enter the governing apparatus where what happens (the *result*) is equivalent to what you wanted to obtain (the *aim*). If the aim is not reached, that means there has been an error somewhere. In that case new tasks are set and we work out guiding actions which are directed on reducing more and more the gap between the aim and the result.

When they coincide (or we get an acceptable gap) the result is evaluated by the control apparatus (coach) as *useful*, which is transmitted to the performance apparatus (in our case the gymnast). For example, after a number of unsuccessful repetitions of the exercise, the coach finally says to the gymnast: 'This is what you have to do.' According to the theory of functional systems of P.K.Anokhin [2,3], the useful result is a system-forming factor. Here the processes taking place in the black box (in our case these are psychological, physiological and biomechanical processes) form a functional system. This in the first approximation is one of the basic mechanisms for forming the habit of correct execution of gymnastics exercises of any complexity, correct technique or required physical attribute. In our conception it is taken as the basis.

The above-examined processes are taught in special scientific disciplines, viz. *biomechanics, physiology, sports psychology and sports pedagogy.* It should be said, however, that these processes do not have precisely marked boundaries. They develop over time, gathering information and somehow interacting. This imprecision and interaction of the borders between processes ensures that motor activity is due to the presence of inter-disciplinary areas and border scientific directions in which we study the mechanisms of transition from one process to another.

The structure of the interdisciplinary and border directions studying sporting-motor activity is represented in Figure 5. Some of these directions are generally acknowledged (for example, psycho-physiology and pedagogical psychology), others are only developing (physiological biomechanics, psycho-biomechanics). But the mechanism of their formation is the same. We justify it on the basis of the 'black box' methodology and theory of successive approximations.

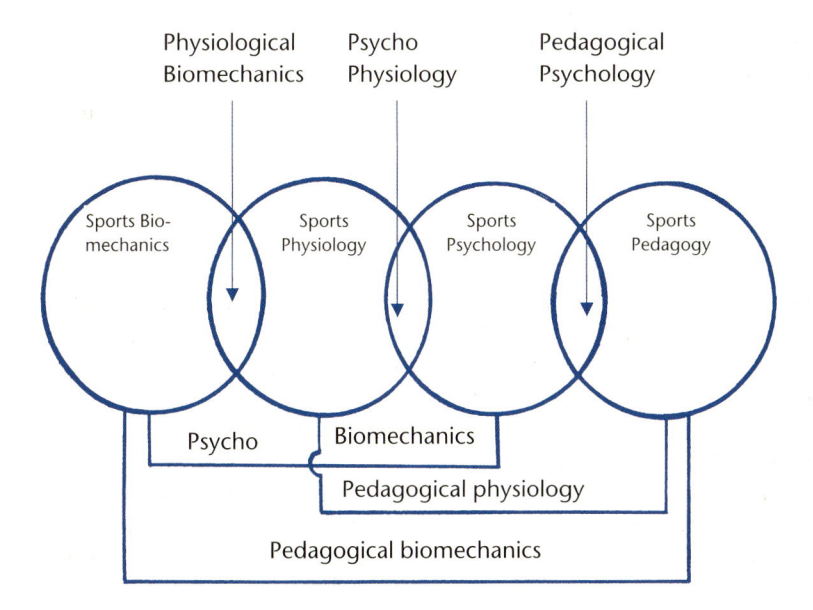

Figure 5 – *Structure of inter-disciplinary trends in sports science*

In our conception we take *pedagogical biomechanics* – ie the black box with a pedagogical entry and biomechanical exit – as one of the major interdisciplinary methodological models. The approach we have developed enables us to use both qualitative and quantitative definitions. The dominant formalised language of pedagogical biomechanics is the language of inequalities (*more or less*). With a qualitative analysis we do not use strict quantitative definitions, but we can with certainty confirm that this parameter is greater or smaller than with any gymnast or any given instruction.

Thus, pedagogical biomechanics in our conception is an objective interdisciplinary scientific direction and at the same time a concrete methodology. As one of the main aims, it sets out to establish close ties between biomechanics and sporting pedagogy. One of the major tasks is to reveal the interrelations between the coach's pedagogical impact and the biomechanical consequences of the gymnast's actions. Pedagogical biomechanics has two overriding tasks – *direct* and *reverse*. The direct task consists of determining the biomechanical consequences of pedagogical actions, while the reverse task determines the pedagogical consequences of biomechanical effects on gymnasts.

Contemporary Russian preparation techniques for top-class gymnasts are based on the classical didactic principles of pedagogics (*gradualness, accessibility, systematic progress, consciousness and firm grounding*) and have sufficient scientific and methodological foundation. They rely on advanced gymnastics experience and the results of research. Russian scientists have established the biomechanical and psychological-pedagogical basis of gymnastic activity, as well as the major aspects of their preparation [69, 46, 15, 56, 63, 30, 44, 53, 73, et al].

Especially important in our conceptions is the problem of integral preparation, organically linking all its forms and components into a single pedagogical technique of a production line of top-class gymnasts. Until recently this problem was resolved mainly at an intuitive-empirical level within the framework of the national team. Only recently have we begun to tackle it on the level of theory [8,9].

The overall methodological bases of our concept of preparing gymnasts are the genetic method, the principle of historicism and the systems approach [23,

60, 63], while the specific bases are the sporting-goal, forecasting prospects approach and the principle of outstripping development realised through creating optimal surplus in our forms of preparation [63, 8, 9]. These methodological principles are our cornerstone. They permeate the entire preparation system, all its forms and the entire set of techniques.

Before setting out the essence of our approach, our methodology, we have to provide some explanation of relative forecasting and prognosis in gymnastics without which we cannot build and justify an effective technique for preparing top-class gymnasts.

We refer to forecasting as foreseeing or foretelling any gymnastics event, result or phenomenon in the future. Thus, gymnastics forecasting establishes a link between the present and the future of gymnastics and gymnasts. When forecasting we may use both *intuitive* (based on practical experience) and *scientific* (based on law-governed, set scientific methods) forecasts. Making forecasts in time may be divided into current (a week, month), short-term (from a few months up to a year), middle term (up to two years) and long-term (four years or more). The difference between the usual and the sports-oriented forecasting are as follows: The former is a probable judgement about what will happen with a given sport and with specific athletes in a certain period, which emerges from an analysis of preceding and current events. The latter is what must happen (and we want to happen) at a given moment of time if we take into consideration the starting conditions and what has to be striven for.

We should mention that the operation of reverse action frequently leads to self-fulfilment or self-destruction of the forecast if we act on the latter. So foretelling a sporting success may cause inspiration and mobilisation of the athlete's powers. Foretelling failures may cause panic in some athletes and actually exacerbate the situation.

An adequate forecast is the basis for timely correction of the preparation programme and elimination of causes of possible negative consequences. So when forecasting we orient ourselves on evaluation of the *probable* (given the condition of maintaining current trends in gymnastics) and the *desired* (given the condition of pre-set norms or results). In forecasting theory this corresponds to *outcome and process* forecasting [53].

How to Create Champions

The speculative forecast in gymnastics is the continuation into the future of observable tendencies as long as they will not be altered by administrative means. Speculative forecasting somehow steadily penetrates into the future, first the immediate, and then the distant future. Its aim is to reveal prospective problems that will need to be tackled given stable extraneous conditions.

Normative forecasting in gymnastics means defining possible paths of tackling problems arising in the preparation process with the aim of achieving a required state of the gymnast on the basis of pre-set criteria or norms.

Prospects are what in principle may be attained in gymnastics. But what interests us most of all is the part which coincides with our objective, set in accordance with a normative forecast, and changing (or directed changes) trends. That part of the prospects which defines the speculative forecast is what happens with a gymnast if trends remain stable and if we compare the parameters of what has been and what are at the present time. But this is far from always what we want to have in the future.

The sports-goal prospect-forecasting approach is based on the following basic concepts:

1. the necessary starting condition for setting adequate goals and tasks for long-term preparation of top-class gymnasts is an analysis of prospects and trends in gymnastics, a forecast of its state and the state of gymnasts in the future;
2. the data from speculative and normative forecasts are compared and used for working out and refining techniques of gymnast preparation, including its modelling, projecting, programming, guidance and supervision;
3. we need to establish strategic and tactical forecasting with a different degree of confirmation in time (i.e. to work out long-term, middle term, short-term and current forecasts) which we need to use for working out and correcting various periods and stages of long-term preparation;
4. compulsory procedures are as follows:
   - regular 'running ahead' and 'looking into the future' through multiple forecasting, modelling and expertise in various timescales;
   - regular comparison of indicators of current conditions of gymnasts with previous, expected and purposive (ie those conditions and parameters which we strive to achieve as a result of the preparation process in accordance with the normative sports-integrated forecast). This means comparing what *is* at a given moment with what *was*, with what *will be*, and finally with what *should be*.

METHODOLOGICAL BASIS

Let us stress that 'looking into the future' is not a single act, it is a process of constant orientation on gymnastics prospects which move on, become complicated and never stand still.

Thus, the sports-goal prospect-forecasting approach is a specific scientific-sporting orientation in a complex integral of programming, which sets and resolves basic tasks in preparing athletes, using overall scientific methods (analysis, synthesis, comparison, forecasting, modelling, projecting and programming). We work out a programme for preparing top gymnasts, and implement it according to an algorithm, the basis of which is set out in [37]. See Chapter 3.3.14.

The senior coach of a national team must constantly work with the drawn-up prospects and forecasts. Often the state which an athlete or team with high probability will attain after a certain period of time training according to the given methods will substantially differ from the purposive state. This is reason for expedient alteration in the training process and corrections to the preparation system.

A sports-goal prospect-forecasting approach is used not only for working out a system and technique of preparing the national team, but also in planning the preparation of junior gymnasts oriented towards attaining high sports results.

Outstripping development and optimal surplus are two functionally connected principles which permeate the whole system of integral preparation, all its components. They are the pivot of our approach.

As with most methodological concepts, these principles have their own historical roots. In our view they find their adequate expression in the popular Russian saying 'hard in study, easy in battle' or 'sow before you reap': the basic tenets of a soldier's actions in the battles to come must be learned in military studies. In this case it will be easier to fight and win.

The most important methodological tenet of preparing gymnasts is: *the paramount parameters of future competitive activity must be learned in training*. This postulate is a tool for implementing the principles of outstripping development and optimal surplus; they apply as much to gymnastics as any other pursuit. This tenet operates in all sports with high medal-earning capacity – ie where athletes of the national team regularly win a high percentage of medals from those on offer in the Olympic Games and World Championships. This tenet is applicable to the whole system of big-time sport.

It hardly needs special proof to see that the battle to come will be easier, more effective and productive if most possible situations are rehearsed in training sessions, and not simply rehearsed, but also many times played through, surpassing the actual demands. Of course, it is impossible to fully foresee and model all possible battle or competitive situations, but we have to strive towards it. We should note that gymnastics, as a sport with a stabilised kinematic movement structure, is much easier tactically than team games or individual pursuits. Gymnastics therefore has more opportunities in this sense.

For example, from a technical viewpoint, the difficulty of a competitive programme should not be at ceiling level. In training the gymnast should learn and be able to perform more complex exercises than in competition. The technique of performing a specific exercise should be ensured by a sufficiently rapid mastery of its more complex modifications.

The specific endurance of a top-class gymnast should be higher than what competitive activity demands. Surplus endurance should be such that in the event of tiredness and nervous stress the gymnast would not make a mistake when executing his competitive exercises and continue his competitive activity as required.

Test indicators of special physical preparation should be higher than what is required for performing competition exercises.

In order to attain the necessary and sufficient psychological surplus, the gymnast should be able to perform the competition programme in training in conditions which are more difficult than in competition. In this event the gymnast will be more stable in the face of the extraneous factors that are inevitable in competition.

Thus, for successful performance in competition we need an integrated optimal surplus comprising a surplus of technical, tactical, physical, functional and psychological components.

In conclusion we quote the opinion of McCullough, the eminent specialist in the mathematical theory of biological reliability; he considers that functional and morphological surplus in the structure of biological systems have as their main attribute and paramount factor their reliability. 'What is surplus,' he maintains, 'is in the same degree that it is surplus, stable. So it is reliable. Only through surplus can we get reliability'[41]. We fully share that opinion and use it in constructing our concept of top-class gymnast preparation.

2.2 The Concept of Preparation

In gymnastics which is oriented towards the highest level of achievement, the major goal of preparation consists of the successful performance at major competitions with the attainment of high sports and technical results which are pre-planned. Competitions and competitive activity here, as in all big-time sport, are primary, while the training activity is secondary and subject to the former.

Therefore, the basic integral model for the entire system of top-class gymnast preparation is the future competitive activity. For that reason it must be carefully studied, forecast and adequately modelled theoretically and practically in the preparation process.

This proposition is a system-forming factor in the preparation process of Russian top-quality gymnasts. Hence the strategy of their preparation comprises multiple modelling in training of the basic parameters of competitive activity over and above the actual requirement. This is achieved by implementing in training the principles of outstripping development and optimal surplus.

A key motto of Russian top-class gymnasts is 'Give high-quality super-complexity', while the proficiency criterion is reliable and requires error-less performance of full-value competitive-class exercises with set productiveness on the basis of virtuoso technique in circumstances of acute sporting contention.

The concept presupposes a constant increase in complexity and refinement in the composition of competitive exercises in all of the gymnastics events with simultaneous improvement in the level of technical-executive skill and competitive reliability. These tasks are tackled through the mastery and inclusion of original super-complex elements and routines in the competitive programme for national team candidates, the application of high volume and intensity of training loads arbitrarily spread in time, and adequate means of restoration.

A dominant concept is the strategic reliance on surpassing foreign rivals on basic parameters (difficulty and originality of exercises, sporting technique, performance proficiency, competition reliability, indicators of technical, tactical, physical, functional, psychological and theoretical preparedness).

The principal distinction between the traditional preparation system and the modern-day Russian technique consists of the following. In the 1960s gymnasts in control training sessions tried to attain only some parameters of competitive activity or even many times surpassed them in volume during weekly micro-cycles, but in conditions very far from competition.

Modern-day technique in training contains the set task of complex optimal surpassing of the basic parameters of forthcoming competitive activity with systemic surpassing of the major foreign rivals in all basic indicators of preparedness.

There are grounds to suppose that the psychological tenet of 'overtaking rivals' is more effective than that of 'Catching up'. A serious rival usually does not wait to be caught. He too forges ahead. As a result the process of reaching the level of a leader who is forging ahead may last for an indefinite period. In some sense this process is like a game of chess where the person playing the black pieces repeats the moves of his opponent playing white. The result is clear: the player of the white pieces claims victory.

We caught the Japanese gymnasts using their methods over some twenty years. Replacing 'catching up' by 'overtaking' with a change in preparation technique in the early 1970s enabled us relatively quickly to overtake everyone and become world gymnastics leaders. So the modern technical concept of preparing Russian top-class gymnasts poses the need for constantly keeping ahead of all rivals under the slogan: 'Keep ahead of all and everything!' both in terms of those who are in front and those who are catching up.

METHODOLOGICAL BASIS

To keep ahead, however, has to have its sensible limits. To achieve high results at the biggest tournaments dos not mean striving to keep ahead of modern-day gymnastics on several fronts at once. Besides this not being rewarded by the present rules and it being fraught with high probable risks, the gymnastics public might not understand and may not accept the innovations of futurist gymnasts, which are far from the realities of today. There have been such precedents in the history of gymnastics.

The world gymnastics community has to mature to reappraise set values and move to a new, higher level of development. Above all, this applies to the FIG technical committees who govern world gymnastics and to the judges who are compelled to carry out the existing rules. Our long-term experience has shown that to win it is enough to overtake rivals in the wheel, as cyclists say.

To attain the highest level of results gymnasts need to carry out large volumes of work over many years. They need to train a great deal, especially at the stage of entering the world of elite gymnastics. We must note that over recent decades there has been a marked tendency to increase training and competition loads for top-class gymnasts.

At the same time scientists and practitioners have noted many times that a purely mechanical increase in volumes of training loads in normal conditions by itself does not solve the problem of increasing the effectiveness of preparation. Moreover, it frequently has an adverse effect on the rate of improving technical proficiency, leads to overloading of the support-motor apparatus and an increase in injuries [23, 52, 63 et al.].

Thus, a contradiction arises between the need to increase training loads to attain high results and the limited psycho-physical potential of gymnasts, and, incidentally, also their environment (equipment). Further, load volumes in contemporary gymnastics are coming close to the limit from psychological, biological and social aspects. So extensive paths of resolving this problem (mechanical increase in load volumes) are to a certain degree exhausted. We have to seek reserves in the intensification of preparation.

The apparent contradiction in our concept may be resolved through constant improvement of methods of teaching and the techniques of integrated preparation, as well as its intensification through increasing work loads in higher zones of intensity. Here we create internal and external special conditions which ensure a fuller and safer implementation of the motor potential of gymnasts. Let us emphasise that it is the technique of integral preparation that is the cornerstone. The major components and versions of this technique have been tested by us in the last seven Olympic cycle, starting in 1973.

Relying on the classical didactic principle of pedagogics, Russian techniques of training top-class gymnasts are supplemented by the requirement to master the complex in the simple. This signifies that when learning a relatively simple element (for example, the tuck somersault), we need to master it not only at the level of error-less performance from a judging viewpoint, but at a parametric level that enables the gymnast swiftly to master the element in a more complex procedure (for example, a double and triple somersault).

In this case the path from the simple to the complex loses its one-dimensional linearity and acquires a sort of shuttle character, by this we mean a periodical return from the complex to the simple with transition of this simple in form movement to a parametrically more complex skill. In this connection what is important in our conception is the purposive basic preparation, whose role in the training process of the national team is actually increasing rather than diminishing.

The block-scheme of the concept of integrated preparation is shown in Figure 6. The structure of basic forms of preparation, in their unity and interconnection, are portrayed in the form of a flower with petals touching one another. Taken together these basic forms of preparation work as a uniform integrated technical system.

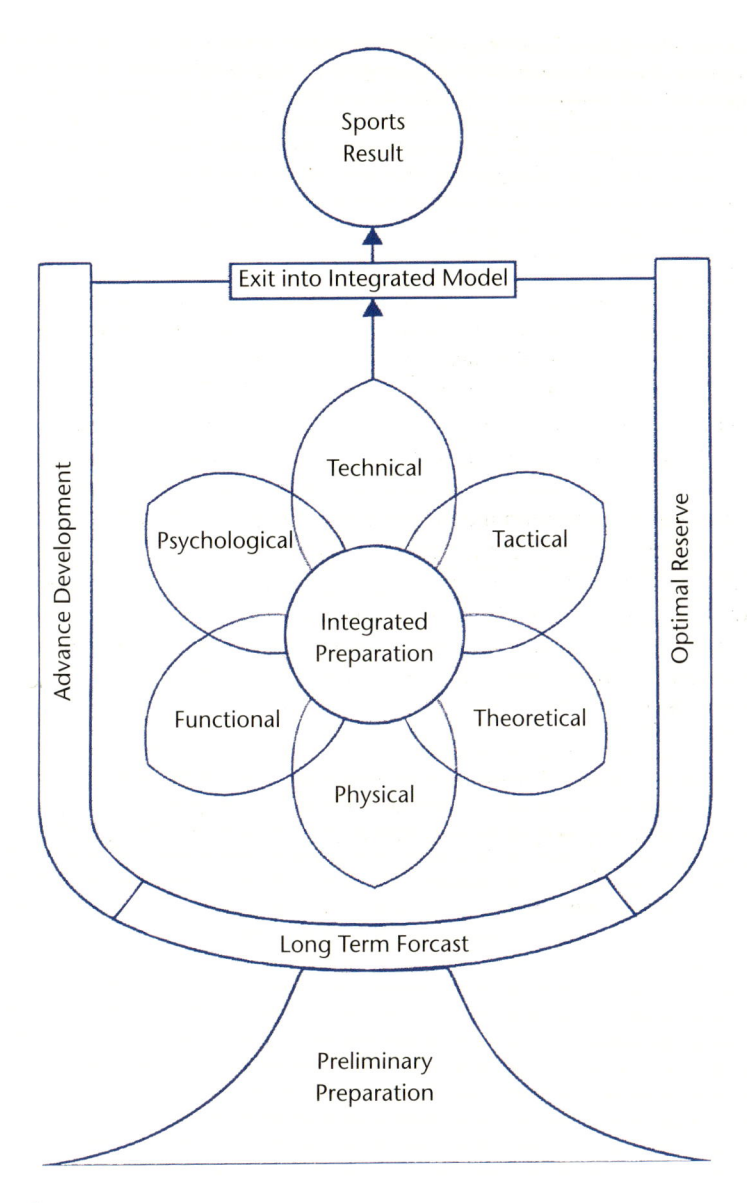

Figure 6 – *Concept of Preparation*

The fundamental rule of gymnastics today, its cornerstone, is physical preparation. A high level of physical preparedness is the first necessary condition for achieving top results in gymnastics. This condition is necessary, but it is not enough by itself.

In the final analysis, the only way to achieve a sporting-technical result is by technical actions leading to movement or fixation of the gymnast's body (or its links) in space and time. Any deviation is a direct result of technical mistakes whose causes may vary. So technical preparation is the 'roof' of the building of integrated preparation, built on the foundation of physical training.

If we view the system of integrated preparation in terms of 'entries' and 'exits', as is accepted in the external description of systems in system analysis we may see technical training as an *exit*, and physical preparedness as an *entry* into the system. From a mathematical viewpoint, the technical preparedness of top-class gymnasts may be represented as the function of a number of independent variables, the main one of which is level of physical preparedness.

Like the processes ensuring sports-motor activity, the forms of preparation represent non-rigid objects. As evident from Figure 6, they do not have strictly drawn boundaries separating them from one another. The forms of preparation interact, harness one another, intertwine and insert themselves into one another, forming indistinct multitudes (fuzzy sets [93]).

The main tasks of the lengthy preparation of the national team consist of the timely transfer to planned sporting-technical results and process indicators represented in integrated models and model characteristics of basic stages of the Olympic preparation cycle.

Formatively speaking, the fruits of the seven-colour rainbow of the integrated preparation have to ripen over time and they have to be picked in time, enabling the stages of preparation with corresponding sports results. In gymnastics slang this is 'timely transfer to an integrated model'.

The strategic aim of overseeing the preparation of the national team consists of ensuring that at the upcoming Olympics the team as a whole and each of its members display their best results. The tactical goals are to attain model indicators of preparedness and planned sports results in the many competitions at the basic stages of the Olympic preparation cycle. The condition of high and supreme top form is the functional condition ensuring the attainment of these objectives.

By management we understand the process of transferring the system to a set (integrated) state through influencing its variables. In our case the variables are indicators of level of preparedness of gymnasts (technical, physical, psychological, etc. – see Figure 6). The main means of influence on these variables in our developed conception are pedagogical methods and devices which are applied in routine with other means of influence and restoration (biomechanical, physiological, psychological, technical, natural, physical permissible pharmacological and medical-biological).

We consider biomechanics, physiology, sports psychology, sports pedagogy and medicine as the basic scientific-sports disciplines whose data we need to use when constructing the system of preparing top-class gymnasts. These disciplines constitute the natural scientific basis of the preparation concept (one of its fundamental constructs). The conception of preparation presupposes the need to use the attainments of sports medicine, biology, engineering and sports management.

Purposive research has to be made in these disciplines (primarily biomechanics and sports pedagogy), as well as in areas connected with them. For the purpose of developing gymnastics and enhancing the quality of scientific-methodology this work should be completed using a gymnastics model, both in experimental and in theoretical aspects.

An important component of integrated preparation is the provision system. Its major forms are: scientific-method provision (SMP), medical-biological provision (MBP), material-technical provision (MTP), financial provision (FP), personnel-resource provision (PRP), information provision (IP) and motivational provision (MP). When drawing up a preparation programme we have to determine *what* and *how much* we need for the preparation of the national team in the Olympic cycle.

The key source of replenishing personnel for any national team is its reserve – youth and junior team members. The preparation concept of Russian top-class gymnasts provides for purposive work with the reserve on the basis of the ideology and methodology described above, but with certain differences in the techniques and methods of preparation.

The preparation system relies on the above-mentioned forms of provision which, together with preparation of a reserve, research and experimental-constructor work (RW and ECW) represent the basic foundation of the concept of integrated preparation of the national team (see Figure 6).

This foundation serves also as a basis for the methodological shell of the preparation technique (*the sport goal prospective-forecasting approach, outstripping development and optimal surplus*) portrayed in the form of a horse-shoe inside which is the model of integrated preparation. The integrated model is the system-forming factor for it, while the actually attainable sports results are the outcome parameters. The criteria of optimising the process of integrated preparation are speed, *quality and reliability of mastering the sport goal models*.

As already mentioned, the basic foundation for drawing up a preparation programme for the national team in Olympic cycles is served by the sports-goal prospective-forecasting models. Modern techniques of the integrated preparation of Russian top-class gymnasts include the use of a whole system of such models (see Chapter 3.3). They are drawn up on the basis of an analysis of the dynamics of technical results in the Olympic cycle, trends in gymnastics (see Chapter 1.4 and 1.5) and the natural growth in complexity of gymnastic exercises (see Chapter 6.6) with account taken of the present level of preparedness of the national team and its major rivals.

We would stress that on the basis of a hierarchically chosen system of sports-goal prospective-forecasting models we carry out planning, programming, control and correction of the process of many years of preparing top-class gymnasts and the national team as a whole.

Models of content, difficulty and quality of performance of exercises by victors at future competitions (team, all around and individual equipment) are system-forming in this hierarchy. When drawing up these models the main task is the optimal outstripping of the forecast complexity, the quality and the reliability of execution of competitive exercises by the main foreign rivals with exceeding the actual functional demand of the upcoming competitive activity.

After working out these models we work out model characteristics of physical, functional and psychological preparedness that ensure the correct conclusion (see Chapter 3.3.3).

We regard model characteristics as variable guides possessing the quality of mutual compensation. So if a gymnast has little strength he may compensate for this shortcoming by excellent technique and vice versa (within reasonable limits).

A key condition for gaining planned results over many years of preparation is to figure out a 'tree of goals', setting specific tasks subordinate to the main strategic objective of successful performance at the major competitions with appropriate results. The main ones are as follows:

- creating optimal surplus (technical, tactical, physical, functional and psychological);
- outstripping possession of new super-complex exercises and on time mastery of the integrated model of the current stage of preparation;
- ensuring reliable and highly-productive activity in conditions that are more difficult than competition, according to the basic parameters.

The paramount object of planning, programming and projecting in our conception of training top-class gymnasts is the training process of the national team in the current four-year Olympic cycle. We manage the planning, programming and projection on the basis of our above-mentioned methodology in the direction *from the end (goal) to the beginning (starting condition)*. The principle of multiple repetition of models worked out in detail of the pre-competition stage of preparation culminating in the respective competitions lie at the core of planning over the four-year Olympic cycle of preparation.

We need to work out a programme for preparing the national team for the coming Olympics immediately after the past Olympics on the basis of a comparative analysis of results, trends, prospects and forecasts of gymnastics development both at home and abroad.

Drawing up models is a science and art simultaneously (see Chapter 3.1). So a creative team of coaches, scientists and specialists in top-class gymnastics must work together on elaborating the integrated parameters and model characteristics, models of periods and stages of preparation, models of training load, and other prospective-forecasting models. It is important for this to be a fairly narrow team of progressively thinking like-minded people (experts, analysts, practitioners) who adequately appreciate the problems of contemporary gymnastics and big-time sport, people who are well versed in their own speciality and preparation techniques. When selecting this team we ought to be governed by the following principle: coaches have to train gymnasts, and not the scientists or doctors, but with their obligatory participation as consultants and with the proofering of appropriate methodological assistance.

Goal models are becoming more complicated in each new Olympic cycle. They serve as the basis of drawing up and selecting new effective technical aids, ways of teaching and training top-class gymnasts. The goal model can be viewed as a 'tree of goals' in which the very top and upper branches of the tree are the structure of top level hierarchy. If the goals of the top levels are clearly marked, we can determine the structure of the entire tree of goals while following it from end to beginning along each branch [53]. The model characteristics of forms of preparedness and other models are fixed in a special document (called a comprehensive integrated programme for preparing the national team to the coming Olympic Games).

A major means of forming optimal surplus in the technique of integrated preparation is the outstripping modelling of basic parameters of competitive activity, i.e. surpassing its actual demand in the training process. With this aim in the integrated preparation we use several types of special training which model competitive activity (see Chapter 3.2).

In the preparation of top class gymnasts for competitions it is sensible to utilise various models of the stages of pre-competition training adapted to the form of the competition and the individual make-up of gymnasts. These stages consist of several weekly micro-cycles of varied direction. As we carry them out in training, we model various conditions of the coming competitive week, creating an optimal surplus of the basic parameters of preparedness and we tackle the tasks of restoration after training loads (see Chapters 3.2 and 5.5). We have tested these micro-cycles many times in the last seven Olympic cycles for the national team.

METHODOLOGICAL BASIS

We have established that to create optimal surplus at the stages of pre-competition preparation, the gymnasts sufficiently exceed the parameters of competition activity by 1.5 to 3 times in the model weekly micro-cycles and analogous training sessions. The lower the gymnast's ranking, the more he needs to exceed the limit. This approach enables the gymnasts to reach a peak of form by the start of competition.

To raise the effectiveness of the training process a necessary condition is optimal management of its course. This becomes possible when taking account and supervision of individual parameters of the training load which must be minimised according to the criterion of information (see 5.2), especially at the stages of direct preparation for competition. The parameters of actual training activity must periodically be compared with the sports goal prospective-forecasting models.

The integrated preparation conception presupposes the tactical correction of training load parameters according to the state and individual traits of specific gymnasts while maintaining the overall strategy of preparation for the team in general.

A major component in the technique of integrated preparation is the selection system of the national team. The sporting principle lies at the core of this (see Chapter 3.3.9).

The professionalisation of modern-day gymnastics is apparent in maintaining a high level of preparation for competitive activity over all the annual macro-cycles. This naturally leads to a shortening of the transitional period by up to two-three weeks a year. Moreover, the gymnasts continue to train fairly actively in this period.

Our many years of experience have shown us that the correct varying of volumes and intensity of training loads plus comprehensive use of pedagogical, physical and medical-biological means enables us to restore and maintain a high level of work during the annual cycle without a marked transitional period.

We tackle the tasks of psychological preparation mainly by pedagogical means. A high level of special physical and technical preparation, as well as multiple modelling of the conditions of competitive activity in the training process (see Chapter 3.2) ensures optimal physical, technical and psychological surplus, which considerably reduces the action of adverse psychological factors in competitions and training sessions.

Therefore, the need for the constant use of professional psychologists in training top-class national team gymnasts is substantially diminished. But from time to time their services and the provision of specialist psychological information are not only very useful but necessary.

We think that educational psychology is the most valuable in preparing top-class gymnasts for inter-disciplinary directions. Personal coaches of outstanding gymnasts who have followed them from childhood are intuitive educational psychologists. This, in our view, provides the best intuitive educational practitioner psychologists.

The principle of centralised preparation (see Chapter 4.8.7) dominates contemporary techniques of integrated preparation of the Russian national team. Many years of experience has proved the expedience of lengthy joint training sessions for the country's top gymnasts at specialised training camps. In training together they grow more rapidly in the sense of sports proficiency and results owing to the natural way of acute competition for a place in the team.

We need to have a comprehensive scientific group (CSG) consisting of highly-qualified scientists and experts with the national team. They coordinate applied research and provide a scientific-methodological preparation for the national team, including taking part in drawing up and grounding each new integrated programme. Active work of a compact and highly-qualified CSG is a necessary condition for successful preparation of any world-class national team.

The system of national team preparation and management over the four-year Olympic cycle is based on an analysis of the course of preparation and on correcting the programme. The material of regular tests carried out by the CSG experts together with the medics (see Chapter 9) provide data for the analysis and current correction of individual plans of candidates for the national team.

On the basis of this material at the end of each preparation year of the current Olympic cycle it is wise to draw up methodological recommendations. It is necessary to put this to a comparative analysis:

- results of all the year's competitions and control training sessions of the main candidates for the national team;
- data of the tests;
- resultant indicators of preparedness and integrated models.

Any deviations provide the reason for drawing up recommendations for correcting individual plans and preparation programmes for the national team.

2.3   Methodological Principles of Preparation

Let us now set out the methodological principles on which we construct the current Russian techniques for preparing top-class gymnasts at the national team level [97]:

- **Outstripping.** This principle stipulates the surpassing mastery of new super-complex exercises by the integrated model of the programmed Olympic cycle, as well as the drawing up, confirmation and inclusion in the training process of new means and methodological devices, training equipment and aids for teaching and training. In accordance with this principle, when selecting candidates for the Russian national team, together with sports results, we take into consideration the prospective competitive programme and the degree of its outstripping the programmes of the main foreign rivals.
- **Surplus.** This principles envisages the creation of optimal surplus on the main parameters of preparedness through the application of high volume and intensity training loads and the method of combined actions ensuring the formation in top-level gymnasts of preparedness and work capacity which should substantially exceed the demands of actual competitive activity. In line with this principle, a strategic objective of preparation should be an optimal surplus in the complexity of exercises, the quality and reliability of their execution, tournament endurance, technical, tactical, physical and psychological preparedness.

- **Professionalism.** This principle means the constant readiness of a top-class gymnast for competitive activity in the annual macro-cycle. It envisages the maintenance of a level of preparedness and form that will enable the gymnast to perform his competitive programme at any moment on demand;
- **Modelling.** In accordance with this principle, the major parameters of the upcoming competitive activity will be modelled many times during the preparation by mainly educational means. The role of such modelling will rise particularly during the stage of pre-competition preparation when we apply special model weekly micro-cycles;
- **Periodisation.** Accordingly an undulating spread of training loads is made in the macro, meso and micro-cycles of the preparation process;
- **Individualisation.** When drawing up personal competitive and training programmes, we consider the individual characteristics of gymnasts. The same goes for selecting the means and methodological devices of special preparation, planning and organizing the pre-competition stages;
- **Scientific-methodological grounding.** When preparing the national team we constantly test and introduce new effective means and methods of special preparation and teaching as well as new equipment and control methods. However, we only reinforce preparation techniques with those that have undergone preparatory testing with other squads of gymnasts and have obtained necessary and sufficient scientific-methodological grounding.
- **Routine of multiple preparation and specialisation.** This principle envisages preparation on a multiple basis for 'universal' gymnasts capable of putting up a successful battle for medals both on individual pieces of equipment and in the overall category. Heightened demands are made on them in terms of difficulty and composition on crucial disciplines;
- **Dynamic.** This principle stipulates ongoing tactical correction to the national team preparation and individual programmes depending on the situation and specific conditions;
- **Management.** Here we work out integrated comprehensive programmes by the start of each Olympic cycle of preparation and ensure their inclusion in all parts of the national gymnastics system by way of documents regulating the mastery of integrated prospective-forecasting models and forming an overall prospective direction for

Russian gymnastics (annual calendars and positions about competitions, programmes for the children's and young people's sports schools, method letters and information material);
- **Centralisation.** This is one of the basic tenets of national team training. It presupposes the predominantly centralised preparation of the main and junior compositions of the national team at specialised training camps;
- **Self-provision.** Here we stipulate purposive work in preparing a reserve for the national team, the preparation and improvement of the qualifications of coaches and the refinement of Russian gymnastics equipment and facilities;
- **A healthy moral climate.** This principle envisages the creation and maintenance of an atmosphere of comradeship, loyalty and mutual help, nipping in the bud any conflicts at the administrative level during the centralised preparation of the national team.

We should note that from 1972 prospective gymnasts began to be attracted to centralised preparation together with their personal coaches (including the junior national team). At the same time we eliminated the flawed institution of transferring talented gymnasts to several coaches in the national team who, to put it bluntly, were creaming off the best for themselves. These measures considerably enhanced the motivation of coaches in the localities, ensured the constant growth of their educational proficiency and encouraged the creation of a healthy moral climate in the process of many years of preparing candidates for the national team.

2.4 Similarities and Differences in Preparing Men and Women Gymnasts

Much of the above goes equally for male and female gymnasts and is used in preparing the men's and women's national teams. At the same time the training of female gymnasts for top achievements does have its peculiarities. We should note that, although most coaches of women's teams are former male gymnasts or former men's coaches, the mentality of women's coaches differs from that of men's coaches. There are usually more conflicts in women's gymnastics.

The main distinction between men's and women's gymnastics is that women have four pieces of equipment, three of which are jumping (the vault, beam and free exercises), while men have six, of which only two involve jumping. Here exercises on the horse and rings do not have anything in common. So men's gymnastics is more complicated from a motor standpoint. Top-class women gymnasts train just as much as do the men (if not more). Times for mastering fully-evaluated routines on all sets of equipment are greater for men and so the path to top gymnastic success is shorter in women's than in men's gymnastics (see Chapter 1.2).

We must note that in recent years a marked coming together has occurred in the character and content of exercises in men's and women's disciplines. For example, the technique of performing acrobatic and support vaults in composition and structure is the same for men and women. It is practically identical also in other similar men's and women's events – eg on the horizontal bar and asymmetrical bars. There are no men's and women's techniques in modern-day gymnastics, just as there is not a national technique. There is good and bad, correct and incorrect technique. The differences depend not so much on sex and age as on anthropometrical data, talent, quality of basic preparation and level of physical preparedness.

At the same time essential differences between men's and women's gymnastics naturally exist. This is due to the constructive characteristics of men's and women's equipment, as much as to anatomical and morphological, physiological and psychological characteristics of male and female organisms. These peculiarities must be taken into account in the process of preparing men and women gymnasts, but they should not be exaggerated. Contemporary men's gymnastics is more athletic, while women's is more plastic and expressive, more artistic, even though it is one and the same sport expressing respectively the art of men and women.

Here we need to say a few words about certain trends which some gymnasts exhibit fairly regularly over the whole of their sporting career irrespective of their sex. By this characteristic (like, for example, for all athletes) we may conditionally separate them into three categories. Those in the first category normally perform in competitions as they do in training. A bit better, a bit worse, but not by much. Competition stress externally is less expressed in their emotions and competitive actions. As they are taught, so they perform.

What they cannot do in training, they cannot manage in competition, and vice versa. This is a reliable, easy to forecast category. In the national teams they are usually good averages.

Those in the second category more often perform in competitions worse than they could. A pre-performance fever and competition nerves are more manifest. They frequently suffer from what we call 'a bear's disease' (metabolic disorientation) which has an adverse effect on their sports and technical results. Among top-class gymnasts we meet this category very rarely.

The third category comprises people who usually do better than normal. These athletes are not afraid of competition or rivals or judges. They enjoy competing, are able to focus their will, capable of getting themselves together at the right moment. They do not suffer from pre-competition nerves. Competitive stress is in their favour, it multiplies their powers. The more acute is the competitive struggle, the more measured and the better they perform. These are very strong-willed people with a strong character and high motivation.

At competitions they often manage what they cannot in training. Even among the world's elite people of this nature are very rare. They include outstanding representatives of Soviet Union and Russian gymnastics, such as Victor Chukarin, Larissa Latynina, Boris Shakhlin, Nikolai Andrianov, Alexander Dityatin, Dmitri Bilozerchev, Yuri Korolev, Vitaly Shcherbo, Svetlana Khorkina. An outstanding representative of this category is the absolute Olympic champion in Sydney Alexei Nemov.

One should organise training of top-class men and women gymnasts with account for their aptitude for one of the three above-mentioned categories. Given other circumstances being equal, one should train second category gymnasts more and more intensively, get them to perform routines as a whole so as to ensure themselves an acceptable store of reliability and required productiveness. We should note that belonging to one category or the other, although it is genetically determined, it is not an absolute given, set for all time. Under the influence of external and internal conditions it is possible to move from one category to another. Only lengthy observations of a gymnast will enable a coach to determine the basic tendency towards one or another psychological category.

Practical experience of work with men and women gymnasts enables us to make conclusions about the presence of a great deal of similarity in work with a mixed sex squad. This similarity is much greater than the differences.

The main difference in training methods consists in the fact that young and older girls need to repeat tasks more often and need more frequent explanations. They more frequently forget and 'lose' what has seemed to be well-mastered elements and routines. Female gymnasts need more refined information, more exact and detailed tasks with concrete explanations for why something needs to be done. These explanations are more emotional than for male gymnasts who require more logical and laconic information. Information for female gymnasts ought to be given in smaller doses than for men.

Let us emphasise once again that there are no basic distinctions in terms of ideology, methodology and technique in preparing men or women gymnasts.

CHAPTER THREE

Preparation Modelling

3.1   Models and Model Characteristics

The principal document of the senior coach is the programme for preparing the team for the upcoming Olympic Games. Determining the technical preparation of the national team, this programme must fairly precisely answer the questions: *where, how, why, for what and through what* we have to do in the years of the Olympic cycle in order successfully to perform at the next Olympic Games. Before getting down to draw up the programme we have to build an adequate integrated model. This is done in the following way.

After a comparative analysis of results from the previous Olympics, the balance of forces, as well as trends and prospects for gymnastics we work out a forecast of distribution of places, points and medals for the next Olympics. After determining the main strategic goal in preparing the national team for the next Olympics we build a tree of goals for the coming Olympic cycle. An obligatory condition here is to build it from the top down, from end to start.

We need to define it step by step *from the end* (date of performance of the team at the next Olympics) *to the beginning* (the current moment) how and through what concretely we will arrive at our main goal, what is necessary to do during the interval stages of preparation. We have to define the principal parameters and structure of changing purposive states of athletes, as well as the model indicators of basic types of preparedness ensuring successful movement from bottom to top up the tree of objectives so that we reach both intermediate and final goals. In detailed form this will be portrayed as a sports-purposive prospective-forecasting model for preparing the national team in the Olympic cycle.

We should stress that attainment of the parameters of pre-set purposive states should ensure an outcome to model characteristics of intermediate preparation stages and ultimately to a model of strategic results in accordance with the normative forecast plan.

When drawing up the programme of many years of training the team and directly in its process of realisation, we, like in other sports, widely utilise the method of modelling. This method includes a series of aspects. The main ones are modelling of the various facets of proficiency and levels of preparedness, as well as an idea of the results of this modelling in the form of purposive models and model characteristics, and the modelling of the principal parameters of upcoming competitive activity in training conditions.

The modelling method is a powerful means of scientific cognition and is widely employed in various branches of contemporary science and technology. By modelling in science is understood the reproduction of characteristics of a certain object in another object specially created for their study and called the *model*.

Modelling is used when direct investigation of the object is difficult, expensive and requires too much time, or is simply impossible to do. For example, even top-class gymnasts cannot compete all the time despite their preparation being a highly-productive and stable competitive activity. Like other athletes, they spend much of their time training, preparing for competition. Their training activity may become a fairly adequate model of competitive activity, or it may not. Everything depends on the conditions we will relate below.

By model in modern sport we mean the totality of different indicators (quantitative and qualitative) of the state and level of an athlete's preparedness causing the attainment of a certain level of proficiency and forecast results. For example, the totality of model characteristics in physical preparation represents a model of the gymnast's physical preparedness.

A certain similarity should exist between the model and the object. It lies in similarity of physical characteristics or functions of the object (for example, *of competitive activity*) and the model (for example, *of training activity*) or in the identity of mathematical description of behaviour of the object and its model.

The model may perform its function only if the degree of its correspondence to the object is determined. If this degree is high enough the model may be considered adequate, and it may be implemented.

Depending on the nature of the model and those facets of the object that are embodied in it, we may distinguish *mathematical and physical* models. Models may have a different, physical side, apart from the modelling object. It is important for certain facets of the model to be described by the same mathematical expression as the modelling attributes of the object. For instance, mechanical variations of the physical body and vacillations of the current in the electrical circuit possess one and the same mathematical model.

If it suddenly seems that the activity of elite athletes, cosmonauts or test pilots may be formulated by the same mathematical expression, these utterly different forms of activity will possess the same mathematical model. It may be used for mathematical and computer modelling and operate with it, setting questions like 'what would happen if...?' Data obtained as a result of that modelling may be used for scientific and practical purposes.

The utilisation of mathematical models and imitation modelling in the preparation of top-class gymnasts is a very promising affair. But it requires work from an entire team of highly-qualified specialists from different profiles (mathematicians, mechanics, programmists).

Owing to the great complexity of a gymnast's motor activity at the present time we model only a few of its aspects. The mechanical-mathematical models of gymnastics movement provides particular interest for modelling [47, 30, 58, 63, 28, 72, 92, 80, 78 et all]. However, wide application of mathematical modelling in the practice of top-class gymnast preparation is a matter for the future, and probably the distant future.

Models may be quantitative as well as qualitative (for example, descriptive) as well and complete or partial. They may represent certain attributes of the object or the function it performs. In the latter, the model is called functional. In certain circumstances the training session or weekly training micro-cycle may be functional models of competitive activity.

The borders between different models are fairly conditional. The method of models based on similarity of functions carried out by objects of a different nature (for example, machines and humans) is the basis of cybernetics. A cybernetic machine, for example, is just as much training equipment as a teaching machine adapted to an automatic external feed-back [17] (see Chapter 10.2.13).

We should particularly underline that selecting and making models is extremely important and a responsible procedure in the system of preparing top-class gymnasts and athletes in general. The correctly chosen and well-worked out model predetermines the success of preparation.

In using the modelling method in sport it is not obligatory to build very complicated and/or only mathematical models (although this is also desirable). Good practical results may be obtained also using relatively simply models in preparing athletes, models which may be created by organisational-educational means. So we conditionally call this type of modelling *sports-pedagogical modelling*.

For example, if as a result of specially organised training and pedagogical actions on the athlete we repeated the basic parameters of competitive activity and provoked conditional psycho-physiological or physical shifts analogous to competition, that means that we have modelled it. Training in such artificially created conditions represents a model of competitive activity or an important aspect of it. If its basic parameters of competitive activity are surpassed, that means that we have modelled it with an outstripping factor.

Results and phenomena occurring in training sessions in this case may very probably be expected in competition as well. If the use of a concrete model in training provides a stable positive result in competition, we may conclude that the established model is pedagogically adequate. Thus, pedagogical modelling of competitive activity actually turns into a means of preparation which we widely use in work with the national team and its reserve.

We ought to note that in the present top-class preparation system the method of modelling is used increasingly widely. In our techniques it has long become one of the major tools and its effectiveness is hard to overestimate. It had been used in the Soviet national team and today is being used in the Russian national gymnastics team, both in drawing up purposive models, planning and programming the preparation process, and directly in practice at every basic link in the training process.

The following methods may be used in drawing up models and model characteristics in sport generally and in gymnastics in particular:

- mathematical modelling;
- imitational modelling;
- methods of mathematical statistics;
- the phenomenological method.

As mentioned above, the first two methods are very promising, but their potential in sport is so far limited. Using methods of mathematical statistics with construction of regressive and correlation models, however, also has considerable limitations.

The phenomenological method is related to a concrete orientation with the best world gymnasts, and with phenomena. Here the best world gymnasts, their exercises, technical performance, indicators of technical and physical preparedness are taken as the model [56]. But this approach is far from being faultless in science and, primarily, from a methodological viewpoint. It is often used in practice because other more correct and strict scientific methods are either insufficiently worked out or inaccessible for use.

When using empirical methods (phenomenological or statistical) for working out integrated models and model characteristics we need clearly to remember that each elite athlete is a vivid and inimitable individual. They all have their unique nuances. Just as it is impossible to find two people with the same finger-prints, so we won't find two elite gymnasts with absolutely identical anthropological and physical data, with the same technique and, even more so, with the same mentality.

So the empirical method should be used with care, not taking it to the methodological absolute which, unfortunately, often happens. When drawing up model characteristics on the basis of experimental data we need to have a sufficient number of uniform observations, while these data have to be accurately processed by methods of mathematical statistics, not forgetting also trends in development.

Let us examine a specific example. In the last Olympic cycle of 1997-2000, the Chinese men's team won the team championship at the last two world championships and the Olympic Games. From a practical standpoint the conclusion is obvious: the Chinese team is stronger than their rivals and the level of their preparedness is higher than their closest rivals. But such a conclusion cannot be regarded as sufficiently substantiated scientifically.

If the team results are solid, the element of chance is very high and for us to draw the conclusion that verifiable differences are present in level of preparedness of prize-winning teams we have to carry out a special investigation of them (see Chapter 9). After a statistical processing of the obtained data we may make a more substantiated conclusion scientifically, while these data may be used as a guide for working out corresponding model characteristics.

However, if investigation of competitive activity of Olympic and world prize-winners (individual or team), something that is difficult to do, but real, then a full profound comprehensive investigation of team winners by independent experts at the present time is very problematical for understandable reasons.

When working out model characteristics there are other difficulties. As already mentioned, a high level of technical preparedness in gymnastics is based, above all, on optimal physical surplus. A gymnast's special physical preparedness depends on many factors. Among them one of the most important is the level of strength preparedness which, primarily, depends on muscle strength. But it is practically impossible to measure the strength of specific muscles of a live person.

We overcome this difficulty when drawing up model characteristics of special physical preparedness (SPP) as follows. As a result of special investigations we determined several exercises according to SPP, whose results have a high correlation coefficient both in terms of strength of specific muscle groups and of sporting results, which were included in the battery of tests. With the aid of this battery we investigated a number of deviations of our team and determined the basic strategic indicators with each test (the arithmetical mean, standard deviation, average error, dispersion, etc.). Insofar as the standard deviation has a plus or minus sign, it can, summing up with the arithmetical mean, both improve and worsen the test results.

As model characteristic for the specific test we normally take the value that is better than the mean. But in accordance with the principle of outstripping development we sometimes take the sum of two standard deviations above the mean. We use this indicator, for example, as the model characteristic for the purpose of stimulating development of particularly important physical attributes and creating optimal physical surplus.

We take an analogous approach also when working out other model characteristics. Orientation on near-the-limit indicators of basic facets of preparedness enables us to avoid and remove disproportions during the individual preparation of gymnasts, pull up lagging indicators of preparedness to the necessary level in time.

This approach ensures also that we gain a certain proportionality and harmony of levels of the basic component parts of sports proficiency. It is especially important for gymnastics to observe the principle of proportionality and harmony of various attributes, capabilities and levels of preparedness in the preparation techniques [73].

We ought to mention that in each new Olympic cycle the composition and structure of tests, as well as the model characteristics are subjected to a certain correction, which is usually a consequence of changes: development trends, correlation of forces and rules of competition.

3.2 Modelling Competitive Activity

To the natural question 'Is modelling competitive activity a science or an art?' we would say that it is both at the same time, rather like medicine. But most of all it is a science.

As we have already mentioned, competitive activity is a crucial object of research and modelling in sport generally. When preparing gymnasts for competitions we have used elements of modelling competitive activity from time immemorial. This is a well known control training which repeats competition conditions. Of course, there are repetitions and repetitions. In spectacular enterprises, for example, besides the usual repetitions we have run-throughs and dress rehearsals. In the traditional system of preparation we normally confine ourselves to run-throughs without getting as far as dress rehearsals. So we have modelled only some aspects of competitive activity, and we have reached surplus only in separate parameters.

As distinct from the traditional system in modern-day top-class gymnast preparation in specially-organised training sessions we model all the basic parameters of the upcoming competitive activity.

Please note that the nature of training and competitive activity differs substantially. It is one thing cooking a meal in a hot kitchen and eating it at the kitchen table with your relatives and friends (*training activity model*). It is quite another using the meal as food at a big banquet with candles and servants, when mistakes in etiquette are not forgiven and open to scrutiny (*competitive activity model*). They are different affairs, but effectively the first is subordinate to the second and is done for the latter's sake.

But if the table is laid with a starched table cloth and guests are invited in evening dress, this family meal will be like the banquet model. To fully reproduce conditions of an official banquet in domestic circumstances is impossible.

It is just the same when using the pedagogical modelling method; we need to remember that it is in principle impossible to reproduce fully conditions of competitive activity in training. It is impossible, for example, to reproduce the psychological stress of world or Olympic finals. Artists know that the dress rehearsal can never replace the premiere.

At the same time we can determine the basic parameters of competitive activity and learn not only to repeat them in training, but also to surpass them – ie to model with outstripping. At first these parameters may be exceeded individually, and then in routines, moreover in artificially created conditions which are more complex than competitive in certain characteristics. In this event we create the very psychophysical and technical surplus that we need for ensuring reliable and highly-productive competitive activity. Practice has shown that with this approach the level of a gymnast's preparedness exceeds the actual competitive demands.

Let us explain on specific examples. When preparing for the 1972 Olympics the reliability of Olga Korbut's performance on the asymmetric bars with at

PREPARATION MODELLING

that time her unique routine was practically a hundred percent. Yet at the Olympics she fell off precisely this equipment. Analysis of Korbut's training activity at the stage of direct preparation for the Olympics showed that all her test attempts on the asymmetric bars were performed in training in conditions far from competitive. After a fine, exhaustive warm-up she had plenty of time to prepare for the control approach, and only when she was completely ready did she signal to the judges that she was ready to be judged. It was not the judges that called her to the equipment, it was Olga who called the judges. This happened the other way round in competition.

As a result of our analysis we concluded that in this case the reason for her mistake could be inadequate modelling of competitive activity. This was taken into consideration when working out the technique of integrated preparation, and this bore fruit.

In 1982, the sixteen-year old Dmitri Bilozerchev, leading in the full events at his first world championship, came out to perform exercises on the horse. There was a delay caused by the judges going into a huddle over the previous participant. While waiting for permission to approach the horse, Dmitri unusually stood for a long time without moving. In this time he could easily have 'overheated' or 'gone cool'. This was an obvious inhibiting factor that could have caused technical errors and enhanced the likelihood of a mistake.

But Dmitri did not overheat or go cool. He executed his very complex exercises on the horse with a result of ten points. Why? Firstly because he was uncommonly talented, a unique gymnast. And secondly we should stress that in preparation of the national team we began in training to model various inhibiting factors that could arise in competition. And we did this with outstripping. So Bilozerchev had experience of performing his work routines in conditions that were more complex than had arisen at the moment of competition [4].

Let us give the example of one of the first attempts at creating artificial inhibiting factors in control training sessions which the gymnasts and coaches initially had their doubts about. The senior coach called the gymnast to start, and then suddenly called for a pause, telling the gymnast 'You stand by the equipment and wait ; don't move.'

The gymnast was all geared up to make an approach and could not understand why there was a delay. He began to get nervous, even irritated (which, incidentally, was exactly what was wanted) and in that artificially created state performed the competitive exercise with the intention of gaining an optimal assessment. The model is simple, but it enables us to prepare gymnasts for unexpected competitive situations and to work out the necessary psycho-physical surplus.

We use various forms of special training modelling competitive activity in our technique of integrated preparation. The main ones are as follows:

- *control training* (performance of competitive exercises with marks);
- *model training* (performance of exercises within the framework of upcoming competitions with test);
- *control-model training* (a fuller possible imitation of the conditions and rules of upcoming competitions with marks given);
- *'shock' training* (performance of competitive routines with double outstripping of the volume of competitive loads on average);
- *model-'shock' training* (the same, but under competition conditions with modelling of inhibiting factors).

In contemporary techniques of preparing top-class gymnasts modelling of weekly micro-cycles has the upper hand over modelling of training sessions (see Chapter 5.5).

Basing ourselves on the idea of the primacy of competitive activity when modelling top-class gymnast preparation, we conducted special investigations before working out model competitive micro-cycles [5,6,7,32].

The object of our investigation was 14 gymnasts in the Soviet national team of whom 7 were merited masters of sport and 7 masters of sport, international class. Their competitive activity was the subject of investigation. The task of the research consisted in establishing its composition, structure and basic parameters. To tackle the set task we used pedagogical observations, chronometer and pulse-meter. The results were processed by standard methods of mathematical statistics used in sports science.

At competitions conducted according to FIG regulations we registered the number of elements and routines with all forms of equipment, the number of support vaults, approaches, elements of high difficulty, and elements of special physical preparation that had actually been performed by the above-mentioned gymnasts. We also registered a number of temporal indicators of their competitive activity.

We determined and analysed the composition and structure of the competitive micro-cycles in which, besides their own competitive activity, included a number of other components. These components had normally been ignored, but we felt that they needed to be taken into consideration for the modelling. So, we analysed the following components of competitive micro-cycles:

- *testing equipment a day before the start of competitions;*
- *training during competition days;*
- *general warm-up before competitions;*
- *special warm-up on all the equipment;*
- *each person's own competitive activity (performance of routines with assessment);*
- *training on rest days between competitions.*

As a result of our analysis of arithmetical indicator means of load in competitive micro-cycles of varying duration we established that all the tested gymnasts belonged to one group. The coefficient of variation of load indicators in individual forms of the full events was relatively small and varied within the bounds of 5.5-12.8%.

Comparative analysis of indicators of competitive load in various forms of the full events showed that the top-class gymnasts performed the greater number of elements in the competitive micro-cycles on the horse, then in the floor exercises, on the horizontal bar and parallel bars (in order). They performed the smallest number on the rings.

We established that in special warm-ups the gymnasts executed routines completely more often on the horse, then on the parallel bars and horizontal bar. In the surveyed selection not once were routines completely performed on the rings and floor exercises. The greatest number of elements in competitive micro-cycles were normally done when tested.

The training load during competitive micro-cycles was considerably higher than the competition itself. Intensity of work in routines at competition was on average substantially higher than at training sessions. This distinguishes competitive activity from additional training sessions during the competitive micro-cycles.

Data on heart beat frequency (HBF) were of particular interest for subsequent modelling of competitive activity; they were registered in control training sessions and competitions directly before the gymnast approached a piece of equipment and immediately after he performed routines on all pieces of apparatus. In most cases the HBF indicators before performing routines in competition were considerably higher than in the training sessions. In those cases when the gymnast performed last on the apparatus, the HBF in competition was lower than in training sessions.

We established that an increase in HBF after performing routines on the various pieces of apparatus varied. The highest HBF was after performing the floor exercises.

On the basis of the data we received we worked out the statistical models of competitive activity for top-class gymnasts for various competitive micro-cycles. As a result of the research we made important conclusions which are still valid today:

- a certain regime of competitive activity with characteristic composition, structure, volume and intensity of load corresponds to each form of competition;
- a *control-model micro-cycle* adequate to the form of upcoming competition and model of the competitive micro-cycle should be built into the structure of stages of direct preparation for competition;
- to create optimal surplus and necessary preparation for competitive activity it is sensible to include in this structure a *'shock'-model micro-cycle* that significantly exceeds the competition in load;
- when performing routines you should register the HBF before and after approaching the apparatus. This enables you to obtain objective information about the psycho-physiological value of the load and on that basis more effectively to control and govern the state of the gymnasts;
- in those cases when possible, it is wise to conduct several model training sessions at the competitive stage (without giving marks, but strictly observing the whole rules of the upcoming competitions). This is particularly valuable for young gymnasts who do not yet have enough competitive experience.

Thus, the main conclusions were that at the stage of direct preparation for competition we need comprehensively to model the conditions of upcoming competitive activity, being guided by a corresponding statistical model of the competitive micro-cycle. Here we need to strive to model it by exceeding all the basic parameters of competitive activity, including not only load, but also its biomechanical, physiological and psychological components.

Our conclusions were many times used when working out models of stages of direct preparation for various competitions which were successfully tested during preparation of the national team in several Olympic cycles.

Let us illustrate the adequacy of one of the conclusions. Before the start of the World Junior Games in Moscow in 1998, the junior Russian team carried out six model training sessions in the competition venue of the 'Olympic' Palace of Sport. But only at the last one did it work like clockwork, successfully having performed all the competitive exercises in full accordance with the regulations of the upcoming competitions. The modelling of competitive activity at the venue enabled the Russian team to win the team and individual championships at all competitions, as well as most gold medals on the apparatus.

3.3 Sports-Goal Prospective-forecasting Models

Modern-day techniques of integrated training of the Russian national team envisages working out and using an entire system of sports-goal prospective-forecasting models.

3.3.1 Normative Forecasting Model

The normative forecasting of distribution and winning of medals is the starting point of planning and programming the preparation of the national team in each new Olympic cycle. It is worked out immediately after the Olympic Games on the basis of a careful analysis of the correlation of forces internationally and development trends. On this basis experts draw up a forecasting plan, and the sports administration draw up a design plan relying on the forecasting plan. The design plan stipulates the minimum number of points and medals which the national team has to win given the most unfavourable set of circumstances, as, for example, happened initially with the Russian team at the Sydney Olympics. So the design plan is usually overfulfilled.

The design plan and the forecast plan are compiled according to a certain form, starting from the end. For example, at the next Olympic Games we must (design plan) and can (forecast plan) win a certain number of gold, silver and bronze medals, including men – certain number, and women – certain number (indicating the programme numbers).

Further, we determine and forecast the basic opponents in the team and individual championship for all apparatus and individual, for both men and women. After that we set the design and forecast plans for winning and distributing medals in years of the Olympic cycle for our main rivals, exceeding the norms that ensure we tackle the key strategic task. All this is accompanied by an appropriate brief grounding.

Thus, we formalise the main strategic goal in preparing the national team during the upcoming Olympic cycle in the normative forecast in numerical form.

Let us give a specific example. In 1989 the Soviet State Sports Committee ratified the normative design plan of the Soviet gymnastics team, according to which the team was supposed to win 15 medals at the Barcelona Olympics, including 7 gold, 5 silver and 3 bronze. The men were to win 4 gold, 3 silver and 2 bronze, and the women 3 gold (1 team), 2 silver and 1 bronze.

In the 1989-92 Olympic cycle we planned also to win a certain number of gold, silver and bronze medals at the world and European championships according to the year of the cycle. We established that the main rivals of the Soviet team in that Olympic cycle were, for the men, East Germany, China and Japan, and for the women – Romania, East Germany, Bulgaria and the USA. We also compiled a design plan for distributing medals by year of the Olympic cycle for the main rivals of the Soviet team.

On the eve of the Olympics experts forecast us overfulfilling the design plan. And so it was. The forecast for our main rivals was fully confirmed, while the design plan for winning Olympic medals was exceeded. In all our gymnasts won 18 medals, including 9 gold (6 for the men, 3 for the women), 5 silver (3 and 2 respectively) and 4 bronze (2+2).

This success to a large extent was due to the tremendous performance of Vitaly Shcherbo who won 6 gold medals, including in the team championship. Not a single gymnast had ever won such a large number of Olympic medals at once. The rules of competition and specifics of the judges helped him in this in that it enabled one and the same medal to be won by two or even three gymnasts.

Here is another example. The design plan of Russian gymnasts at the Sydney Olympics consisted in winning 10 medals (3 gold, 3 silver and 4 bronze). On the eve of the Olympics experts forecast that we would exceed the plan. Despite the successful start (after the first day of competition the men's team was in the lead), circumstances then changed away from us. We lost both team championships (men's and women's – even though we had forecast a gold medal in one of them).

In the final count, however, instead of the planned ten medals, Russian gymnasts won 15 medals at those Olympics (5 gold, 5 silver and 5 bronze). The integrated preparation system had won out.

We should note that making a forecast, like modelling, is both a science and an art. Here much depends on the qualifications and experience of experts.

3.3.2 Model Characteristics of Competitive Activity

The paramount characteristics of competitive activity of top-class gymnasts are as follows:

- content and difficulty of competitive exercises in the various pieces of apparatus;
- technical-performance proficiency;
- competitive reliability.

These characteristics are simultaneously the major indicators of level of preparedness of men and women gymnasts.

For the leading members of the Russian team the purposive model characteristics of competitive activity are expressed in the following indicators: starting assessment – 10 points, deductions for errors – up to 0.3 points, reliability of reproducing in competition the best versions of routines in training – 98%.

3.3.3 Model Characteristics of Olympic Champions

3.3.3.1 Winning Team Model

This model depends on the rules and tenets of competitions. At Sydney the men's and women's national teams consisted of six gymnasts in each. In the team competitions 5 gymnasts competed on each apparatus. In the team score the four best results were taken for each apparatus.

In that event the winning team model was determined by the following:

- all team members had to have a difficulty of exercise significantly higher than that required by the rules of FIG international competitions;
- the team had to have three interchangeable gymnasts capable of making the individual final for all events and taking 1-6 place in the competitions;
- one of the multi-event gymnasts was the team leader and captain;
- the leader had to perform his exercises faultlessly, had to have no fewer than two 'shock' events and display stable high results in the pre-Olympic season;
- one of the two remaining multi-event gymnasts had to be ready to take on the role of leader if need be;
- each multi-event gymnast had to have an average starting assessment of 10 points and 2-3 'shock' events in which he could count on making the final in individual events of the multi-event competition. Routines in the 'shock' events had to include 2-4 groups of Super-E difficulty;
- the remaining members of the team should not commit more than one small error, should have 1-2 'shock' events with a difficulty of 2-4 group E and a starting mark of 10 points no less than in any event of the multi-event competition.

3.3.3.2 Model of Absolute Olympic Champion

Olympic multi-event champion or absolute champion is the most honourable title in gymnastics. Its purposive model includes the following:

- full-value competitive exercises in all forms of the multi-event competition, corresponding to all the requirements of the competition rules with an average starting mark of 10 points;
- a high level of technical-executive proficiency in all multi-events with an average mark not lower than 9.6;
- a high level of tournament endurance, ensuring 18 faultless starts over the three days for men (3x6=18) and 12 starts for women (3x4=12);
- 100% reliability both in preliminary qualifiers and in the final multi-events;
- successful performances and high rating in the multi-events in the pre-Olympic season.

3.3.3.3 Model of Olympic Champion in the Multi-events

To win a gold medal in any multi-events the gymnast must satisfy the following criteria:

- the exercise must contain 3-4 group Super E, his own unique elements or routines in the highest group of difficulty, giving maximum additions to his points score;
- a starting mark of 10.0 points;
- perfect technique of performing all elements and routines;
- virtuoso execution proficiency;
- absolute reliability of performance in the qualifiers and finals in the given form of the multi-event competition (100%);
- successful stable performances with high results in the given form of the multi-event competition at big international competitions in the pre-Olympic season.

3.3.4 Forecast Model of Sporting-technical Achievements

The replacement of the compulsory programme in 1997 and the new rules for international competitions of FIG 1997 provoked a jump in difficulty of competition programmes for the world gymnastics elite. But exercises on all apparatus became more monotonous (see Chapter 1.6).

The new version of the rules, ratified by FIG in 2000, enables world gymnastics to develop a little more harmoniously given that the rules will operate without any change for the entire Olympic cycle. As a result of devaluing the difficulty of a number of strategic elements, most participants in the world championships and Olympic Games will find it hard to master the full-value competitive programme and accumulate a difficulty that will ensure a ten-point starting mark. For that they need a higher level of special physical, technical and psychological preparedness.

The major long-term gymnastics trends affecting greater complexity in exercises (see Chapter 1.4) maintain stability not only in the 2001-2004 Olympic cycle, but also in the distant future. The competitive exercises of the world gymnastics elite will become more complex, varied and rich than in the previous Olympic cycle.

The difficulty of exercises will rise mainly along the lines of mastering trick elements of high complexity, as well as concentrating complex elements in time and space. Repetition of complex elements will disappear from competitive exercises. Simple connecting elements will gradually be squeezed out of routines; when they perform them gymnasts may be able to correct any faults and get ready for performing the next complex element.

Trick elements of record complexity (triple somersault in floor exercises, triple somersault forward and back with turn from the horizontal bar and rings, etc.) will again appear in the top world and national tournaments. It will not be that far into the future that we shall see the quadruple somersault which will first be performed on the horizontal bar. In the near future we may expect further growth in technical-performance proficiency through mastery of modern techniques by an increasing number of gymnasts and a raising of special physical preparedness.

As with any living organism, gymnastics will develop by its own laws in accordance with the trends natural to it. But the competition rules they dictate are determining the highway of gymnastics development until such a time as they cease to operate. World gymnastics is forced to adapt itself to these rules as any living organism adjusts to external conditions of the environment.

Specialisation permitted by the rules in various pieces of apparatus will lead to a substantial growth in the complexity of competitive exercises in the all-around competition. Here we may see the appearance and/or successful performance of several complex elements and routines.

Men

Floor exercises:

- forward somersault with turn of 720° and 1080°;
- double forward tuck somersault;
- triple back somersault;
- 1/2 turn and triple forward somersault;
- double tuck somersault with turn of 720° and 1080°;
- back somersault with turn of 1080° and 1440° (triple and quadruple twist);
- lengthy series (including reverse routines including elements of group D, E and Super-E).

Pommel Horse:

- modified travels over all parts of the horse with the legs circling together and in flairs with dismounts through handstand with turns and lowering into circles;
- varied circles with turns of 1080° and more on the body and handles, between handles and on one handle.

Rings:

Further progressive development of exercises on the rings is being held back by the FIG competition rules. The level of technical readiness and special physical–preparation of top-class gymnasts even now enables them to perform much more complex and varied routines than finalists showed in Sydney.

We should expect to see successful performance of the following elements and routines:

Swing elements:

- Guzcoghy straight in various routines;
- giant swings with parallel arm positions;
- giant swings in back hang;
- Honma straight;

Dismounts:

- double straight back somersault with turn of 720° and 1080°;
- triple back somersault in tuck and piked after the Guzcoghy;
- back somersault with turn of 360° with following double tuck somersault;
- double forward somersault with turn of 540° and 900°;
- triple tuck forward somersault with turn of 180°.

Strength elements:

- press lifts from horizontal back hang into 'swallow';
- press lifts from 'swallow' into horizontal position and inverted cross;
- reverse "swallow";
- turns from cross into lateral Azaryan crosses;
- series of three and more different elements of high difficulty of a type swing-static-press.

Owing to specialisation in various forms of multi-event competition we expect on the rings a considerable improvement in the gymnast's body lines and geometrical figure in strength static positions. They will be kept with minimal deviation from the ideal. Accordingly, deductions for any errors in elite groups will be reduced.

Vault:

- handspring and 2.5 forward tuck somersault with turn of 180° before landing and of 360° in the first or first two somersaults;
- hanspring and 1.5 forward piked somersault with turn of 720° and 1080°;
- Tsukahara with 2.5 tuck backward somersault with turn of 360°;
- Tsukahara piked with turn of 720° and 1080°;
- Yurchenko with 2.5 back tuck somersault with turn of 360°;
- Yurchenko piked with turn of 720° and 1080°;
- Cuervo with 2.5 back tuck somersault with turn of 360°;
- Cuervo piked with turn of 720° and 1080°.

Parallel bars:

- double forward and double back piked somersaults from support into upper arm hang;

- long swing double back tuck somersault into support;
- long swing double piked somersault into upper arm support and into hang;
- forward and backward somersaults above the bars with turns of 180° and 360° into support and upper arm hang;
- front uprise and back somersault over the bars into handstand;
- front uprise and Diamidov with turn of 540° into handstand on one bar;
- from swing back somersault to handstand with a turn of 360°;
- Tippelt forward tuck somersault into handstand.

Dismounts:

- double back somersault with turn of 360° (Tsukahara);
- double somersault: first with turn of 360°, the second in tuck (full in back out);
- double piked forward somersault with a turn of 180°;
- double forward tuck somersault with turn of 540°;
- triple back somersault and forward in tucked position.

Horizontal bar:

- Tkachev with turn of 360° (Lyukin) in series;
- Tkachev and forward tuck somersault into hang;
- backward long swing and a piked forward somersault with turn of 360° (Winkler);
- long swing forward and a back piked somersault with turn of 540° (Deff);
- Kovacs piked + Kovacs tuck with turn of 360°;
- Kovacs straight and with turn of 360°;
- long swing forward and a double back tuck somersault in front of the horizontal bar with 180° turn into hang;
- double forward tuck somersault in front of the bar into hang ;
- double forward somersault over the bar with turn of 360° into hang in undergrasp;
- long swing backwards, a back tuck somersault in front of the bar into hang;
- long swing forward, a forward tuck and piked somersault (Xiao Ruizhi-Marinich), with 180° turn into backward swing;

- arch-somersault forward in tuck and piked position, with 180° turn into hang and into long swing backward; long swing backward in L – grip, after backward long swing turn of 180° into under-grasp and Czech long swing (turn from Russian into Czech swings);
- series of three or more different flights and elements with release and recatch of group D and higher.

Dismounts:

- double back straight somersault with turn of 1080°;
- triple back somersault: the first with turn of 360° with straight body, the second and third in tuck (full in back out triple);
- triple back somersault with turn of 360° and 720°;
- triple forward somersault with a turn of 180°;
- triple somersault showing different body shapes in combination- straight-piked-tucked, or vice versa.

Women

Vault:

- handspring – 2.5 forward somersault;
- handspring – 1.5 forward tuck somersault with turn of 1080°;
- Tsukahara straight with turn of 1080°;
- Yurchenko with turn of 900° and 1080°;
- Yurchenko – 2.5 back tuck somersault;
- Yurchenko – 2.5 back tuck somersault with turn of 360°.

Asymmetric bars:

- straight back somersault with a turn of 540° into hang (Deff);
- Tkachev with turn of 360° (Lyukin);
- Balabanov- forward straight somersault into hang;
- Forward straight somersault with turn of 360° (Winkler);
- Tkachev + Deff;
- series of three or more flighted elements;
- on top bar facing inwards, turn 180° from Russian into Czech longswings.

Dismounts:

- double back tuck somersault with turn of 720° (Tsukahara);
- straight double back somersault with turn of 720°;
- double forward somersault with turn of 540°;
- triple somersault.

Beam:

- turns of 1080° on one leg;
- push off with two jumps and turn of 540° and more;
- back somersault with turn of 360° in tuck and straight position in series;
- straight forward somersault in series;
- straight forward somersault and forward tuck somersault to land on two feet and side somersault;
- forward somersault with turn of 180°, 360° and 540°;
- series of three somersaults;
- handspring and forward somersault.

Dismounts:

- double back half-tuck somersault with turn of 360° (Tsukahara);
- double back half-tuck somersault with turn of 720°;
- double back straight somersault;
- double back straight somersault with turn of 360°;
- double forward tuck somersault with a turn of 180°;
- double forward piked somersault.

Floor exercises:

- double back straight somersault with turn of 360° and 720°;
- double back semi-tuck somersault with turn of 720°;
- double twist in transition;
- half turn of 180° and double forward somersault;
- double forward somersault in transition;
- triple back somersault;
- long 'reverse' series with two or more D elements.

3.3.5 Technical Preparedness Model

For members of the Russian national team we take the following parameters for the purposive technical preparedness model:

- excellent technique in performing all elements and series of the competition programme;
- excellent technique in performing the basic elements of various levels from initial to the highest;
- confident mastery of no fewer than two elements of Super E difficulty, three elements of group E and five elements of group D on the best apparatus;
- confident mastery of series of very complex elements providing maximum additions to the base mark on all apparatus with positive dynamic reduction in deductions for performance over the Olympic cycle years;
- confident mastery of two vaults of top difficulty of various structure with positive dynamics of reducing deductions for performance over the Olympic cycle;
- technical surplus expressed in mastery not only of faultless, but also prospective technique enabling the gymnast if need be to quickly increase complexity of the competition programme;
- an ability precisely to reproduce at the necessary moment an optimal faultless version of the competitive programme in circumstances when off-putting and unfavourable factors occur, including competition stress;
- high tournament endurance in 'shock' and model micro-cycles;
- high reliability of performing the competition programme, both in control training sessions and at various levels of competition, primarily during the control, knock-out and major competitions of the season;
- good prospects for technique and the competition programme, as dynamics of productive control training sessions and competitive activity, which are one of the most important indicators for debutants in the national team.

3.3.6 Model of Special Physical Preparedness (SPP)

The SPP model for top-class gymnasts is represented in Tables 3 and 4.

Table 3
Tests and model characteristics of SPP for top-class gymnasts

MEN

No.	Test	Parameter	Unit of Measure	Model Characteristic
1.	Running (controlled)	20m	s(seconds)	3.0-3.1
2.		Speed in last 5m	m/s	7.8-8.2
3.	Vertical Jump	From the spot, swinging arms	cm	60-65
4.	Rope climb	4m without leg help	s	5.0-5.5
5.	Round off, flic flac, back somersault	Flight time	s	0.95-1.0
6.	Cross on rings	Holding time	s	5.0-6.0
7.	Front horizontal hang	Holding time	s	5.0-6.0
8.	Horizontal Support (planche)	Holding time	s	5.0-6.0
9.	Inverted cross	Holding time	s	5.0-6.0

Table 4
Tests and model characteristics of SPP for top-class gymnasts

WOMEN

No.	Test	Parameters	Unit of Measure	Model Characteristic
1.	Running	20m	s	3.2-3.3
2.		Speed on last 5m	m/s	7.4-7.6
3.	Vertical Jump	From spot swinging arms	cm	52-56
4.	Vertical Jump	From spot, no arm swing	cm	42-43
5.	Standing Long jump	From spot	cm	220-225
6.	Depth jump	With jump off	cm	61-62
7.	Rope climb	3m without leg help	s	5.6-5.8
8.	Round off, flic flac Back Somersault	Flight time	s	0.85-0.9
9.	Support half lever	Holding time	s	28-30
10.	Back horizontal hang	Holding time	s	28-32
11.	Front horizontal hang	Holding time	s	20-23
12.	Handstands	Holding time	s	90
13.	From support half lever, lift to handstand with straight arms and bent body	Number of repetitions		8-10
14.	From swing on low bar upstart to handstand and repeat.	Number of repetitions		10-12
15.	Flexibility test	Deductions	Points	0.5-0.6

We should note that from one Olympic cycle to another there is a tendency for a growth in model characteristics and real indicators of SPP for top-class gymnasts. The most conservative are indicators in 20m run and jumps, as well as sprinting speed over the last 5m. of the run. At the same time our comparative biomechanical analysis has shown that top-class gymnasts today on average run faster than gymnasts did 20 years ago.

3.3.7 Functional Preparedness Model

The model characteristics of functional preparedness determine the parameters that are forecastable and diagnostical by the criteria of the functional state of the organism [29,74]. They include indicators of the state of the following basic systems:

- cardio-vascular system (CVS) characterised by heart contraction frequency (HCF), arterial pressure (AP), electro-cardiogram (ECG) ;
- neuro-muscular apparatus (NMA) characterised by a electro-stimulator test, which is aimed at defining the following:
    - relaxing tonus (RT),
    - tension tonus (TT),
    - relaxing volume (RV),
    - maximum volume of tension (MVT);
- internal organism medium (IOM or homeostasis) characterised by such biochemical indicators as lactate (mg/%), acidic balance (AB), pyrovate (mmol/l), inorganic phosphorus (mg/%).

Each of the above-mentioned indicators is measured on a ten-point scale. On that basis we work out an integrated evaluation. The goal model envisages a state of high functional preparedness. The range deviations from the model are diagnostic criteria of faults in the limiting systems of the gymnast's organism. Top-class gymnasts must have each of the parameters and the overall integrated indicator assessed with no less than 8.0 points with women, and 7.5 points with men.

A guiding basis for working out the model characteristics of the functional state may be the average indicators of reactions of the organism's systems of practically healthy top-class gymnasts with a double performance of standard floor exercises of the compulsory programme type with three-minute rest between attempts, (special test).

As an example, Table 5 shows the model characteristics of the functional preparedness of top-class gymnasts [74].

Table 5

Model characteristics of the functional state of top level women gymnasts

\multicolumn{6}{c	}{Cardio vascular system}	\multicolumn{2}{c	}{Neuro Muscular apparatus}	\multicolumn{8}{c}{Biochemical constants}
Special test bts/min	Score	Special Test AP	Score	ECG	Score	RT, TT, RV, MVT	Score	Lactate Mg/%	Score	AB	Score	Pyrovate mmol/l	Score	Non organic phosphorus	Score
185	8	105	8	Fault in the repolarisation process	8	58	8	11.5	8	7.35	8	0.1	8	2.5	8
170	8.5	110	8.5	Migration of the rhythm source Sinus Bradicardia	8.5	60	8.5	11	8.5	7.346	8.5	0.09	8.5	3	8.5
160	9	115	9	Fault in the inter stomach conductivity	9	66	9	10.8	9	7.33	9	0.07	9	3.5	9
150	10	120	10	Sinus rhythm	10	70	10	10.2	10	7.328	10	0.04	10	5	10

3.3.8 Psychological Preparedness Model

This model includes indicators of individual-psychological peculiarities of the personality, motivation level, speed of processing visual information and psycho-motoristics. All these indicators must be no lower than 8.5 points on a ten-point scale. As an example Table 6 shows the model characteristics of top-class gymnast readiness drawn up by Kalinin and Nilopets.

Table 6
Model characteristics of the psychological readiness of top level male gymnasts

Psycho diagnostic procedures		Model characteristics, score
Tests, methodics and means		
Evaluation of Individual psychological specifics of the gymnast		Catell's 16-PF Test
Evaluation of the motivation for sports activities	Interview	7.5
Cognitive functioning	Series of cognitive tests	7.5
Evaluation of the precision of a simple movement	Pursuit tracking	7.5
Evaluation of motor memory.	"Labyrinth"	7.5

3.3.9 Selection Model for the National Team

Forming the national team is one of the strategic procedures in the technology of integrated preparation of top-class gymnasts. First of all we should note that selection of an Olympic team is not a single instance, it is whole complex which is done by stages over the entire Olympic cycle. The sporting principle has to dominate the national team selection system. Our long experience has demonstrated that forming the national team on the basis of the sporting principle is the most effective, transparent and democratic means. In selecting candidates for the team we must be governed by the following criteria:

- sports results;
- difficulty and prospects of the competition programme, its degree of correspondence with model characteristics;
- dynamics of competitive results over a yearly cycle with account for the rates of growth and personal level of sports-technical attainments;
- stability of performances and competitive reliability;
- level of special physical and technical preparedness;
- degree of correspondence of indicators of preparedness in terms of model characteristics;

- state of health;
- performance of the individual preparation plan and performing discipline;
- psychological characteristics of personality.

In our experience those gymnasts who in the past year have the lowest total of places occupied at *control and knock-out* competitions are primarily made candidates for the Russian national team.

Selection for taking part in world and European championships and cups is done on the basis of sports-technical results shown in the major annual selection competitions. Selection of the Olympic team is made with account of the basic factors determining the success of a gymnast's competitive activity during the entire Olympic cycle and, in particular, at the final stage or preparation.

The most important criteria of selecting the Russian Olympic team are:

- level and dynamics of sporting results in the previous and current year;
- degree of correspondence of competitive programme (difficulty, start value, executive ability, reliability) and level of preparedness (technical, physical, functional) to model characteristics;
- level of will power qualities, fighting character.

On the basis of these criteria we selected four main participants for the men's and women's national teams. The fifth and sixth participants are decided by a coaches' council by the method of expert assessment according to the results of control-model training sessions and special selection competitions at the final stage of preparation.

3.3.10 Pre-competition Preparation Stage Model

The pre-competition preparation stage is direct and purpose-designed preparation for competition whose duration depends on the scope of competition (see Chapters 4.8.10, 5.5 and 5.8). Its key task is to bring top-class gymnasts to the peak of their form. As an example Table 7 shows a model of the pre-competition preparation stage which was drawn up while preparing the national Russian team for the 34th world championship in China (1999).

At this championship the Russian team won more medals than all the other teams, including 5 golds. The structure of micro-cycles is shown in Chapter 5.5.

Table 7

Model of pre-competition preparation of top-class men and women gymnasts for major competitions

Name of Weekly Micro-Cycle	Number of routines per week Men	Women	Number of routines per day Mon	Tues	Wed	Thurs	Fri	Sat
1. Restoration	10	10	M:0 M:0	W:0 W:0	M:1*5 M:1*5	W:1-1-3 W:1-1-3	M:0 M:0	W:0 W:0
2. Catching up	20	20	M:1*5 M:0	W:1-1-3 W:0	M:0 M:1*5	W:0 W:1-1-4	M:1*5 M:1*5	W:1-1-3 W:1-1-3
3. Stabilisation	25	25	M:1*5 M:0	W:1-1-3 W:0	M:1*5 M:1*5	W:1-1-3 W:1-1-5	M:1*5 M:1*5	W:1-1-3 W:1-1-3
4. 'Shock'	40	50	M:2*5 M:0	W:2-3-5 W:0	M:0 M:2*5	W:2-3-5 W:2-3-5	M:2*5 M:2*5	W:2-3-5 W:2-3-5
5. Model	30	60	M:1*5 M:1*5	W:2-3-5 W:2-3-5	M:1*5 M:1*5	W:2-3-5 W:2-3-5	M:1*5 M:1*5	W:2-3-5 W:2-3-5
6. Stabilisation	25-30	50	M:1*5 M:1*5	W:1-3-5 W:0	M:1*5 M:1*5	W:1-3-5 W:1-3-5	M:1*5 M:1*5	W:1-3-5 W:1-3-5
7. Stabilisation	25-30	50	M:1*5 M:1*5	W:1-3-5 W:0	M:1*5 M:1*5	W:1-3-5 W:1-3-5	M:1*5 M:1*5	W:1-3-5 W:1-3-5
8. Toning Down	20	24	M:1*5 M:0	W:1-3-5 W:0	M:0 M:1*5	W:0 W:1-3-5	M:1*5 M:1*5	W:1-3-5 W:1-3-5

Note: The following signs in the table signify:

- M – men; W – women
- M:0 or W:0 means that on that day men and women do not perform competition routines;
- M: 1*5 and 2*5 means that on that day men perform one or two competition routines each on the five apparatuses (altogether corresponding to 5 and 10 routines a day at training session);

- W:1-1-3, W: 1-3-5, W: 2-3-5 means that on that day the women perform on three pieces of apparatus that number of routines which corresponds to the figure set by a hyphen. The first figure decides the number of routines on the asymmetric bars, the second on the beam, and the third in the floor exercises;
- the upper index in the last figure (for example 5) means that the routine is executed according to individual indices (see Thursday in six and 7 micro-cycles).

The number of vaults during a control training session normally fluctuates between four and six. This parameter is individual and therefore varies greatly.

Three training sessions are held daily in the weekly micro-cycle except Thursday. On Thursday we have two morning sessions. Sunday in each micro-cycle is rest day and features no training at all.

3.3.11 Competition Preparation Model

Table 8 gives an approximate model of the competition training of men and women gymnasts of the timetable of the Russian national team in the 1997-2000 Olympic cycle.

Table 8

Model of competition preparation of the Russian national team in the 1997-2000 Olympic cycle

Year	Jan	Feb	Mar	Apr	May	June	July	Aug	Sept	Oct	Nov	Dec
1997		AC	IT, RC	IT	EC		RC		WC	IT	IT	IT
1998		AC	IT, RC	IT	EC		RC		WC	IT	IT	IT
1999		AC	IT, RC	IT	EC		RC		WC	IT	IT	IT
2000		AC	IT, RC	IT	EC		RC		WC	IT	IT	IT

NB: AC = area championships, IT = international tournaments, RC = Russian championships, EC = European championships, RC = Russian Cup, WC = world championships, OG = Olympic Games.

This model is added to by the competitive load model for members of the Russian national team in the same cycle, as shown in Table 9.

Table 9
Model of the competitive load of the Russian national team in the 1997-2000 Olympic cycle

Indicators	1997	1998	1999	2000
Number of Official Competitions (out of "training controls")	6-8	6-8	6-8	6-8
Number of starts (number of visits to the apparatus or podium)	M:48-112 W:40-95	M:48-122 W:40-95	M:48-122 W:40-95	M:48-122 W:40-95
Number of days of competition	16-20	16-20	16-20	16-20

3.3.12 Competition Micro-cycles Model

Table 10 shows the load model in competition micro-cycles of varying duration.

Table 10

Load model in competition micro-cycles of varying duration (CMC)

Load indicators	CMC duration		
Number of elements:	4 days	6 days	8 days
• in the CMC period as a whole	694	1277	1762
• during training	264	645	870
• directly in competition	430	632	892
Total time on apparatus (hrs/mins):			
• in the CMC period as a whole	7hrs 40 mins	12hrs 6 mins	17hrs 15 mins
• in training	2hrs 5 mins	4hrs 32 mins	7hrs 15 mins
• directly in competition	5hrs 35 mins	7hrs 34 mins	10hrs 0 mins
Load intensity by element (el/min)			
• in the CMC period as a whole	1.5	1.76	1.7
• in training	2.11	2.37	2
• directly in competition	1.28	1.39	1.48
Summary indicators:			
• number of routines	14	21	27
• number of elements of CMC	10	56	111
• top difficulty elements (%)	26.9	15.5	16.9

3.3.13 Goal Exercise Models

These models include biomechanical models of goal exercises (elements, connecting parts and routines) and pedagogical models of their mastery. Therefore, we call these models pedagogical-biomechanical.

Table 11 represents an example of a goal biomechanical model of a quadruple somersault from the horizontal bar. This is a new, super-complex dismount which as far as we know, no one has yet tried at official FIG competitions. Its model characteristics are calculated on the basis of experimental biomechanical data and mathematical model-making [63].

Table 11
Goal biomechanical model of dismount by back tuck quadruple somersault from the horizontal bar

Modelling Level	Parameters	Model Characteristics
Geometrical	Length of flight (distance from bar)	1.80m
	Height of lift over the bar	1.45m
	Horizontal movement in flight	1.05m
	Absolute height of flight	1.56m
Time	Flight time	1.38sec
	Tuck time	0.25sec
	Preparation for landing time	0.20sec
Kinematic	Absolute speed at moment of dismount	5.79m/s
	Initial vertical speed in flight	5.74m/s
	Horizontal speed in flight	0.76m/s
	Angle of dismount	81°
	Angle speed in position of fixed tuck	3.2 turns per min

The overall model for learning a quadruple somersault includes the following components:

Initial base of learning:

- high, well rounded triple somersault with stable landing onto mat to competition standard;
- landing after triple somersault with over-rotation on the back into a foam-rubber pit;
- biomechanical parameters of the triple somersaults approximate to the model characteristics of the quadruple somersault.

Preparatory exercises:

- accelerated giant swings gathering maximum speed in the second rotation;
- technically competent release into back somersault by conscious directed actions in the shoulder and hip joints;
- high, with quick rotation in flight somersault in tuck, semi-tuck, as well as with straight body and arms lifted high in flight (no lower than shoulder level), landing into over-rotation.

Gathering exercises:

- high, well rotated triple somersault with quick and tight tucking in flight, early and full stretching, and landing on the back in a foam pit with significant over-rotation;
- high, well-rotated triple somersault with semi-tuck (its degree of openness gradually increases) with somewhat slowed tuck in flight and landing in the foam rubber pit with a marked rotation on to the back;
- three triple somersaults in a row on the trampoline using a safety harness;
- quadruple back tuck somersault from the trampoline into the foam pit with perfect landing and over-rotation;
- quadruple back tuck somersault from the horizontal bar:
  - using safety harness into the pit;
  - also without harness with the coach's help on exit;
  - also on foam rubber mats with safety harness on entry;
  - also independently;
  - also in competition standard;
  - also in connecting elements;
  - also in working routine;
  - also at competitions.

3.3.14 Model for Elaborating and Directing the Preparation Programme

The process model of elaborating and directing the national team preparation programme in the Olympic cycle includes the following operations (at the basis of which is the algorithm suggested in work [37]):

- analysis of balance of forces;
- comparative analysis of the result dynamics;
- analyses of tendencies and perspectives of gymnastics development;
- forecasting;
- comparison of data outcome and process forecasting;
- modelling up a tree of goals;
- elaborating of sport- goal and prospective forecasting models;
- modelling preparation;
- planning, programming and projecting preparation;
- elaborating a comprehensive preparation programme;
- assessing the value of a preparation programme;
- ratifying the preparation programme;
- selecting candidates for preparation;
- implementing the preparation programme;
- investigating the team;
- control of preparation;
- comparative analyses of sport-goal and real psycho-physiological and physico-technical state of athletes at the conclusion of stages of preparation;
- correcting the preparation;
- selecting the team;
- performing in competitions;
- correcting preparation;
- performing at major competitions.

Besides the above-listed models we use projecting models of the training process in the national team integrated preparation system, as well as training load, ensuring preparation and other purposive models (see Chapters 5 and 9).

CHAPTER FOUR
Integrated Preparation System

4.1 Ways and Means of Preparation

4.1.1 Ways of Preparation

The theory of physical education and sports training differentiate five principal ways of preparing athletes: technical, tactical, physical, psychological and theoretical. In recent times we have noticed a trend towards highlighting functional preparation as an independent section. This is due to the fact that an organism's function has to be specially trained and adapted to the specifics of a given sport, which from the standpoint of big-time sport is fully justified.

Moreover, contemporary theory and methodology in gymnastics differentiate also a number of additional ways and varieties of preparation, such as *basic, linked, rotary, jumping, acrobatic, choreographic, centralised, middle-high altitude, pre-competition, competition, etc.*

Physical and technical preparation are the main points of support through which the central axis of the integrated preparation system passes. Around this axis, as around a solid rod, the remaining forms of preparation are grouped and their structural interaction is built.

Ways of preparation do not have precise boundaries that sharply differ from one another. In interacting they permeate and, so to speak, pass through each other, forming imprecise objects, successive approximations and linked ways of preparation (Figure 6). The multilateral linking of different forms of preparation and, primarily, the technical-physical linking is one of the major trends of development of the integrated preparation system. This is what differentiates it from classical preparation in which the analytical principle of clear separation of forms of preparation dominates.

4.1.2 Means of Preparation

Choosing means of preparation depends on those tasks whose resolution ensures timely arrival at the purposive model of competitive activity and the attainment of the forecast results in the upcoming Olympic cycle.

Exercises of *special preparation (exercises typical of competitive activity in the given sport)* must prevail among training means applied in the integrated preparation system. After all, for a gymnast to jump high, he has to jump a lot, and not run a lot, swim or cycle a lot. This track aphorism is totally applicable to gymnastics.

The following means of preparation should be used in training top-class gymnasts:

- *competitive exercises in all the events (competitive routines altogether);*
- *parts of competitive exercises (elements and series from competitive routines);*
- *vault (as a whole and by stages in easier and harder conditions);*
- *training exercises (routines, series, elements, phases, jumps);*
- *basic, profile, linked, special and preparatory exercises;*
- *SPP exercises for developing and/or maintaining the necessary level of strength, force and velocity qualities, speed, flexibility and special endurance;*
- *Acrobatic exercises;*
- *Jumping on the trampoline;*
- *Choreographic exercises (for women);*
- *Additional means of preparation.*

Ways and means of preparation are also linked to one another. The tackling of special tasks of various forms of preparation runs parallel and simultaneous while performing the same exercises. A closer and multiple linking of them is one of the leading trends of development of the system and techniques of preparing top-class gymnasts in the current Olympic cycle (2001-2004).

Exercises of general physical preparation (team games, running, swimming, etc.) are used in limited amounts predominantly as means of recovery, and psycho-physical unloading. The share of general physical preparation may grow somewhat by the end of the main competitions of the year.

4.2 Technical Preparation

4.2.1 Sports Technique and Technical Skill

Technical skill takes shape and improves in the process of technical preparation and plays a particularly important role in gymnastics. *Technical skill* is a process of learning various gymnastics exercises, technical actions and guiding movements. Teaching gymnasts is linked inexorably with forming and improving sports technique and technical skill, where we set and deal with the classical pedagogical problems of 'what to teach?', 'how to teach?' and 'why to teach?'.

It is in the process of technical preparation that the educational ability of the coach and his professional qualification as a gymnastics teacher especially come out vividly. Therefore we may say with some conviction that technical preparation is the most educational form of preparation. Let us note in particular that any system of learning, besides one's own learning, always involves the teaching of a pupil [40].

Sporting technique is one of the most important concepts of technical preparation. The term technique comes from the Greek 'techne', meaning 'art', skill. The technique of performing gymnastics exercises includes a multitude of factors: biomechanical, physiological, pedagogical, psychological, aesthetic, etc. Refinement of technical skill is a crucial component in the technology of integrated preparation. In the final analysis, only through technical actions, by technique, will the gymnast attain sports-technical results and the goal model (Figure 6). A high level of physical, functional and psychological preparedness is a necessary condition of possessing optimal technique.

The forming and refining of technical skill is associated with acquiring the technique of performing various exercises. This process has a cyclical character. It begins each time with the setting of goals and tasks, is accompanied by educational inputs from the coach and ends at each specific stage of a gymnast's movements – ie by a biomechanical process which will lead to the set result. This result compares with the goal and the coach's and gymnast's efforts are set on making the difference between them as small as possible and, ultimately, making the attained technical result the same as the goal (more precisely with the goal model).

If the basic biomechanical characteristics of movement vary over a wide scale – if from start to start there is a big difference (for instance, in length and height of flight) the forming of technique is not completed. Narrowing and stabilising of the scale of variation of technique involving the basic characteristics with transfer of most elements of self-control to an automatic level testify that the performance of technique of the given exercise has taken shape and that the motor (technical) ability has become a habit. However, the technical results here will not necessarily be high, while the mastered technique may be optimal. The gymnast has simply mastered it, making it automatic. Whether the technical version of performance mastered by the gymnast is good or bad is quite another matter.

Thus, any technical result is a consequence of technical actions by which a gymnast realises a particular technique. Technical actions on the outside are expressed in characteristic body movements with a certain dispersion of his body in space and time. It is precisely according to the external picture of movements performed by the gymnast that we judge whether the technique is good or bad.

That is why we compare the result achieved by the gymnast (in the broad sense) with the goal (or purposive model) and the movements of other gymnasts. In that way we compare various versions of technique of performing specific exercises (elements, series, routines). The procedure for comparing what was with what now and what should be is one of the most important in teaching and its invariable attribute. This applies equally to teaching in general and to the mastering of exercises of any complexity in particular.

Sporting technique (in our case the technique of performing gymnastic movements) is a central concept of technical preparation. There exist a multitude of definitions of technique with their own pluses and minuses [23,16,63]. This is beyond our book. Without going into detail, we provide here our own definition of sporting technique which lies at the basis of this book.

By technique we understand the sum total of automatic habits for tackling motor tasks through purposive technical actions resulting in an ordered dispersion of the athlete's body and (or) his links in space and time – ie typical movements. The result that he achieves is the means of assessment of performed movements. This assessment includes a number of components: judging, coaching, expert, public, as well as the gymnast's own self-evaluation.

The goal model of technique is the ideal a priori image of how and through what a given exercise should be performed. This model in one way or another (often in contracted form) exists in the consciousness of the coach and gymnast until they begin some sort of practical actions. The contracted model takes shape especially and is associated with the acquisition of additional information. As motor experience is accumulated as a result of multiple performances of exercises, their purposive models more and more become detailed and specific. At the stage of refinement of technical skill they again become more general.

The mechanism of acquiring and refining technical skill in the process of technical preparation provokes particular interest theoretically and practically. Let us set out our view on this. The acquiring and refinement of technical skill in gymnastics is, in our view, a matter of the forming in the cerebral cortex of a sort of data base whose elements are a multitude of functional systems. This is a meta-programme consisting of control of concrete movements programmes.

The same gymnastics exercise cannot be repeated twice in the same way. The biomechanical characteristics of even firmly embedded optimal technical structure always vary, even in a fairly narrow range. As a result of multiple repetitions of exercises, an optimal programme of movement control is worked out in the cerebral cortex for each specific routine of changing external and internal conditions (starting position, balance of basic biomechanical parameters of movement, physical conditions, degree of fatigue, etc.). This includes a whole series of components: the purposive model, commands given by the central nervous system to the muscles, their contraction, movement of body links, reverse action, control, correction, etc.

Programmes whose realisation provides a useful result are remembered by the gymnast and put away in his motor memory as in a computer in the form of basic elements of data of a positive type, like 'I must do that if...' (ie in particular circumstances). Those programmes which do not bring useful results are also stored in the motor memory, but now as elements of negative experience of the type 'I shouldn't do that if...'

In certain external and internal conditions the prepared programme of movement control is taken out of the motor memory and implemented in an automatic regime. Thus, a particular programme of movement control is included according to what has been created by specific circumstances when performing the exercise.

Evidently, with such a selection of cerebral cortex as the main coordinator, a certain physiological apparatus (apparently vestibular) must be found that registers and evaluates the basic parameters and concrete conditions of movement made during its specific performance. After that the brain selects a sub-programme of movement control adequate to these conditions from the data base formed as a result of a multitude of repetitions – ie from the existing meta-programme it selects an adequate sub-programme which it implements. And all in the blink of an eye.

For example, when performing a triple somersault as a result of a technical error in support the gymnast has created insufficient angular momentum and has begun 'to hang' in flight. Sensing insufficient rotation, he starts tucking tighter, holds the tuck longer and thereby compensates for the support action mistake. This is done unconsciously, on 'auto-pilot', which takes shape with a gymnast as he acquires motor experience as a result of multiple performances of a given class of exercise.

The greater the experience and motor erudition of a gymnast, the richer the data base at his disposal. The more talented the gymnast, the fewer number of repetitions he has to do to form an adequate meta-programme of movement control. A gymnast's talent, like tactics, is determined by his ability adequately to react to conditions created while performing exercises, including extreme conditions that he has not so far met in his motor experience.

A number of terms and concepts are used in the theory and method of technical preparation which require further definition.

Technical actions are actions connected with implementation of a certain technique of performing an exercise. They include controlling actions, operations controlling movements (main and correcting) and elementary movements in the joints. Besides that, they include the control movement component being realised by the central nervous system in the process of higher nervous activity. The sum total of technical actions determines the technique of performing gymnastic exercises and their technical structure (see Chapter 7.2).

Control actions are actions connected with control of specific movement, including biomechanical, physiological and psychological components.

Control movements constitute an external mechanical manifestation of control actions on the basis of the joints. They are divided into *major* and *correcting actions* (46). The major control movements always provide great mechanical effect. One may in principle get by without correcting movements. The simultaneous performance of major and correcting control movements in the joints increases the total mechanical effect if they are performed in one dimension.

The technical basis is the stabilising skeleton of the structure of technical actions (otherwise technical structure) typical of all movements of the given structural group.

The technical means is a variant of the technique of performing a gymnastics exercise with stabilising technical and biomechanical structure.

Among technical means of performing relatively simple exercises are those whose technical structure and basic parameters are highly similar to the given type of a very complex exercise. These means have to be learned particularly carefully and brought to technical refinement in the process of basic special technical preparation – ie this will enable the gymnast in future more quickly and with greater quality to master increasingly complex exercises and, more rapidly to gain complexity in the competitive programmes.

By increasing the major parameters of movement as he perfects the technique of relatively simple exercises, the gymnast is able to form the necessary conditions for mastering the most complex. For example, when increasing the height of flight and speed of turn in a double somersault he can acquire the basic parameters of flight necessary for performing a triple somersault.

To test one or the other, the gymnast ought to perform two test exercises landing in a foam rubber pit: 1. double somersault with straightening of the body in flight and 2. double somersault in maximum open position (tuck). If the gymnast in both cases lands in the pit with an obvious over-turn in the somersault, then after a preliminary 'overturn' on the trampoline he can transfer to mastering the triple somersault. His basic flight parameters have been formed.

4.2.2 Conception of Technical Preparation

The strategic objective of technically preparing top-class gymnasts consists in the perfect mastery of the optimal technique of performing full value and competitive exercises and their reliable performance in conditions of top competitive struggle, attaining planned results. This objective, like a law, sets the character and direction of the process of extensive technical preparation, its content and structure.

The object of technical preparation in contemporary gymnastics consists in forming and perfecting technical actions whose complexity increases. Its object consists in motor habits of progressive complexity. These habits ensure an increasingly quality performance of already mastered exercises and the mastery of increasingly complex elements, connecting movements and routines.

One of the important factors of attaining high and stable results is the constant refinement of the technology of mastering exercises and of technical preparation as a whole, which represents a progressively developing sub-system within the integrated preparation system.

The ways and means of technical preparation in modern technology of integrated preparation normally move in tandem with other forms (especially physical and functional, as well as psychological and tactical). At the stage of reinforcing the motor habit, this is done so that in training the gymnast it ensures an exceeding of basic parameters of technical preparedness necessary for successful competitive activity.

The strategy of perfecting technical skill takes shape within the terms of 'outstripping' development. But, if the strategic tasks of learning over many years of technical training are set and tackled as purposive development tasks, then the technical tasks are set as model technical indicators which become progressively more complex over time.

The peculiar feature of our approach to technical preparation consists in it being set on mastering increasingly complex exercises, movements and technical actions with increasing results over many years of training gymnasts.

This should not be understood as a call for an immediate storming of the heights of complexity. We do not mean that, having mastered, for example, a double somersault, one should straightaway move on to learning a triple somersault; and once having mastered the triple right away moving on to a quadruple. One should adapt the mastered movement to growth in complexity through purposive refinement of the technique of its performance with the aid of special tasks. One must make the technique of performing the mastered exercises more complicated parametrically and structurally.

We have in mind primarily the increase and more precise concordance of the basic flight parameters being set from support (the vector of speed of the overall centre of body mass at the end of connecting movement with support is the main kinetic moment (see Chapter 6.3.1). If we refine the technique of performing relatively simple exercises with the goal of bringing it only to a faultless level according to the judge's marks, this frequently becomes a brake on mastering more complex exercises of this type.

For example, a well-mastered somersault technique (stretched somersault) for which the judges make no deductions in the junior rankings will be a brake on mastering more complex somersaults (a double and a triple, for example) if during flight the arms are immediately let down, while the body is considerably 'convex' (bent). This pose is characterised by a smaller moment of inertia of the gymnast's body in relation to his transverse axis by comparison with a fully straightened body and requires less angular momentum given from support. Ultimately less effort of interaction from support is required to perform this stretched somersault.

It is another matter when a gymnast performs a stretched somersault at maximum height with fully straightened body in flight and arms raised up. This technique is more promising from the viewpoint of mastering a double somersault. But, to master it the gymnast needs to increase the basic parameters of flight given from support. In other words, the simple stretched somersault should be complicated parametrically. One should develop the parameters of more complex movement element in a more simple form.

Now about the double somersault. Parametrically a purposive refinement of technique of its execution means that the goal should be to master this by technical means, which:

- ensures a swift completion of second somersaults across the horizontal bar;
- with an early and full straightening of the body in flight with maximum height;
- with a steady and stable (perfect) landing at a given point.

Evidently, we require a more refined technique for this performance, a higher level of development of force velocity qualities and (or) a fuller use of them. Many years of experience testify to the fact that a forced storming of complexity without previous parametrically purposive refinement of the technique of already mastered exercises (and, above all, the basic) only leads to slowing down the mastery of more complex movements and reducing improvement of mastery.

That is why any (especially super-complex) exercise has to be learned not only with the aim of including it in the competitive programme faultlessly, according to judging requirements, but also with the initial objective of mastering increasingly more complex modifications without loss of quality.

Hence the conclusion that learning relatively simple exercises means building from a technique of performing very complex movements of a given type. Thus, the objective of learning relatively simple exercises (a somersault, for instance) consists in forming a technical basis that has a high degree of similarity to the most complex movements of a given type (for example, a triple somersault).

Our research and practical experience have shown that to reach this goal ensures a rapid and qualitative mastering of more and more complex exercises, including super-complex. This by no means signifies that learning a relatively simple movement ought to start with mastering the most complex technical variants of its execution. We are only emphasising the need for constant orientation on such variants during the technical refinement. We must learn to master the complex in the simple, and the simple in the complex.

Naturally, with such an approach a relatively simple exercise will become technically more complex, and the process of learning under the motto 'master the complex in the simple' is more lengthy and work-intensive, especially in forming the technical basis of fundamental exercises at the stage of beginning technical mastery. However, loss of time in the initial stages is subsequently repaid with interest. We have paid testimony to the fact that ultimately the mastery of movements of progressive complexity with this approach takes place more effectively with substantial gaining of time (see Figure 1).

We do not recommend taking the technique of new elements to the absolute in isolated execution. In that case problems arise when including a well-mastered element separately into connecting movements and routines. This is caused by the fact that the element is being mastered and refined only in the most favourable conditions (a convenient and stable starting position, lack of tiredness, etc.). The technique of performance becomes stable in 'warm' circumstances which are very rare when performing this element in routines at competitions.

The technical habit taking shape loses its flexibility and adaptability necessary for competitive conditions. When including it in routines this habit has to be broken, adapting the stabilising technique to conditions not always favourable, including very unfavourable, which can be modelled in training. That is why we recommend perfecting the technique of the mastered element in connecting movements and routines at the level of incomplete stabilisation of the motor habit.

We feature the following zones of intensity in the technical preparation process:

- small (training by elements);
- medium (training by series);
- big (training by routines);
- sub-maximum (training by routines in a competition regime);
- maximum (training by routines in a regime exceeding the competition).

The extent of mastery of each zone of intensity has two indicators: mean assessment (m) and performance reliability (R) which may be expressed in the formula:

$$R = n/N$$

Where n is the number of successfully performed exercises, and N is the number of attempts at performing the given exercise (element, series or routine).

In each zone of intensity there are five levels of mastery:

- 1. mean mark is 1 with reliability of up to 0.2;
- 2. mean mark is 2 with reliability of up to 0.2-0.4;
- 3. mean mark is 3 with reliability of up to 0.4-0.6;
- 4. mean mark is 4 with reliability of up to 0.6-0.8;
- 5. mean mark is 4.5 with reliability of up to 0.8-1.0.

We recommend mastering the following zone of intensity after reaching indicators of the fourth level of mastery of the previous zone on condition that conservative technical faults are absent.

In accordance with the planned weekly micro-cycle of load at training sessions of various forms we carry out 'shuttle' transfers from the lower zones of intensity to the higher and back. In the final case we set the task of attaining maximum indicators of the fifth level of mastering the given zone of intensity (5 marks given R=1.0).

4.2.3 Basic Technical Preparation

Basic technical preparation (BTP) is a process of mastering technically the basic exercises of varying complexity, the forming and refinement of basic technical habits of various levels. BTP is a necessary condition for acquiring necessary technical surplus. It has a long-term purposive character and is carried out according to a multi-year programme which is drawn up with account for trends in gymnastics development and forecasting of technical achievements in the Olympic cycle. It also envisages a planned and consistent mastery of key habits necessary for successful progression during a gymnast's sporting career. The quality of basic technical preparation is an indicator of success in training top-class gymnasts. As a rule, successes or failings of national gymnastics schools are primarily connected with the quality of basic technical preparation.

The objective of BTP lies in the technically perfected mastery of a minimised circle of exercises, the technical basis of which is most adequate for the most complex movements of the major structural groups. These exercises are called profile or basic. The basic physical qualities and technical habits necessary for their successful mastery remain fairly stable over many years. They may be divided into general (necessary for successful mastery of exercises on all apparatus) and specific (necessary for each particular apparatus).

The basic technical elements (and then also the basic control in movement and actions) are defined on the basis of the law-governed growth in complexity (see Chapter 6.6) through gradual climbing down the ladder of complexity with a simplification of technical structure of the most complex movements, but with distortion of the technical basis. Starting at the early stages of forming technical mastery, BTP is actively conducted at the level of the national team. This is an important and significant part of the integrated preparation of top-class gymnasts, being the top level of the BTP hierarchy.

BTP is constructed on the basis of the following principles:
1. concentration of movements and actions in space and time;
2. repetition of movements and actions (one and the same actions, elements and connecting movements are done several times in a row);
3. economy and automatic performance and technical actions.

BTP includes mastery of profile routines on apparatus which are a special form of structural teaching systems of movement. The elaboration and constructing of profile routines is done also on the basis of the principle of concentration. Here we have in mind concentration of basic elements and technical actions in space and time which ensure their execution.

The basic components of technical actions needed for rapid assimilation of increasingly complex exercises of the main structural groups on each apparatus must be contained in the profile routines in simplified form. The characteristic feature here consists in that these relatively simple technical actions are done in well-known complicated conditions.

Profile routines are built up mainly so that each successive element can be done only in the correct technique of performing the previous element. For this purpose all the simple connecting elements in the process of performing which the gymnast can use to correct any mistakes are excluded from the profile routine.

With this approach it is not the coach's instructions or emotions, not internal, let alone external conditions that condition the correct technique. The very construction of the profile routine a priori reduces the probability of committing significant technical mistakes – ie it becomes unfulfilled in the opposite case.

As an example we show the profile routine we have worked out on the horizontal bar:

1. back swing forward swing shoot to handstand and hop-change to undergrasp;
2. swing back and hop change to overgrasp;
3. swing forward and hop change to undergrasp;
4. swing backward in undergrasp and half-turn to undergrasp;
5. long swing forward and squat in, dislocate into handstand and long swing in rotated grasp (Adler);
6. hop change to overgrasp and short clear circle to handstand (Felge);
7. giant swing forward in overgrasp half turn to undergrasp (blind change-Keller);
8. long swing in undergrasp half turn with maximum amplitude into overgrasp;
9. swing forward, "back- away" with straight body and arms stretched upward, landing at a distance of 1.5 to 2m. from the horizontal bar.

NB
- elements 4 and 7 are repeated 2-3 times in a row;
- series from elements 8 and 9 are repeated 2-3 times in a row with large extension of the free arm to the side each time;
- all the repeating elements are done with increasing amplitude and the last end in a position close to hand-stand;
- all changes of grip are always done simultaneously;
- all elements are done one after the other without any 'dilution';
- dismount by back somersault alternates with forward somersault which is done with big back swing immediately after the Keller turn with the same requirements.

It is clear that this routine may be done to the end without stopping only with perfected mastery of the technique of performing each element. This technique must be flexible, well adapted to unfavourable circumstances. Evidently, a technical error in the previous element worsens the conditions for correct execution of the subsequent element. The gymnast must instantly react to the situation and correct his actions straightaway.

Here the possibilities for correcting any technical errors and the adopting of a favourable starting position for performing the following element in this routine are reduced to a minimum because of a lack of simple connecting elements where this error may be easily corrected during the movement. If we 'compensate' for this routine by long swings, it at once loses its profile character. The possibility of correcting technical errors immediately appears and the probability of committing them radically increases. Our experience demonstrates that if a potential for error occurs, gymnasts invariably take it no matter what you say. The path of least resistance is always the path of the majority.

To successfully execute the given profile routine the gymnast must master well the basic technical actions necessary for mastering the technique of all complex turns, flight elements and dismounts performed with long swing on the horizontal bar. In turn this ensures rapid technical progress in mastering movements of progressive complexity. This routine is constructed on the principle of artificially controlling the environment [52] and the principal of determination of internal conditions by the external, which in psychology is called the internalisation principle [40]. Here the internal actions take place from the exterior.

Profile routines of this type are simplified models of contemporary compulsory series of complex elements which are enriched by bonus from the judges. If utilised at early stages of technical preparation they prepare and orient young gymnasts on mastering these routines. We began to use such profile routines when preparing the national team and its reserves (primarily) a long time ago – more than twenty years ago. At first they were used as integrated technical models, then as teaching and control exercises and, finally, as special warm-ups on the apparatus.

In the BTP we differentiate *initial, intermediate, high and top levels*.

The initial level envisages mastering basic technical habits and abilities, of correct dynamic carriage, by basic control actions and movements during the process of mastering relatively simple exercises.

At the intermediate level gymnasts master basic elements and profile exercises.

The high level is connected with mastering basic elements of high complexity and models of strategic connecting movements. Without mastering them it is impossible to build a full value and competitive routine and reach the level of the sports-goal prospective-forecasting model of technical achievement. The profile routines of high, and then the top level which, nevertheless, become more complicated over time consist of these elements and series.

They are constructed, like the above-mentioned profile routine, on the principle of concentration of movements and actions. These routines represent a number of consecutive approximations to the goal model of technical mastery. Their perfected mastery is the goal and point of the BTP of the top and very individualised level.

We should note that the starting base of gymnastics remains stable in volume and structure; such has been the case for many years. That can certainly not be said about the top levels of BTP. Its volume and structure are not set in stone. As gymnasts master what at a given moment are complex exercises, an increasing number of gymnasts tend to devalue them. What at a given moment are complex elements over time become routine. From one Olympic cycle to the next we notice a trend towards complication of the technical basis of the topmost levels (see also Chapter 3.3.5).

4.3   Physical Training

4.3.1   Physical Qualities

The sum total of motor possibilities reflects a gymnast's motorics. The *physical qualities* of a gymnast are different aspects of his motorics [22]. For successfully mastering full value modern exercises top-class gymnasts have to have a high level of development of basic physical qualities. They include: *strength, speed, endurance, flexibility and dexterity*. All physical qualities are genetically determined and depend on development, but in differing degrees. The level of development of physical qualities necessary for performing full value and competitive gymnastics exercises is determined by model characteristics of the SPP (see Chapter 3.3.6).

4 INTEGRATED PREPARATION SYSTEM

Strength (force) is one of the most important physical qualities of gymnasts. Research demonstrates a close connection between the level of development of strength and sports-technical results. Other physical qualities are directly dependent on level of muscle power development. Parallel with the term *strength* and *strength qualities* we also use the terms *muscle power, strength potential* and *strength ability*.

The strength qualities are a sum total of several components which are interconnected and mutually conditioned. These are *static strength, dynamic strength* (slow and fast) and *strength endurance*. These varieties of strength attributes are necessary for performing different exercises, like swings as well as purely strength movements. They apply to the following:

- static exercises (angle, horizontal support and forward and backward hang, 'cross', 'swallow' inverted cross etc.);
- slow power movements up and down (so called 'presses' or power lifts or lowering);
- exercises of the 'swing-power' type (swing movements ending with power static, for example, lift by long swing into 'cross', 'swallow' horizontal support);
- power marathons (see Chapter 4.3.3).

It is hard to draw precise borders between components of strength attributes. They intertwine and permeate one another (Figure 7). They are unique moveable objects that mathematically can be represented in the form of imprecise multitudes or fuzzy sets [93].

Figure 7 – *Structure of strength qualities*

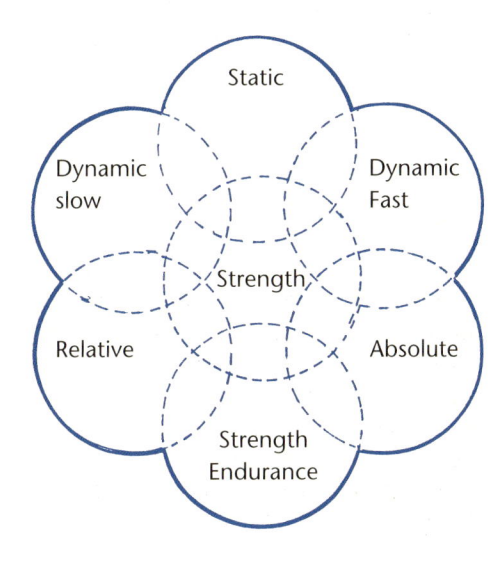

For men and women gymnasts alike, what is important is not absolute, but relative strength (ie per 1 kg of weight, when the absolute magnitude of an indicator of strength is divided by the gymnast's weight- see Chapter 1.2). The level of manifestation of strength qualities determined with the aid of special test exercises, is an important informational indicator of a gymnast's preparedness and his prospects at all stages of selection.

A high level of strength qualities and, above all, relative strength, is typical of both general and top-class gymnasts. To determine this level we use special test exercises (see Chapter 3.3.6).

To develop strength qualities and maintain them at the necessary level top-class gymnasts have systematically to perform a big volume of special strength exercises. These exercises are done in lightened, normal and more difficult regimes – a) with the help of the coach or a partner, b) independently and, c) with an artificial aid. In the last case we use a belt, vest and lead weight or sand weight of varying amounts. To develop particular muscle groups we have to use special apparatus of the Minigym variety.

Speed-strength qualities play an important role in contemporary gymnastics. They are apparent in the gymnast's ability to demonstrate high strength in a short period of time. They are necessary for performing exercises of an 'explosive' nature: thrusting off, landing, leaving and arriving at the apparatus, sharp swings and other sharp movements. We use the same regimes to develop them. Top-class gymnasts usually possess a fairly high level of speed-and-strength qualities. But achieving them is a serious problem since they to a large extent are determined genetically – ie either you have them from nature or you haven't, and to develop them by certain methods is very difficult.

Exercises used in SPP must be chosen by the principle of dynamic correspondence (specifity) (14). As applied to strength and speed-and-strength preparation the essence of this principle consists in making the special exercises for promoting strength and speed-strength qualities in a structured way and parametrically similar to those exercises for the successful mastery of which the qualities are developed.

Above all, they must be similar to the purposive exercises that are part of the competitive programme and the technical preparation programme, according to parameters like direction of movement, amplitude, regime of muscle work, speed of developing maximum strength, its amount and extent in time and space. We should note that the principle of dynamic correspondence does not contradict the principles of outstripping development and optimal surplus, but combines well with them.

The physical quality of speed characterises the gymnast's speed potential, his ability to carry out motor (technical) actions in a minimal possible time for the given conditions. We distinguish the following basic types of manifestation of speed qualities: speed of single movement, frequency of movements and latent time of motor reaction [22]. These indicators are independent of each other – ie the gymnast can have a high first indicator and a low second, and vice versa.

Speed qualities are manifest mainly in the run-up when performing support and acrobatic jumps. Speed at the moment of vault on to the vault table in support vaults, frequency of paces in the 'running on the spot' test exercise, number of circles, longswings, somersaults from stand or any other dynamic elements performed in a unit of time are all also indicators of a gymnast's potential. Top-class gymnasts must possess a high level of speed qualities (see Chapter 3.3.6).

Another important indicator for gymnasts is speed or speed of developing strength which is called *gradient of force* in biomechanics. Speed is sometimes confused with sharpness. But this is not the same. Sharpness is a speed-strength force-velocity quality characterised mainly by a high gradient of strength. It is a very important quality for performing elements of high complexity, especially jumps/swings, releases. Being a quality that is inherent it is very difficult to develop.

The 'speed-strength' dependence is in inverse proportion: the higher the speed, the less the strength. For example, in a test of maximum amount of arm flexion per unit of time with maximum load, the maximum speed of movement will be reached when the load is equal to nil (no load on the arm). The minimal speed (equal to zero) will be achieved when the weight taken by the arm will be maximal. The gymnast will be able to hold it on a straight arm, but not in a state of bent arm. The average indicators of speed are reached with roughly average expenditure of strength.

Flexibility is also an important physical quality of a top-class gymnast. But the level of development of flexibility, like other attributes, must be not the maximum possible, but the optimal – ie corresponding to the principle of optimal surplus. This level, for example, is considerably lower than in modern rhythmic gymnasts. Extreme flexibility in gymnastics is more harmful than useful because gymnasts who are too flexible by nature usually have insufficient strength. Moreover, we know that very great mobility in the spinal cord is an unfavourable factor for attaining top sports results and performing high training loads without which we cannot achieve what we need to in gymnastics.

We distinguish static (in rest) and dynamic flexibility (in motion), as well as active (through one's own muscle efforts) and passive (under the impact of external forces) flexibility, which is always greater than the former. The difference between them is called a shortage of active flexibility [22].

This indicator may be reduced through special strength and speed- strength exercises performed with maximum possible amplitude. A growth in strength and speed-and-strength attributes in this case leads also to an increase in indicators of active flexibility which depends on a number of conditions (time of day, warm up, temperature in the hall and level of preparedness). With a low temperature in the hall and insufficient or poor warming-up of the body, the flexibility indicators diminish.

Being largely genetically determined, an innate quality, flexibility develops fairly well in childhood and youth. With female gymnasts it is considerably higher than with males. As one gets older the flexibility indicators usually worsen without special training. Sufficient mobility in the joints is a necessary condition for mastering a refined technique for performing exercises. The best age for developing flexibility is 7-10.

Circus artistes who perform as 'rubber men/women' or 'female snakes' demonstrate a level of flexibility close to the limit, as well as rhythmic gymnasts. But, as mentioned above, optimal flexibility which is somewhat higher than the actual need of an individual competitive programme is necessary to achieve top results in gymnastics.

Dexterity is one of the major physical qualities of a gymnast. By dexterity we mean the ability of fine differentiation and precise coordination of one's physical efforts and technical actions in time and space in conditions of complex orientation and lack of time, as well as a marked ability to learn fast new complex exercises. Dexterity of a top-class gymnasts is specific and has practically little in common with the dexterity of a juggler, fencer or boxer.

Endurance is a crucial physical attribute in modern sport, and is manifest in an ability to carry out physical exercises for a fairly long time without reducing the productiveness despite fatigue. By endurance we mean the ability to carry out the required physical work in a set intensive system. In gymnastics the anaerobic mechanism of energy supply of muscle activity predominates, and this is a very powerful system (see Chapter 1.2). The threshold of anaerobic supply (TAS) in competitive and training activity is normally never attained.

Special endurance is a paramount factor for achieving high and stable results. It is apparent in a gymnast's ability many times to perform competitive exercises without substantial technical errors and with a set level of productiveness in conditions of various intrusive factors, including competitive stress.

Gymnastic endurance is a complex and multi-component quality. It is a profoundly gymnastic quality depending on many factors. A necessary condition of a high level of special endurance is optimal work, above all of the cardio-vascular system, ensuring the arrival of feeding substances to the working muscles and accelerating metabolism.

Endurance depends on the functional state of the gymnast's support-motor apparatus and its neuro-muscular components, level of coordination abilities and technical skill, physical qualities and will power preparation. A gymnast's *general endurance* takes shape using means of other sports (cross country running, swimming, skiing, football).

Special endurance which is a limiting factor in growth of skill acquires a dominant role with top-class gymnasts. To promote special gymnastic endurance we need to use exercises adequate for competition – ie similar to those in the biomechanical structure and training routines. The latter may be easier than the competition in difficulty, but longer and vice versa.

Research has shown that such an important quality as high gymnastic work capacity is closely associated with special endurance. This indicator is one of the most important factors directly affecting sports-technical results.

To enhance gymnastic work capacity and promote special endurance we pay particular significance to methodologically well programmed and projected preparation as a whole and, above all, methodologically correct planning and control of training loads (see Chapter 5).

We should note that it is also difficult to draw a line between the above-mentioned physical qualities. Being interconnected and interdependent they intertwine and permeate each other (Figure 8). Research has shown that a high level of development of strength is closely associated with a high level of special endurance and jumping ability. Yet flexibility, for example, correlates poorly with them. The physical qualities of gymnasts within certain parameters possess the quality of mutual compensation. That is why the model characteristics of SPP are not a dogma.

NB In the specialist literature we use the term physical condition. In the theory and method of physical education and sports training the term physical qualities is also applied. But in addition to that various mechanical states of the gymnast's body enter the concept of physical condition.

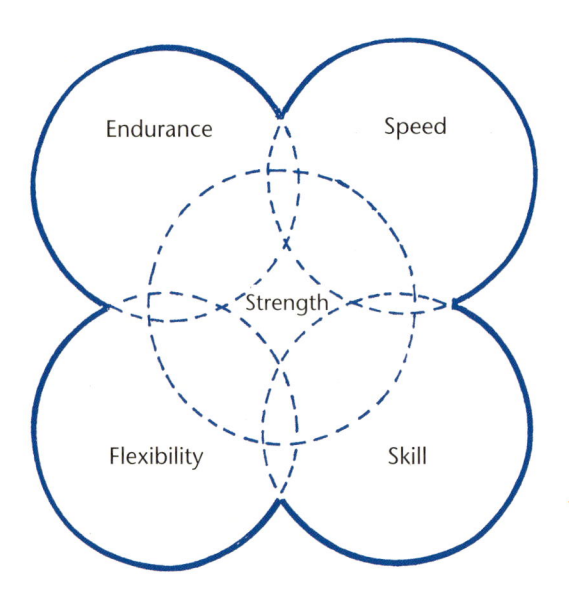

Physical training of top-class gymnasts is directed at developing physical qualities to the set level and then retaining them at that level.

Figure 8 – *Structure of physical qualities*

4.3.2 Physical Preparation Conception

Physical preparation is the foundation on which the entire system of integrated preparation of top-class gymnasts and all gymnasts who set their sights on high sporting achievements is built (Figure 6). It is aimed at developing the physical qualities ensuring successful mastery of complex gymnastic exercises. The ultimate goal of physical preparation consists in promoting physical qualities up to the level of optimal physical surplus that ensures high quality and reliable mastery of a full value and competitive programme with a set level of productiveness.

Physical preparation of top-class gymnasts includes general (GPP) and special (SPP). Other sports (cross country running, swimming, skiing, team games) are means of the former. In modern-day high achievement sport we notice a marked tendency to reducing the share of GPP and an increasing share of SPP in training top-class gymnasts. Thus, when preparing for the 26th Olympic Games and the 33rd and 34th world championships, the share of GPP in the overall load of the Russian national team in the preparatory and competitive periods comprised 3-5%.

It has been established that physical qualities developed using exercises from other sports that radically differ from gymnastics are poorly carried over into the structure of purposive gymnastic exercises. For example, endurance developed in cross country running adds practically nothing to special gymnastic endurance necessary for worthwhile performance of routines in the competitive regime. However, the role and share of GPP are considerably higher in the lower ranks of gymnasts.

The role of SPP is extremely high and has a marked tendency to rise. Its share in the overall load of the Russian national team is as much as 60% in the preparatory period and about 40% in the competitive. In the pre-competition and competitive micro-cycles this share may diminish to 15-20%. But this occurs by no means with all gymnasts, and this indicator is very individual. For example, in a four-week cycle of preparation for top competitions it may vary from 5% to 50%. The remaining part of the training load is taken up by technical preparation.

We may develop the major physical qualities of gymnasts both isolated from each other and together. The method of combined effect is a very effective method in the latter case. We widely apply this method in the integrated preparation system both in the process of combined development of technical-physical preparation, and in the process of combined development of the physical attributes themselves, when several physical qualities are developing simultaneously (see Chapter 4.3.3.1).

The combined actions method elaborated by Dyatchkov [23] and Ratov [52] ensures the development of physical qualities together with mastering the technique of execution. Following this method including exercises SPP, we recommend performing gymnastics exercises of cyclical type while wearing weights. For instance, Stalder and Endo performed on high bar, one after another, until refusal.

Any result in gymnastics ultimately comes only from technical actions. But these actions themselves may be done in an optimal regime only with a high level of special physical qualities or, in other words, with optimal physical provision.

The word *optimal* here is used in the sense that the level of physical preparedness must exceed the actual physical demands of those elements and routines which the gymnast carries out in training and competitions. It must be higher than that minimum of physical qualities which is necessary for successful resolution of motor tasks in training and competitive activity. For without optimal physical surplus it is impossible to ensure high reliability in performing modern gymnastic exercises.

It is natural to ask 'By how much should we exceed it?' By way of elucidation, for example, it would not be sensible to put a jet engine in an ordinary motor car. So a gymnast does not need the strength of a weightlifter, the speed of a sprinter or the endurance of a marathon runner. He needs the optimum of specifically gymnastic physical attributes. What is this optimum?

To answer this question so far we have no sufficiently strict theory. Chapter 3.2 shows how the problem is tackled in the technology of integrated preparation.

Unfortunately, we have to say that in practice even top-class gymnasts are beginning to master new exercises (elements and routines) in a state of local physical insufficiency. We have in mind a lack of specific physical qualities necessary for mastering a given element (say, arrival after a double back somersault over the bars on the parallel bars).

This happens very often in the junior ranks. In this case the special physical qualities needed to maser purposive exercises are developed directly in the process of mastering these exercises. Here the tasks of physical preparation are resolved in the process of technical preparation, and not the other way round, as follows from theory (see Figure 6). The absence of optimal physical surplus leads to violation of the principle of 'outstripping' development. As a result the process of mastering purposive exercises takes much longer than it should.

Moreover, because of the lack of this surplus gymnasts master purposive exercises with technical faults. At best they adapt their technique to their own local physical inadequacy, thereby reducing its reliability and likelihood of success. At worst they get injured and lose any real prospect of rapid and quality mastery of more complex exercises in this given structural group.

One of the important aspects of basic SPP and functional preparation is the development of the gymnast's abilities to control the mechanical state of his body while performing exercises. To perform successfully he requires various body conditions – from being relatively relaxed to extremely tense (like a powerful spring or as hard as a stone). The mechanical state of the body and its physical conditions are very important factors in controlling movement.

The necessary body conditions and habits of controlling its mechanical state have to be formed in the process of basic combined technical-physical and functional-rotating preparation (see Chapter 4.8.3). Unfortunately, this is rarely done while preparing even top-class gymnasts consciously, purposefully and correctly.

As a result, local physical and functional inadequacy arises and begins to increase. In turn this leads to adverse consequences in the process of technical preparation, including injury. Let us stress once more that optimal physical and functional surplus has to take shape before any real need for it arises during technical preparation. Here lies the essence of the principle of 'outstripping' development as applied to SPP.

It requires the creation of a physical surplus that precludes many difficulties that arise during technical preparation when learning and perfecting the technique of exercises of any complexity. Optimal physical surplus, therefore, is the first necessary condition of successful technical preparation of top-class gymnasts. Let us emphasise that this condition is necessary, but that is not all.

Our prepared method of SPP outlined below ensures strengthening of the support-motor apparatus and development of the basic physical qualities while simultaneously refining the technique of basic exercises. It has been tested and improved over several Olympic cycles.

4.3.3 Special Physical Preparation

Over many years of preparing top-class gymnasts we conclude that they need daily to perform a large amount of SPP training load. With a centralised preparation of top-class gymnasts we recommend the following SPP parameters in a weekly micro-cycle:

- *6 morning training SPP sessions;*
- *6-12 daily individual 'pumps';*
- *2 circuit sessions for SPP (Wednesday and Saturday);*
- *10 hours is the total duration of SPP work;*
- *amount = 1800 elements a week.*

This amount of work done weekly all year round provides a good educational result and ensures maintenance of a high SPP level.

4.3.3.1 Morning SPP Training Session

With centralised preparation SPP ought to be done in the first morning training session. The content and structure of SPP exercises, as well as the combined physical-technical training during the session, are represented in Chapter 5.7.1.

4.3.3.2 SPP at the End of the Training Session

At the end of the second or third training session we recommend daily, for 10-15 minutes, to perform special SPP exercises. In gymnastics slang we call this 'pumping'. With men this consists of a set of power exercises performed on the rings and parallel bars. At the end of each 'pumping', we do rope climbing of about 5 m with the legs in straddle-piked position (1-2 times).

Elements and routines that are part of the 'pumping' are selected on a strictly individual basis with account for the characteristics of the gymnasts and their level of SPP. In the preparatory period these routines have approximately the same amount of the order of 50 elements. They are 2-3 times less in the competitive period.

4.3.3.3 Circuit SPP Training

Circuit training is one of the effective ways to intensify the training process. Circuit training in SPP which we have used in the technology of integrated preparation for several decades has recommended itself as a powerful means of intensifying development of the necessary physical qualities and SPP as a whole.

We recommend top-class gymnasts to do this twice a week on Wednesday and Saturday during their evening training. The all-round SPP training we now use includes 10 stations and takes 35 minutes. It consists of two rounds of 5 stations in each. At each station for three minutes all gymnasts perform the same exercises (except exercises on the rings in the second round).

Constant physical work of high intensity at each station is done for three minutes. Before the start of all-round training the gymnasts are divided into several equal groups (maximum of 5), so that the stations are not crowded or underused. The optimal number of gymnasts in a group is 4. All gymnasts work simultaneously on their station. Their personal coaches if need be can lend a hand. Change of stations comes at the command of the senior or duty coach.

First Round (15 minutes)

First station. *Acrobatic runway:*

- here they perform long jumps from deep squat (3 runways of 20m). At the end they do a forward somersault.

Second station. *Rope climbing:*

This is done without leg assistance twice up 7m with body piked and legs either straddled or together.

Third station. *Exercises on the pommel horse:*

- the following routine is performed:

1) 5 high straight crossings (single leg cuts),
2) 5 reverse crossings (single leg cuts),
3) 5 circles with two on the handles,
4) transfer to support on body and handle,
5) 5 circles on the body and handle,
6) turn into crosswise support on the body,
7) 5 circles in crosswise support
8) turn into support on the handle and body,
9) 5 circles in support on the handle and body,
10) transfer into support on handles, 5 circles in support on handles.

Fourth station. *Exercise on the rings:*

The gymnast does a routine of 15 power elements of the type typical of rings in the third part of the first morning training session (see Chapter 4.3.3.1).

Fifth station. *Exercise on the parallel bars at the ends of the bars:*

The gymnast does a routine consisting of the following elements:

1) back swing bending arms,
2) forward swing straightening arms,
3) back swing bending and straightening arms in hand-stand,
4) forward swing.

The gymnast should repeat the exercise ten times.
After the first round the gymnast may rest for five minutes.

Second Round (15 minutes)

This is a repetition of the first round (the same five stations) in number of stations and content of exercises with the only difference that on the rings and parallel bars other routines are performed.

The power routine on the rings is composed depending on the gymnast's individual capabilities and level of SPP. We select power elements from the power marathon in the third part of the first morning training session (see Chapter 4.3.3.1).

The following routine is done five times in a row on the parallel bars:

1) from upper arm hang, uprise forward to support,
2) swing backward to handstand,
3) pirouette forwards,
4) swing forward to stutzkehre to support.

Gymnasts in the Russian national team do not practice general circuit training in SPP at the present time. They perform individual 'pumping' circuit at the end of training. For top-class gymnasts we recommend a 'pumping' circuit consisting of the following five stations:

First station: *Standing apparatus:*

- here we perform a power exercise consisting of the following elements:

1) 'Spichagi' – from support half-lever lift with straight arms and bent body to handstand,
2) planche press with straight arms; straight body,
3) horizontal supports (hold-press); planche,
4) press back in handstand.

Amount of routines – up to 40 elements.

Second station. *Low rings:*

- here we perform power exercises consisting of the following elements:

1) front lever (hold),
2) press into bent (piked) hang,
3) lower into back lever (hold),
4) press into hang bent (piked).

The exercise is repeated five times in a row without a rest.

Third station. *Rope:*

- climbing rope of 5m once without leg assistance in straddle pike position (or pull-ups on a bar 15 times).

Fourth station. *Pommel horse:*

- on this apparatus we do special exercises to develop trunk muscles, lying lengthwise on the body of the horse and holding on to the handle:

1) lifting legs up, lying on the stomach (developing strength of the muscle-bending spine);
2) raising legs up, lying on the back (developing the stomach muscles and back flexibility);
3) raising legs up, lying on the right, then the left side (developing trunk muscles).

Fifth station. *Weights:*

- here we do deep squats with weights of 20-30kg on the shoulders.

The exercises at all stations are performed until the coach calls 'enough' and he orders a change of station.

4.4 Tactical Preparation

By contrast with team games and individual sports, tactics in gymnastics seem more simple. This is due to the fact that gymnastics is a sport with a stabilised kinematical structure of movement. There is no direct contact with a rival during competition. Therefore, the tactical preparation of top-class gymnasts reduces to the formation of the following:

- varied thinking;
- readiness to perform successfully in competition in any form;
- ability to stand up to diverting factors and stress;
- development of habits of successful competitive struggle in unfavourable circumstances;

- ability quickly and adequately to react to unexpected situations;
- ability if necessary swiftly to change the routine while performing it.

For example, if the gymnast makes a technical mistake precluding performance of the next complex element, he must instantly react and perform another element, reworking the routine during the movement. This has to be specially taught in training with the aid of artificially-created diverting factors. Successful improvisation in competition is, after all, the result of adequate repetitions. Dmitri Belozerchev, twice absolute world champion and three-times Olympic champion, possessed wonderful varied tactical thinking.

Tactical preparation of top-class gymnasts is combined with technical and other forms of preparation. Here the various conditions of competitive activity are modelled (see Chapter 3.2).

4.5 Psychological Preparation

We do not conduct psychological preparation as a separate form of preparation in the Russian national team. Its basic tasks associated with psychologically ensuring reliable and highly-productive activity for team members are dealt with mainly by psychological-educational means using combined effects (see also Chapter 3.3.8). Psychological preparation is combined with other forms of preparation (technical, physical, functional, etc.).

The techniques of multifarious educational modelling of competitive activity during the training process using basic parameters in excess of the actual requirement have been worked out and tested in several Olympic cycles and enable us to reach a level of psychological readiness that is needed for successfully conducting competitive activity at the topmost level without the involvement of professional psychologists.

We believe that the assistance of professional psychologists is necessary in those sports where the athletes are not tested in training or cannot reach the basic parameters of competitive activity and show their best results, where these parameters are not exceeded and not modelled. When performing record attempts at big competitions these athletes are entering the world of unknown sensations simply because they have not been able to test these record-breaking regimes in training. So these athletes really do need professional psychologists since the probability of a natural attempt at a record or their best result in competition is small.

Things are quite different in gymnastics. We reproduce the regimes of upcoming competition in control training sessions, we test them in various ways and exceed them in the basic parameters at a level of high and supreme productiveness.

Let us return to the example given in the section of modelling competitive activity (see 3.2) where during model training the senior coach, having called the gymnast to the apparatus to perform a routine, suddenly calls out 'Everyone stop and listen!' and keeps him at the apparatus or uses other intrusive factors. There was a time when people thought this excessive. But now coaches and gymnasts in the team understand that these are psychological devices by which we can model possible competitive situations. We thereby deal with one of the important tasks of psychological preparation and form psychological stability in the face of extraneous factors.

In training top-class gymnasts we use the old tried and tested carrot and stick methods.

Let us reiterate that we regard pedagogical psychology the most sensible approach in training top-class gymnasts in inter-disciplinary events. The best pedagogical psychologist-practitioner for such gymnasts is the coach who has trained them since childhood and brought them to top results. Such coaches are gifts of the gods, like the coaches of Olympic champions Nemov, Khorkina and Zamolodchikova – merited coaches Nikolko, Pilkin and Maslinnikova who know all the psychological nuances of their charges from back to front.

In our sport the problem does not consist in attracting professional psychologists to training the national team on a permanent basis, but in organising adequate psychological training of coaches in the sense of communicating the necessary amount of theoretical and practical knowledge from the area of pedagogical psychology and teaching them actively to use this knowledge in sporting practice.

We believe that it is easier to make a practical pedagogical psychologist out of a top-class coach than a gymnastics specialist out of a professional psychologist. Without knowing the specifics of gymnastics his efforts are unlikely to be productive enough.

This does not mean that we fully ignore professional psychologists when training top-class gymnasts. We think that we have to rely on them when defining and working out indicators of individual gymnast personalities, their psycho-motorics, level of motivation and so on. Particularly valuable are psychograms of team members, showing their psychological profile at the concluding part of training. At this stage we can certainly use psychologists individually.

We should make the point that most top-class gymnasts are very strong personalities. Having passed through so much over many years of centralised and competitive preparation, most team members possess practical habits of psycho-regulation at an intuitive level without special teaching.

4.6 Functional Preparation

The basic task of functional preparation is to develop physiological functions necessary for successfully mastering complex exercises and competing at the top in circumstances of extraneous factors. For example, the function of the cardio-vascular and respiratory systems must ensure performance of intensive anaerobic muscle work of great capacity in a 'rushing' rhythm with a pulse value of up to 220 beats a minute.

Usually these functions develop up to the level necessary while performing various exercises and competitive routines during training For the purposes of forming an optimal functional surplus we use models exceeding the actual needs of competition. Such, for example, as repeat performance of competitive routines after artificially shortened rest, doubled-up somewhat simplified competitive routines, repetition of super-complex elements and routines in a single approach.

The quality of 'twisting' is formed through special training on a vestibular apparatus during functional, rotating and other forms of preparation. Functional preparation is combined with physical, as well as with rotational and acrobatic forms of preparation.

An important aspect of functional preparation is the formation and development of the ability to control the physical state of one's body through changing the aggregate state of the muscles when performing exercises. Habits of control over the physical-mechanical state of one's body have to be formed specially in the process of combined functional-rotational preparation (see 4.8.3).

Functional preparation, like other forms of preparation, has to be built on the basis of the principle of 'outstripping' development and optimal surplus. The presence of optimal functional surplus is a necessary condition for dealing with the basic tasks over many years of training top-class gymnasts (see also Chapter 3.3.7).

4.7 Theoretical Preparation

A coach working with top-class gymnasts has to have a higher sports education at the level of a sports institute or academy. Besides gymnastics, the coach must have enough firm knowledge in the area of biomechanics, physiology and psychology of sport, sports education, the theory and method of physical education, sports training and the theory of sport.

Gymnasts, too, must possess knowledge in these areas, but in more limited amounts. This knowledge is obtained in the process of theoretical preparation which is usually done directly during training. In our view special sessions in theoretical training should be given, above all in the techniques of performance of the methods of teaching exercises of progressive complexity – from basic to super-complex.

The training process of top-class gymnasts (including the topmost level) must be provided with the necessary scientific information and teaching aids (posters, film and videos, special computer programmes). A video recording is obligatory. We also need to use computerised video-analysis of sports techniques (see Chapter 10.2.12).

For successfully developing gymnastics and raising the effectiveness of national team training we should pay particular attention to raising the qualifications of coaches and specialists. To these ends one should periodically (for example once every two years) hold national conferences on gymnastics. At these conferences it is useful to have reports from scientists and specialists, sum up experience, discuss achievements, shortcomings and proposals for improving the system of training gymnasts, including the national team.

It is also sensible periodically to hold special scientific seminars and symposiums for coaches. It may be convenient to do this, for example, during big competitions. During training camps it is also very valuable now and again to conduct sessions with coaches and put on lectures for them on the major problems of training top-class athletes and on sports science. One may invite as lecturers outstanding specialists in sports science and educationalists, biomechanics specialists, biochemists, physiologists, psychologists, doctors, specialist coaches (acrobats, choreographers, etc.).

Once every four years one should hold courses for raising the qualifications of coaches with the issuing of appropriate certificates upon the writing of special essays and taking examinations. These documents should be taken into consideration when giving coaches testimonials.

4.8 Various Forms of Preparation

4.8.1 Basic Preparation

Basic preparation (BP) is a process of creating the necessary technical, physical, biomechanical, physiological and psychological prerequisites for successfully tackling the basic tasks of major stages of long-term training. The basic task is to form a basic technical, physical, functional and psychological surplus at a given stage of preparation. The criteria of effectiveness of basic preparation are timely arrival at parameters of the model of the current stage of training, as well as speed, quality and reliability of mastery of the purposive basic models.

The principal component of basic preparation is special basic physical-technical preparation accomplished by the method of combined effects. The foundation of basic preparation (basic physical qualities and technical habits) over many years remains stable. It has a multi-level hierarchical structure which, relying on a stable foundation, progressively develops upwards in a spiral in accordance with trends in gymnastics development.

Before the start of major cycles of long-term preparation we establish the composition, volume and structure of the basic qualities of knowledge and habits of the top level through analysis of gymnastic trends. On that basis we correct the composition and structure of the basis which has four levels: initial, intermediate, high and topmost.

The composition and structure of the basis are not absolutely fixed at the highest levels. As the gymnast masters the most complex exercises in ever increasing number there is a natural devaluation of their difficulty. So after a certain time these exercises move from being complex and even very complex to becoming basic high level exercises. Thus, the basis develops and becomes more complicated in line with gymnastics development without a final fixing of its topmost level in the foreseeable future.

As confirmation of this let us note that after the Sydney Olympics the men's and women's technical committees of FIG devalued the difficulty of many exercises, reducing their difficulty group (see the table of groups of difficulty in the FIG Competition Rules for 1997 and 2001).

Like the basic elements of technical preparation, the basic exercises in a broad sense are defined through analysing the existing competition rules, trends in gymnastics development, the natural complexity of exercises (see Chapters 1.4 and 6.6) by means of a gradual movement down the 'ladder of complexity'. Moreover, starting from the physical requirements of basic exercises, we establish the basic physical qualities, motor knowledge and technical habits necessary to master them.

4.8.2 Rotational Preparation

Rotational preparation is a type of special preparation on the trampoline (including 'trampoline-foam rubber pit'), as well as on the apparatus and training equipment using straps and belts. The gymnasts perform multiple rotations around the axis of the apparatus (for example, the grip of the horizontal bar), as well as round the transverse and longitudinal axes of the body in simplified conditions (for example, on a special hanging belt) (See Chapter 10.2.4). Here the amount of work considerably (1.5-3 times) exceeds the actual requirement in competition in terms of rotating elements in routines.

The rotational preparation tasks are: 1) developing habits of controlling rotating movements in support and in flight, and 2) creating functional surplus in rotating movements.

For example, the requirement of competitive activity in horizontal bar exercises constitutes ten elements of a rotational nature (according to competition rules). In their morning training national team members perform on this apparatus cyclical routines on straps which include from 20 to 30 such elements. Thus, the requirement of competition on this apparatus is exceeded 2-3 times.

Similarly we perform in one approach in the same training session on the trampoline a number of somersaults in a row 'from point to point' which several times surpasses the competition requirement both in the floor exercises and on the horizontal bar. And such approaches are multiple (see Chapter 4.3.3.1). As a result we form an optimal rotational-functional and technical-physical surplus.

Being a component part of functional preparation, rotational preparation, as a relatively independent area, by the end actually comes close to physical preparation, but it is not the same. At the other end of the scale it comes close to technical preparation. There takes place a rotational-functional, technical-physical routine. Thus, our methodology operates effectively both here and in all other forms and varieties of preparation.

4.8.3 Combined Preparation

As already mentioned above, various forms of preparation usually combine with one another, including at the level of basic preparation. This provides a considerable training effect. At the present time routine of the forms and varieties of preparation is becoming particularly intensive in the technology of integrated preparation of top-class gymnasts. We use several varieties of combined preparation.

4.8.3.1 Basic Combined Technical-physical Preparation

To successfully master modern-day complex gymnastics exercises the gymnast's body must possess the capabilities of a powerful spring whose hardness and springiness change over a fairly wide spectrum depending on the form of exercise and specific conditions. This spring must have a large reserve of rigidity and effectively work when wound up (in 'shock' movements) and let go.

The modern technique of most exercises and jumps is built on control movements of the 'courbette' (snap-up) and 'anti-courbette' spring types. Movements of this type have a big speed-and-strength and energetic requirement. Basic technical habits and physical qualities necessary for their formation develop in the process of combined technical-physical preparation.

To develop the muscles that ensure a correct dynamic carriage and performance of control actions of the courbette and anti-courbette type we use the well-known 'boat' exercise. In the warm-up it is useful to perform also side somersaults turning the body around the longitudinal axis (one diagonal of the mat for the floor exercises). Here from a 'boat' position on the back the gymnast transfers through side bend into a position of arms straight up, etc.

A good additional means we would recommend is the 'wave' (Figure 61) training device. Exercises on it are done in static (isometric) and dynamic regime in a position of face up, face down, to the right and to the left.

First exercise: hold the body as much in the concave position as possible (lower 'boat').

Second exercise: hold the body as much in the upper convex position as possible (upper or overturned 'boat').

Third exercise: as slow a rise as possible into the position of 'overturned boat' with subsequent lowering into a position of 'lower boat' (exercise is performed to the limit).

Fourth exercise: as rapid a rise as possible into the position of 'upper boat' with subsequent lowering into a position of 'lower boat' (exercise is performed to the limit).

Fifth exercise: 5-10 repetitions of the second exercise, 5-10 repetitions of the third exercise in each of the four above-mentioned body positions.

NB

1. the first four exercises are done in all four positions: facing upwards, facing downwards, to the right and to the left;
2. all four exercises may be done with different weights – from 2kg to 30% of the gymnast's own weight.

Instead of the usual strap the gymnast may use a rotating strap (twisting belt) enabling him freely to turn around the body's longitudinal axis. In this case it is sensible in one approach to turn about this axis 'pumping' in turn the forward, left side, back and right side surface of the muscles.

4.8.3.2 Basic Combined Functional-rotational Preparation

This form of combining of the functional and rotational preparation creates the basis for performing exercises with a free flight phase. Its task is to form a basic functional and rotational surplus for mastering and perfecting such exercises and technical actions that ensure their performance.

The basic combined rotational-functional preparation includes multiple purposive performance of special exercises on a special training apparatus. Its main detail is a wide and strong safety belt with a soft inner base and ropes attached to it. This belt is hung on a high horizontal bar, to the rings or the ceiling. High quality ball bearings fitted into the belt ensure free rotation of the gymnast's body around its transverse axis (Figure 62) and, if a twisting belt is used, also around the longitudinal axis.

Work with this device involves the following. The gymnast stands on a special stand and is fixed in this belt. The stand is taken away and the gymnast, having taken a comfortable initial position, begins to execute through his own efforts multiple rotations of the forward and back piked somersault with a good conscious control of the actions, poses and body position in space (See Chapter 7.2). Initially the coach carries out the control, then it is done independently.

If a twisting belt is used, enabling the gymnast freely to turn around the longitudinal axis, multiple somersaults with twists can be performed on the training apparatus.

At the start all rotations are done slowly, with halts, under tight control, then faster and faster. Finally the gymnast adopts rotating regimes exceeding by 2-3 times the requirement of actual competitive and training activity when performing complex unaided rotations.

Thus, top-class gymnasts may rotate 2-3 times faster than when actually performing a double piked somersault. This is done as a result of optimised technical actions and purposive control of one's body by mechanical means (see Chapter 6.1), as well as of help from coach or partner.

Using this training apparatus top-class gymnasts in one approach can perform in the order of 40-60 forward and back rotations in various routines. They can perform from 1 to 5 approaches to the apparatus depending on the period and stage of preparation. The number and speed of rotations can be regulated depending on the period and stage of preparation, as well as the level of preparedness of the gymnast. He is able to rotate both faster and longer than in normal conditions.

Work with this apparatus is particularly useful for young gymnasts when forming correct control actions and dynamic carriage in the flight phases of exercises. It is useful also for more mature gymnasts in maintaining their form.

In all circumstances the use of this apparatus enables us to intensify the process of preparation and create optimal basic surplus for mastering and perfecting unaided rotations. As a result the process is more rapid and qualitative, thereby implementing the 'outstripping' principle.

4.8.4 Jump Preparation

This preparation is a division of SPP associated with development of spring and preparation of gymnasts for big jumping loads. Modern gymnastics demands a high level of springiness. Performance of complex jumping exercises is associated with considerable compression forces on the support-motor apparatus.

An increase in jumping load in conditions of technical and (or) physical insufficiency usually leads to overloading of the support-motor apparatus and injury. As a result of frequent repetition of powerful interactions with standard support of a 'shock' nature when performing acrobatic and support vaults, as well as dismounts from equipment, gymnasts damage the spine, joints and muscle-ligament apparatus. Most injuries occur precisely here.

Contradictions arise in the training process; the main ones are:

- contradiction between the need to increase the jumping load for enhancing results and the limited potential of the gymnast's support-motor apparatus;
- contradiction between the actual motor potential and the impossibility of its complete utilisation with standard pieces of apparatus and equipment.

To resolve these contradictions during morning sessions of SPP and training circuits we conduct special work on strengthening the gymnast's support-motor apparatus, adapting it to high jumping loads in amount and intensity, and developing springiness (see Chapters 4.3.3 and 5.7.1). Moreover, we do a lot of work in mastering complex unaided rotations in simplified conditions on the trampoline and training apparatus (see above), which enables us to reduce the amount of hard surface jumping loads in training.

Another effective means of resolving the contradictions is to use pneumatic pieces of apparatus with regulated resilience [26,61,90,91] (see Chapter 10.2.8 and Figure 66).

4.8.5 Acrobatic Preparation

Acrobatic preparation is done while mastering and perfecting the technique of executing acrobatic jumps of progressive complexity on the acrobatic runway and the mat for floor exercises. The preparation is an important component part of technical preparation. In cases when the amount and intensity of acrobatic preparation is great enough, it is combined with special physical and other forms of preparation, primarily with functional.

The importance of acrobatic preparation lies in the trends in recent decades to 'acrobatise' gymnastics:

- packing floor exercises and beam exercises with complex acrobatic jumps;

- packing competitive routines on the apparatus (above all on the asymmetrical bars and the horizontal bar) with complex elements and routines, in the free flight phase;
- complicating the flight phases of elements on the apparatus, dismounts and support vaults with complex rotations.

Acrobatic preparation encourages mastery of the correct technique for controlling movement in flight which is then used for performing exercises with a flight phase on the apparatus. A high level of acrobatic preparation is necessary for mastering complex exercises in the flight phase.

Acrobatic preparation consists in mastering and perfecting various somersaults of progressive complexity, forward, backward and sideways, with turns and without (in tempo, in tuck, piked, straight, with twists, single, double, triple). These varieties of somersault are done after a round off, or handsprings and tempo saltos forward and back, from the spot and after a run-up.

The content of basic acrobatic preparation is set out in Chapters 5.7.4.

4.8.6 Choreographic Preparation

We do not do choreographic preparation in the Russian men's team because top-class gymnasts already possess a culture of movement sufficient for successful competitive activity.

With the women's team, however, we use the following:

- classical ballet expertise at the bar – 30-45 minutes daily (duration depends on the preparation period);
- choreographic 'water' from the competitive routine on the beam – 5-6 times daily completely;
- choreographic 'water' from floor exercises – up to 10 times daily.

This amount of choreographic preparation is greater in the women's youth team. Besides this it includes special choreographic expertise for the beam and separately for floor exercises.

4.8.7 Centralised Preparation

The principle of centralised preparation (see Chapter 2.3) predominates in training top-class Russian gymnasts.

Centralised preparation is the preparation of gymnasts in conditions of training camps conducted at specialised bases. A base consists of a specialised gymnastics hall with a rehabilitation-hygiene block (shower, sauna, swimming pool, massage facilities, etc.), hotels, dining room and medical section. It is sensible to site the base out of town but close to big cities. The Soviet team had at its disposal three preparation bases: Lake Krugloye near Moscow, Lower Esher on the Black Sea near Sukhumi (Georgia) and Tsakhkadzor in the hills near Yerevan (Armenia). Today the Russian team has only the Russian Olympic Centre at Lake Krugloye where all the best gymnasts have been trained for over twenty years.

We consider that the most effective form of preparing top-class gymnasts and, above all, of a national team, is centralised preparation for a total of about 250 days a year. The recommended balance between centralised preparation and local preparation for national team members in an annual cycle is 7:1, where the 5 of the 7 parts is with centralised preparation, and the 1 with local training, while the remaining 2 parts account for taking part in competitions. It is sensible to conduct in the order of ten training camps (TC) a year.

The TC lasts for 2-3 weeks (usually 3) with a break of 7-10 days during which the gymnasts undergo training where they live. At the stages of pre-competition preparation for the top international competitions of FIG (Olympic Games, world and European championships), the TC duration is 4-8 weeks or more.

At the beginning and end of each TC (normally in the first and last days) it is expedient to hold control tests for technical and physical preparation which enable us to determine what level of preparedness the gymnast is at when coming to the TC and what he has achieved by the end, what shifts he has made. An analysis of the dynamics of the results of these control tests enables us better to evaluate the quality of work each month in the annual cycle.

After the Sydney Olympics the Russian team went over to a year-round centralised preparation.

4.8.8 Altitude Preparation

Altitude preparation is a form of special preparation that is conducted at training camps at between 1300 and 2500 above the sea. This is an effective means of enhancing the work capacity and special endurance of the gymnasts. For top-class gymnasts such preparation is not particularly pressing, but it is thoroughly warranted. For this squad one or two training camps for three weeks is sufficient. This encourages the formation of an additional reserve of functional surplus in the annual cycle of preparation.

When conducting training camps at a high altitude location one should take account of the following. As a result of special research [57] it has been established that acclimatisation to high altitude takes approximately 14 days. There are two waves in this period.

The toughest for training are from the second to the fifth day and the 13th-14th days after arriving. During acclimatisation the speed-strength qualities do not alter, while ability to perform aerobic and strength work rises. The acclimatisation peak is the 8th or 9th day.

In the first 5-7 days it is not recommended to perform heavy anaerobic work. It is better to reduce the volume and limit the SPP training round. Speed qualities in the first few days do not diminish. Then they grow and their increment ends by the 14th day. In the period of acute acclimatisation during the first 7-8 days the delicate coordination of movement is violated.

Work capacity worsens when performing exercises lasting more than two minutes.

Work on endurance may be performed without any limitation and harm, beginning from the tenth or twelfth day. Intervals of rest between sessions in the first week should be doubled, and in the second week should be increased by 1.5 times by comparison with sea level conditions. In the third week they come back to the norm. Technical indicators usually improve after the second week.

In the second week after returning to sea level there is a thickening of the blood. At this time there is a heightened danger of injury. Gymnasts find themselves in a slightly excited state which should be taken account of when planning and correcting the preparation programme.

After returning to sea level the best days for entering competitions are the 2nd, 3rd, 4th and 5th days. It is not recommended to perform on the 8th 9th and 10th days. On these days the peak of re-acclimatisation occurs and competitive results fall by up to 50% of the potential. The best results can be displayed in the period from the 18th to 25th days after the training camp at high altitude [57].

For our high altitude training we have used the Tsakhkadzor base in Armenia, 1980m above sea level. For various reasons (primarily financial difficulties), the Russian national team has not been able to use high altitude for the last ten years.

4.8.9 Pharmacological Preparation

We have never used and do not use any pharmacological preparation as such for the Russian national gymnastics team. This goes against the moral and ethical principles of our Federation. We do use permitted pharmacological provision for the national team (see Chapter 9.5).

4.8.10 Pre-competition Preparation

Pre-competition preparation is a stage of direct preparation for competition. We utilise a number of tested models of pre-competition training adapted to the type of competition and individual capacities of the gymnasts (see Chapters 3.3.10 and 5.8). The duration of the pre-competition stage varies from 2 to 8 weekly micro-cycles depending on the competition ranking. The higher it is the longer the duration of this stage. In the technology of pre-competition preparation we use weekly micro-cycles of varying orientation. Each weekly micro-cycle has a special purpose, name and tasks (see Chapter 5.5).

4.8.11 Competition Preparation

This is an important integrated part of the technology of training top-class gymnasts. Competition preparation for candidates of the national team must be seen as annual participation in a series of competitions which, depending on the adopted classification [56], may be classed as basic and auxiliary.

Basic competitions in turn are divided into major, selection and control.

Major competitions of the year are the biggest international tournaments, such as the Olympic Games, the world and European championships, and other continental championships and the World Cup. The country's top gymnasts take part in these competitions and they have the following tasks:

1) to display their best result in the entire competition and (or) in their best events;
2) to achieve victory in the team championship and (or) in other planned events in the programme.

The Olympic Games, the world championships and the World Cup are normally held in the middle of the second half-yearly macro-cycle of preparation (September-October), the European championships are held at the end of the first half-yearly macro-cycle (April-May).

Selection competitions for taking part in major competitions of the year are the national championships and the national cup, as well as special selection contests within the national team. The national teams for the Olympics and world championships are formed on the results of these competitions.

Control competitions for candidates for the national team are official international tournaments. Participants have the following tasks:

1) achieve a planned result;
2) perform exercises corresponding to the individual model of the preparation stage;
3) acquire international competitive experience.

In addition, candidates for the national team take part in auxiliary competitions which are in turn divided into those leading up to the control competitions.

Lead-up competitions are the All-Russia, regional and international tournaments that take place in the period of preparation for the major competitions of the year. Various candidates for the national team according to individual attributes take part in these competitions. Their basic tasks are:

1) acquiring competitive experience and
2) implementing basic elements of the competitive activity model.

Control auxiliary competitions take place in conditions of the centralised preparation of the national team. All candidates for major and control international competitions take part in them. For candidates for the national team these may be internal, but they are very important competitions that are part of the selection system (see Chapter 3.3.9).

In the four-year Olympic cycle of preparation it is wise to plan two competitive periods in each annual macro-cycle. Thus, for example in the four-year cycle of preparation of the Russian team for the Sydney 2000 Olympics, the competitive periods in each annual macro-cycle normally lasted from February to May and from September to January.

In February candidates for the national team took part in regional lead-up competitions, in March in the Russian championships, in April in international tournaments and in May in the European championships. In September-October gymnasts participated in the main competitions of the year – the world championships and the World Cup (in 2000 the Olympic Games). From October to January the Russian team took part in various international tournaments. In July and August they took part also in the Russia Cup.

Altogether we envisage each candidate for the national team taking part during the annual cycle in 6-8 big competitions (48-122 starts for men and 40-95 starts for women) which on average took up between 16 and 22 competitive days (see Chapter 3.3.11).

How to Create Champions   5

CHAPTER FIVE
Planning and Projecting Preparation

5.1 Methodics Basis

Success over many years depends on correct planning and management. The training process is of crucial importance; in planning it we normally identify *macro, meszo and micro-cycles*, then subsequently, *training days and training sessions* [42].

The duration of macro-cycles usually is from six months to a year, meszo-cycles from a few weeks to a few months, and micro-cycles a week. Within the macro-cycles we distinguish periods of training of varying length – *preparatory, competitive and transitional* [42,67]. The *preparation stage* constitutes several weekly micro-cycles (for example, the pre-competition training stage. Work done in training, the training day, week, month, year and Olympic cycle as a whole is measured in units of training load.

To attain top results today's gymnasts must possess not only a high level of special physical qualities, perfect technique and will power, but also high work capacity and fantastic love of hard work. The history of gymnastics knows enough examples when talented gymnasts with excellent coordination were unable to reach the heights owing to insufficient application and desire to work hard.

High work capacity, by which we understand the ability to perform large amounts of physical work and swiftly recover from it, is a hereditary and an acquired attribute. Being to a certain extent conditioned genetically, it develops quite well when using high training loads. To cope with this load the gymnast should have high application which is developed from childhood. We should note, however, that highly-developed work capacity is not always linked with a liking for hard work which defines the training load that a gymnast performs in training.

5.2 Training Load Structure

The effectiveness of training depends on correct planning and managing training loads. *Volume* and *intensity* are some of its key indicators.

The volume of training load is normally determined by the total amount of performed elements and routines. It depends on the duration of training sessions and the number of attempts. In the preparatory period the load volume largely depends on the number of attempts and elements performed in a single attempt. In the competitive period it mainly depends on the number of performed routines. Research has shown that a high dependence exists between the overall number of elements, the number of routines and the number of high complexity elements performed in training [27].

Intensity is determined by the number of elements or routines performed per unit of time (minute or hour). Correspondingly we distinguish intensity of training load by elements and routines.

By deliberately changing the volume and intensity, as well as those parameters of training load which permit considerable variety, we may establish a pleasant work regime ensuring timely attainment of training objectives and resolution of its major tasks, including those associated with effective recovery after large loads.

It has been established that the higher the intensity of load when performing an equal amount of special work, the stronger will be the physiological effect on the organism and the higher will be the training effect. This law is common to all sport. However, a maximum of training loads is not an aim in itself. Here, as in any big enterprise, we need a sense of proportion. Otherwise we may push the gymnast into a state of being overtrained.

Planning

When planning training loads and implementing plans we should be guided by the principle of Quantum satis – as much as is necessary (doctors sometimes write that on their prescriptions when indicating how much of the ingredients to put in the medicine). Russian gymnasts have long trained under the slogan of *'Work not as much as you can, but as much as you need'* – having in mind successful performance with topmost results.

We provide below specific data and recommendations in planning and managing training loads based on thirty years of experience of working with the national teams and on research findings.

5.2.1 Training Load Indicators

To successfully plan and manage training loads one should start with defining and registering them. We register the following indicators of training load:

- *training days;*
- *training sessions;*
- *training time;*
- *number of performed elements;*
- *number of performed routines;*
- *number of performed routines in stable state;*
- *number of performed vaults;*
- *intensity by element;*
- *intensity by routine;*
- *intensity by vault;*
- *intensity of training load;*
- *total number of attempts;*
- *number of SPP elements;*
- *number of SPP attempts;*
- *SPP intensity;*
- *number of elements in technical training;*
- *number of attempts in technical training;*
- *number of elements of top difficulty groups;*
- *number of elements performed on the trampoline;*
- *number of attempts on the trampoline.*

As a result of special research (7,32) into the training load structure we have separated out five factors with varying contribution to the total dispersion:

1) *number of performed routines (50.8%);*
2) *number of performed elements and vaults (14.7%);*
3) *time indicators (9.8%);*
4) *special physical training (8.1%);*
5) *trampoline training (4.9%).*

The following are the most informative parameters of training load at the pre-competition training stage before important competitions:

- *number of performed routines;*
- *total number of performed elements;*
- *training time;*
- *number of SPP elements;*
- *number of top difficulty elements;*
- *intensity of training load;*
- *percentage of successfully performed routines and support vaults.*

We have established that in the last two weeks of pre-competition training stage the number of informative indicators of training load and the level of reliability of their interconnection with results rises.

5.2.2 Basic Training Load Parameters

We recommend the following basic training load parameters per year for gymnasts aiming for prize-winning positions at the world championships and the Olympic Games:

- *number of training days* • 300-310 (including competition)
- *number of training sessions* • 850
- *number of training hours* • 1500
- *number of elements* • 180 000-200 000
- *number of routines* • 1600-1800 + or − 100 (1600 a year in the first two Olympic cycle years, 1800 in the two last)
- *number of vaults* • 2600-3000 (2600 a year in the first two Olympic cycle years, 3000 in the two last)

5.3 Structure of Olympic Cycle of Training

The Olympic cycle is divided into four annual training cycles. It is sensible to put relatively stable amounts and intensity of training load according to the year of the cycle in the training programme of the national team. The load somewhat rises by the third year. In the fourth year it stabilises at the third year level.

Behind national team training planning in the Olympic cycle we put the principle of multiple repetition of a detailed model of the pre-competition training stage ending in top competitions. This enables us to model the final six-month macro-cycle and its concluding stage (which lasts from the final selection competition to the start of performance in the Olympics) in the seven six-month macro-cycles of the Olympic cycle.

Thus, we model the last training macro-cycle together with the final stage seven times in the Olympic cycle. Altogether the Olympic cycle includes eight six-month training macro-cycles. Their main direction is shown in Table 12.

Table 12

Direction of six-month macro-cycles in the four-year Olympic training cycle

No. of training macro-cycle	Direction
1st six-month macro-cycle	Raising the level of special physical training
2nd six-month macro-cycle	Learning new complex elements and combins.
3rd six-month macro-cycle	Modernising the competition programme
4th six-month macro-cycle	Raising the level of special physical training
5th six-month macro-cycle	Raising the level of technical skill and stability
6th six-month macro-cycle	Growth in results, stabilisation of high level performing skill and reliability
7th six-month macro-cycle	Final determination of competition programme, acquiring tournament endurance, modelling, selecting double composition of Olympic team
8th six-month macro-cycle	Modelling the Olympics, elaboration of competition reliability, final selection of Olympic team

This training programme must be seen as preparation of both national team members and its closest reserve – the junior team.

5.4 Structure of Macro- and Mezzo-cycles

Each annual training cycle for the national team is normally divided into two training *macro-cycles* lasting approximately six months. They, as a rule, culminate in a big international competition and a short transitional period lasting a few days. For example, the first macro-cycle ends with the European championships (May-June), while the second ends with the world championships or Cup (October-November).

Each six-month macro-cycle consists of three periods: *preparatory* (1-2 months), *competition* (3.5-4.5 months) and *transitional* (up to two weeks).
    The preparatory period for top-class gymnasts is relatively brief. Usually it is January-February and July-August. We normally tackle the tasks mainly of physical preparation and perfection of technique.

The competition period is longer. Usually it is March-June and September-November when we mainly deal with the tasks of bringing the athletes to the selection and main competitions. We pay particular attention to:

- raising special tournament endurance through multiple performance of competition routines as a whole;
- enhancing reliability of performing competition routines, using methods of pedagogical modelling of upcoming competition conditions (see 3.2).

This periodisation is not fixed for all time. The periods indicated (both macro and mezzo-cycles) do not have once and for all set time boundaries. In that sense they are not absolutely fixed. Depending on the competitive calendar we may put three instead of two macro-cycles in the structure of an individual annual cycle and, correspondingly, three preparatory and three competition mini-periods or mezzo-cycles a year.

This attempt is typical when planning the individual training of specific athletes, which depends on the periods of their participation in regional, national and international competitions. The shortest are the *transitional periods* which in recent Olympic cycles comprise up to a week and a half.

The classical transitional period usually looks as follows:

- substantial reduction in training loads for a fairly long time;
- reduction in the level of special preparation;
- leaving a state of being in good form;
- active relaxation.

However, our long-term experience of working with top-class gymnasts has shown that comprehensive use of pedagogical, medical-biological and physical means of recovery in the technology of integrated training enables us to maintain a high work capacity in the annual macro-cycle without a marked transitional period which today does not exceed more than a few days with top gymnasts. A substantial reduction in training load exists only with a few gymnasts (usually the veterans) after the Olympic Games.

Such a powerful reduction of the transitional period is due to the action of such developmental trends as professionalisation of gymnastics, which means that top-class gymnasts have to be permanently ready for competitive activity (see Chapter 1.4) on the motto of 'Always be in form'.

Each six-month macro-cycle is divided into mezzo-cycles (usually of a month), and these in turn are divided into weekly micro-cycles in which we put periods and stages of training.

The most effective form of training top-class gymnasts and, primarily, the national team is *centralised training* conducted in training camps (see 8.7). The training camp together with training days in the localities can be seen as a training mezzo-cycle.

5.5 Structure of Training Micro-cycles

Weekly micro-cycles are the most precisely planned and well managed units of training. Altogether the annual training cycles contains 52 weekly micro-cycles. Each weekly micro-cycle has its own number coinciding with the number of the week in a given year.

Typical micro-cycles last seven days. Their uniform structure envisages two waves of growth in training load. The first wave lasts three days (Monday to Wednesday). On Thursday the load is substantially reduced (to 50%). On the fifth and sixth days of the week (Friday-Saturday) the load again mounts to a maximum or sub-maximum level (second wave). Sunday is a free day for active relaxation, fully precluding any means of special training. Altogether in a typical weekly micro-cycle we have *6 training days, 17 training sessions and 33-36 hours of training time*

In training we should utilise weekly micro-cycles of varying direction with the following rough indicators of training load:

- *pulling up* (20 routines, 12 000 elements, 20-40% of SPP elements in total training load). This micro-cycle ought to be conducted in the first and second week of January, in the 21st, 22nd and 23rd week of June and the 43rd, 44th and 45th week of October-November after the world championships;
- *basic* (30 routines, 12 000 elements, 20-40% of SPP elements). This micro-cycle ought to be conducted in the 3rd, 4th, 5th, 14th, 15th week, from the 24th to 32nd and 46th to 52nd week of the annual training cycle;
- *model-shock* (35-40 routines, 14 000 elements, 20-40% of SPP elements). This micro-cycle should take place in the 11th, 12th, 13th, 16th, 17th, 36th, 37th and 38th week of the annual cycle;
- *model-tuning* (30-35 routines, 11 000 elements, 10-30% of SPP elements). This should take place in the last weeks before competition, for example, in the 18th, 19th, 39th and 40th weeks of the annual cycle;
- *recovery* (10-12 routines, 10 000 elements, 20-40% of SPP elements). This micro-cycle should take place after competition, for example in the 20th, 41st and 42nd week of the annual training cycle.

Besides those listed above we also use other micro-cycles (for example, adaptation-tuning). The number of routines and their dispersal over the training days of the weekly micro-cycles of varying direction is shown in Figure 9.

In the preparatory period we mainly use *pulling up, basic, shock and model-shock* micro-cycles. In this period the most important typical micro-cycle for creating necessary surplus is the *shock*. Here we widely utilise various means of training, including special physical training (SPP) exercises and exercises on training equipment. We also use close to the maximum training loads with average indicators of number of routines.

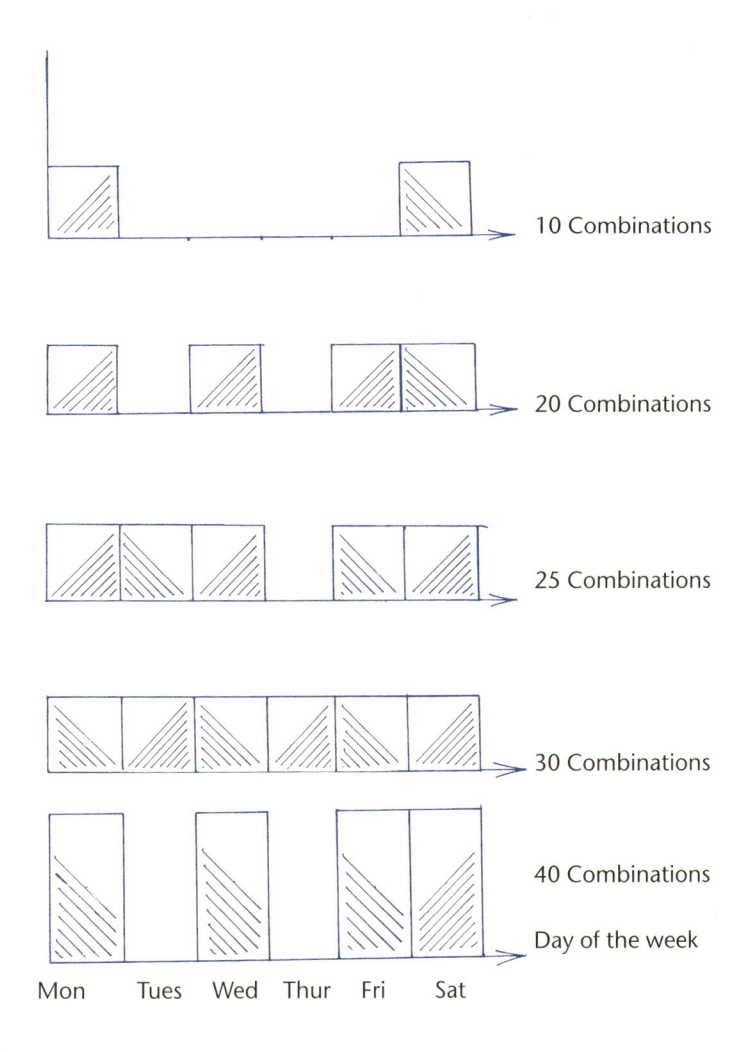

10 Combinations

20 Combinations

25 Combinations

30 Combinations

40 Combinations

Day of the week

Mon   Tues   Wed   Thur   Fri   Sat

Figure 9 – *Number of Combinations in weekly micro cycles of differing orientation*

The share of SPP exercises consists of from 20% to 50% of the total amount of load. A large part of the load goes on individual elements, routines and SPP exercises that may constitute up to 50% of the total load. These micro-cycles ensure the accumulation of motor potential and the creation of a basis for subsequent implementation in the competition period. Shock micro-cycles alternate with basic micro-cycles. Together they comprise the basis of the preparatory period.

The most important for the competition period are the model-shock and model-control micro-cycles. The model-shock micro-cycles are applied in the first half of the preparatory stage. Their main task is to create a high level of special work capacity and functional surplus.

In the two main training sessions conducted in the first and second half of the week (Tuesday and Friday), we model competition conditions with complete observance of the rules of the upcoming competition. We have in mind the rigidly fixed time for warm up on the apparatus, the precise alternation of warm up and tested attempts for evaluation, and we practice an artificial delay in permitting exercise performance after the call to the apparatus.

On Wednesday and Saturday we hold shock-model training which envisages a double amount of work on routines as a whole by comparison with the competition. In this micro-cycle we use near-the-limit loads in volume and intensity. Here we perform close to the maximum number of elements and routines. The share of SPP exercises constitutes 15-30% of the total amount.

Two to three weeks before competition the model-control micro-cycles are of crucial importance. We can more fully model in them all the conditions and rules of competition, as well as training conditions on days between competitions. It is very important for each gymnast and his coach to know their role and place in the team and, in line with that, to base their behaviour on that (turn and length of warm up on the apparatus, preparation of equipment within the competition rules and conduct between starts).

Recovery micro-cycles are used mainly after competition. Their key tasks are recovery, active relaxation, analysis of results and taking stock of the situation for the next stage of preparation.

Such parameters as number of performed elements, routines, support vaults and SPP elements can vary within a fairly broad spectrum at various stages of training and in different micro-cycles. These parameters determine the dynamics and intensity of training load. They reach a maximum 1-2 weeks before major competition, and then they diminish. They reach their lowest magnitude in the transitional periods which should be termed micro-periods as a result of their brief duration.

The share of SPP in the training load normally falls most significantly (up to 10%) during gymnast participation in major competitions. At all the remaining stages it changes within 20-50% of the total load.

5.6 Structure of Training Day

Our long experience of experimentation has brought us to what we think is the optimal structure of a working day which has not changed for many years at the training camps (TC) for Russian national team members. This training day regime enables us successfully to cope with the main tasks of preparation in TC conditions. The men's team has the following working day regime:

- 6.45 get up, morning toilet;
- 7-8.25 first training session;
- 8.30-9.00 breakfast;
- 9.00-10.20 rest;
- 10.30-13.00 second training session;
- 13.10-13.45 lunch;
- 13.45-16.45 rest;
- 17.00-19.00 third training session;
- 19.10-19.40 dinner;
- 19.40-23.00 study and spare time;
- 23.00 bed.

The structure of the women's training is similar to that of the men, but the time slightly shifts:

- 7.30-9.00 first training session;
- 11.00-14.30 second training session;
- 17.00-19.30 third training session.

Similarly breakfast, lunch and dinner shift by half an hour.

This regime is identical for all days of the week except Thursday and Sunday. For both men and women only two morning training sessions are held on Thursday, so the gymnasts have more free time (immediately after lunch) on that day. On Sunday the gymnasts always (apart from competitions) completely relax; there is no special training and eating times are the same with the exception of breakfast which is half an hour later.

This daily regime may be used as a model for organising the working day in training camps. In principle it is useful as a guide also for organising training in the localities if gymnasts are not involved in study or it is organised without any constraints.

If it is impossible to ensure three training sessions a day in the gymnastics hall when training where the gymnast lives the first morning SPP session should be done at home. The gymnast can use a 'video-coach' as instructor. This is particularly useful for young gymnasts who do not yet have sufficient experience. Of course, the effectiveness of such training is considerably less than in a training camp. Nevertheless it is better than nothing.

If the gymnasts have to study intensively, it is sensible to conduct the morning training in the gymnastics hall and begin it immediately after morning toilet and breakfast. One should conduct the second training session after lunch. In this case it is the major session and lasts longer than in a training camp.

On Saturday and Sunday training sessions can be conducted according to the TC working day – ie as in the camp. So the free day will be Thursday. The weekly training load is less than in the TC. But it is important to spread it with two peaks that coincide with the days relatively free of study.

5.7   Structure of Training Sessions

Top-class gymnasts must work every day and on average up to six hours a day. With centralised training each day of the week, apart from Thursday and Sunday, there are three training sessions. On Thursday there are two sessions, on Sunday none.

Every day one training session is the main one (it lasts 2.5 hours) and two others are auxiliary (1.5 and 2 hours respectively). Normally at TC the first morning and last evening sessions are the auxiliary, and the second morning session is the main one (except when we are modelling conditions of upcoming competition micro-cycle).

Each session consists of three parts:

1. preparatory part or warm up (7-10 mins before auxiliary and 35-40 mins before main sessions – the warm up includes general developing exercises and basic acrobatic jumps of varying level, including top level);
2. basic part (normally this is work on the apparatus);
3. concluding part (10-15 mins, usually of SPP and recovery procedures).

5.7.1   First Training Session

We changed the traditional morning warm up at national team training camps to a full value first training for SPP and strengthening of the support-motor apparatus [57].

The men's team begins this morning auxiliary training at 7 am, and the women's at 7.30 am. It normally lasts 1.5 hours, but can be more or less depending on the period and stage of training (respectively from 1 hour 15 mins to 1 hour 45 mins). The training load comprises some 300 elements. The main part of the training is normally preceded by a group warm up lasting 7-10 minutes. The major tasks of the first auxiliary morning training session are:

1. activating and strengthening the support-motor apparatus;
2. special physical training for developing and maintaining necessary physical qualities;
3. combined physical-technical improvement.

Because the content and structure of this first morning session is not ordinary and is compulsory for all members of the team we explain it fully. The session includes 18 independent sections or parts devoted to resolving special tasks. Regular holding of this training in centralised preparation has given us good practical results.

1. The first part consists of five stations and is totally dedicated to strengthening the support-motor apparatus. In the men's and women's team this part included circuit training consisting of five stations of 45 seconds in each (without a pause):

    - First station – running on the spot on a thick foam rubber mat at average tempo;
    - Second station – jumps on the wave-style device (See Chapter 10.2.2; Figure 60);
    - Third station – jumping over a gymnastics bench (20 jumps x 3 sets = 60 jumps);
    - Fourth station – squats, one leg held horizontally forward, holding on to the lower bar (2 attempts 10-15 times);
    - Fifth station – jumps from two legs on the acrobatics runway (4 times 20-80m and finishing with a forward somersault).

    Rest after this part is for 3-4 mins. The content of the morning session now differs for men and women in terms of SPP.

2. The second part for men is devoted to strengthening shoulder joints with simultaneous development of flexibility and strength. The exercise in Figure 1 optimizes the rear hang position. It is useful to perfect Russian and Czech long swings on the horizontal bar and women's asymmetric bars.

    Starting position: hands behind back, holding a standard weight of 20kg, with the bar touching the hips from behind. The exercise consists of performing forward inclines bringing the bar up and back as far as possible with subsequent return to starting position (Figure 10). This exercise is repeated 10 times.

    Figure 10

3. The third part is devoted to combined development of special strength attributes necessary for successful performance of complex strength exercises on the rings. The exercise we use enables the gymnast to develop static and slow dynamic strength, as well as strength endurance. The exercise contains 35 strength elements, not counting the static strength exercises. In

PLANNING

gymnastics slang this is called a strength marathon. The exercise is once only performed on the lower rings with the help of the coach:

1. from standing hang, gripping the rings lift into inverted hang;
2. raise to inverted hang upstart to half lever;
3. bent arm straight body forward roll, then press to handstand (hold 2 sec);
4. inverted cross (hold 2 secs);
5. press back to handstand;
6. lowering into inverted cross (hold 2 secs);
7. lowering into Maltese (hold 2 secs);
8. lowering into back lever (hold 2 secs);
9. lift to inverted hang;
10. upstart to half lever;
11. straight arm straight body press to handstand;
12. lower to inverted cross (hold 2 secs);
13. press to handstand;
14. lowering into inverted cross (hold 2 secs);
15. press back to handstand;
16. inverted cross (hold 2 secs);
17. lowering into Maltese (hold 2 secs);
18. lowering into back lever (hold 2 secs);
19. pull to inverted hang;
20. upstart half lever;
21. bent arm straight body forward roll, then press to handstand with bent arms and straight body (hold 2 secs);
22. inverted cross (hold 2 secs);
23. press back to handstand;
24. inverted cross (hold 2 secs);
25. lowering through horizontal support into cross (hold 2 secs);
26. press out to support;
27. lowering into cross (hold 2 secs);
28. press out to support;
29. lowering into cross (hold 2 secs);
30. lower to front hanging scale (front lever);
31. upstart half lever;
32. swing Maltese (hold 2 secs);
33. lowering into back lever (hold 2 secs);
34. pull to inverted hang;
35. lower forward into front hanging lever (hold 2 secs).

4. The fourth part is the technical-physical perfection of the run up. The run up is performed with acceleration using artificial weights (twice of 50m). We use a motor car tyre as our weight. It is tied to the gymnast's waist by a flexible rope; he then tows it along.

5. The fifth part is devoted to technical-physical perfection of support vaults/jumps. We do 3-8 jumps of the somersault type, 2.5 (Roche) forward somersaults, a straight Tsukhahara, a Tsukhahara with turn of 720o.

6. The sixth part is devoted to technical-physical perfection of the basic exercises on the parallel bars performed with weights (a girdle weighing 2-2.5 kg). The exercise with repetitions includes 27 elements:

   - from swing in support, swing to handstand;
   - forward swing;
   - back swing into handstand (hold, repeat 5 times);
   - Diamidov, swing forward (repeat 5 times in a row);
   - forward swing;
   - back swing into handstand (hold, repeat 3 times);
   - Diamidov forward swing (repeat 3 times);
   - from handstand turn with forward pirouette (hold, repeat 2 times).

7. Seventh part is the control approach for stability and adaptability of technique on the lower parallel bars (without weights but with coach's help):

   - swing in support, swing to handstand;
   - forward swing;
   - back swing into handstand;
   - Diamidov to forward swing;
   - salto backwards to handstand.
     (Repeat all routine 2-3 times in a row).

8. The eighth part is devoted to technical-physical perfection of the basic elements in support on the hands using the 'Parallel Bars – Brusya (Figure 63) training apparatus (see also Chapter 10.2.5).

   First exercise:
   1. from swing in support, front somersault to support;
   2. swing back and hop pirouette (repeat twice).

Second exercise:

1. from handstand or forward swing from support into salto backwards with straight body into handstand and
2. push into front salto from handstand.

9. The ninth part is devoted to combined technical-physical perfection of the basic exercises in support on the hands and in support on the high parallel bars. Both exercises are performed in one go.

First exercise:

- from swing in support on the upper arms back uprise to handstand;
- swing forward;
- lowering into support on the upper arms;
- back uprise to handstand (repeat 7 times);
- forward swing;
- back swing into handstand (hold, repeat 10 times with strict control of the quality of performing handstands).

Second exercise:

- front uprise;
- swing backwards and hop pirouette into handstand;
- forward swing and stutzkehre;
- lower onto upper arms and front uprise, swing back into hop pirouette;
- forward swing and stutzkehre.
  (Repeat exercise 7 times).

10. The tenth part is devoted to combined development of slow dynamic strength and flexibility. The exercise is repeated three times:

    1. from handstand on one bar bend the body and lower the legs between the arms to pass through half lever and Russian lever into Manna;
    2. from Manna lift to handstand with straight arms and straight legs.
       (Repeat 3 times).

11. The eleventh part is devoted to combined technical-physical perfection of the basic elements of a high level on the horizontal bar. The exercises have a cyclical character and are performed in loops on a polished horizontal bar.

1. in overgrasp, big forward swing through handstand, revolution into support on straight arms and rotation backwards into handstand (Stalder legs together, repeat 10 times with no reduction);
2. in undergrasp (Endo with legs together, repeat 10 times with no reduction).

12. The twelfth part is devoted to combined technical-physical perfection of the basic exercises on the pommel horse:

First exercise: 50 inward loops;

Second exercise: 20 outward loops;

Third exercise: Magyar and Shivado exercises (performed on handle-less horse).

All three exercises are performed with the accent on parallel placement of the hands on the body of the horse.

Fourth exercise:
1. circle in support on the body and handle, one hand on each;
2. Stockli 'B' in to handles (the middle);
3. circle on the handles;
4. rear out;
5. Stockli 'B' in to the handles (middle);
6. circle on the handles.

All exercises are repeated twice.

13. The thirteenth part is devoted to technical-physical perfection of the basic acrobatic jumps. The following jumps are performed:

1. from handstand on springboard, snap down (Courbette) and tucked back somersault;
2. from handstand on the springboard a courbette-tucked back somersault and contra-tempo forward somersault tucked;
3. snap down, flic flac, tuck back or straight somersault;
4. round off, flic flac, straight back somersault;

5. round off, whip, straight back somersault;
6. handspring, forward tucked or straight somersault.

In a single approach we recommend performing no fewer than five elements, landing on foam rubber mats at a height of 20 cm.

14. The fourteenth part is devoted to combined rotational-functional training on the trampoline. Here we perform from 20 to 50 elements in the following routines:
    1. forward straight somersault from the same landing and take off point (5 times in a row);
    2. forward straight front somersault to double forward somersault (repeat 2-3 times in a row) connected;
    3. forward straight somersault with a 360° twist to double front somersault (5 times in a row);
    4. straight back somersault same landing and take off point (5 times in a row);
    5. double straight back somersault with turn of 720° landing in a foam rubber pit. "Double double straight."

After that the gymnasts may perform individual routines. The choice of elements and their order depend on individual characteristics of the gymnasts and the current training tasks. For example, to enhance precision of landing it is recommended to perform single, double and triple somersaults from the trampoline with emphasis on precise landings on the mat upon the floor or on mats spread in the foam rubber pit.

Then the somersault may be complicated with twists. After that the emphasis is on performing rotations in flight, adequate dismounts and acrobatic jumps that are part of the gymnast's competitive programme. Here it is necessary to model actual conditions of specific dismounts and jumps in height and length of flight. The number of elements in these routines depends on the period and stage of training, as well as on the level of the gymnast's preparedness. All in all he may perform from 10 to 40 elements.

15. The fifteenth part is working on landings. The exercise consists of the following: the gymnast places on his shoulders a bar weighing 110% of his own weight and during one minute on half-bent legs fixes the lowest position of the landing phase after dismount and jumps with high flight.

16. The sixteenth part is devoted to developing the strength of specific muscle groups. For this we use strength training apparatus of the 'Minigym' type with a weight of up to 50kg. He repeats the exercise 10 times.

17. The seventeenth part consists of strength exercises on the low rings performed initially in more difficult (with weighted belt), then with easier conditions (arms are placed into the ring straps):

    First exercise (weight of 2-3 kg):

    1. from handstand lowering into inverted cross (hold 3 secs);
    2. lowering into Maltese (hold 3-5 secs);
    3. lowering into cross (hold 3-5 secs).

    Second exercise (arms placed into straps under the rings):

    1. from handstand lowering into cross with inverted cross;
    2. press lift into handstand (hold).

    This exercise is performed 3 times and repeated 'to the limit' in each phase.

18. The eighteenth and last part of the first morning training session involves rope climbing 7m (performed once without leg help in half lever position).

Here the team's first morning session ends. Its composition and structure may alter depending on the period and stage of training, as well as the level of gymnast's preparedness.

Characteristics of the women's first training session

The number of profile elements in latter-day women's gymnastics is more than with men, especially on the asymmetric bars and the beam. So the first morning session for national team women is somewhat longer. While having the same tasks as the men, it includes the following components:

- running with weights (see the 4th part of the first morning session for men);
- support vault (4-6 attempts). The gymnasts should perform vaults in the structure group which they perform at competition (rotation,

round off and round off, flic flac), including also such complex jumps as somersault with turn of 720°. The jumps are done in both easier and harder conditions (onto and over a pile of mats into the foam rubber pit).

For example, when training for top competitions of the past Olympic cycle Russian women gymnasts in the morning session performed such jumps as the Tsukhahara in tuck, Tsukhahara with turn of 360° with straight body, the Tsukhahara with turn of 540° with straight body (twice), the Tsukhahara with turn of 720° with straight body forward revolution, forward piked somersault, round off, flic flac, piked somersault, also with turns of 360°, 540° and 720°. They repeated the jumps 2-3 times.

Exercises on the horizontal bar:

The horizontal bar is an important auxiliary apparatus for performing exercises on the women's asymmetric bars. During the morning session it is recommended to perform the following elements and routines.

1. pike hang, lift, rotation into stand (repeat 5 times) undershoot;
2. cast to handstand (5 times in a row);
3. Stalder from support to stand (5 times in a row);
4. longswings backwards (5 times in a row) Giants;
5. preparatory exercise for Tkatchev actions (5 times in a row).

Routines of some 30 elements which the gymnasts perform in straps are made up of these exercises. For example, the lift, upstart, cast, Stalder, Giants, Tkatchev action etc. Each element is repeated several times in a row according to the cyclical principle. (see Chapter 5.2.3).

Exercises on the beam:

We recommend the top-class gymnasts to perform up to 100 elements altogether on the beam in various routines. Each gymnast has her own routine, including the flic flac and somersault, round offs and flic flacs, round offs and somersault, round offs, flic flacs and somersaults of varying complexity, other acrobatic jumps from the individual competition programme, as well as various basic turns, choreographic jumps and elements for balance.

Work on the beam includes exercises at competition standard, on the low and double high beam. Here we use landings on a pile of mats placed level with the beam and higher. To increase reliability and avert becoming accustomed to 'one's own' apparatus, we recommend performing the competition exercise on different beams (convenient and inconvenient).

For the purpose of working out optimal surplus in part of the special routine endurance we recommend performing doubled competition routines with lightened acrobatics including the dismount. This equally applies to the free exercises. It is useful also to perform on the beam several basic routines in a row with simplified basic acrobatics (up to 5 routines).

5.7.2   Second Training Session

This is the main one. Usually it lasts two hours. We deal with the following training tasks:

1. work on integrated routines and big connecting movements in all the multi-events;
2. establish technical surplus;
3. acquire special endurance;
4. maintain level of constant readiness to perform the competition programme in the annual cycle;
5. individual SPP (personal 'pumping').

At this session men and women normally go through all the events – 6 for men, 4 for women. This session lasts the longest (usually 2.5 hours) and has the highest average intensity (2-3.5 elements a minute and up to 6 routines an hour).

In terms of their overall aim and character the major training sessions, like the weekly micro-cycles, may be catching up, shock, control, model, developing, recovery, etc. (see Chapter 5.5).

5.7.3   Third Training Session

At the auxiliary third training session we mainly work on the technique of performing separate elements and routines, as well as developing and perfecting special physical qualities. Here we cover not all the apparatus, only those pieces that show the weak spots or on which complex new elements are being learned. The duration of the third session in TC conditions is usually two hours.

On Wednesday and Thursday we have circuit strength training in the third session, where the intensity of additional training is a very high endurance circuit (up to 25 elements a minute).

5.1.4 Characteristic Features of the Preparatory Part

5.1.4.1 Main Tasks

Preparation for training or warm up is an important component part of the training session which must not be ignored. Warming up deals with a number of special tasks, the major being:

- establishing an organised start;
- preparation for the main part of the session;
- general warming up and activation of the support-motor apparatus;
- guarding against injury;
- working on correct co-ordination tuning posture;
- working on and activating habits of performing basic control movements;
- working on basic control poses and major positions;
- background technical-physical tuning;
- basic repetition of stable landings;
- perfecting the technique of the basic and the learning of new acrobatic jumps.

Observations made at the top international competitions have shown that coaches hardly ever warm up their charges with people around, with the exception of the Russian team. Evidently this happens because the coaches undervalue the importance of general warm up, or they do not know how to do it, or they do not want to, or they are lazy, or whatever. We think that gymnasts, including top-class gymnasts, should warm up as a matter of course collectively, and our long experience testifies to the high pedagogical effectiveness of this approach.

We make special demands on the set of exercises that are part of the general warm up. Besides dealing with the above-enumerated special tasks this set should:

- cover all groups of muscles, ligaments and tendons that are actively to work when performing the training programme;
- be carried out mainly without a halt;
- be performed by all members of the team simultaneously under the coach's command;
- remain stable over a long period.

5.7.4.2 Warming up before Basic Training

We reproduce below the warm up created by L. Arkaev as a model of the preparatory part of the basic training session. Its general developing parts under the author's direct command and with his participation as senior coach for more than 25 years have been performed collectively and daily by all generations of the Soviet and Russian men's teams before beginning the basic training session.

The warm up includes three parts that are performed on the carpet for the floor exercises. The first part is done in movement, the second on the spot. The third part is an acrobatic warm up and at the same time a basic acrobatic preparation.

Part 1. General developing exercises in motion: In this part of the warm up the gymnasts are in constant motion, moving one behind the other around the carpet.

1. walking in a circle at a constant pace (twice round the carpet);

2. starting position (SP): fingers interlocked, arms in front of the chest.

   - arms forward with hands forward;
   - return to SP;
   - arms up above the head;
   - return to SP.

The exercise is repeated 4 times (4x4=16).

Planning

3. SP basic stance, arms by the side.

   - 1-4 – four circles with arms forward;
   - 5-8 – four circles with arms backward.

The exercise is repeated 4 times (8x4=32).

4. SP arms bent hands clasped in front of the chest.

   - left foot forward turning arms and trunk to the left;
   - right foot forward turning arms and trunk to the right.

The exercise is repeated 6 times (2x6=12).

5. SP basic stance.

   - take a step forward with the left leg and move both arms to the side and upwards above the head;
   - take a step with the right leg and circle the arms downwards;
   - take a step forward with the left leg and circle both arms upward and forward;
   - take a step forwards with the right leg and circle arms downwards to the side.

The exercise is repeated 4 times (4x4=16).

6. walking with toes inward to count of 16;
7. walking with toes outward to count of 16;
8. walking on tiptoe to count of 16;
9. walking on heels to count of 16;
10. running at constant pace (one circle);
11. running lifting knees high (1 circle);
12. running bending legs back (1 circle);
13. running with paces inwards legs crossing (1 circle);
14. running with paces outwards legs crossing (1 circle);
15. ordinary running (1 circle);
16. running at accelerated pace (half a circle);
17. ordinary running (half circle);
18. running with acceleration (half circle);
19. ordinary running (half circle).

Part 2. General developing exercises on the spot

In this part of the warm up the gymnasts are spread in a circle on the carpet for floor exercises. The coach is in the middle showing the exercises that they are to perform as a group.

20. SP basic stance.

- placing right leg back toes to the floor, bring arms in a circle forward and up;
- return to SP;
- placing left leg back toes to the floor, bring arms in a circle forward and up;
- return to SP.

Repeat 4 times (4x4=16).

21. 1-4 – four circles with arms forward;

5-8 – four circles with arms back.

Repeat 3 times (3x8=24).

22. SP – basic stance, arms bent at the elbows before the chest.

- turn trunk to the left with arms swinging sideways;
- SP;
- turn trunk to the right with arms swinging sideways;
- SP;
- turn trunk to the left with arms swinging upwards;
- SP;
- turn trunk to the right with arms swinging upwards;
- SP.

Repeat 2 times (8x2=16).

23. SP – stand with legs apart, right arm up, left on the hip.

- circle with right arm inward;
- three springy inclines to the left;

- change SP with circle of the left arm inwards;
- three springy inclines to the right.

Repeat 2 times (8x2=16).

24. SP – basic stance.

- 1-4 circle movements with the head to the left;
- 5-8 circle movements with the head to the right.

Repeat 2 times (8x2=16).

25. SP — basic stance.

- turn head to the left (as far as it will go);
- turn head to the right (as far as it will go);
- 3-4 repeat.

Repeat 4 times (4x4=16).

26. SP – basic stance.

- lunge to left with turn to left with arms up;
- 2-4. three springy movements with arms back bending the legs;
- 5-8. also in other direction.

Repeat 2 times (8x2=16).

27. SP – stand with legs apart, hands on hips.

- turn trunk to left with sharp movement with left elbow back;
- turn trunk to right with sharp movement with right elbow back.

Repeat 6 times (6x2=12).

28. SP – stand with legs apart, hands on hips.

- 1-4. full circle movements of pelvis to left;
- 5-8. full circle movements of pelvis to right.

Repeat 2 times (8x2=16).

29. SP – stand with legs apart, arms to the side.

- 1-4. four springy inclines forward;
- 5-8. four springy inclines back.

30. SP – stand with legs apart, arms to the side

- incline forward bending with turn to right touching the right ankle with left hand;
- back incline bending to the left, touching the right calf with the left hand;
- forward incline bending with turn to the left, touching the left ankle with right hand;
- back incline with turn to the right, touching the left calf with right hand.

Repeat 4 times (4x4=16).

31. SP stance with arms up.

- 1-4. circle movements of trunk to right (keeping pelvis still);
- 5-8. circle movements of trunk to left (keeping pelvis still).

32. SP – stand with legs apart, incline forward, arms bent in front of chest.

- turn trunk to right with sharp movement of the right elbow back;
- turn trunk to the left with sharp movement of left elbow back.

Repeat twice.

33. SP – basic stance.

- 1-4 bend legs, make circle movements of trunk to the right (keeping pelvis still);
- 5-8 bend legs, make circle movements of trunk to left (keeping pelvis still).

Repeat twice (8x2=16).

34. SP – stance, bending legs.

- 1-4. circle movements in knee joints to right;
- 5-8. also to left.

Repeat 2 times (8x2=16).

35. SP – basic stance.

- incline forward touching the floor with fingers;
- squat, straighten the legs, fingers still touching the floor;
- stand up;
- squat, touching floor with fingers, straighten the legs fingers still touching the floor;
- squat touching floor with fingers, stand up.

Repeat 3 times (8x3=24).

36. SP –basic stance arms forward,

- 10 squats on full sole of foot.

37. SP – squat hands on the floor.

- 1-4 rising on half-toes turn foot to right and left (warming up ankle joints).

Repeat 4 times (4x4=16).

38. SP – sitting with legs bent, knees apart, heels together.

- 1-4 four springy knee movements pressing the knees towards the floor.

Repeat 4 times (4x4=16).

39. SP – sitting with legs bent in support hands behind the back resting on the floor.

- turn knees to right touching floor with right knee;
- turn knees to left touching floor with left knee.

Repeat 6 times (2x6=12).

40. SP – sitting in back support, left leg bent, right leg straight. (exercise for co-ordination).

- swing right up;
- lower and bend right, straightening left (change to SP);
- swing left to the left;
- lower and bend left, straightening right (return to SP);
- swing right to the right;
- lower and bend right, straightening left (change to SP);
- swing left up;
- SP.

Repeat 3 times (8x3=24).

41. SP sitting in back support with legs apart.

- swing left to the right, touching floor behind the right;
- SP;
- swing right to left touching floor behind left;
- SP.

Repeat 3 times (4x3=12).

42. SP – the same.

- turn to left into splits;
- SP;
- turn to right into splits;
- SP.

Repeat 3 times (4x3=12).

43. SP – the same.

- turn shoulders to the left and backwards;
- SP;
- turn shoulders to the right and backwards;
- SP.

Repeat 3 times (4x3=12).

Planning

44. SP – the same.

- swing left arm to the right;
- SP;
- swing right arm to left;
- SP.

Repeat 3 times (4x3=12).

45. SP – the same.

- bend left arm, sharp movement with elbow back to the left;
- SP;
- bend right arm, sharp movement with elbow back to right;
- SP.

Repeat 3 times (4x3=12).

46. SP – sitting legs apart, arms in front of chest.

- turn trunk to left;
- SP;
- turn trunk to right;
- SP.

Repeat 3 times (4x3=12).

47. SP – sitting legs apart, left arm up, right down.

- incline and bend forward to right;
- change to SP;
- incline and bend forward to left;
- change to SP.

Repeat 3 times (4x3=12).

48. SP – the same.

- incline trunk to left;
- incline trunk forward; as close to the floor as possible;

- incline trunk to right;
- SP;
- 5-8 also in other direction.

Repeat 2 times (8x2=16).

49. SP – sitting legs together, stretched knees, arms to the side and upwards.

- raise legs up;
- SP;
- raise legs up;
- SP.

Repeat 4 times (4x4=16).

50. Roll on to the back legs straight and close to the face.

- 1-4 springy movements to touch floor behind the head with feet.

Repeat 3 times (4x3=12).

51. SP – lying on back, left arm at waist supporting the body, elbow leaning on floor.

- 1-7. slowly rotate and bend to left;
- 8 change to SP.

Repeat in other direction.

52. SP – lying on back with legs apart and flexed behind the head, catch hold of heels from inside with hands.

- 1-12. springy movements with legs and trunk towards each other (preparatory exercises for Stalder on the horizontal bar).

53. SP – lying on left elbow and left side with legs together (side rocks).

- 1-7 straightening arm, make springy inclines to left, rocking body (feet move off the floor);
- 8. change SP.

Repeat in other direction.

54. Sitting with legs together, palms under pelvis (buttocks).

    - 1-8 rocking with turns to right and left.

55. SP – front support on the thighs.

    - 1-4 arch and stretch coming to kneeling support (Koshechka);
    - 5-8 slowly return to SP with opposite curve of the spine.

Repeat 3 times (8x3=24).

56. SP – lying on stomach and elbows, bent legs at right angles, feet flexed.

    - turn ankles and head to right;
    - SP;
    - turn ankles and head to left;
    - SP.

57. SP – lying on back with arms to sides.

    - turn left shoulder to right;
    - SP;
    - turn right shoulder to left;
    - SP.

Repeat 3 times (8x3=24).

58. Lying on stomach with arms forward.

    - spreading legs turn to left until you touch the floor with left shoulder;
    - SP;
    - spreading legs turn to right until you touch the floor with the right shoulder;
    - SP.

Repeat 4 times (4x4=16).

59. SP – lying on stomach with arms forward.

- raise left leg and right arm;
- lower;
- raise right leg and left arm;
- lower.

Repeat 4 times (4x4=16).

60. SP – lying on back with legs together, arms forward.

- 1-30 rocking in a dished position.

61. SP – sitting on knees, arms forward, chest touching floor.

- 1-12 springy inclines with pelvis to right and left alternately.

62. SP – support position on hands and knees.

- swing left leg back;
- swing left leg to left and side;
- swing left leg back;
- SP;
- 5-8 with other leg in the other direction.

Repeat 3 times (8x3=24).

63. SP – sitting on heels in crouch position.

- sitting on the right heel;
- sitting on the left heel;
- sitting on the right heel;
- SP;
- 5-8 four springy rockings on soles of feet forward and back.

This exercise for warming up the soles of the feet is repeated twice (8x2=16).

64. Headstand 6-8 secs.

65. SP – front support with bent arms.

- 1-30 Stepping from one foot to the other.

This exercise lasts for 30 secs and is for warming up the Achilles tendons.

66. SP – the same.

- 1-16 Jumps on hands and feet simultaneously.

16 jumps in all.

67. SP – stance with arms up.

- swing with one leg, push off with other to handstand (hold 60 secs).

68. SP – basic stand.

- 1-4 raise arms up, shaking the hands; relaxation
- 5-8 lower.

Repeat 3 times (8x3=24).

69. SP – basic stance.

On the spot back tuck somersault into 'dostok' (landing with no error). The exercise is repeated until the gymnast makes the 'dostok'.

After that the gymnasts pair up.

70. SP – sitting down with partner sitting on the back, legs across shoulders.

- rise on half toes and fix this position, lightly rocking back and forward for 10 seconds;
- lower on to heels as low as possible, and fix this position, lightly rocking back and forward for 5 seconds;
- repeat for 15 seconds;

- 5. rise on half toes;
- 6. lower on to heels.

Repeat 5. and 6. for 30 seconds rotating knees.

All the exercises are performed for 60 seconds.
Change places with the partner and repeat the exercise.

71. Shaking the extremities for 15 seconds.

Here the general developing exercises end. This part of the warm up lasts 12 minutes. After it begins the last section of the preparatory part of the training session – the acrobatic warm up which includes basic elements of the basic acrobatic preparation of all levels.

Part 3. Basic gymnastic-acrobatic warm up

All basic elements and exercises have a cyclical character – ie they are repeated several times each. The exercises are performed along a diagonal of the carpet for floor exercises. Its length is about 17 m and this distance limits the number of repetitions of a specific element or routine in a single approach. The gymnasts in turn, one after the other, perform the following exercises:

1. jump to handstand, roll forward, stand up with straight legs;
2. kick to handstand, handstand, three bounces on two arms, roll forward;
3. kick to handstand, hop half turn, lower to crouch roll backwards into handstand with full turn;
4. backward roll with hop half turn to handstand, forward roll into support, legs apart, in tempo Endo roll to handstand, pirouette and repeat etc.;
5. series of handsprings and flysprings from run up;
6. handspring and a series of forward somersaults (2-4 in a row);
7. from run up 2-3 forward straight somersaults in a row (1-2 attempts);
8. forward straight somersault with turn of 720°;
9. forward straight somersault and forward straight somersault with turn of 720° (3 attempts);

10. double forward somersault from run up (3 attempts): 1) from acrobatic runway into foam rubber pit, 2) on acrobatic runway and 3) on mat for floor exercises;
11. forward straight somersault and double forward tuck somersault (3 attempts);
12. handspring, forward straight somersault, forward straight somersault with turn of 360° and forward straight somersault with turn of 540° (handspring, straight, full, 1.5 twist);
13. round off and series of whip back somersaults up to the edge of the runway (2 attempts);
14. round off, flic flac, whip somersault, flic flac, whip, etc. up to the end of the runway (2 attempts);
15. round off, whip back somersault, back somersault with turn of 540° and forward somersault with turn of 360°;
16. round off, flic flac, double straight somersault (double blanche) (1-2 attempts);
17. round off, flic flac, double back somersault: the first one full in back out, the second in tuck (twist more to the back) (1-2 attempts);
18. individual ending of the floor exercises (1 attempt).

Here the general warm up ends. For both men and women it normally lasts 35 minutes. The difficulty of the final acrobatic jumps of the basic acrobatic warm up is not fixed. By measure of their mastery and perfection of technical skill, the difficulty of the jumps may increase in order (for example: not a double straight somersault, but a double straight somersault with twist, and then also with two twists). This vividly confirms our thesis that the top level of the base cannot be fixed for a fairly long time. It develops and becomes more complex together with the perfection of technical skill and gymnastics development (see Chapter 4.2.3).

5.7.4.3 Warm up before Auxiliary Training Sessions

Before beginning the main part of auxiliary sessions with the national team we also carry out a group warm up lasting 7-10 minutes. It includes a shortened (by comparison with that described above) set of general developing exercises and basic acrobatic jumps. Individual warm up for 5-7 minutes may precede the group warm up, and it is not part of the time of the auxiliary training session.

5.8 Structure of the Pre-competition Training Stage

As already mentioned, the pre-competition training stage is the direct preparation of top-class gymnasts for specific competitions. Depending on the scale and ranking of the competitions this stage may last from two to eight weekly micro-cycles (4 on average). An obligatory condition of these training stages is modelling of the conditions of coming competitive activity while exceeding its major parameters.

We began actively to draw up and test models of pre-competition training stages at a technical level in the late 1970s and early 1980s. We did one of the first tests of modelling the competition micro-cycle (CMC) at the pre-competition training stage of Nikolai Andrianov for the 1976 Olympic Games. This experience was very successful: Andrianov won 4 Olympic golds and the accolade of being named the best athlete of the year.

The first pedagogical experiment using the shock-model micro-cycle we had drawn up was done in the men's national team at the pre-competition training stage for the Friendship-84 international competition [7,32].

We set out here in rather more detail its course and results since the data we gathered represent historical and scientific value for the theory and method of gymnastics, and we used the laws we had worked out many times in practice. In fact, they have retained their actuality up to today.

The aim of the experiment was to reveal the effectiveness of a principally new for the time, structure of the pre-competition training stage for big tournaments. The tasks of the experiment were the following:

1. to work out the structure of the shock-model micro-cycle and demonstrate its effectiveness;
2. to work out the structure of the direct training stage for big tournaments in three training sessions a day with account for the individual characteristics of the gymnasts and to show its sports efficacy;
3. to evaluate the influence of the experimental training load on the functional state of gymnasts.

The results of the Druzhba (Friendship)-84 competitions were the criterion of efficacy. The programme's effectiveness was assessed by comparative analysis of the results of this stage with those of analogous stages in which the same gymnasts had taken part.

We used the following methods of research to tackle the set tasks: pedagogical observations, pedagogical experiment, chronometry, myotonometry, heart beat frequency, orthostatic test, cluster dynamometry, self-assessment and self-control.

Six gymnasts took part with over ten years experience behind them; of these, five were merited masters of sport and one master of sport, international class. The stage of pre-competition training included four weekly micro-cycles; each micro-cycle, in turn, comprised six training days and one rest day.

The optimal spreading of training load, its composition, structure and dynamics are of crucial importance at the pre-competition training stage. What particularly interested us were the parameters of training load of the team leaders, Bilozerchev, Artemov and Balabanov who had taken the first, second and third places in the multi-event at Druzhba-84.

In the four-week dynamic Bilozerchev reached his peak of training load by element in the second week, Artemov in the third and Balabanov in the second and third weeks. In number of routines performed in the weekly cycle Artemov's and Balabanov's peak came in the same weeks, while Bilozerchev's came in the third week.

The dynamics of number of performed routines in the weekly micro-cycles with these gymnasts was also individual (apart from the shock model cycle when for all gymnasts the amount of training load in number of routines was the same). In the final week of training Bilozerchev performed 28 routines, Artemov 6 (he sustained an injury) and Balabanov 19. Such a wide gap may be put down to the fact that Bilozerchev had to acquire a greater reserve of competition reliability than the others insofar as he had not taken part in competitions for ten months owing to an ankle injury.

Artemov successfully performed in a number of preliminary competitions in that season, so it was enough for him to perform 78 routines in the third and second micro-cycle weeks to attain a high level of functional readiness for the coming competitions. In the final week we paid particular attention in his training to quality of performance of individual elements and routines. With account for his injury the performance of six routines in that last week seemed fully adequate for maintaining a high level of special endurance and technical preparedness by the start of the competitions.

Balabanov's training load indicators were in the middle between those of Bilozerchev and Artemov.

As we came closer to the competitions the indicators of training load in number of SPP elements, number of attempts to the apparatus and intensity of training by element diminished with all gymnasts in the final week. The amount of technical training somewhat fell correspondingly.

The dynamic of such an important indicator as stability in executing competition routines was of particular interest to us. In the fourth week (first week of the pre-competition training stage) it was high with all gymnasts, reaching 92.3-95.2%. In the last week it reached its maximum of 100%.

For the first time in the structure of the direct training stage before big international tournaments we included the model-shock micro-cycle that we had worked out. Its main tasks were to exceed the loads of the competition micro-cycle and to model the coming competition activity. Here we modelled the order of events at the competition and order of performance in the team, the behaviour and actions of team members between starts, as well as the time of performances and duration of the competitions. The time for general and special warming up was strictly limited in line with the rules of the coming competitions.

We conducted the model-shock micro-cycle in the second week of the stage (of the start of competition). For the first time it included 17 training sessions in the three times a day regimen except Thursday and Sunday. On Thursday we conducted two training sessions. Sunday was rest day. The second session each day was the main one, the first and third were auxiliary. Control training sessions in which we modelled the coming competition activity took place in the main sessions throughout the week. A team of top-class judges allotted marks for performance of competition exercises according to the current competition rules.

To determine the effectiveness of the proposed regime of load dispersal we had a systematic supervision of the state of the gymnasts, using the above-mentioned pedagogical and medical-biological methods of investigation.

Pedagogical observations of the gymnasts and a chronometer of their training activity enabled us to establish actual individual indicators of training load. The training loads by such indicators as overall number of elements and routines performed in the model-shock micro-cycle were considerably higher than in competition. In number of elements they were higher by 38.3% (the competition micro-cycle had 1762 elements), while in number of routines they were 33.3% higher (the CMC had 27 routines).

All tested gymnasts except one had two load peaks by elements. The turning points on the graphs of training loads for the week normally came on the third and sixth day of the weekly micro-cycle. The minimum load for all gymnasts was on the fourth day, and the maximum on the sixth day of the week.

As the experiment demonstrated, using such a variant as dispersal of training load in the weekly micro-cycle enabled us to work out the pedagogical tasks and enhance the functional preparedness of the gymnasts.

Such parameters of training load as number of training days, training sessions and training time for all gymnasts in the national team were the same in the model-shock micro-cycle. Roughly the same were the number of performed routines, the total number of attempts and the percentage of stable performed routines.

The only exception was Pogorelov who had a somewhat smaller number of performed routines, but the greatest number of elements and attempts to the apparatus. This was due to the fact that his competition programme contained unique elements and routines. For the purposes of increasing the stability of their performance we paid particular attention to Pogorelov's training in the auxiliary sessions to the quality and reliability of performing precisely these elements and routines.

The volume of training load in the model-shock micro-cycle (7 days) comprised on average some 30% of the volume of training load of the entire four-week pre-competition training stage (28 days). All those taking part in the experiment in this micro-cycle performed the maximum number of high complexity elements, which attested to its high intensity.

Each national team member had his own individual set of SPP exercises constituted on the principle of combining technical and physical training. As already shown above, SPP is one of the most crucial factors in training top-class gymnasts; the number of performed SPP elements is a very informative indicator at the pre-competition training stage.

What struck us was that with the winner of the multi-event Druzhba-84 championship, Bilozerchev, this indicator was markedly higher at the experimental stage of training 733 elements of SPP than with the outsider of the team, Balabanov (344 elements of SPP). We ought to note that Balabanov had a very high SPP level, yet not much greater than Bilozerchev.

The average ratio of technical and physical preparation used in our experiment was on average 4:1 (79.4% and 20% respectively). However, on an individual basis this indicator varied over a fairly wide spectrum: from 2.5:1 with Bilozerchev to 6:1 with Balabanov.

We found that the pulse of the gymnasts before and after the control training sessions in the free programme was on average higher than after the compulsory programme. But even before the control training session in the compulsory programme the gymnasts' pulse was higher than normal, and comprised 87 beats a minute. Evidently this was caused by pre-start nerves modelled in the training process conditions. The pulse of all the gymnasts was within normal bounds in the subsequent control sessions.

Before the start of the control sessions in the free programme the pulse of some gymnasts was higher than normal in the model-shock micro-cycle. For example, on Tuesday and Thursday it reached 90 and 96 beats per minute with Balabanov and Artemov respectively. This was due to the imminent performance of complex elements and routines in the free programmes. The modelling of extreme conditions in the model-shock micro-cycle enabled us subsequently to make appropriate corrections and to hold the concluding control sessions of this micro-cycle at a high level. It was precisely on Friday and Saturday that the gymnasts showed their best results.

Analysis of the tests, using orthostatic test, cluster dynamometry and myotonometry showed that all those taking part in the experiment were in good form and dealt well with the training loads. We should note that despite the objective indicators positively characterising the changes in their organisms, their subjective self-assessment was fairly high. In all probability this was due to the fact that they had not had such high demands made on them before in preparing for competitions. This was borne in mind when preparing gymnasts for future competitions.

The comprehensive use of pedagogical and medical-biological methods of investigation enabled us to work out the positive influence of this variant of dispersal of training load on the functional stage of the organism and sports-technical skill at the pre-competition training stage. After the shock-model micro-cycle the gymnasts needed only their Sunday rest to fully restore their functions for the next weekly micro-cycle.

Sports-technical skill, its reliability and productiveness in the team reached its maximum in the final days before competition and remained just as high as they progressed.

Thus, as a result of our experiment we showed that our model of pre-competition training stage with the built-in model-shock micro-cycle structure is effective from a sports viewpoint. It enabled us more fully to implement the principle of 'outstripping' development and optimal surplus, to bring the team to the peak of form directly by the start of competitions and to attain high sporting results. The high level of functional, physical and technical surplus attained as a result of the experiment ensured high competition reliability and productiveness both for the team and for its leaders. The gymnasts of the Soviet team won in the team and individual championship in the multi-events and won most gold medals on the apparatus.

Analysis of the experimental results allowed us to draw the following conclusions:

1. the results of the Soviet men's team at the Druzhba-84 championships confirmed the effectiveness of our variant of constructing the four-week stage of pre-competition training;
2. when working out and refining models of training stages for various competitions we should take account of the major features of upcoming competitive activity, the indicators of training load and the individual characteristics of the gymnasts;

3. introduction into the structure of the pre-competition training stage of the model-shock micro-cycle enabled us to acquire a high level of functional preparedness, to establish optimal physical, technical and psychological surplus and a fuller adaptation of the gymnasts to the conditions of upcoming competitions;
4. training loads in the model-shock micro-cycle should substantially exceed the parameters of competition load at the coming competitions;
5. the regime of training load and the mechanism of their dispersal in our experiment corresponded to the functional potential of the gymnasts and was adequate to the level of their physical and technical preparedness. After performing the planned load in the weekly micro-cycles of the pre-competition training stage they needed only Sunday for rest to fully restore their work capacity.

These conclusions were many times used when working out and refining the contemporary technology of training Soviet and Russian top-class gymnasts.

Subsequently, using models of upcoming competitive activity, we worked out four variants of constructing the pre-competition training stage for various competitions. The main difference between them was that the maximum training load came at different weekly micro-cycles of the four-week pre-competition training stage, as shown below:

- first variant – first micro-cycle (last week from start of competition);
- second variant – second micro-cycle (second week);
- third variant – third micro-cycle (third week);
- fourth variant – fourth micro-cycle (first week of the stage).

Bearing in mind the increasing competition internationally we made a further intensification of the training process. This is apparent in a further increase in the load and intensity of training loads in the weekly micro-cycles by including a special set of SPP exercises in the first morning sessions to develop strength and speed-strength qualities.

The share of technical training exercises was also increased. We corrected the dynamic of training load in the weekly micro-cycles so as to, as fully as possible, model the regimes of the coming competitive activity in conditions of training at the stage of pre-competition training; and we redistributed the training load in the weekly micro-cycles. Of the total number of performed elements 32.5% were performed in the first training sessions, 41% in the second and 26.5% in the third.

In a subsequent pedagogical experiment we made a pedagogical test of the effectiveness of various variants of the pre-competition training stage before such important tournaments as the USSR championships and Cup, the European championships, University Games of 1985, and World championships. Twelve members of the Soviet national team took part (8 merited master of sport and 4 masters of sport, international class). Each person tested three variants of the pre-competition training stage.

In all cases the gymnasts on average performed the same number (11 500 elements) at the same intensity (2.6 elements a minute) in terms of training load spread over weekly micro-cycles according to the 2nd, 3rd and 4th variants (see Table 13).

Table 13

Average training load indicators in various variants of the pre-competition training stage

Variants	Load Indicators	MC No4, %	MC No3, %	MC No2, %	MC No1, %
2nd	Number of elements	20	26	31	3
	Number of combins.	20	24	36	20
	Intensity, el/min	2.38	2.5	3.08	2.64
3rd	Number of elements	28	30	25	17
	Number of combins,	22	3	25	16
	Intensity, el/min	2.57	3.04	2.76	2.24
4th	Number of elements	31	28	20	21
	Number of combins.	31	27	18	24
	Intensity, el/min	2.96	2.81	2.5	2.37

Analysis of the results of the subsequent pedagogical experiment revealed that by comparison with previous data (indicators of training load at pre-competition stages before conducting this experiment) on average there was an increase in training load indicators like volume (by 39%), intensity (by 21.9%), number of SPP elements (by 59.8%), elements of technical training (by 28.7%), attempts (by 30%), support vaults (by 23.1%) and stable performed routines (by 4.1%). The effectiveness of training was expressed in an authentic improvement in sports-technical results. The highest results came when using the third variant of pre-competition training stage.

The following conclusions were drawn as a result of the subsequent experiment.

Use of the second variant is advisable if we need to create tough conditions at selection competitions conducted within the country (the national championships and cup). Its structure included the following weekly micro-cycles: catching up (MC No.4), basic (MC No.3), shock-model (MC No. 2) and control-model (MC No.1). During this pre-competition training stage up to the start of competition inclusively the gymnasts are in centralised training.

The third variant should be applied when training for big international and the major competitions of the year (World and European championships, Olympic Games), when the athletes have to train for a week at the competition venue. This variant included the following weekly micro-cycles: basic (MC No.4), shock-model (MC No.3), control-model (MC No. 2), adaptation-tuning up (MC No.1).

The fourth variant is effective at the start of the competition period, when after a big load and intensity of load in the previous preparatory period the gymnasts are faced with a competition period in which they have to take part in several contests with short intervals in between of 1-2 weeks. This variant comprised the following weekly micro-cycles: shock (MC No.4), shock-model (MC No.3), recovery (MC No.4), control-model (MC No.4). It was useful mainly for young gymnasts who first took part in control competitions (for example, in international tournaments), and then in selection at national championships and national cups.

These conclusions were used in preparing the Soviet team for the 1988 Seoul and 1992 Barcelona Olympics, where our gymnasts performed with flying colours (in Seoul the men's team won 12 medals – 8 gold, 3 silver and 1 bronze, while the women won 7 (3+2+2); in Barcelona the gymnasts of the combined team of the former USSR also won 12 medals in the men's events (6+4+2) and the women won 6 (3+1+2). So in just two Olympics we won 20 gold out of the 28 on offer). The models worked out are used in somewhat modified form even today within the system of integrated training of the men's and women's Russian teams.

How to Create Champions   6

CHAPTER SIX

Biomechanical Basis of Technique

6.1 Main Concepts and Terms

The laws of teaching gymnastics exercises are closely associated with the laws of mechanics. Gymnasts and coaches need to know the laws of mechanics in order to understand the basic mechanisms underlying the technique of performing gymnastics exercises and the methods of their mastery [85, 22]. They cannot be ignored. If they are, the coach will be setting the gymnast unperformable tasks and demanding the impossible. So biomechanics occupies a special place in the structure of sports science (see Chapter 2.1).

Movement is one of the fundamental scientific concepts. The biomechanics of sport studies the mechanical movement of an athlete's body when performing physical exercises. A gymnast's movement is a biomechanical process accompanied by a change in the position of his body and (or) its links in time and space. Any dynamic gymnastics exercise or any part of it is always expressed externally in mechanical movement.

Mechanical movement may be translational (linear) and angular (circle or turn). In turn, each of them may be constant, accelerated, slowed down, one- or multi-dimensional, reverse, varying, as well as simple and complex. All these types of mechanical movement exist when performing gymnastics exercises. This applies both to the gymnast's body as a whole and to the movements in the joints, with the only exception that as a result of his anatomical structure, only rotating movements can be performed in the joints.

When analysing movement we define the position of the body in space at various moments in time and compare them with one another. For this we use various systems of coordinates, also called calculating systems. Normally we use right-angled (orthogonal) systems of coordinates well known from school. Some of these are fixed in relation to the earth. For example, the systems of coordinates rigidly connected with a motionless gymnastics apparatus. Such calculating systems are called motionless or inertial. Others are rigidly connected with a moving body (for example, a gymnast's body). They are called mobile systems of coordinates. This includes when a body moves unevenly (speeding up); the systems of coordinates connected with this are called non-inertial.

To describe the movement of an object (say, a gymnast's body) we need to define where the body is, how quickly and where it is moving, as well as whether this movement is slowing down or speeding up. In terms of biomechanics this means that we need to define the position of the body in space, its movement and direction, as well as its speed. This applies both to the body as a whole, as well as to its individual parts when the mutual location of these parts in relation to one another alters, as happens when performing gymnastics exercises.

Movement ought to be differentiated from action. The concept of action in mechanics and psychology is significantly different. A gymnast's actions in the psychological sense do not always lead to mechanical movement (as, for example, when performing powerful static exercises), while movement is not always a sign of a gymnast's active actions. One is a target change in the mutual location of links of the body as a result of control movements in the joints or holding a particular pose.

However, the very fact of changing the pose does not always mean a sign of controlling the movement. A pose may change also when a gymnast exerts no active muscle effort (see Chapter 6.2). On the other hand, controlling movements by a gymnast may not be reflected in the parameters of his movement. A gymnast may move with constant speed or with acceleration under the action of external forces, irrespective of whether he performs some sort of controlling movements or not (see Chapter 6.3).

The concept of *inertia* is one of the crucial concepts of mechanics. By inertia in mechanics we mean the ability of any physical bodies to maintain velocity or state of rest equally unchanged in the absence of external influences. *Inertia* is the quality of bodies to put up resistance to a change in their mechanical state. To bring the body out of a state of rest or alter the nature of its movement some external effort has to be applied. The quality of inertia is contained in Newton's first law of motion.

In their technique top-class gymnasts intuitively use the quality of inertia much more effectively than low level gymnasts. In the course of performing exercises they often exert less effort, while the effect is substantially greater. In the technique of top-class gymnasts the phases of movement where inertia dominates alternate with phases where active effort precisely allocated in time and space is exerted.

The section of biomechanics studying inert qualities of an athlete's body is called *mass geometry*. This studies so-called *mass-inertia characteristics* (MIC). This includes *mass* and *centre of mass coordinates*, as well as *moments of inertia* of an athlete's body, his anatomical parts and biomechanical links. One must know the mass-inertia characteristics to determine the *dynamic characteristics* of a gymnast's movement (see below).

The mass of an athlete's body is characterised by the amount of matter within it. It is a measure of the body's inertia in translational movement. The greater the athlete's mass, the more his weight and the greater effort he requires to begin movement or to change his velocity. Light, small and strong gymnasts normally have the advantage over heavy and tall gymnasts because the latter in the mechanical sense are more massive and, consequently, have more inertia. To perform gymnastics exercises, other things being equal, they need to exert more effort, while their relative strength is usually less than that of light gymnasts (see Chapter 1.2).

An athlete's body mass is the total mass of his anatomical parts or biomechanical links. In a first approximation it is one tenth of the athlete's weight (weight = mass × acceleration due to gravity (≈ 10)). When performing gymnastic and any other physical exercises the mass of the athlete's body links is considered constant and evenly distributed throughout the link which, in biomechanics, is regarded as a rigid body.

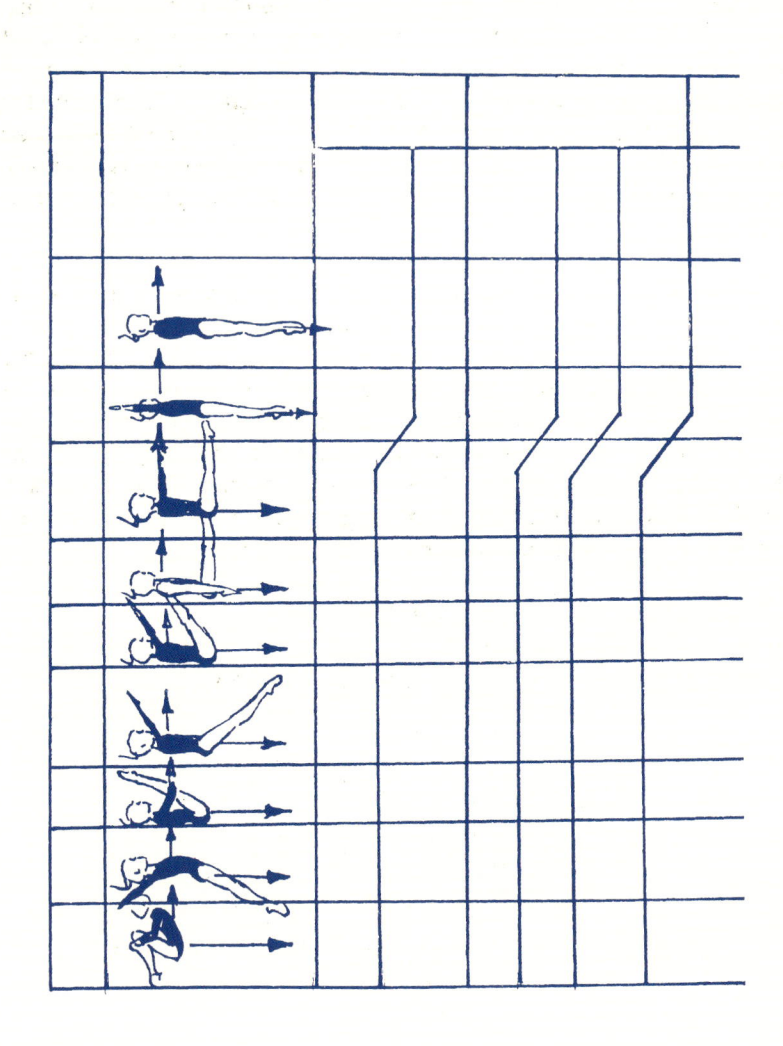

Figure 11 – *Basic mass inertia characteristic of a gymnast's body in various poses*

BIOMECHANICAL BASIS

Every body has a centre of gravity (it is the centre of mass) by which we understand an abstract point through which the resultant of all gravitational forces applied to the body acts. The position of the centre of mass of a rigid body does not change relative to it. A gymnast's body consists of many anatomical parts, each of which has its own centre of gravity. Since the body's anatomical parts are considered rigid bodies, the relative position of their centres of gravity does not change when performing gymnastics exercises. However, the mutual location of a gymnast's body links generally changes significantly.

The equally acting point of all forces exerted on a person's body is called his general centre of gravity. This point is the same as the overall *centre of body mass* (CoM). The CoM of a normal person in the anatomical position is at the centre of gravity of the body which is situated a few centimetres below the belly button. When changing position he also changes the CoM position in the system of coordinates connected with the athlete's body (Figure 11). For instance, in a bent position, the CoM is outside the gymnast's body. The most general laws of technique of performing gymnastic exercises are manifest when analysing the CoM movement of the gymnast's body.

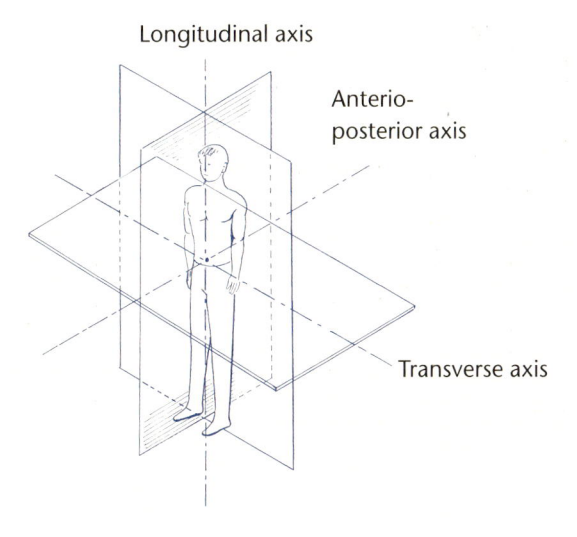

Figure 12 – *Principal axes of the human body*

The moment of inertia is the measure of resistance of the gymnast's body and his links in rotational movement. Most gymnastic and acrobatic exercises have a rotational component. Therefore, the moment of inertia of a gymnast's body and his links, like the mass, is an important biomechanical parameter. The magnitude of the moment of inertia depends on the *distribution of mass relative to the axis*, to which it is determined, and the pose which substantially changes when performing exercises generally.

One may have an innumerable number of axes through any body, including that of an athlete, but only three will be major. The major axes passing through a body's CoM are called the central axes. When rotating around one of these axes there is no dynamic pressure on the axis from the body.

An athlete's body has three main axes formed by intersecting the three major planes of the body passing through its CoM —longitudinal, transverse and anterior-posterior. In the anatomical position these axes are determined fairly simply (Figure 12). But given a change of pose the position of the body's main axes also changes. Their orientation relative to a person's body in free stance, as well as the value of moments of inertia, may be determined by the experimental-analytical method [58] (Figure 11). At the same time, the position of the main central axes of an athlete's body links relative to them remains unchanged.

If we take two bodies of identical mass – rod and sphere, it will be easier to rotate the sphere around the transverse axis up to a set speed because the sphere's moment of inertia is less, inasmuch as the particles of the sphere are more grouped around the transverse axis than with the rod. If we rotate these two bodies around the longitudinal axis, the rod will be easier to rotate because its moment of inertia relative to that axis will be less than with the sphere for the same reason. The dynamic equivalent of the rod is a stance with arms up or a handstand, while the sphere is a firm tuck position (Figure 13).

Core/rod)

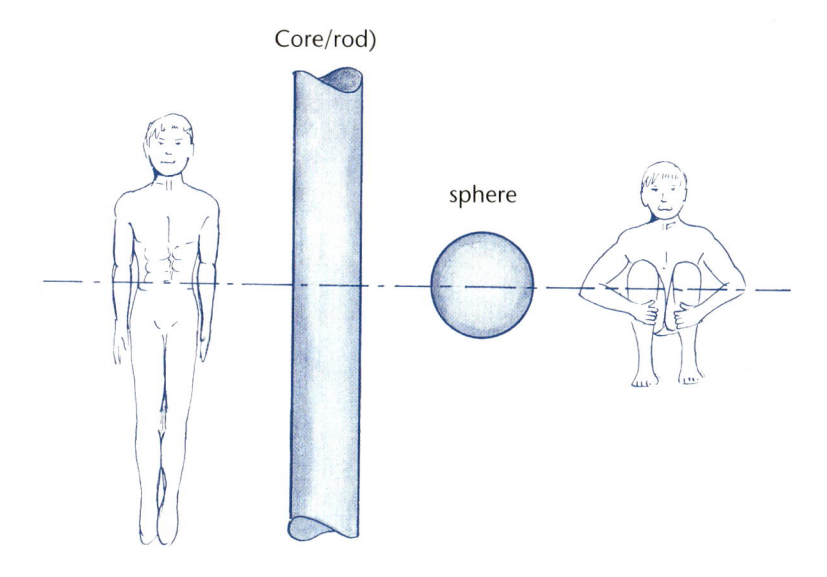

sphere

Figure 13 – *Moments of inertia in different shapes*

The moment of inertia of a gymnast's body in the anatomical position relative to the longitudinal axis is roughly 12 times less than around the transverse. The moment of inertia relative to the transverse axis in the tuck position is over four times less than in a handstand. In changing the stance, and thereby also the magnitude of the moment of inertia of his body relative to the axis of rotation, the gymnast may govern the angular velocity of movement (see Figure 11 and Chapters 6.2 and 6.3).

The principle of independence of movement is one of the most important principles of mechanics. Let us illustrate this in the following example. While performing exercises gymnasts perform simple and complex movements. Complex movements in mechanics are analysed, dividing them into *transferable* (for example, translational movement together with CoM) and relative (for example, rotating movement in relation to CoM). Their sum total represents absolute movement. According to the principle of independence of movement one may study the translational and relative movement independent of one another.

So, for example, when performing exercises in the flight phase the gymnast's body completes a complex movement. In analysing technique it is expedient to split it into two component parts. The translational movement is made by the progressive CoM movement of the body in flight, while the relative movement is the rotating movement of the body around its CoM. Following the principle of independence of movement, these two movements can be studied independent of each other. The difficulty of analysis of a rotating movement is that, by contrast with a rigid body, a gymnast's body pose in flight substantially changes. For example, when performing a triple somersault the gymnast tucks himself, fixes the tuck position and then straightens out. This difficulty can be overcome by representing the body's movement in the form of three programmes (see below).

Both simple and complex rotating movements may also be made in the joints. This depends on the anatomical peculiarities of a specific joint and the nature of the exercise. Control movements may be performed both in a single joint and in several at once.

When making a biomechanical analysis of technique one should use three systems of coordinates. One is immoveable or inertial, which normally is associated with the gymnastics apparatus (reference points), and the two others are moveable (non-inertial), connected with the gymnast's body. Their beginning is combined with the base point. Normally this is the CoM of the gymnast's body or the point of approximation to it, for example the axis of the hip joint centre (Figure 14).

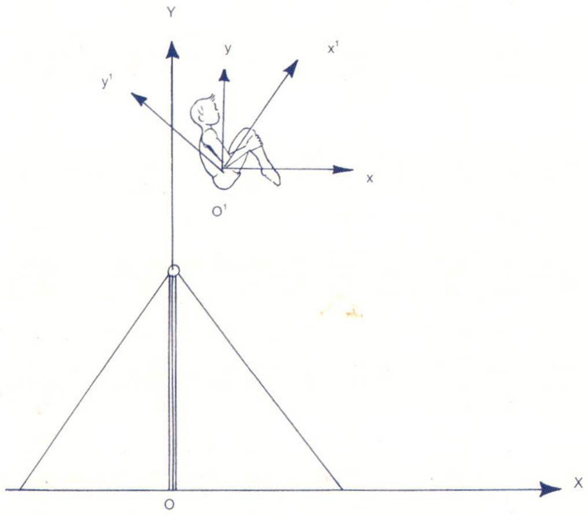

Figure 14 – Three systems of coordinates X,O, Y – static (inertial) x, o^1, y and x^1, o^1, y^1 – dynamic (mobile)

One of the moveable systems of coordinates moves parallel with the first immoveable system of calculation. This enables us to analyse progressive movement of the gymnast's body as a whole. The second system of coordinates normally is strictly linked with one of the three main axes of the gymnast's body or one of its links which change their orientation in space. So the third system of coordinates normally rotates relative to the second. This enables us to analyse the rotating movement of the gymnast's body and its links while performing exercises.

We may use various models of the gymnast's body for a biomechanical analysis and modelling of the technique of gymnastics exercises – from the material point (for example, when investigating the trajectory of CoM in flight) and the rigid body (for example, when investigating the gymnast's movement in motionless pose) up to multi-link spatial models with altering configuration. The latter represents the gymnast's body in the form of an abstract mechanical system consisting of mechanical links, combined with ideal hinges whose form models the joints (Figure 15). The mass-inertia characteristics of the links of the model normally correspond to the body links of a person.

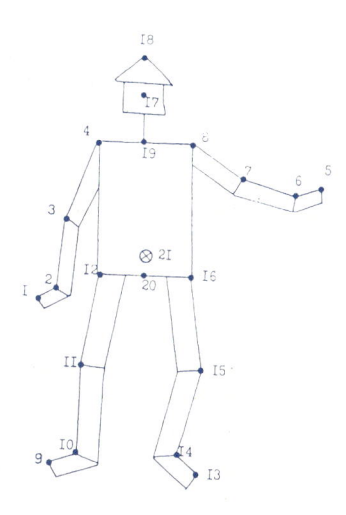

Figure 15 – *Mathematical model of a gymnast's body*

When performing many gymnastic exercises the rules of competition demand holding the arms and legs straight. Here movements of the right and left extremities often are symmetrical (for example, giant circle). In these circumstances it is enough to use three-link models of the gymnast's body for revealing the common biomechanical laws and modelling technique (for example, a model consisting of the arms, trunk together with the head).

Analysis of technique begins with determining the position of the gymnast's body at various moments of performing the exercise and comparing them. This position becomes fully determined if we know where (in what place in space) at a given moment the gymnast's body is, how it is oriented in space as a whole and in what pose it is. The indicated parameters determine the programme of the gymnast's movement when performing exercises.

This programme consists of three components: *the programme of place* (determined by change in coordinates of a certain base point of the gymnast's body in an immoveable system of coordinates, usually CoM), *the programme of orientation* (determined by change in orientation in space of the main body axes) and *the programme of stance* (determined by the nature of change in mutual alignment of links) [46]. The programme of place defines the transferable progressive movement of the gymnast's body as a whole, while the programme of orientation is its relative rotating movement as a whole. The programmes of place and orientation together comprise the overall programme of movement [34, 46]. The programme of stance from without reflects control of movement made by the gymnast.

Dynamic posture is an important biomechanical concept. We take it to be the act of holding an immoveable mutual alignment of body links in a variable force field [46] or the posture in basic working positions. For example, when performing a giant circle on the horizontal bar, when moving from the top downwards gravity acts in the same direction, and from the bottom upwards the moment due to gravity acts in directly the opposite direction. From the gymnast's standpoint the force of gravity in relation to his body seems to alter his direction.

In fact it is the gymnast's body that changes its position in relation to the vector of gravitation oriented constantly and directed towards the centre of the earth. To maintain a straightened dynamic posture in the horizontal position facing upwards and downwards the gymnast needs tension from directly opposite muscle groups. One of the principal requirements of the technique of performance according to the judges' rules is observance of correct dynamic posture when performing exercises.

Analysis of technique is associated with defining the *biomechanical characteristics* and *parameters of movement*. This definition may be quantitative and qualitative. In the first case we use special measuring instruments – from tape measure and stop watch to computerised measuring instruments. With their assistance we may determine the quantitative measures of movement in numerical form with varying degrees of accuracy. A qualitative definition of biomechanical characteristics is based on theoretical images, without using any numbers as a rule.

As applied to gymnastics biomechanical characteristics are measures of the mechanical state of the gymnast's body while performing exercises. They objectively reflect the process of achieving a result accessible to external observation. The interconnection between biomechanical characteristics and parameters of the gymnast's movement while performing exercises is called the *biomechanical structure*.

Biomechanical characteristics are divided into *kinematic* and *kinetic* (dynamic). With the aid of kinematic characteristics we can objectively describe an external picture of the gymnast's movements without account of the reasons that cause them. There are three levels within the kinematics of gymnastics exercises: *spatial, temporal and spatial-temporal*.

At the spatial level we view the geometry of movement, determine the coordinates of points, distances between them, various alignments, angles and trajectories. At this level we answer the questions of 'what?' and 'where?' which take place when the gymnast is performing the given exercise. An idea of the exercise's geometrical structure is provided, for example, by the kinogram or video recording, reproducing one frame after another.

At the temporal level movement is determined in time and provides an answer to the question 'when?'. To temporal characteristics belong duration of movement, its beginning, end, a moment of time during the performance, tempo and rhythm.

At the spatial-temporal level are determined changes in points in time, as well as velocity and acceleration of various links and points of the athlete's body, including CoM. At this level we gain an answer to the question 'how?' (how fast are the position and speed of the gymnast's body, its links and points changing).

The reasons for movement are defined in kinetics. Here we distinguish two levels: *force and energy*. Here the kinematic characteristics are associated with mass-inertia. At the force level are determined force and force moments, number of movements and kinematic moments, force impulses and moments of force. Here we get an answer to the question 'why?' from the given movement. For example, linear acceleration arises because an external force has acted on the body or an angular velocity arises because moments of force have acted on the body.

At the energetic level is determined the work of strength, power and mechanical energy. Here we receive an answer to the question 'through what?' the given movement occurs. (For example, a movement done as a result of mechanical work or expended energy.)

When performing gymnastic and any physical exercises the energy from one form changes into another. Thus, as a result of biomechanical reactions the chemical energy accumulated in the gymnast's muscles turns into mechanical potential energy of elastically deforming muscles. Being caused by its presence the force of pull of the muscles performs the mechanical work. As a result of this work and that of external forces on the potential energy of elastically deformed muscles, and on the gymnast's entire body and the apparatus, the potential energy is transformed into kinetic energy of movement.

When moving from below upwards into the field of earth's gravity in an unsupported position we lose kinetic energy, while the potential energy increases until the accumulated kinetic energy is all spent. At the moment when the vertical velocity of CoM of the athlete's body is equal to zero, potential energy reaches its maximum. The kinetic energy again expands, while the potential diminishes after reaching the dead point of flight when moving from the highest point downwards in the process of free fall.

In interaction with the apparatus the accumulated kinetic energy once more turns into potential energy of elastic deformation of the extended muscles and ligaments, as well as the deformed working surfaces of the apparatus. In further interaction with the apparatus, the accumulated potential energy once again turns into kinetic energy of movement of the apparatus and the gymnast's body, etc. When landing after a dismount the kinetic energy of the gymnast's body movement is absorbed by the landing surface and the gymnast's support-motor apparatus, turning into heat energy and disperses.

To understand the mechanisms at the basis of the technique of performing exercises we have to know the basic laws of mechanics. This, primarily, means Newton's three laws of motion, well known from physics, and the three laws of conservation.

Newton's first law: *the body retains a state of rest or even linear movement until an external force acts upon it.*

The gymnast's body CoM in flight moves in the horizontal direction evenly with constant velocity unless an external force acts upon it – ie if the coach does not provide the gymnast with direct physical assistance. Under the action of gravity in this case the gymnast's body CoM moves in the vertical direction upwards but constantly slowing, and after reaching the top point of flight (called the dead point) it speeds up on its way down.

Newton's second law: acceleration is directly proportional to the force acting upon the body and inversely proportional to the mass or otherwise: the force is equal to the product of body mass and the acceleration (F=ma).

The greater the gymnast's mass, the greater the external force has to be on it to attain the required acceleration.

Newton's third law is normally called the law of action and reaction. It goes as follows: with the interaction of two or more bodies of each force acting on another body, a reactive force counteracts it, being equal to the first in magnitude and opposite to it in direction.

When the gymnast pushes off from support, he acts on it with a certain force. The support, in turn, exerts on him an effect with a force equal to the first in magnitude and opposite to it in direction.

The three laws of conservation come straight from Newton's three laws.

The law of conserving kinetic energy states: *if the sum of work of all external and internal forces exerted on the system is zero, the kinetic energy of the system will remain unchanged.*

When performing swing movements on the horizontal bar the gymnast is performing internal work associated with the shift of his own body mass in relation to the apparatus, which increases the kinetic energy of his body. In tucking and then straightening in an unsupported position, the gymnast also performs internal work associated with a shift of his body mass in relation to CoM. Here the magnitude of moment of inertia of his body changes in relation to the axis of rotation passing through the CoM. Similarly, the kinetic energy of a rotating movement in flight initially increases (in tuck) and then diminishes (on landing).

When moving in the vertical direction in a fixed pose in flight, no internal mechanical work is performed. The force of gravity being the external force in relation to the gymnast does the work (negative when moving from below upwards and positive when moving from above downwards). In accordance with this the vertical component of kinetic energy of progressive movement of the gymnast's body in flight at first diminishes, and after reaching the highest point of flight then increases. In a horizontal direction in flight the work of the force of gravity is zero. So the horizontal component of kinetic energy remains unchanged.

The law of conserving an amount of movement states: *if the sum of all external forces exerted on the system is zero, its amount of movement remains unchanged.*

This event has relevance in the above-mentioned gymnast's body movement in the horizontal direction in the flight phase of gymnastic and acrobatic exercises. The amount of horizontal movement given from support does not change here.

In a vertical direction, however, the force of gravity comes into effect and so the amount of movement in this direction changes.

The law of conservation of angular momentum states: if the sum of moments of external forces exerted on the system is zero, the magnitude of its angular momentum remains unchanged.

In an unsupported position the moment of external forces in relation to the gymnast's body CoM is zero. According to the theorem of change in angular momentum, the law of conservation acts here. The mechanisms of controlling complex rotating movement in the flight phase of gymnastic and acrobatic exercises are based on the law of conservation of angular momentum in an unsupported position (see Chapter 6.3).

The mechanisms of control of movement when performing gymnastic or any other physical exercises (see Chapters 6.2 and 6.3) are based on the theorems of change in these parameters and laws of their conservation. Changing the mass-inertia parameters of one's body, through altering the pose is a result of the action of internal forces and interaction with the support; the gymnast controls the speed of his own movement.

The physical state of the gymnast's body, defined by such mechanical conditions as hardness, toughness and flexibility of muscles, exerts a certain influence on this speed (primarily on angular velocity) when holding the pose. We noted that, other conditions being equal, the gymnast's body in a strongly tense state rotates faster than in a relaxed state. The mechanism of this phenomenon is illustrated in the following example.

If we take two hen's eggs of identical size (one hard boiled, the other raw) and transmit to them the same rotating impulse (spin), the hard boiled egg will turn faster and longer. This takes place because inside it is harder in a certain sense than the raw egg. In the hard body the connections between the particles are hard and therefore the distance between them is constant. The particles of the body (the masses of the raw egg) placed close to the centre of gravity move to the periphery (closer to the hard external egg shall), which increases the body's moment of inertia relative to the axis of rotation. Since the principal moment of external force applied to the body in its rotation is in this case equal to zero, then owing to the conservation of angular momentum the angular velocity of the raw egg diminishes. It begins to turn more slowly than the hard boiled egg.

A situation similar to the raw and hard boiled egg arises in a gymnast's body when changing his aggregate state from relaxed to strongly tense. In this event the gymnast's body becomes more like the boiled egg than the raw egg in the fixed pose.

Experiments have confirmed these pedagogical observations. They have demonstrated that given identical conditions of flight set from support, the strongly tense gymnast's body turns faster than a relaxed body when performing multiple somersaults [25]. So an ability to control the physical state of one's body is an important element of gymnastic technique.

Most control movements when performing swing and take-off exercises are based on the so-called 'stretch-reflex', which shows that muscles previously stretched to an optimally aroused state possess optimal contractual effect.

So, when performing control actions of the swing-throw type, the courbette and anti-courbette, optimal stretching of the muscles should always precede the active contraction of the muscles of the body's working surface (front and back). This leads to accumulation in the muscles of energy of elastic deformation, in the same way as pulling a bow before releasing an arrow does.

Coaches and gymnasts must know that too strong or weak, too long or short stretching of the muscles diminishes the effectiveness of their subsequent contraction. Similarly any pause between stretching and contracting of the muscles has an adverse effect.

A gymnast's control actions from without are evident in bending and straightening movements in the joints or in holding them (in one or several joints or pose as a whole). When performing control movements of a total character (for example, pushing off from support) there is a change in magnitude of angles simultaneously in several joints, including between the vertebrae. Movements in the latter arising out of contraction of the muscles surrounding the spinal column (above all the long muscles of the spine) play an exceptionally important role in technique. Although in each vertebral joint they are fairly small, taken together they produce a big mechanical effect.

When building up the technique of exercises one should follow the principles of natural and simple attempts: the smaller the amplitude of joint control movements the better when striving for the desired effect as a whole – as long as this does not involve a worsening of the external picture of movement and other aesthetic or mechanical effects.

6.2 Movements in Support Position

6.2.1 General Laws

All dynamic gymnastic exercises are either rotational or have a rotational component. Control movements in the joints are only rotational. Newton's second law for rotational movement has the form of

$$*T = I\alpha$$

Where M is the moment of external force relative to the axis of rotation; J is the moment of inertia of the body relative to this axis; and a is the angular acceleration. This is the basic equation of rotation. Thus, the appearance and acceleration of rotation of the gymnast's body in support are caused by the action of the moment of an external force relative to the axis of rotation. The moment of force is equal to the product of a force and its moment arm:

$$F = Fd$$

---

*T = Angular momentum

Where M is the moment of force, F is the force and d is the moment arm of force equal to the shortest distance from the line of action of the force to the axis of rotation.

To illustrate the basic biomechanical laws underlying the technique of performing rotating movements in support, let us look at a very simple case – movement from handstands without change of pose on the horizontal bar.

If we disregard friction and air resistance, we may think that only the external force of gravity acts on the gymnast. It is equal to the gymnast's weight and is applied to his CoM. The moment arm in this case will be the shortest distance from the gymnast's body CoM to the vertical passing through the support point. In the starting position the gymnast's body CoM is located on the support vertical (Figure 16). The moment arm at this point is equal to zero and, consequently, its moment is also equal to zero. The gymnast's body is in a state of unstable equilibrium.

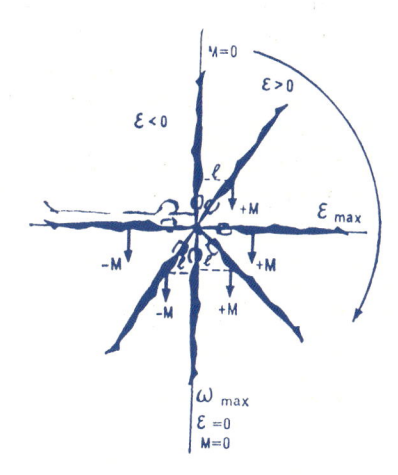

Figure 16 – *Gymnast's movements on the horizontal bar*

As we see from Figure 16 when coming out of a state of equilibrium the moment arm increases from zero. Relative to the support axis passing through the horizontal bar grip, a moment of gravity forms. We get an angular acceleration (α) and the gymnast's body begins to turn around the bar in a direction of top downwards.

The magnitude of angular acceleration (α) is inversely proportional to the moment of inertia of the gymnast's body relative to the axis of rotation. The greater the moment of inertia, the less this acceleration given the same weight of gymnast and, consequently, the higher the gymnast goes, the more slowly will his angular velocity grow.

Figure 16 shows us that as a result of movement around the axis of rotation the moment arm (d) begins to increase. The bigger it is, the greater the moment of force provided by the gravity and the greater the effect for increasing the angular velocity of the gymnast's body. The moment arm reaches its maximum magnitude in a horizontal position, after which it falls. The moment arm is zero in the upper and lower vertical positions.

After passing the extreme lower vertical position the moment of force due to gravity also changes its sign and becomes negative, putting a brake on. Inasmuch as the moment arm increases, the moment grows in absolute magnitude, reaching the maximum in the horizontal position from the front. After that it diminishes and becomes zero in the upper vertical position.

In connection with this the angular acceleration of the gymnast's body behaves as follows. When moving from the top downwards from the upper vertical position it increases and reaches its maximum in the horizontal position from behind. Then it diminishes and becomes equal to zero in the extreme lower vertical position. After passing this position the angular acceleration becomes negative. It grows in absolute magnitude, reaching its maximum negative value in the horizontal position from the front, after which it diminishes. In the vertical position a = 0.

Angular velocity (ω) here changes as follows. In the starting position ω = 0. When moving from the top downwards it continually increases and becomes maximal in the extreme lower vertical position. When moving from the bottom upwards it continually diminishes. The angular velocity changes fastest in the horizontal position from the rear (grows) and from the front (diminishes). In this position the increment of angular velocity in absolute magnitude is maximal.

In the extreme upper vertical starting position the gymnast's body possesses the largest supply of potential energy. When moving from the top downwards it diminishes, turning into kinetic energy. The kinetic energy reaches its maximum value in the extreme lower vertical position. Potential energy at this moment is at its lowest. With the start of movement from the bottom up, the picture changes: kinetic energy falls, and the potential energy increases. If the gymnast does not change his pose, then in the extreme upper vertical final position all the kinetic energy once again turns into potential energy and the velocity of movement again is zero.

Let us now see how a change of body position is reflected in the gymnast's movement. A change of body position causes a change in distance from the gymnast's body CoM up to the axis of rotation. It reaches its greatest magnitude in a fully straightened body position with arms upwards (so called full stretch). Overall bending or straightening of the body in any case diminishes this distance. Here equivalently the moment arm and, correspondingly, its moment (besides the upper and lower vertical positions where the moment of force due to of gravity is always equal to zero) diminish. In the light of the above, when moving from top downwards the gymnast should all the time retain a maximum straightened body position with full stretching in the shoulders. However, in that position the moment of inertia of the gymnast's body relative to the axis of rotation will also be maximum. As follows from equalisation of the rotating movement, the angular velocity here will be less.

Therefore, in taking a 'wind-up' before dismounts and fly-overs (release and catch elements), today's gymnasts pass from the upper vertical to the horizontal position, retaining angles in the shoulders and hips (Figures 17 and 18). After completing the main control action in the phase of thrust they do not immediately straighten their body and, avoiding the vertical position in handstand, they straighten out only in the horizontal position. Moreover, they do not fix that straight body position, but pass it to a position of bend, this being the final position of the swing phase.

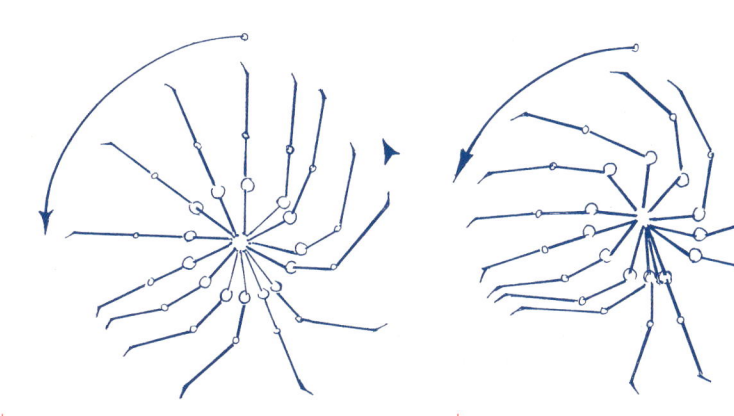

Figure 17 – *Classical giant circle on the high bar*

Figure 18 – *Preparatory giant circle on the high bar*

Thus, the classical phase of dispersal (movement with straight body from handstand to horizontal and onwards) is reduced. After the thrust phase almost at once they perform the swing phase which has a more marked character and is performed somewhat more sharply and earlier than usual. Here the horizontal bar experiences a stronger dynamic deformation than with the classical technique of performing a giant rotation. Figure 19 shows a dynamogram of the efforts of a gymnast's interaction with the bar when performing a backward giant circle on the basis of the thrust technique and in the classical version (without thrust).

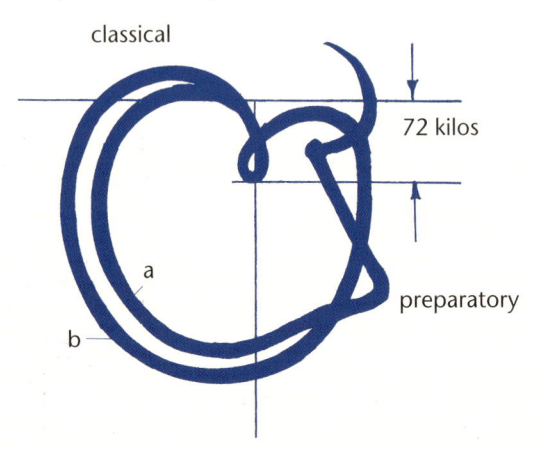

Figure 19 – *Dynamogram of efforts of interactions with the bar when performing a circle on the high bar a) with thrust technique b) with classical technique*

We have to say that the modern technique of performing giant rotations is biomechanically sound and sensible. In the classical version the speed lost by the gymnast in straightening the body after thrust is regained when exiting from handstand after passing the upper vertical. In the modern version the speed accumulated by the end of the thrust when passing the upper zone of movement is lost to a much less degree. Moreover, the gymnast has no need to 'catch' the moment of the start of the swing phase. He straightaway falls into the necessary position. What is more, a more powerful interaction with the bar at the moment of the so-called thrust receives correspondingly a more powerful gain from the bar in the following phase of movement, which helps the CoM thrust.

When moving from below upwards the overall bending and straightening of the body brings the gymnast's body CoM closer to the axis of rotation, which lessens the magnitude and action of gravity's pull (Figure 20). Therefore such technical actions are advantageous.

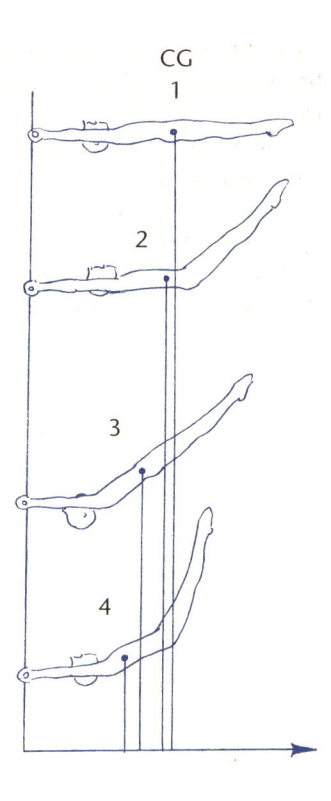

Figure 20 – *Bringing the centre of gravity closer to the axis of rotation when changing body position*

Without going into detail, let us note that bringing the body's mass of links and its CoM towards the axis of rotation accelerates rotation, and taking it further away slows it down (Figure 21). Intensive overall bending or straightening in the lower vertical zone produces the largest increment of speed of rotation. Thus, by actively altering the body position, the gymnast may control the speed of body rotation around the support axis.

We should make special note of the fact that movements in the joints located closer to the axis of the body's rotation, other things being equal, are always more effective from a mechanical viewpoint. Thus, if the gymnast bends in the shoulder joints from a straightened position, this to a large degree will bring his CoM closer to the axis of rotation than the same movement in the hip joints (Figures 21 and 22).

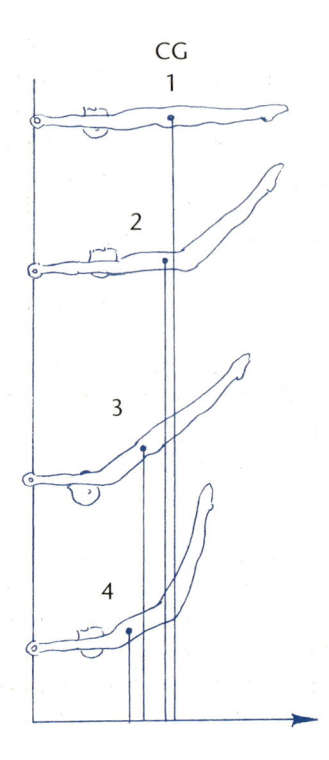

Figure 21 – *Changing the distance of centre of gravity from the axis of rotation when bending in 2) hips 3) shoulders 4) hips and shoulders*

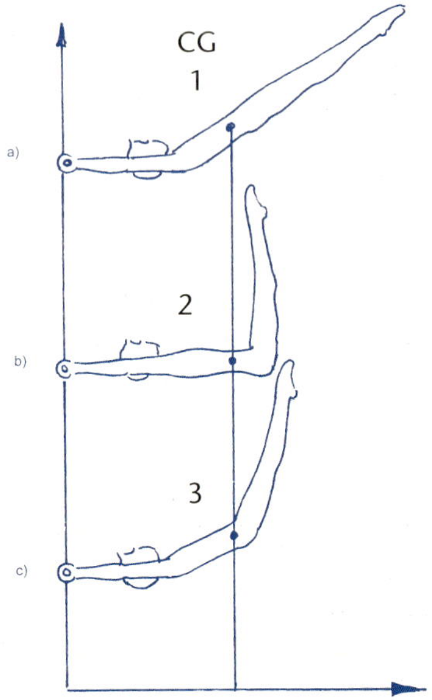

Figure 22 – *The same mechanical effect of bending in different joints*

One and the same mechanical effect when performing movements in long hang swing may be obtained through movement both in the shoulders and in the hips. In the latter case the gymnast needs a big amplitude of movement (Figures 22). Here the gymnast's body position will change more noticeably. The greater the speed of movement in both cases, the more will be the mechanical effect.

If both movements are carried out together, adding movement in the vertebral joints, the total effect will be greatest (21.4). Therefore, the basic control action is rarely localised in just a single joint.

For the muscles to contract more effectively, they should be previously stretched to a state of optimal arousal (see the stretch-reflex in Chapter 6.1). To these ends we perform a so-called 'start of a wave' when performing movements of big swing before the start of the main work action (thrust). This is active pulling away from support, hanging in the shoulders during the movement with simultaneous general bending and straightening of the body. By doing this we stretch the muscles of the front and back surface of the body (depending on what surface is the work surface).

As we showed in Chapter 6.1, the full kinetic energy of the gymnast's movement is equal to the sum of work of external and internal forces. The appearance of internal forces and their moments in the joints as a result of muscle work causes a shift of centres of mass and the links and gymnast's body CoM towards the axis of rotation. The mechanical work performed increases the kinetic energy of the gymnast's movement. The angular velocity of the body increases as a whole.

As a result of active change in body position after passing through the lower vertical, the gymnast compensates for the natural loss of kinetic energy through 'pumping' energy from inner sources. In this case at the moment of passing through handstand he has a supply of positive speed. Thus, as a result of contraction of previously stretched muscles in the appropriate joints there arise moments of force under the action of which the body's links begin to turn around their joint axes.

In which direction is it more favourable to turn – towards rotation of support links or in the opposite direction? At first glance it does not matter at all. General piking and arching produces a lessening of the distance from the CoM to the axis of rotation (Figure 20 b,c). In both cases the magnitude and action of the braking moment of the force of gravity will diminish. But that is only at first glance.

Let us look at control of the angular momentum of the multi-link system. In simplified form it may be represented in the form of a sum total of produced moments of inertia of the body's links and their angular velocity relative to the axis of rotation.

Analysis of this equation enables us to draw the following conclusions. If all or most mass links of the gymnast's body will turn around their joint axes towards the rotation of the link attached to the support, then the angular momentum of the gymnast's body will increase, and if in the opposite direction, it will diminish. So to increase this parameter and accelerate the gymnast's body rotation in forward swing he should bend in all joints, while in the back swing he should, conversely, straighten up.

For example, for a successful performance of a double and triple somersault backwards in tuck from the horizontal bar or a Kovacs fly-over we must create a big angular momentum at the moment of release. To do this the gymnast should bend in the shoulders, hips and vertebral joints in the phase of forward thrust (in forward swing) (Figure 23a). To perform the same dismounts with back swing in the phase of rear thrust the gymnast should quickly straighten up, arching in the shoulder and hip joints.

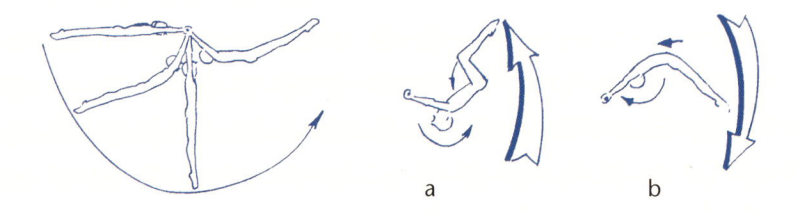

a   b

Figure 23 – *Acceleration (a) and deceleration (b) of rotating movements of the gymnast's body*

To slow down the swing he should act in a directly opposite way. For example, if at the end of the thrust in forward swing the gymnast actively straightens up, arching in the shoulder and hip joints, he can stop the body's rotation, and after ending connection with the support even begin to rotate in the opposite direction. This law is used when performing elements with change of direction of body rotation at the moment of exit from support.

At the core of the technique of performing such elements lies a powerful counter-tempo in the work stage of movement. Here he performs a so-called anti-courbette characterised by a total straightening during the release phase (Figure 23b) in the forward swing after total bending of the body in the thrust phase. Exercises of this type include such elements as the Tkatchev, the forward swing and forward somersault into hang (Xiao Ruizhi), swing forward and forward somersault dismount.

When performing similar forward swing exercises the reverse sequence of control actions comes into play. In this case the gymnast performs the so-called courbette. Exercises performed with back swing with counter-tempo include flight, fly-over of Voronin, Markelov and Yamawaki, back swing back somersault into hang (Figure 24).

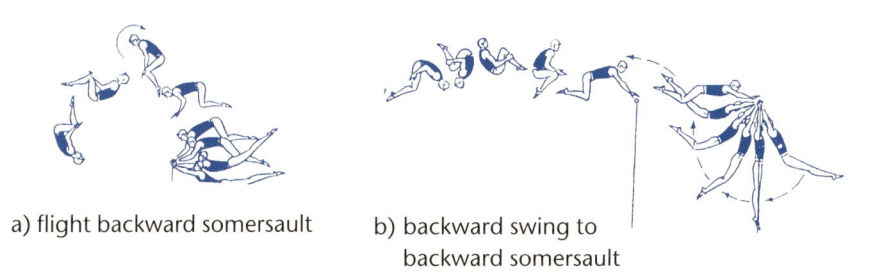

a) flight backward somersault

b) backward swing to backward somersault

Figure 24 – *Elements executed using the courbette*

Counter-tempo at the end of the forward swing is an important detail of the technique of performing the Tippelt on the parallel bars (Figure 25) which gymnasts often perform with loss of tempo when exiting into handstand. This error is caused by the fact that at the end of the forward swing the gymnast often forgets or does not have time to begin movement in the direction opposite to the thrust. Many do not even know that before lowering the arms they should begin to straighten out.

a) to handstand position

b) with forward somersault

Figure 25 – *The Tippelt*

When teaching the Tippelt, coaches usually do not pay enough attention to the final anti-courbette. This small control movement before lowering the arms enables us to perform the Tippelt without loss of tempo. In the opposite case gymnasts are forced to use strength when exiting into handstand, which results in reduction in marks. Coaches and gymnasts ought to remember that the Tippelt model on the parallel bars is a well-rotated Tkatchev with high arrival.

To perform a simultaneous change of grip from below into handstand by big forward swing on the horizontal bar the gymnast at the end of the thrust must sharply arch in the shoulder joints. If he does this fairly actively and timely, it will stop him precisely in the stand. If he does this too actively and early, he will not reach the stand.

If he does not do it at all, he will pass the position of handstand without stopping after changing hands, and this is a serious error. The same on the rings: if when performing a giant back rotation the gymnast does not arch his shoulder joints in time when exiting into handstand, he will not be able to stop and he will over rotate.

If when performing a vault of handspring and 2 and 1/2 forward somersault the gymnast begins early to tuck as he pushes off with his hands on the body of the horse, the most mass links of his body (trunk and legs) will begin to turn in a direction opposite to the overall body rotation (Figure 26b). Here the angular momentum of the gymnast's body at the moment of ending the connection with support will not increase, but decrease. The gymnast in flight will turn insufficiently quickly and will 'hang in the air' despite all his efforts. As a result he will not be able to perform a double somersault and land successfully. His landing normally ends in a large error.

When performing this vault, the links of the gymnast's body when he pushes off the body of the horse should turn in the direction of the body rotation in the next flight. Correct dismounts usually end with straightening the body at the moment of release. Here the reaction of the support is directed along the line connecting the point of support with the gymnast's body CoM (Figure 26a). This enables him to attain optimal combination between the initial velocity of flight and the angular momentum. He needs to tuck quickly, but only after ending connection with the support.

BIOMECHANICAL BASIS

A similar picture occurs when performing acrobatic jumps (27). If when thrusting off from support, for example, into a back somersault the arms are raised up, they turn in the direction of the turn of support links of the gymnast's body and his angular momentum increases at the moment of take-off. If these and other links (for example, the trunk) turn in the opposite direction, it diminishes.

When performing a take-off to forward somersault after a run-up or a handspring, the gymnast normally arrives in support in a somewhat arched position, and he leaves it in a straight position. In the interaction with support in the shoulder and vertebral joints he performs a rapid arching through to straightening (from an arched position), and performs a rapid straightening up in the hips and knees. In the ankle joints at this time he performs a quick extension of the foot (the angle in the ankle joints increases). With a good take-off the distal links of the gymnast's body turn forward at that moment. Here the angular momentum increases.

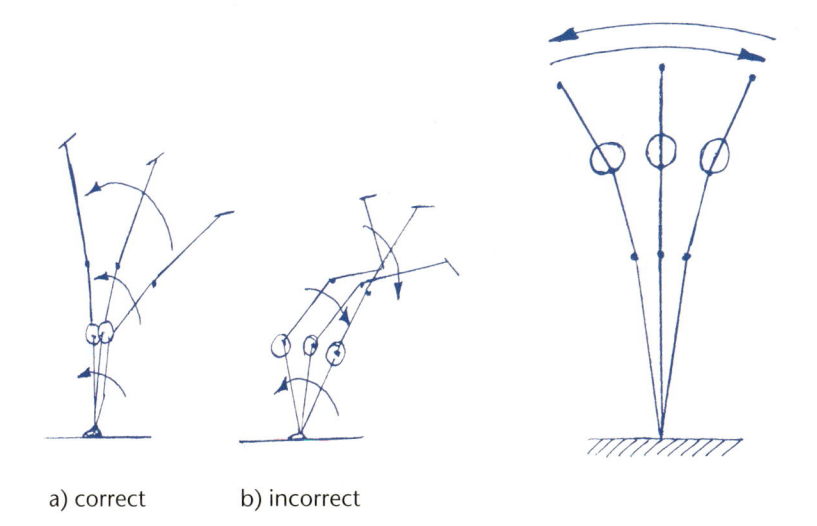

a) correct   b) incorrect

Figure 26 – *Push off from the horse*

Figure 27 – *The structure of take-off position when performing acrobatic somersaults*

It is important to understand that to increase (or decrease if necessary) the angular momentum provided from support on any apparatus what is important is not the angle of turn of the link or links, not the angular path that the gymnast passes through, but the angular velocity at the moment of letting go of the support.

Women coaches often forget this when teaching the Tkatchev fly-over on the asymmetrical bars. Many of them put the accent on magnitude of straightening at the moment of exit, and not the speed of overall straightening of the body at that moment (Figure 28). This is wrong, for, once having attained the anatomical maximum, the overall straightening of the body stops at the moment of letting go of the support. The links of the body stop turning towards the body rotation in flight. As a result the gymnast moves to an unsupported position with woefully insufficient rotation: she 'hangs in the air' and poorly (slowly) turns in flight.

This equally applies also to creating angular momentum relative to the longitudinal axis when double and triple twists are performed from support. Fairly often the gymnast turns a twist early from support. Here the speed of rotation of links around the longitudinal axis at the moment of letting go of the support begins to diminish, and even becomes zero because the reserve of turn of links around this axis is exhausted.

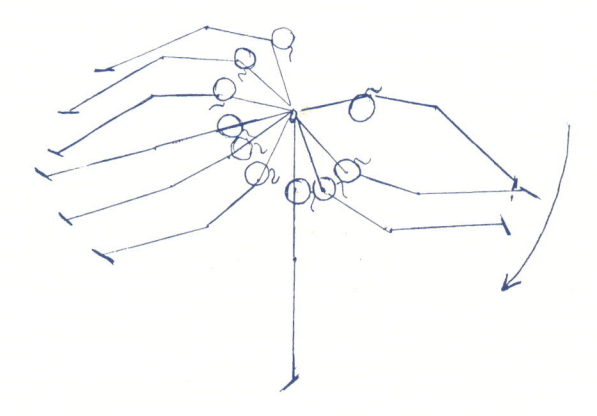

Figure 28 – *The Women's Tkatchev*

As a result insufficient angular momentum relative to the longitudinal axis is provided from support, the gymnast performs twists in flight insufficiently quickly and at the moment of landing normally does not come out of the twist in time. Moreover, early initiation of a twist in support considerably reduces the effectiveness of thrust off. This reduces both the height of flight and the speed of rotation in somersault. Insufficient twist in this case normally ends in an incomplete somersault.

So gymnasts should always strive to perform a full value take-off into somersault and only turn the twist at the end of it. Bearing in mind that all thrust off from support lasts in the order of 0.1-0.2 seconds, it is fairly difficult even for top-class gymnasts to correctly coordinate their actions in such a brief time.

The coach's maxim in this event should be: 'first come out of the somersault and only then do the twists immediately afterwards.' This maxim takes into consideration the mental state as well, in that with shortage of time gymnasts usually try to exceed the implementation of the coach's maxim. They usually work to outstrip what is necessary. In attempting correctly to carry out the coach's command – i.e. to perform twists straight after leaving support, they still start the rotation around the longitudinal axis in support, but now not early, but at the right moment. In this case the maximum angular velocity around this axis is attained precisely at the moment of take-off. As a result an angular momentum is given from support, which is necessary and sufficient for performing multiple twists in flight. All this equally applies to similar exercises in all forms of men's and women's multi-events.

The mechanism of thrust off from support when performing jumps/vaults lies in the following. The overall straightening of the gymnast's body as a result of contracting the appropriate muscles in interaction with the support causes acceleration of the CoM upwards. As this emerges there is a force acting downwards. This leads to an additional dynamic support reaction force acting upwards. If the gymnast raises his arms up as he thrusts off from support, he will gain additional constituent acceleration of the CoM upwards.

As a result, the efforts of interaction with support increase. As soon as the vertical reaction force exceeds the gymnast's weight, the vertical acceleration exceeds the downward acceleration due to gravity (9.81 m/s^2), and flight begins. The greater the initial vertical velocity of flight, the higher it will be. The work of the force of contracting muscles causing CoM acceleration upwards is precisely the reason for thrust off from support. The support reaction by itself does not cause movement upwards. It is not a moving force, but without it the vertical acceleration of the gymnast's body CoM could not happen.

Thus, direction and speed of rotation of the gymnast's body links in interaction with support are of crucial importance, especially at the moment of leaving the support.

We ought to make the point that even with a switched off system of internal self-control (the muscles do not work, the joint moments of force are zero) movement of a multi-link model of the human body under the action merely of external forces is very hard to forecast at the level of common physical sense. It is practically impossible to forecast how it will conduct itself mechanically, how it will change its configuration. For that we need to work out a mathematical model, write down movement equations, compile a program and generate movement models on the computer.

We have managed to reveal the following very interesting facts and laws by mathematical, computer and physical modelling of free movement of a three-link gymnast's body model (arms + trunk + legs) around the horizontal bar in the above-mentioned conditions, together with Khasin and his collaborators [72].

Both the physical and mathematical models of the gymnast's body when switching off internal self-regulation perform the same movements as the great bulk of gymnasts starting independently to master forward swings. The picture of actual and model movements in all cases was identical in structure (Figure 29).

It was as follows. Moving from a horizontal position from above downwards in a circular motion, individual (distal) links both of the physical and the mathematical models of the body begin to lag behind the support (proximal) links. Here the legs lag behind the trunk, and the trunk behind the arms. Their longitudinal axes form a broken bending line pointing downwards. An overall straightening of the body takes place. Thus, under the influence of only external forces both body models perform a typical phase of preparatory actions.

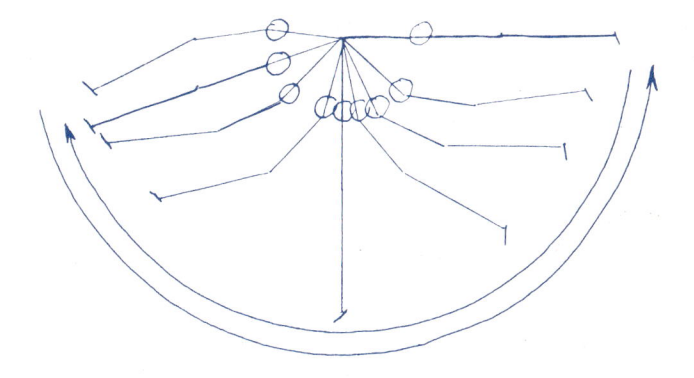

Figure 29 – *Structure of free swings on the high bar (real and model)*

When coming close to the lower vertical the legs begin to overtake the trunk, and the trunk the arms. The gymnast's body bends in the shoulders and hips, forming a broken concave line with a tendency to fall. This is a typical final position of the phase of basic work of actions (thrust) when actually performing forward swings on the horizontal bar.

Coming close to the end of the swing to the front horizontal, the legs and trunk of the physical and mathematical models of the gymnast's body again begin to lag behind the arms, forming a convex line of body with a tendency to move down. Both models perform a sort of lazy anti-courbette. The same is done by the great bulk of young gymnasts beginning to master swings. This is the most typical technical mistake when learning forward swings and giant swings backward in both men's and women's gymnastics. Here the coaches who teach the technique of giant swings normally tell their charges: 'Don't stick out your stomach at the end of thrust, keep it in.'

What is interesting here is that the structure of the first two phases of movement of the actual gymnast and his physical and mathematical models identically coincide with the normal technique of performing a giant swing on the horizontal bar. Once again we would underline the fact that movement of the models is done by switching off control and acting only by external forces. Hence the following conclusions:

- for a gymnast the natural movement is that with switched off internal self-control (joint moments are zero) and under the impact only of external forces. Here the form of the body and its configuration changes;

- the correct technical structure of the first two phases of the forward swing coincide in structure with the natural movement of the gymnast's body;

- in mastering swings gymnasts unconsciously switch off internal control of the movement. They relax their muscles and move under the influence of external forces;

- when learning giant swings the natural movement at the end of the swing leads to a technical error;

- by contrast with the natural movement, gymnasts perform the thrust actively and energetically;

- a more early and powerful straightening at the end of the forward swing typical of natural movement is replaced by a late and smooth straightening of the body while holding angles in the shoulder and hip joints after the thrust (if this is a giant circle). In the latter case the thrust is done seemingly with late straightening of the body in the horizontal position.

Interestingly enough, the above-described scheme of natural movement passively reproduces the technical structure of the support period of the Tkatchev. Only with a technically correct performance of this element on the horizontal bar are the above-described movements done later, more sharply and with great amplitude. Thus, against a background of natural uncontrolled movement the gymnasts create controlling joint moments of force. An increase in kinetic energy of movement in the direction of its natural development results from the inner muscle work they have done.

We should also note that gymnastic apparatus is elastic and this elasticity is regulated by competition rules [81, 82, 88]. The interaction of gymnasts with apparatus represents a variety of elastic interactions.

Each apparatus possesses its own frequency of vibration. When a gymnast performs an exercise on the apparatus, a biomechanical system of 'gymnast-apparatus' is formed which also has its own frequency of vibration. The gymnast's interaction with the apparatus causes the emergence of necessary vibrations in this system. The gymnast performs active technical actions in a set time and has his own frequency. If the frequencies of free and compulsory vibrations of the system coincide, there arises the phenomenon of resonance. Here the amplitude of vibrations of the system, its speed and kinetic energy sharply increase.

For example, when a gymnast hangs on the horizontal bar, there is formed a system of 'gymnast-horizontal bar'. This elastic system possesses its own frequency of free vibrations. We can observe them if we pull the gymnast by the feet. If we take the gymnast out of equilibrium and give him an initial swing, he will begin to swing like a pendulum with the frequency of his own oscillations. If the gymnast starts to perform bending-straightening movements during the swing, he will sharply increase the swing's amplitude in the event that the frequency of free and compulsory vibrations of the system coincide.

If we change the time and magnitude of efforts when performing control movements, we may select the variant when the frequency of free and compulsory vibrations of the system will be fully synchronized and then the kinetic energy of movement will considerably rise. The effectiveness of control movements in the sense of emergence of resonance depends on the elasticity of the apparatus, the gymnast's biological characteristics and his mass, as well as the time, point of application and magnitude of effort of interaction with the bar.

The mechanism of resonance phenomena underlies the technique of performing movements of the thrust off and pulling in type, as well as all swing exercises on the apparatus [30, 59, 80, 76, 78 etc].

The biomechanical laws we have seen with the example of the horizontal bar apply also to other apparatus. But in each multi-event the exercises have their specific peculiarities.

6.2.2   Exercises on the Parallel Bars

The specifics of exercises performed with swing in support on the parallel bars consist in that as the gymnast performs them the shoulders together with the arms make a return-progressive movement like an inverted pendulum relative to the bars on which the hands are fixed. Here the gymnast's body makes a rotating or pendulum-type movement of his body around the axis of the shoulder joints. Thus, a double pendulum may serve as a mechanical model of exercises of this type. The shift of arms together with shoulders may be seen as a transferable movement, while the rotating movement of the body around the axis of shoulder joints is a relative movement.

In the relative rotating movement the moment of the force of gravity in relation to the axis of the shoulder joints acts on the gymnast's body, which causes rotation of the trunk together with the legs around that axis. In moving from above downwards this moment overtakes the gymnast and he must not resist its action. When moving from below up it slows down the movement and the gymnast must actively work to create control moments of force in the shoulder joints so as to accelerate the swing (Figure 30).

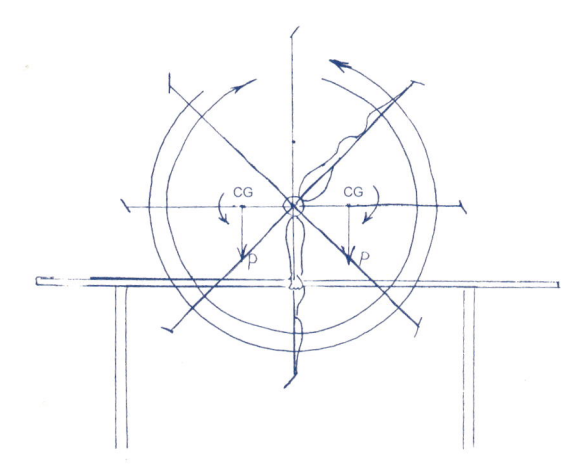

Figure 30 — *The relative movement of the gymnast's body around the shoulder axis when performing swings on the parallel bars*

BIOMECHANICAL BASIS

In the transferable movement the moment of force of gravity of the gymnast's body is applied to the support axis passing through the point of grip. It turns the gymnast's body around that axis clockwise when he moves from above down and in the opposite direction when he moves from below up (Figure 31).

If, when moving from above down, the gymnast tries all the time to hold back the shoulders above the support, the moment of force of gravity will be so great that the gymnast will not be able to hold on to the bars and will fall back (Figure 31). Therefore, at the start of the movement from handstand the gymnast must slightly let his shoulders forward so as to ensure a free, rapidly accelerating swing with a good feel for the support. The less the shoulders go forward, the more the amplitude of swing and the more fully external forces will be used.

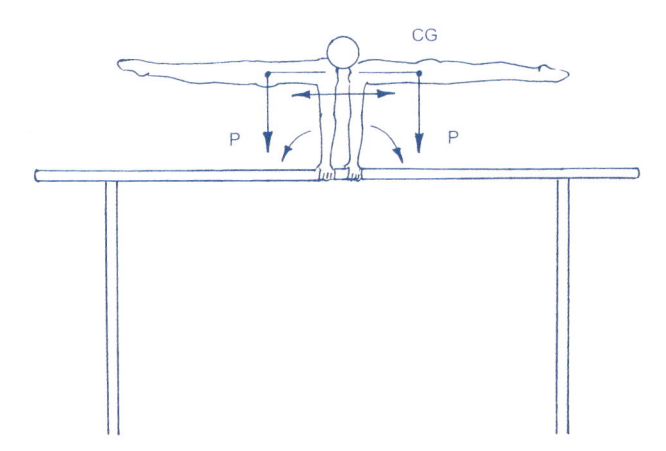

Figure 31 – *Transfer movement when performing swings on the parallel bars*

The maximum angle between the arms and the vertical varies within the boundaries of 30°. It comes at the moment when the gymnast's body passes the horizontal position (Figure 32). After that the shoulders must start to move in the opposite direction (back). If that does not happen, at the moment of or after passing the lower vertical position there arises a negative moment of force due to gravity and the gymnast will be pressed against the bars and he will fall with shoulders forward.

Figure 32 – *Technical structure of the forward swing on the parallel bars*

At the lowest point of swing the shoulders must be above the support point. If with the start of the movement from below upwards the gymnast tries to hold the shoulders above the support or lets them forward again, the speed of rotation of the body will begin to diminish. To avoid that, the gymnast must continue the shoulder movement back and end it at the moment when the body will be horizontally oriented.

Following that, actively pressing on the bars, the gymnast must let the shoulders forward i.e. begin their movement in the opposite direction, trying to swing as high as possible with a good grip on the support.

Pendulum-like arm movement may be coordinated so that the gymnast's body CoM all the time shifts along the support vertical. Here the moment of force of gravity relative to the support axis will all the time be zero. This is not advantageous when the movement is from above down, since the angular momentum of the gymnast's body will be determined only by rotation of the links around his CoM. And when moving from below upwards this is advantageous. There is no negative angular velocity and the angular momentum is retained. Here the vertical velocity of the CoM at the moment of release for the somersault will be directed vertically upwards, which ensures maximum height of flight.

Figure 33 –
Photo-cyclogram of somersault above the bars

The gymnast should let his shoulders forward when moving from handstand to the horizontal position to a lesser degree than when moving them back after passing the lower vertical position. At the moment of passing the horizontal position from the front the gymnast should stop letting the shoulders back and start moving them forward. If he does not do this and continues to move the shoulders back, the body CoM in the flight phase will be moved back and it will be very hard to arrive precisely in handstand or landing.

Figure 33 shows a photo-cyclogram of a Stutz, obtained by the method of stroboscopic stereo-photography. As we can see, the trajectory of movement of the gymnast's body support points represent practically correct ellipses which testifies to what was said above. When performing movements of back swing in support the picture is repeated in reverse sequence (Figure 34).

Figure 34 – *Technical structure of the backswing on the parallel bars*

Exercises performed with swing from support on the upper arms represent rotating movements of the body (trunk together with the head and legs) around the axis of shoulder joints which are fixed by the hands on the bars. The laws here are the same as on the horizontal bar. The specifics here is that with uprises into support the gymnast actively presses his hands on the bars.

The greater the amplitude of the swing and the stronger the hand press, the greater the speed with which the gymnast arrives in support and the greater the possibilities immediately after the uprise to perform the following complex element in support. For example, uprise with forward swing and turn round into handstand, also + Diamidov (Richards), also + somersault over the bars, uprise with back swing + 'behind the feet', etc. In support on the upper arms the gymnast may perform also elements in counter-tempo (for instance, uprise with back swing and back somersault into upper arm support (Figure 35)).

Figure 35 – *Backward swing and backward somersault from upper arm support*

6.2.3 Exercises on the Rings

A characteristic of movements performed with giant swing on the rings is the presence of two supports: mobile (rings) and fixed (the frame to which the rings are attached). By contrast with all other apparatus, the gymnast interacts with a fixed support through an auxiliary mobile link. The pendulum-type movement of the rings represents a transferable movement, while the gymnast's movement about the rings is relative.

If in the starting position the rings are fixed and there is no movement, when performing swing exercises the CoM trajectories of the gymnast's body represent vertical sections located in the plane of the rings suspended below its central axis.

When performing giant rotation from handstand the ropes of the rings incline forwards from the vertical position. Here the moment of force of gravity whose magnitude changes just as on the horizontal bar arises relative to the axis of grip. As a result its actions in moving the gymnast's body away make an accelerated rotating movement around the rings, while its CoM falls downwards, shifting along the vertical straight and the perpendicular axis of the rings frame.

The inclining of the rings forward reaches its maximum at the moment when the gymnast passes the horizontal position. Then the ropes of the rings shift in the opposite direction and, at the moment when the gymnast passes the vertical position at the lowest point of the swing, the rings again take a vertical orientation. Here the moment of force of gravity relative to the rings is zero. After that it changes its sign, putting a brake on the speed of movement of the gymnast's body CoM.

When moving from below up, the picture is repeated in a mirror image: the ropes of the rings continue to bend from the vertical backwards. After that the rings change direction of movement into the opposite direction and, moving forward, again take a vertical orientation at the moment when the gymnast again fixes the handstand.

A certain similarity exists in ring movement with hand movement when performing swings in support on the parallel bars. In both cases there is a transferable pendulum-type movement, coinciding in phase. Only on the rings this movement is uncontrolled, irrespective of the will and action of the gymnast, while on the parallel bars it is directable: here the gymnast can control the shifting of shoulder joints forward and back.

When moving from above down the vertical velocity of progressive movement of the gymnast's body CoM increases. At the lowest vertical position it should return to zero, otherwise the gymnast will fall off the apparatus. Here the gymnast's body experiences a dynamic impulse when one part of the kinetic energy of the progressive movement shifts into the rotating component, while the other is absorbed by the 'gymnast-apparatus' system and moves into other forms of energy.

If the gymnast will fall freely downwards from handstand without changing body position, he is likely to fall from the apparatus below. To lighten the action of the dynamic impulse and use it for the good, the gymnast should perform certain control movements. If his body at the moment of dynamic impulse was not straightened fully, under the impact his joint angles will quickly be eliminated. Here there arises additional angular velocity of the links. When their direction coincides with that of the dynamic rotation of the body, the angular momentum of the gymnast's body increases. In the opposite case the rotation of the body slows down.

The gymnast straightens up to lighten the dynamic impulse downwards when performing movements with big swing forward. Here the body together with the arms take a convex shape. When performing the movements with a big swing back they arch so that the body takes a concave form. Thus, as on the horizontal bar, a swing is performed followed by thrust. And these movements are also natural, as on the horizontal bar. A specific feature of the swing when performing a giant rotation on the rings is that it is performed earlier than on the horizontal bar with an accent on hanging in the shoulders.

When moving from below up after the downwards swing the body's CoM repeats its trajectory in the other direction. The appearance of vertical CoM velocity directed upwards after it has become zero at the moment of passing the lower vertical position is caused by the body's rotating movement around the rings. It continues in the same direction thanks to the angular momentum created from handstand as a result of the action of the moment of force of gravity.

However, if the gymnast remains in the straightened position, the speed of rotation and the vertical speed of CoM begin quickly to diminish. Therefore, at the moment of passing the lower vertical the gymnast performs a swing with arching in the shoulder and hip joints, accelerating rotation around the rings. The swing is completed with straightening the body at the time that arching in the shoulder joints still continues until an angle of roughly 45° in relation to the trunk. After that the gymnast turns the rings round and, powerfully pressing on them with the hands, performs a movement in the other direction in the shoulder joints. Through this he arrives in handstand (Figure 36a).

When performing a giant rotation forward the described picture is repeated in reverse order (Figure 36b). Figure 37 shows the actual trajectory of the gymnast's shift in CoM while performing the giant forward rotation. One should draw attention to the fact that when passing the lower vertical position, the sequence drawing of the gymnast's body shift forms a typical loop enabling him to reduce the consequences of the dynamic impulse.

The biomechanical experiments we have conducted have shown that the magnitude of efforts of interaction with the support in doing giant rotations from handstand diminishes and becomes zero in 0.5 seconds after the start of the movement away. In another 0.3 seconds the reaction of support becomes equal to the gymnast's weight. After that in 0.1 seconds it reaches its maximum in the lowest vertical position (330 kg) and in the following 0.1 seconds it again becomes equal to the gymnast's weight in absolute magnitude. In another 0.5 seconds the reaction of the support returns to zero. In the final position it again becomes equal to the weight of the gymnast. The dynamic part of the exercise lasts some 2 seconds. Figure 38 shows a dynamogram of the giant back rotation on the rings [45].

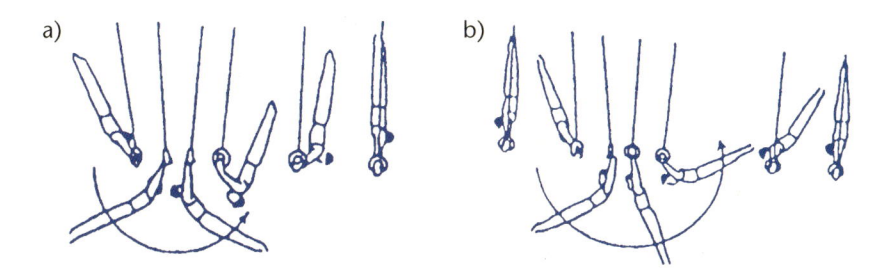

Figure 36 – *Technical structure of giant circle on the rings a) backwards b) forwards*

How to Create Champions

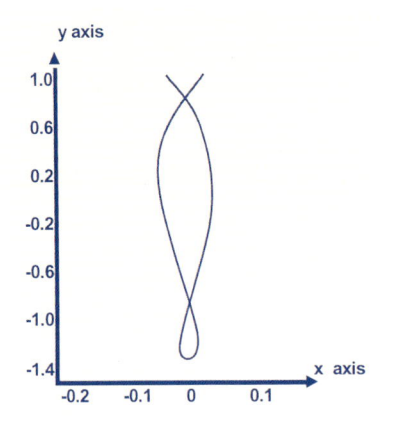

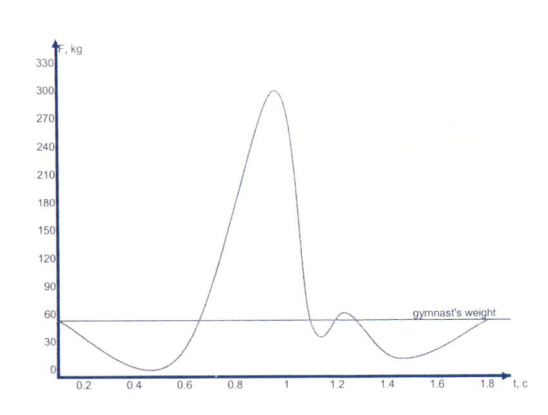

Figure 37 – Trajectory of Centre of Gravity when performing giant circle on the rings

Figure 38 – Dynamogram of the giant circle backwards on the rings

When performing the push away from handstand the gymnast's body CoM vertical velocity grows in absolute magnitude. It reaches its maximum (4.0-4.5 ms^{-1}) in 0.85 seconds after the start of the giant rotation when the gymnast is roughly in the middle of the second quadrant. Then in 0.1 seconds it becomes zero in the lowest vertical position. After that, having changed its direction into the opposite way, the CoM speed in 0.14 seconds reaches its maximum (in the order of 5 ms^{-1}) at the moment when the CoM is roughly at the level of the rings. In 0.5-0.6 seconds it becomes zero. The horizontal velocity of the gymnast's body CoM while performing exercises all the time is close to zero as long as the rings do not shake. Figures 39 display graphs of the absolute velocity of the gymnast's body CoM when performing giant swing forwards on the rings.

Figure 40 – Velocity of the Centre of Gravity while performing a giant circle forwards on the rings

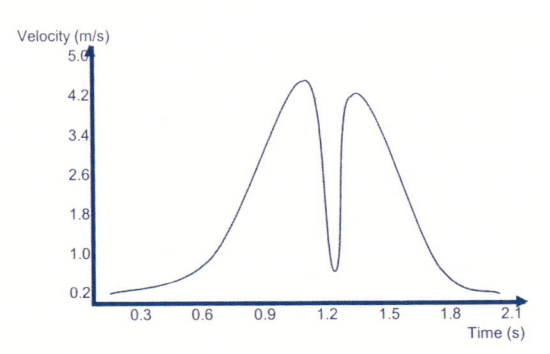

260

6.2.4 Exercises on the Asymmetric Bars

Exercises on the women's parallel bars are exercises on two unequally-high horizontal bars (as in the circus). The difference consists in that these horizontal bars are bigger in diameter. The second specific feature is that when performing giant swings mature women gymnasts have to bend at the hips or straddle their legs when leaving the top bar so as not to make contact with the lower. The third feature is the presence of a large number of fly-overs from the top bar to the lower bar and back. The technique here changes, but not so much as to become acutely different from the technique of performing exercises on the horizontal bar.

6.2.5 Exercises on the Beam

Exercises on the beam are a variety of acrobatic jumps with choreographic elements and turns. The technique of acrobatic jumps on the beam is similar to jumps on the runway with the only difference that these jumps are done on a narrow and hard support. Here the legs are not together, but one behind the other. An important part of the technique on this apparatus is retention of balance. For the gymnast not to fall from the beam as a result of losing balance she needs acrobatic jumps and combinations that are fairly fast, without stopping.

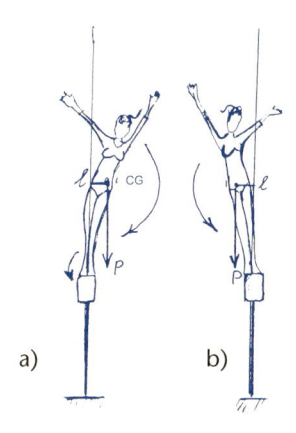

Figure 40 – *Losing balance on the beam (fall off moments)*

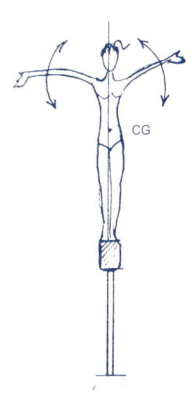

Figure 41 – *Balancing with the arms to retain equilibrium on the beam*

Loss of equilibrium is characterised by the fact that the gymnast's CoM leaves the effective base of support and forms a toppling moment of force of gravity (Figure 40a and b). To return to a position of equilibrium the mechanically most effective movements are in the joints close to the support. However, the slightest mistake when performing a control movement in the ankle joints leads to falling to the other side. So the gymnast normally balances on the beam, using arm movements the performance of which makes the scope of acceptable movements wider (Figure 41).

6.3   Movement in Flight

6.3.1   Basic Parameters of Flight

When performing exercises with a flight phase the objective of the technical actions in support consists of creating conditions necessary for executing a required form of movement in flight. What conditions are they? At speeds with which the gymnast's body CoM moves in flight (less than 10 ms^{-1}) air resistance is taken as being negligible. In that case the only external force acting on the gymnast in flight is the force of gravity applied to its CoM.

The gymnast's movement in the unsupported period of exercise is complicated. It includes transferable progressive movement together with the gymnast's body CoM and the relative rotating movement about the CoM. According to the above-mentioned principle of independence of movement we can view them independently of each other.

The path of the CoM is defined by the velocity at the moment of losing contact with support, while the rotating movement is the angular momentum. Both these parameters are vector quantities – ie they have a magnitude and a direction. They are given from the support. The gymnast cannot change them by his actions in flight. So the velocity of the gymnast's body CoM at the moment of letting go of support and its angular momentum are the basic parameters of flight. The first parameter gives the trajectory of CoM movement in flight, its height, length and time, while the second represents the gymnast's body rotating movement.

6.3.2 Projectile Movement

No matter what the gymnast does in flight he can no longer alter the trajectory of projectile movement of his CoM. He needs some external force to act on him in flight (coach, partner). In general the trajectory of the projectile movement of the gymnast's body in flight represents a curve which we call parabolic (Figure 42). Its form depends on the mechanical state of the gymnast's body at the moment of letting go of the support. This state is determined by the velocity of the gymnast's body CoM, its direction (angle of fly-off) and CoM coordinates at the moment of departure.

In movement in a horizontal direction no force at all acts on the gymnast in flight. So the law of conservation of amount of movement in the horizontal direction comes into play. So the horizontal component of the velocity of projectile movement of the gymnast's body CoM in flight does not change.

In the first part of flight the gymnast's body CoM shifts upwards with negative acceleration (equal to -9.81 ms^{-2}). Accordingly, we have a passive loss of vertical CoM velocity independent of the gymnast's will and actions. At the upper point of flight it becomes equal to zero. The kinetic energy of vertical projectile movement after departure turns into potential energy which attains its maximum in the dead phase of flight. The vertical component of kinetic energy of the body's projectile movement at that moment turns to zero.

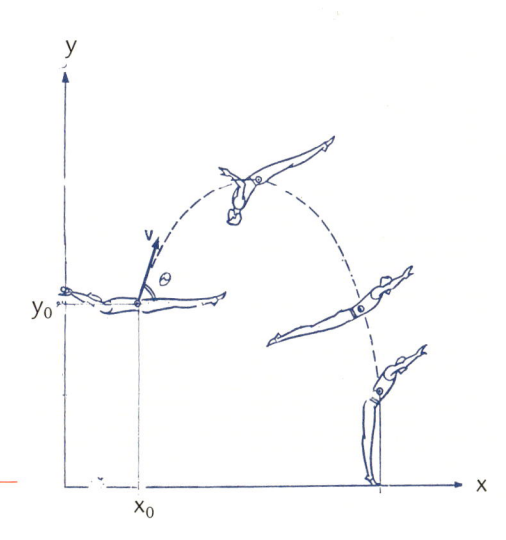

Figure 42 – *Trajectory of the centre of gravity in flight*

In the second part of flight we have a passive transfer of potential energy into kinetic energy of free fall that does not depend on the gymnast's will and action. This is caused by a uniformly accelerated increase in the vertical velocity of the gymnast's body CoM with an acceleration equal to +9.81 m/s^{-2}. Owing to this the gymnast's body trajectory in flight is divided into two branches – the rising and the falling.

If we define the magnitude and direction of CoM velocity at the moment of take off, we may forecast its coordinates at any moment of flight, including its maximum height and length. If the CoM height at the moment of arrival and take off are the same (as, for example, when performing acrobatic jumps well), then the time of CoM rise to the dead point is equal to the time of free fall from this point. Calculations have shown that the increase in the full time of flight from 1.0 s to 1.05 s (+0.05 s) gives an increment in height of the rise of 12 cm. If we increase the height of the apparatus by 1 m, this increases the time of flight by 0.17 s, while its increase by 2 m gives an increment of time of flight of 0.31 s.

A large part of the form of movement that determines the name of the flight or dismount normally is performed above the apparatus. Thus, for example, gymnasts do two and a half somersaults above the horizontal bar when doing a good triple somersault.

6.3.3 Rotating Movement

The second component of the gymnast's movement in flight is rotating movement. According to the principle of independence of movement, this movement may be seen around the gymnast's body CoM as acting about an immoveable point. The body's rotating movement is determined by the second basic parameter of flight – the angular momentum which is fixed at the moment of losing contact with the support. The gymnast cannot change its magnitude and direction by his actions in flight. To do so we need an external moment of force to act on him. It can arise as a result of the coach's help after the gymnast has left the apparatus.

With rare exceptions top-class gymnasts perform flight without external assistance. Since the only external force equal to the force of gravity is applied to the CoM, its moment relative to this point in flight all the time is zero. So the law of conservation of the angular momentum (H) of the gymnast's body operates in flight (see Chapter 6.1).

$$H = I\omega \text{ (const)}$$

Where I is the moment of the body's inertia, ω is the angular velocity, const is constant.

In the unsupported position gymnasts perform a rotating movement of two types – the simple and the complex.

6.3.3.1 Simple Rotating Movement

A simple rotating movement is rotation only around one main central axis (usually around the transverse, more rarely around the anterior-posterior and longitudinal). When performing simple rotations the direction of the angular momentum given from support coincides with one of these axes. An egg turning on the table around a fixed point gives some idea of a simple rotating movement by the gymnast's body (Figure 43).

By contrast with the linear velocity of progressive movement of CoM, the gymnast may control the angular velocity of his rotating movement in flight. The principle of control of rotating movement is based on the law of conservation of the angular momentum. Its mechanism becomes clear if the equation of the angular momentum is written as follows:

$$\omega = \frac{H \text{ (const)}}{I}$$

Where the letters are as designated above. By changing his body position the gymnast changes the magnitude of moment of inertia (J) relative to the rotating axis. Accordingly he changes his angular velocity (ω) in relation to that axis.

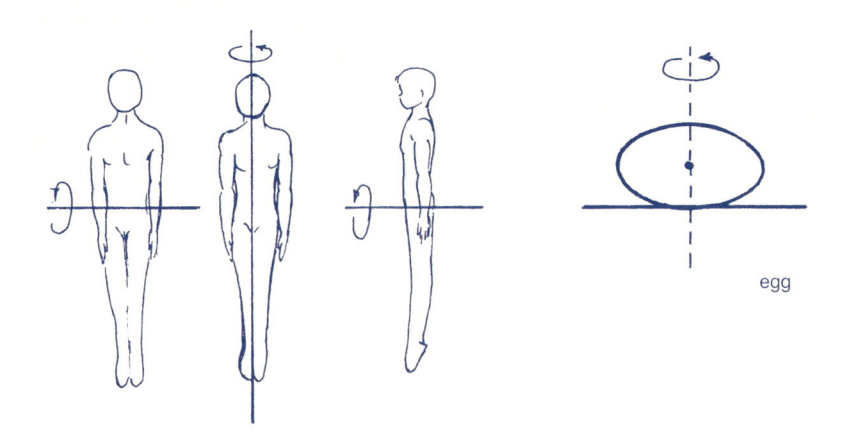

Figure 43 – *Simple rotating movement*

For example, when tucking from a straight position in flight, the gymnast reduces the moment of inertia of his body relative to the transverse axis three-fold. Owing to the law of conservation of angular momentum the speed of rotation of his body will increase by the same amount. In straightening out after landing he increases the moment of inertia and thereby reduces the speed of rotation. The lowest value of moment of inertia relative to the transverse axis of the body is in a position of compact tuck, and the highest is when the body is fully straightened out with arms upwards.

If, for example, when doing a triple somersault, the gymnast slowly tucks/groups and fixes his body position with a non-compact tuck, then, other things being equal, he will have to straighten out later in flight. In the opposite case he will have to give from support a big angular momentum for a timely completion of the triple somersault in flight. With the same angular momentum in flight the angular velocity may be increased if the gymnast's body is taut during rotation (see Chapter 6.1).

If the angular momentum is given from support around the longitudinal axis, then as the gymnast straightens his body and presses his arms to it in flight, he reduces the moment of inertia relative to the longitudinal axis. The speed of rotation around it grows. Spreading the arms to the sides while bending and straightening the body increases the moment of inertia. The angular velocity around the longitudinal axis slows down. But it is impossible fully to stop rotation in flight in this case.

Sometimes when observing various tuck somersaults we gain the illusion that some link in the flight stops rotating. For example, this picture may be seen with a good execution of a support vault with turn into 2.5 forward somersault. After leaving the horse in the process of tuck, the hips somehow stop their rotation in flight, and the trunk catches up with them. This illusion is the result of the formation of angular velocities. Here the angular velocity of the body's rotation caused by the angular momentum set from support is summarised with the angular velocity of rotation of links relative to each other, arising as a result of tucking in flight.

Coaches and gymnasts must know that in the unsupported position they must not bring the legs towards the trunk or, conversely, the trunk to the legs. Because of the law of conservation of the basic angular momentum in flight when bending the trunk and legs will shift in counter directions (see also the second means of forming a complex rotation in the next section). Here the angular velocities of the trunk and legs will be roughly equal in magnitude and be in the opposite direction.

However, when performing a given support vault, the support gives the angular momentum through which the gymnast's body in flight rotates forward. If the gymnast does not change his body position after leaving the horse, the angular velocities of trunk and legs will be equal. If the gymnast against the background of general body rotation bends forward or tucks, the trunk and legs will have additional angular velocities of the opposite direction. Here the relative angular velocity of the trunk merges with its transferable velocity, and the angular velocity of the trunk grows. In the meantime the angular velocity of the legs diminishes – ie their transferable angular velocity will take into consideration the relative speed of bending where the legs turn in the opposite direction (Figure 44). If the angular velocity of transferable and relative movement are the same, we get an illusion of the legs stopping rotation in flight where the trunk seems to catch up with them [56].

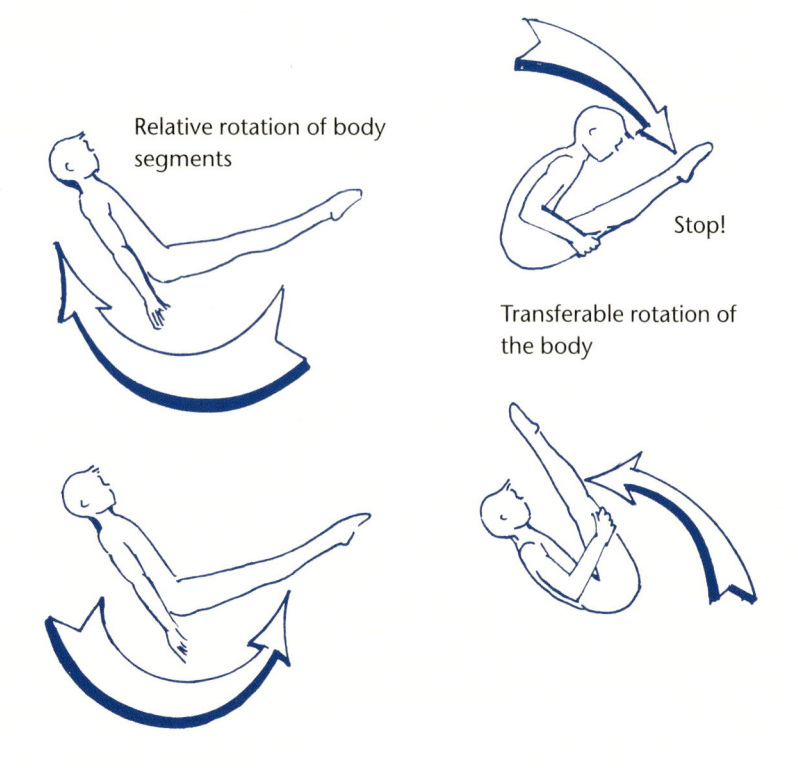

Figure 44 – *The effect of tucking on angular velocity*

Thus, the mechanical essence of the coach's advice is: 'In flight place your legs on your shoulders, and bring your shoulders up to your legs.' He is requiring the gymnast to coordinate his actions so that the angular velocity of his body as a whole, and the angular velocity relative to leg movement in the opposite direction, arising as a result of tucking in flight, are equal.

Other things being equal, the angular velocity in flight depends on the nature of the gymnast's interaction with the support and the mechanical state of his body at the moment of losing contact with it.

6.3.3.2 Complex Rotating Movement

A complex rotating movement generally represents a simultaneous turn immediately around three body axes: *precession, nutation and one's own rotation* (Figure 45). In mechanics this is regarded as the body turning around a point. For example, the gymnast's body in free flight does a complex rotating movement around a point coinciding with its CoM. This is typical of a somersault with turns around the longitudinal axis. One may get some idea of the complex rotating movement of the body in flight from observing a children's top (Figure 46). The top turns around its own longitudinal axis with an angular velocity of its own rotation. This axis in turn does a conical rotating movement around the vertical axis with an angular velocity of precession. The angle between these two axes generally also changes with an angular velocity of nutation.

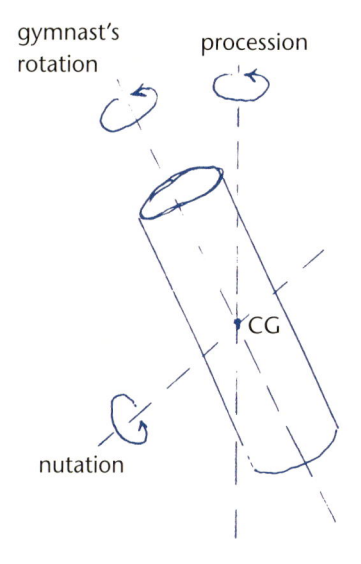

Figure 45 – Complex rotating movement

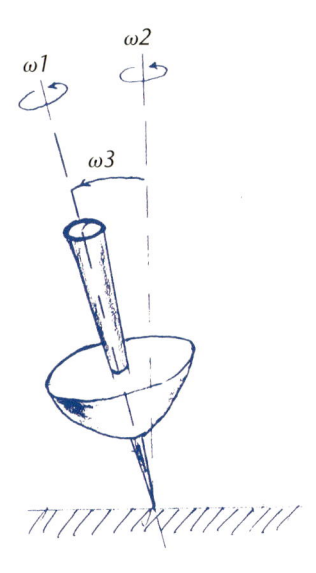

Figure 46 – The movement of the spinning top ($\omega 1$ – angular velocity of one's own rotation, $\omega 2$ – angular velocity of precessions, $\omega 3$ – angular velocity of nutation)

We know three principal ways of creating a complex rotating movement in an unsupported position:

1. setting simultaneous rotation by somersault and by twist from support;
2. bending movements in the spinal column of the 'hula-hoop' type in flight;
3. asymmetrical movement of the arms in flight.

They are all based on the law of conservation of the basic angular momentum, but they have different mechanisms. Normally either all three at once, or the last two are used together and simultaneously.

6.3.3.2.1 First Means of Forming a Complex Rotation

When setting a simultaneous rotation in somersault and twist from support, the longitudinal axis of the body describes in flight a conical surface inclining towards a plane in which the CoM shifts. If we look at it full face we see that the gymnast seems to lie on his side in flight, and then before landing straightens out. This is particularly clear when performing a somersault with turn of 720° and 1080° (from support (Figure 47) [58,59]. Coaches, gymnasts and judges have precisely to understand the mechanism of this phenomenon. Otherwise the objective laws of the complex rotation in flight may be qualified as errors.

When the rotation is set from support immediately around the transverse and longitudinal axes, the gymnast's body in flight turns around an instantaneous axis of rotation whose direction in space and in the gymnast's own body constantly changes. By contrast with a simple single axis rotation, the body in this case turns around a point.

A free movement of a heavy hard body around a point coinciding with it is called the Euler-Puanso case. It has a classical geometrical interpretation giving a simple and visual idea of the form of the body's movement in space. The central ellipsoid of inertia is the major operating entity in Puanso's structure. In its form it is rather like a regular egg repeating the gymnast's body configuration. In the anatomical position it is extended in the direction of the longitudinal axis and flattened in the direction of the transverse and anterior-posterior axes.

If the rotation is created in support simultaneously around the transverse and longitudinal axes of the gymnast's body, angular momentum will arise relative to them. The basic angular momentum is their geometrical sum total at the moment of losing contact with the support. By contrast with a simple rotation, its direction no longer coincides with one of the body's principal axes (Figure 48).

As applied to a gymnast's movement in flight, the essence of Puanso's geometrical interpretation consists in the following (Figure 49) [58,59]. Let us construct a plane perpendicular to the direction of the main vector of the angular momentum and place it so that one of its points touches the central ellipsoid of the body's inertia at the moment of losing contact with the support. Since the basic angular momentum in flight retains a constant direction, this plane, called the Puanso plane, will also retain a constant orientation.

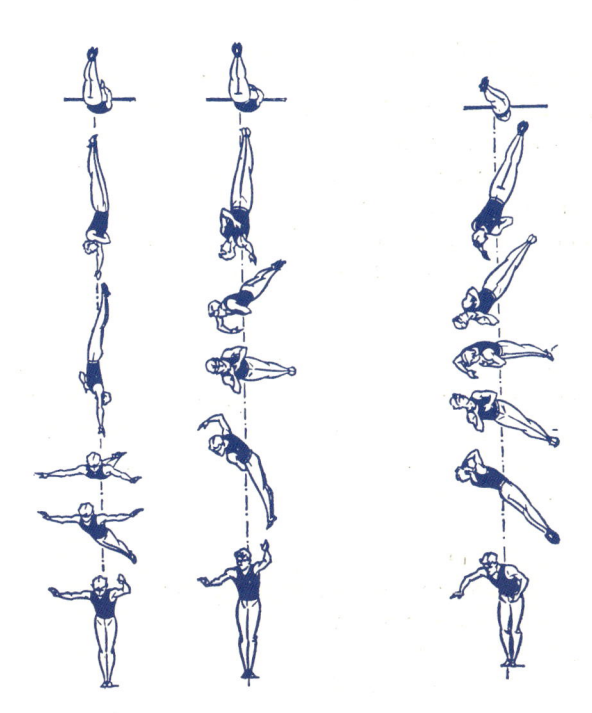

Figure 47 – *Dismounts with twists from the horizontal bar from the front (Suchilin, 1972)*

Now, if we roll along this plane without slipping in an ellipsoid of inertia so that the distance from its centre to the plane remains unchanged, we obtain a visual image of the body's rotating movement in flight in a fixed position.

The line connecting the centre of the ellipsoid with the point where it touches the Puanso plane determines the direction of the instantaneous axis of rotation.

A sideways inclination of the longitudinal axis when performing a somersault with twists done from support is an inevitable phenomenon. The more the rotation around the longitudinal axis is given from support, the more this axis will incline away from the plane in which the body's CoM shifts in flight and the more the gymnast will lie on his side from the standpoint of the fixed observer (Figure 47). And this must not be regarded as an error.

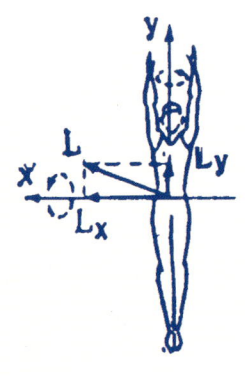

Figure 48 – *Resultant vector of the angular momentum*

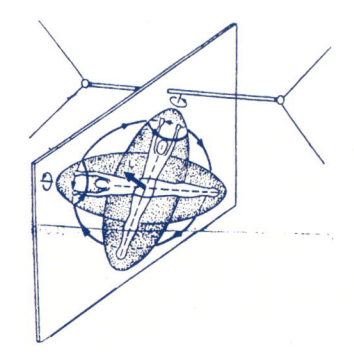

Figure 49 – *The Puanso structure on the horizontal bar*

It ought to be stated that, by contrast with acrobatic jumps, when performing dismounts with twists from the apparatus (horizontal bar, parallel bars, rings), the gymnast lets go of the support at the moment when his body is oriented horizontally or near it. In this case he performs not a full turn of 360° around the transverse axis, not a full somersault, but only three quarters of it. So the longitudinal axis of the gymnast's body at the moment of landing does not return to the starting position and remains inclined towards the plane of CoM transference, which makes a stable landing difficult. When performing full somersaults in free exercises the longitudinal axis when landing returns to the starting position. It is therefore easier to stick the landing.

Theoretical calculations we have made show that when observing the full spectrum of acrobatic somersaults with turns from support of 360°, 720°, 1080° and 1440°, the maximum angle of incline of the longitudinal axis of the gymnast's body in flight towards the horizontal will vary within the bounds of 10°-18°, 28°-50°, and 37°-63° respectively. When observing the same dismounts from the horizontal bar, rings and women's asymmetric bars the scale of the angle of incline will be quite different: 13°-23°, 25°-45°, 37°-63° and 48°-79° respectively. Thus, when giving a twist rotation from support the minimal sideways incline of the longitudinal axis of the gymnast's body in flight should come into effect when performing a somersault with a turn of 360°, while the maximal will be when performing a somersault with a turn of 1440° (four twists).

The body has its maximum sideways incline after performing half a somersault, when the gymnast's orientation in flight is close to the horizontal. After that when doing acrobatic jumps it falls to zero, and when doing dismounts the somersault with triple and quadruple twists remains very significant before landing (as long as the necessary twist rotation is given from support and the body position in flight does not change).

If the turn from support is done to the left, the upper part of the body in flight will lean to the left, and if to the right then it will lean to the right. This will happen from the viewpoint of a person observing the flight full face from the front when the gymnast moves towards the observer. How these theoretical tenets coincide with practice may be seen in Figure 47 where we see contourograms of actual dismounts from the horizontal bar taken from the front.

Let us underline once again that the speed of twist rotation from support will depend not on the magnitude of angle of body turn and its links around the longitudinal axis at the moment of losing contact with the support, but on the magnitude of their angular velocity at that moment. Turning the body's links relative to each other and the entire body around the longitudinal axis in support has an anatomical limit. As soon as it is reached, rotation ends and all the gymnast's efforts to create a fast twist rotation from support will be in vain.

The gymnast can perform a twist in an unsupported position without giving the rotation around the longitudinal axis from support. For this we use the second and third means.

6.3.3.2.2 Second Means of Forming a Complex Rotation

This means consists in performing conical movements with the legs relative to the trunk or conversely, in an unsupported position (which in terms of mechanics is one and the same thing, but different psychologically). When using this means it does not matter whether any angular momentum is given from support or not, whether there is rotation by somersault in flight or not.

To understand the mechanism that lies behind this means of creating twist rotation by this method let us look at the following task. Let us imagine a cosmonaut in a state of weightlessness, when no external forces are acting on him, and let us say that he is motionless in the starting position. Let us note that in weightlessness, just as in the flight phase of gymnastics exercises, the law of conservation of basic angular momentum operates which in this case is zero.

Let us now allow that the cosmonaut tries to raise his legs up to his trunk. Because of the law this automatically leads to a counter shift of the trunk in the motionless system of coordinates. If now the cosmonaut begins to perform a conical movement with his legs relative to the trunk to the right, from the viewpoint of a fixed observer his pose will also change as when swinging a hoop round the waist (hula-hoop). To analyse how this is reflected in the cosmonaut's orientation in space, let us imagine his body in the form of a model shown in Figure 50a.

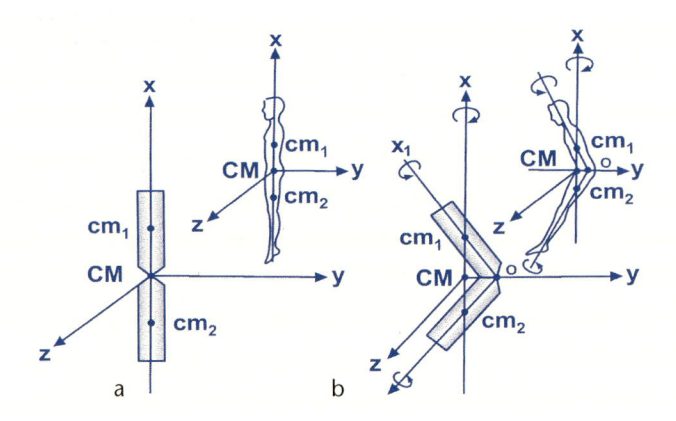

Figure 50 – *Model of the mechanism governing movements of the hula hoop type action (Suchilin, 1972, 1978)*

6
BIOMECHANICAL BASIS

The first link here is with the mechanical model of the trunk together with head and arms, the second is with a model of the legs together with hips, while the hinge is with the model of the vertebral joint. The links represent identical circular cylinders with conical surfaces. Their tops join together in a special hinge. There is a rocking through the relative movement of one link along the surface of the other. As a result the speeds of the points of both links on the general forming cone are equal.

Insofar as the attempt to bring the legs up to the trunk has resulted in a counter movement, the model of the cosmonaut's body in the fixed system of coordinates will be located in space, as shown in Figure 50b. The longitudinal main central axis of model X passing through the centres of gravity of both links will not change its initial orientation. The conical movement of a hula-hoop type will not in any way be reflected in its orientation. However, as a result of these movements the longitudinal axes of links x_1 and x_2 themselves will begin to describe around the longitudinal axis of model X the same conical surfaces with the same angular velocity, which we call the speed of precession. Owing to the constructive peculiarities of the model this will be a regular precession arising under the impact of internal forces. Instantaneous angular velocity of regular precession is represented as follows:

$$\omega = \omega 1 + \omega 2$$

Where $\omega 1$ is the angular velocity of precession (the conical movement of the longitudinal axis of each link x_1 and x_2 around the longitudinal axis of model X), and $\omega 2$ is the angular velocity of its own rotation (the angular velocity of rotation of each link around its own longitudinal axis x_1 and x_2).

Since the rotating movement of the system in the starting position was absent and owing to action of the law of conservation, its angular momentum is constant and zero ($H = I\omega = 0$ const), then the full angular velocity of the system (a) should all the time be zero. Otherwise we will violate the law of conservation of the angular momentum, which cannot happen, other things being equal. Thus, for each link there must be the equation:

$$\omega = \omega 1 + \omega 2 = 0$$

From which it follows that

$$\omega 1 = -\omega 2$$

275

The minus sign tells us that in the process of conical rotation of the legs relative to the trunk, both these links will rotate around their own longitudinal axes x_1 and x_2 in the opposite direction. Since in our case the conical movement is done to the right, the cosmonaut's entire body, when bending, will rotate to the left around a convex axis x_1-x_2 (Figure 50b). From the outside this movement will be seen as a typical twist rotation.

This movement cannot continue by inertia. The cosmonaut only has to stop movement with his legs and fix any pose and the twist rotation will immediately stop. A natural question arises: how many cycles of such control movement do we need to perform to complete a single twist and what must be the scale of these movements? Theoretically it is sufficient to perform a little over one cycle of movement of the hula-hoop type, for a double twist, etc. To complete the twist quickly they should be performed with maximum possible speed with a moderate scale of the order of 20°-30° [58,59].

To test this exercise it is enough to hang on one ring, keep balance, and then begin conical rotations with the legs around the trunk. Here the whole body will turn in the opposite direction. Halting leg rotation and holding the pose will straightaway cause the pirouette rotations to stop.

If we increase the number of links of the model to the number of vertebra in the spinal column, the nature of the described movement will not alter owing to the law of conservation of angular momentum. Bending movements in the spinal column will occur simultaneously in a single direction as a result of harmonious contraction of the trunk muscles (primarily the long muscles surrounding the spinal column).

This will lead to a synchronised ring-like deformation of the inter-vertebral discs ensuring a mutual rocking of the vertebra bodies along both their perimeters. The precession of vertebra relative to each other arising through internal forces will cause their synchronised reactive counter-rotation around their own longitudinal axes. Here the bending longitudinal axis of the spinal column will precess around the longitudinal main central axis of the body's inertia, and by itself thanks to the law of conservation it will begin reactively to turn around this bending axis in a direction opposite to the precession.

Gymnasts do not normally recognise the slight bending-straightening movements of the hula-hoop type with a correct performance of the twists. They are poorly differentiated even with a visual observation from the side. They are fairly marked only when analysing them with a specially built kinogram.

Figure 51 shows contourograms of control movements when performing actual dismounts with twists from the horizontal bar [58,59]. Progressive and rotating movement by somersault is artificially excluded. Film frames are produced showing that the longitudinal axis of the gymnast's body in all cases was oriented vertically. All dismounts are performed with a turn to the left, except the flight with twist (third contourogram).

As we see from the Figure, the control movements when performing flight with twist are done to the left, and the whole body of the gymnast turns around the longitudinal axis to the right. In the other dismounts the control movements of the hula-hoop type are done to the right, while the body turns to the left. In some frames, the gymnast's body looks fully straightened, but in reality at this moment it is bent in a plane that we cannot see, perpendicular to the plane of the sketch.

Thus, the images of the contourogram testify to the presence of control movements of the hula-hoop type when performing dismounts with twists (about which the performer himself had no idea). They also testify that the model we have used is adequate. From the viewpoint of a rotating movement both the cosmonaut in weightlessness and the gymnast in flight find themselves in identical conditions. In both cases we have the law of conservation of angular momentum.

Besides hula-hoop movements, Figure 51 clearly shows asymmetrical shift of the arms subordinate to the law. Especially at the start of the turn around the longitudinal axis is this clear.

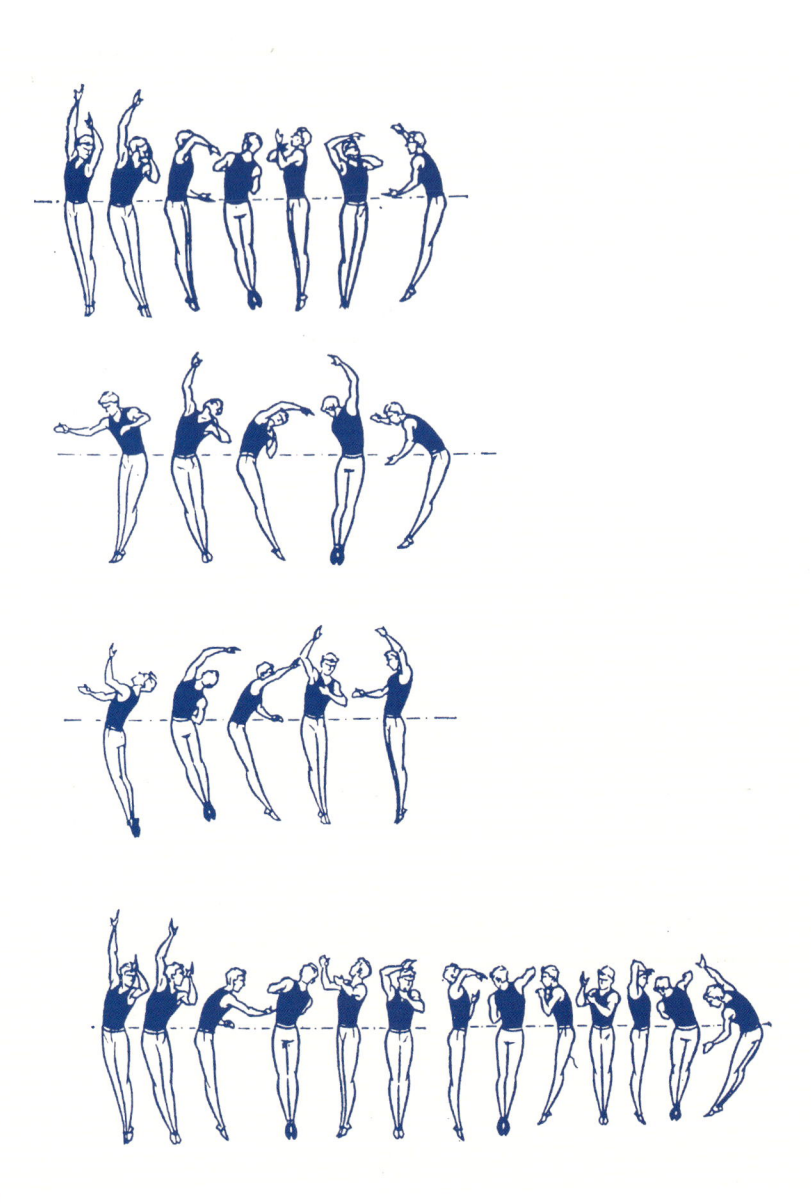

Figure 51 – *Structure of control actions when performing twists (Suchilin, 1972)*

Our research has demonstrated that asymmetrical shifting of the arms at the start of flight with subsequent holding of the pose by itself may produce a complex rotating movement of a completely different mechanical origin.

6.3.3.2.3 Third Means of Forming a Complex Rotation

When using this method the presence of rotation by somersault is obligatory. The vector of angular momentum given from support at the start of the flight coincides in direction with the transverse main central axis of the gymnast's body. The gymnast performs a simple rotating movement around this axis. Then he performs an asymmetrical shift of arms in flight and produces a complex rotating movement. This is the basic method in diving into water with twists.

We justified this method after tackling a theoretical task formulated as follows: does the orientation of main central axes of body inertia change if the person changes his pose asymmetrically in a state of weightlessness? The conditions of the task were analogous to investigating a mechanism of control movements of the hula-hoop type (see the second means of forming a complex rotation) with an asymmetrical change of pose. The same cosmonaut in a state of weightlessness served as a model when no external forces were acting on him.

Our investigation showed that their orientation generally does not change. Thus, for example, if the cosmonaut in weightlessness lowers his left arm from a straightened position with arms upwards, from the standpoint of a motionless observer his longitudinal axis will incline to the right by approximately 6°-10°, and if the right arm, then the same amount to the left (Figure 52) [59].

Let us again refer to Puanso's construction. If from outside the cosmonaut is given rotation around the transverse axis, the vector of his angular momentum will be directed along that axis and he will not change his orientation no matter what he does (because of the law of conservation). The central ellipsoid of the cosmonaut's inertia will touch the Puanso plane at a point coinciding with one of its three main foci which, in the given situation, will be located on the transverse axis.

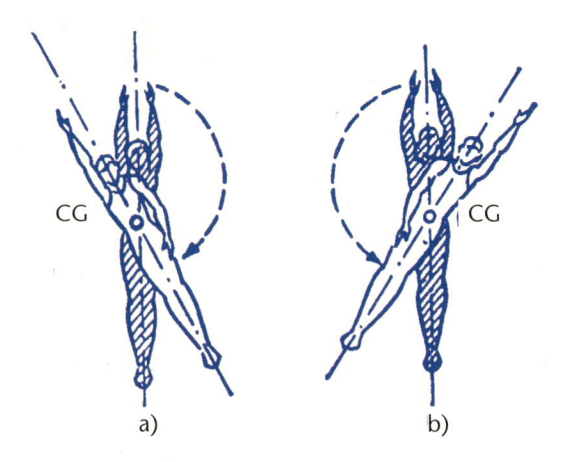

Figure 52 – *The effect of arm movements in flight*

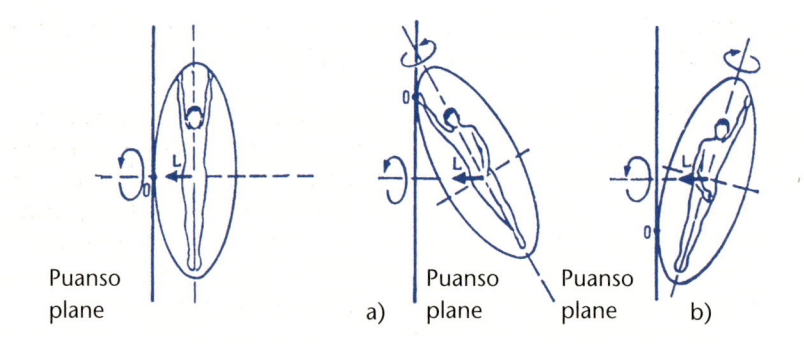

Figure 53 – *The mechanism of creating a complex rotation in flight using asymmetrical arm movements*

The rotation will be simple: the ellipsoid of inertia will turn around its transverse axis touching the Puanso plane at one of its points (Figure 53).

If now the cosmonaut lowers an arm, his ellipsoid of inertia will change its orientation in space and the longitudinal axis will incline to the vector of angular momentum (Figures 53a and b). Its projection on this axis will become different from zero.

Now the ellipsoid of inertia will touch the Puanso plane at the point that does not coincide with any one of its foci. Consequently, after changing the pose, the ellipsoid will roll along the Puanso plane – ie we shall have a situation analogous with the first means of forming a complex rotation in flight (see above). Thus, the simple rotating movement around the transverse axis in unsupported position as a result of lowering one hand will turn into a complex rotation around the CoM with simultaneous turn around the three axes.

Let us apply the cosmonaut case to a gymnast rotating around the transverse axis in flight. In both cases the body's rotating movement around the CoM can be correctly seen as around a fixed point. The moment of external forces relative to the CoM is zero. Our law of conservation of angular momentum of the system comes into force.

Which arm should we lower? Analysis of the Puanso construct shows that we should lower the right arm given a rotation of forward somersault to create a twist movement to the left, and in performing a back somersault – the left arm. To create a twist rotation to the right we need to act in the directly opposite way: when performing the forward somersault we need to lower the left arm, and with a back somersault the right [59].

If in the initial position the arms are spread to the sides in flight, simultaneously with lowering the corresponding arm we need to raise the other arm. This may increase the incline of the longitudinal axis and correspondingly the speed. If there is time, after completing the required number of twists, the gymnast may again turn a complex rotating movement into a simple rotation by somersault – if only around the transverse axis. For this the gymnast has to have time to shift his arms in the opposite direction before landing.

To test these theoretical conclusions we conducted a special experiment [59,63]. Top-class gymnasts did a series of jumps of forward and back somersaults, straightening the body with arms up without twisting in support, landing on the mat in the foam rubber pit. This was done from the trampoline. After letting go of the support each gymnast was told 'Right!' or 'Left!', according to which they had to lower their right or left arm in flight in a certain way. The object of our observation were the facts of emergence of the twist rotation after lowering the arms, its direction and the angle of turn around the longitudinal axis in flight. We analysed only those attempts in which there was no rotation in twist given from support and the gymnasts in flight precisely performed the command given them from the floor.

The conclusions have been confirmed as a result of mathematical modelling of twisting without support [92]. The approach we applied [58] in the research of the technique of performing twists (Figure 47; "hula-hoop" device- Fig. 50; cinegrammes with divided positions-Fig.51), was later applied in work [77, 84, 89].

We established that, when doing a forward somersault, a precise and timely lowering of the right arm (in a direction of forward and down to the left hip) on command in flight caused a twist rotation to the left, while the lowering of the left arm was to the right. When performing a back somersault, the twist rotation to the left arose in flight after lowering the left arm back and down in a circle, and the rotation was to the right after lowering the right arm. In the overwhelming number of cases this was sufficient to perform a turn of 360° and more around the longitudinal axis in flight without creating a twist rotation from support.

The following circumstance was extremely remarkable during the experiment. The gymnasts who never before had done a twist in the 'alien' direction (usually to the right) performed it for the first time without any preliminary intentions merely through the correct movement of the arm in flight (to their own amazement). Thus, the results of the experiment fully confirmed the reliability of the above-mentioned theoretical propositions.

As a result of the research we also established that, by contrast with hula-hoop type movements, arm movements in flight are more precisely internalised and controlled. Therefore, when teaching unsupported twists one should pay particular attention to correct arm work.

When performing multiple twists from support, the three means we have outlined are normally used together. In interaction with the horizontal bar on release the same arm is normally lowered as when creating a twist rotation in flight by the third method. Given the presence of rotation in somersault and the lack of twist rotation for its creation, the third method is more effective (asymmetrical shift of arms in flight). The faster the rotation in somersault will be, the faster will be the rotation in twists. However, the second method (hula-hoop) is more universal because it does not demand an initial rotation in somersault.

We should note that among the above-mentioned mechanisms there is an internal contradiction. Spreading the arms to the side, hula-hoop movements, bending and straightening in flight increase the moment of inertia relative to the longitudinal axis of a gymnast's body. If the rotation around that axis is given from support, its speed in flight in these cases will be less than in a fully straightened position bringing the arms to the body. However, this is compensated for by the effect which an asymmetrical shift of arms in flight gives in routine with control movements of the hula-hoop type.

The latter given their small scale (and this is more effective) may not be appreciated by the gymnasts themselves and not grasped by coaches and judges. Therefore in practice multiple twists are performed by the combined method – ie by twisting in support with subsequent lowering of one arm and a small hula-hoop movement in flight. Twisting of links in support is done in the direction of the twist, while funnel-type movements (hula-hoop) in flight are done in the opposite direction. Correct arm movements in flight when entering into the twist are particularly important when performing multiple somersaults. An asymmetrical shift of the arms to a certain extent stimulates movements of the hula-hoop type.

6.4 Landing

Landing is called a contact interaction with support after the flight phase of dismounts, acrobatic jumps and support vaults/jumps. It takes place in a type of non-resilient impulse when, on making contact, the efforts of interaction with support sharply increase to the maximum, and then diminish, but now more smoothly.

A complete halt to movement is the particular task of landing at the end of a gymnastic exercise. On landing with a jump the velocity of CoM of the gymnast's body sharply diminishes to zero. Here the entire kinetic energy of movement accumulated in flight changes into other forms of energy, is absorbed by the system of 'gymnast-surface of landing' and is dissipated.

Given correct technical actions in the support and unsupported periods the landing should not cause any special difficulties. All the same, this happens infrequently. Usually gymnasts incur errors both in support, and in flight, and on landing. So precise landing after complex dismounts and jumps is a fairly rare occurrence. It is here that top-class gymnasts, including at elite level, continue to sustain weighty and fairly long-lasting losses throughout many years.

So as not to lose precious tenths of a point, gymnasts scrupulously polish the technique of exercises, only to lose marks on landing. Only by precise landing do gymnasts have a real possibility of increasing their scores in the multi-events by 0.5-1 point or over. For example, the absolute champion of the 22nd Olympic Games, Alexander Dityatin, made not a single mistake in landing in 24 starts in Moscow competitions Nos. 1, 2 and 3.

By contrast with the technique of support and flight actions, the landing technique from the outside looks more simple. But the support-motor apparatus of gymnasts here experiences a very high impulse. Technical faults in landing often lead to injuries in the extremities and the spine.

After completing the required form of movement in flight during the phase of preparation for landing the gymnast straightens out. Before placing the feet on support the arms are raised up, the trunk and legs are straightened (but not fully), the foot is bent, the toes are stretched (but not to the limit). The gymnast's body is taut and has a slightly concave or convex form – depending on the direction of rotation in flight.

As a rule the gymnast touches the surface of landing with his toes in a zone + or – 15 cm from the vertical axis of his CoM on the landing surface. When making contact with the support there is a forceful interaction of the gymnast's support-motor apparatus with the landing surface. The legs take the main shock load, and then the spine. The entire support-motor apparatus takes part in deadening the shock.

In the active phase of landing the gymnast performs a squat in a powerful yielding regime (Figure 54). Pressing his feet on the support, he actively resists the action of external forces and their moments which tip him over and press him to the support. After holding the position of maximum squat, when the CoM velocity is zero, the muscle work regime changes to an overcoming regime. The gymnast fixes the landing and straightens out into a basic stance.

Figure 54 – *Structure of landing*

When placing the feet on support relative to the point of contact there arises the moment of force of gravity and toppling over moments caused by the horizontal shift of the body and its turn about the transverse axis in flight (Figure 55a). When doing jumps and dismounts with turning in flight backwards around the transverse axis and with moving forward, as well as with turn forward and movement backward these toppling over moments have the opposite direction (Figures 55b and c). They neutralise each other in composition. If the direction of turn and the horizontal shift in flight coincide, these moments have an identical direction. Their joint action is increased and it is more difficult to land without taking a step or steps forward.

In the event of not turning enough in the twists, a twisting moment acts on the gymnast, caused by the angular momentum not coinciding in direction with a single major central axis of inertia. If there is a sideways incline to the plane of CoM movement, there arises also a side toppling-over moment of force of gravity (Figure 55c). The load on the joints and side leg ligaments here grows considerably.

It becomes asymmetrical, which substantially complicates a stable landing (Figure 55d).

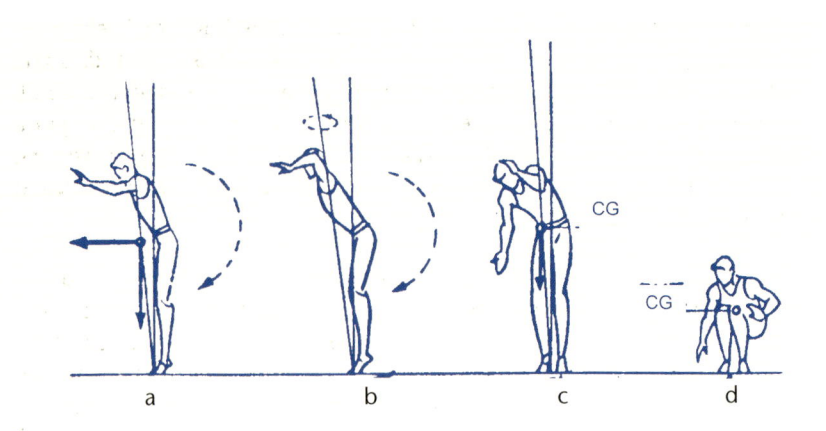

Figure 55 – *Toppling moments when landing*

All the moments of external forces acting on the gymnast are summed up by the rules of vector composition which form a resultant moment applied to the point of support. By their technical actions in landing the gymnast must minimise and neutralise this resultant moment, cutting the speed of movement to zero.

In flight the gymnast must take the optimal position for landing, correctly putting his feet on to the support and, through muscle effort, creating the moment of force equal in magnitude and counterposed in direction to the resultant toppling moment. He has to create a yielding regime of muscle contraction which reliably neutralises the blow and the speed of movement, and thereby ensures a stable landing.

In the event of landing into a hop this is done at the end of the squat. In its process the gymnast's body CoM must be within the bounds of the support area. If not he produces a toppling moment of force of gravity. Experienced gymnasts artificially increase the support area, landing on slightly spread feet and then swiftly bringing the heels together when landing in the basic stance. In the squatting process the gymnast's body CoM shifts downwards. The distance from CoM to the support shortens, which ensures a diminishing of the toppling moment if it is a squat.

If the gymnast has not managed fully to extinguish the horizontal velocity in the squatting process and it continues to pull him forward, as he stands up he has actively to press his toes into the support by means of bending the feet. If this pulls him backwards, there are no reserves left and he is obliged to put a foot back. With a high horizontal speed straightening of the body increases the toppling moment. In all these cases he is bound to take a step or steps forward with the resultant loss of points.

If the gymnast does not have time to straighten out before landing and (or) insufficiently tenses the muscles when placing his feet on to the support, the spring attributes of his support-motor apparatus sharply diminish. It is impossible now to extinguish and then disperse the kinetic energy accumulated in flight. To hold the landing, gymnasts are obliged to switch on additional support. Being unable to deal with the horizontal velocity and (or) with the action of the toppling moment, at best the gymnasts can only make a step forward; at worst they fall over.

Imprecise landing penalised by the judges may be the result of three factors. These are technical faults committed by the gymnast:

1. in the support period;
2. in flight and
3. directly in landing.

In the event of serious errors in the preceding phases the gymnast cannot make a stable landing, even if his actions in landing are correct. It is therefore useless to improve the landing technique. The gymnast has to correct the errors in the preceding phases.

The major mistakes in landing are as follows:

- insufficient straightening of the body at the moment of placing the feet on support;
- insufficient tensing of the muscles;
- incorrect placing of feet on support (insufficient or too far taking them forward or back);
- landing on weak or too hard feet;
- insufficient convex or concave body line;
- inadequate speed of yielding regime of muscle work in the squat.

In the first phase of landing, when the gymnast's CoM moves down, a quickly slowing up, 'sucking in' step of a powerful piston pump may be used as an integrated model of work of the support-motor apparatus. It is valuable for the gymnast to have this model or image in mind when working on the technique of stable landings.

Correct work with the arms is an essential feature of landing technique. Being raised up and tensed at the moment of contact with the support, they are also part of the yielding regime downwards. Here the kinetic energy of movement becomes energy of a springy deformation of the muscles as long as they are tensed sufficiently.

On landing after smooth dismounts (without turns) the movements of the arms are asymmetrical. If the turn in flight is done to the left, the right arm is lowered by a circle inwards in front of the chest.

The following rules are typical of landing:

- the higher the flight, the deeper and more continuous the squat;
- the greater the magnitude of the angular momentum in flight, the farther from the CoM projection on support area are the feet placed on it (from the front from it when turning forward and back – when turning backwards);
- the less the horizontal speed in flight, the closer to the CoM projection on support area are the feet placed. When doing dismounts with super-rotating (double and triple somersault) the feet are placed closer to the apparatus by contrast with dismounts with normal rotation in somersault;
- if the horizontal velocity of flight is great, and its direction coincides with the direction of rotation in somersault, the feet are put farther from the CoM projection on to support in relation to the apparatus. The same is typical of dismounts when the horizontal velocity of flight is extremely slight, and the angular momentum is great (for example, triple somersault from the rings). When performing all other dismounts the feet are put on to support closer to the apparatus from the projection on it of the gymnast's body CoM;
- in order to make a stable landing the gymnast needs to have time to straighten his body in flight before landing, slightly stooping in the

middle part of the spine and straightening the legs, leaving small angles in the hips and knee joints. The arms must be raised higher than the shoulders. He must bend his feet and lightly stretch his toes before placing his feet on the support. Orientation of the longitudinal axis of the body at the moment of planting his feet should be close to the vertical;
- the earlier and fuller the gymnast can straighten up in flight, the higher the class of dismount, fly-over or jump, the easier it will be for him to orient himself, correctly placing his feet on to the support and make a stable landing;
- landing with fully straightened spinal column and (or) on straight legs is extremely dangerous in terms of injury.

It is sensible to work out the technique of landing using the 'trampoline-foam rubber pit' system. Jumps that are similar in technical and biomechanical structure to integrated elements are performed from the trampoline into the pit in which mats are put on a level with the floor. The task here is to land properly.

Here it is necessary to model not only the actual height and length of the flight, but also the direction and velocity of horizontal movement, as well as the direction and velocity of rotation. At first the conditions of landing are made easier, then they are brought up to those closely resembling competition standard, and then they are made even more difficult by reducing height and, correspondingly, the time of flight, and also increasing the horizontal velocity of flight.

In comparison with landing after dismounts and jumps, the arrival of apparatus in the middle of a routine takes place according to the type of not fully springy shock. The main task here consists not in extinguishing the energy of movement accumulated in flight, but in retaining part of it and converting it into potential energy of springy deformation of the 'gymnast-apparatus' system. The difficulty consists in that in the process of arrival at the apparatus, the gymnast simultaneously is preparing to perform the next swing element. While performing the first part the potential energy of the springy deformation of the 'gymnast-apparatus' system again becomes kinetic. This may be a deeply support element or an element with a flight phase. In the latter case the gymnast immediately prepares for a fresh departure from it in the process of arrival into support.

When performing elements with a big swing, which end with complex power static elements (for example, the giant rotation into cross on the rings), the whole kinetic energy becomes potential energy.

6.5 Complexity and Difficulty of Gymnastic Exercises

The complexity and difficulty of gymnastics exercises are close concepts, but not identical. Complexity comes from the word 'complex' (for example of parts), while difficulty means effort, time, work spent on something. In the social sense the complex is normally difficult, and vice versa. But work exerted on learning a gymnastics exercise is a relative criterion. The work capacity of learning depends on the abilities and level of preparedness of gymnasts, the qualifications and experience of the coach, the methods he or she uses, external and internal conditions, and other factors.

To determine the complexity of gymnastics exercises we may use biomechanical, physiological, psychological, pedagogical and sociological criteria. Their degree of objectivity increases in a direction from sociological to biomechanical criteria.

The complexity of an act of movement may be characterised by the number of elements in it, but not utterly. A short exercise may be more complexly long by virtue of a higher concentration of complex elements and technical actions.

Difficulty in the gymnastics sense is a relative concept. It is liable to devaluation. For example, in the 1950s the ceiling of complexity in gymnastics was the double somersault which was performed by only a tiny handful of gymnasts. In the 1960s it became quite common, and in the 1970s tended to turn into an event for kids and juniors. Evidently the objective biomechanical and physiological complexity of the element did not change. But its pedagogical and psychological complexity, the accessibility and difficulty in the sense of work and time spent on learning it inevitably changed. We gained new scientific knowledge about the biomechanics and technique of execution and methodology of learning complex exercises. There appeared foam rubber pits which considerably reduced the stress factors. As a result, the methods for mastering this and more complex elements were substantially improved.

We should note the relativity of physiological criteria of difficulty. We know from biomechanics courses that one and the same result may be displayed with radically different energy expenditure. Top-class swimmers, for example, show a given result at a given distance with substantially less energy expenditure than other swimmers. Thus, one and the same result can have a different physiological energy demand depending on level of squad preparedness.

At the same time it is apparent that, other things being equal, it is always more complex and difficult to lift 100 kg than 50 kg, to run 100 m in 10 seconds than in 15 seconds, to jump 8 metres than 4 metres. It is always more difficult and complex to do the triple somersault than a single somersault. In all cases irrespective of the subject it requires either a great amount of mechanical work or a great power and energy, or a big impulse of force, or all of those things together. In turn it requires a higher level of the athlete's preparedness. Therefore, biomechanical criteria are the most objective for adequately determining the complexity of gymnastics exercises.

Let us also note in passing that the complexity of exercises is in itself an indicator that is principally more objective than difficulty.

6.6 Laws of Growth in Complexity

The general laws of growth in complexity of gymnastics exercises are vividly manifest in analysing the gymnast's body CoM movements. The centre of a section joining the hip joints is the closest point to it. When we analyse the technique of exercises it is important to reveal how this point moves.

As a result of our research we have established that with the growth in complexity of exercises we may observe a clearly marked trend towards increasing the basic biomechanical characteristics of movement. Above all this relates to the velocity of the body's CoM and the angular momentum.

Simultaneous with this is the reduction in technical methods for high-quality execution of the more complex exercises and a narrowing of the scope for variety of their basic biomechanical characteristics.

The model of growth in complexity of exercises may be seen in the form of a funnel narrowing at the top (Figure 56). The simpler the exercise the more technical methods for its performance and the wider the scope of variety of biomechanical characteristics. And conversely: the more complex it is, the less the scope. By improving the technique of performing specific exercises the same laws apply: the basic biomechanical parameters of movement grow and the spectrum of their variety narrows. This in principle applies to gymnastics exercises of any group of difficulty .

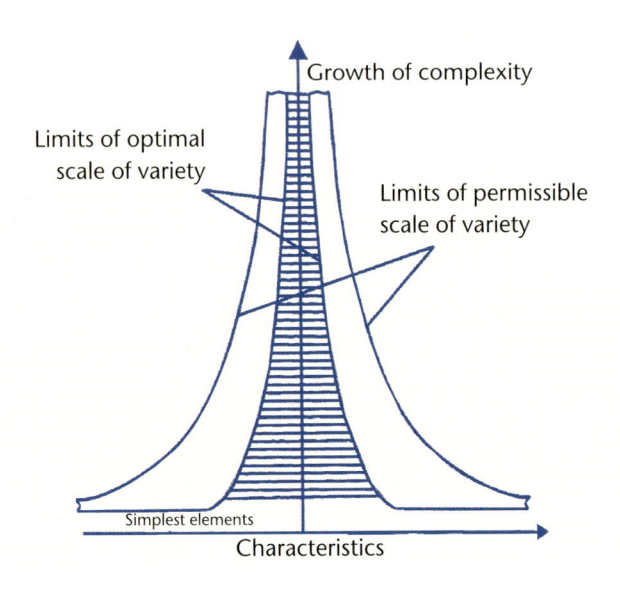

Figure 56 – *Funnel of complexity model*

The technique also of single-type exercises performed in opposite directions is practically the same for the whole group of movements of this type with the exception of just a few nuances. The technical and phase structure of exercises being performed in a certain direction is on the whole a sort of mirror of movements in the opposite direction with an analogous scale of joints in motion. Compare, for example, giant rotations forward and back, the Stalder and Endo, dismounts by forward and back somersaults, the Hecht flight and Tkatchev, straight and reverse intersections, circles and twists to the left and to the right, etc.

BIOMECHANICAL BASIS

The gymnast has control of his movement as a result of interaction with support and a change in magnitude of the moment of inertia relative to the axis of rotation. The laws of its change with top-class gymnasts have a general character irrespective of age and weight data. What we have in mind here is performance of the same elements, elements of increasing complexity of one and the same structure of the group in one and the same and opposite directions, and similar elements on various apparatus.

The optimal technical basis of single-type exercises is most clearly manifest when analysing the most complex. Their technical structure may serve as a guiding integrated model for mastering all movements of progressive complexity of a given structural group (for example, the technical foundation for a triple somersault for all dismounts of a given type).

The complexity of gymnastics exercises is growing in structural and parametric directions (see Chapter 1.6). The parametric direction of growth in complexity expresses the same consistency as a single somersault, double somersault and triple somersault. The order of complexity determined by the angle of turn of the gymnast's body around its transverse axis in flight serves as the parameter in this circumstance. With growth in complexity this parameter changes immediately to the order of 360° (single somersault), 720° (double somersault), 1080° (triple somersault), etc.

In each order of complexity of somersault four levels of complexity are distinguished, determined by their shape in flight: 1. in tuck, 2. piked, 3. straight and, 4. straight body with arms up. Transfer to the next level of complexity involves an increase in the moment of inertia of the gymnast's body relative to the axis of rotation in flight (Table 14).

Table 14

Level of complexity of unsupported rotations

Pose	Mean value of moment of inertia about the transverse axis, kgm^2	Range of values of moment of inertia, kgm^2
In tuck	3.9	3.8-4.0
Piked	7.0	6.5-7.0
Straight	12.0	11.0-13.0
Straight arms raised	17.2	–

By contrast with the order of complexity, the transfer to the next level of complexity occurs less sharply. The position of half-open tuck enables the gymnast to make this period at as small a pace as he likes of increment of magnitude of moment of inertia relative to the transverse axis in a scale of values of 4-9 kgm^2.

Thus, the complexity of simple body rotations in an unsupported position may be determined by the help of two indicators:

- angle of body turn around the axis of rotation in flight and
- moment of inertia relative to that axis in the dominating position.

To perform a more complex form of movement in flight, other things being equal, we need the support to give a higher height of flight and (or) bigger principal angular momentum that ensures a faster rotation in flight. This requires from the gymnast great effort of interaction with the support and (or) a more precise and finer coordination of them.

The parametric growth in complexity of the mastered element takes place with an increase in basic parameters of flight as a result of improved technique.

At any level of complexity movement in flight may be complicated by a turn around the longitudinal axis (by twist). The greater this turn, the more complex it is to perform it.

Between 'twist' and 'somersault' complexity there are certain contradictions. Objectively the somersault with straight body is more complex and difficult to learn and carry out than a tuck somersault, yet to master the twist in the first case is simpler.

A structural growth in complexity takes place as a result of concentration of a growing complexity of elements and (or) technical actions in time and space. The structural complexity of movements executed in the support position is growing mainly in the following directions:

1. complexity of the working position (for example, hang on two hands, hang in reverse grip, hang from the back, hang on one hand);
2. performance of complex elements without previous acceleration (for example, the Stalder routine and in tempo triple somersault into dismount on the horizontal bar);

3. the combination of several complex elements in a row (for example, the Stalder with legs together and turn round + Endo with legs together and turn of 360° into reverse grip, rotation forward in back hang (Russian rotation), turn of 180° into back rotation in rear hang (Czech rotation), lift with forward swing and turn round into handstand with grip from above, swing over bent and forward rotation with turn of 180° into handstand);
4. executing a cascade of complex fly-overs (for example, the Kovacs + Tkatchev with legs together and straight body + the Tkatchev with turn of 360° (Lyukin) + Gienger with turn of 360° (Deff)).

The structural growth in complexity of exercises is leading to a considerably greater complexity of conditions for performing initial (preparatory) and final (culminating) phases of technical actions of a given element as a result of their being 'sewn together' with corresponding phases of other complex elements. The apotheosis of this direction is a cascade of super-complex elements or tricks.

When performing exercises with flight phase, the objective of technical actions in support consists in creating initial conditions necessary and sufficient for performing the required form of movement in flight. The gymnast's task is not to increase the basic parameters of flight (of the starting velocity of CoM flight and the angular momentum) to a possible limit, but to make them optimally accord in magnitude and direction with the moment of letting go of the support. With growth in complexity these parameters have a tendency to rise. However, in the initial stages of mastering the most complex exercises the height of flight may fall. Thus, for example, the height of the double piked somersault is often lower than the double tuck somersault.

We must all take into considerations these laws when mastering gymnastics exercises of progressive complexity.

How to Create Champions

CHAPTER SEVEN
Structure of Gymnastics Exercises

7.1 Methods of Technique Analysis

The principal functional unit in the system of training top-class gymnasts is the 'coach-gymnast' subsystem; in which information constantly circulates in direct and feed-back channels. Direct communication is from coach to gymnast; these are commands, instructions and explanations. Through direct communication the coach explains what the gymnast has to do and sets objectives and tasks.

Feed-back is information coming from the gymnast to the coach. Through that communication the coach receives information on what the gymnast has done, how he did it, what was the result of carrying out his instructions. When teaching and improving technique the most important and objective information is what the coach receives visually. He observes the gymnast's actions and through an external picture of executed movements is able to judge how correctly the gymnast is able implement his instructions. This information becomes more objective when using a video recording and other instrumental means of immediate objective information.

Visual feed-back is enhanced by verbal information. For example, when the gymnast explains to his coach his actions (successful or not), and tells him about his sensations. Moreover, the coach listens for the sound that comes from the interaction between the gymnast and the apparatus. For an experienced coach this is valuable additional communication enabling him to judge the degree of improvement of the rhythm-tempo structure of the gymnast's technical actions, the accents of his efforts of interaction with the apparatus and even their magnitude when performing exercises.

The coach compares the objective and tasks, measures it against the performance and determines further commands to reduce the difference between the performance and the instructions. After the result has become stable, coinciding with the objective, the teaching process passes to the stage of improving technique. This described process has a cyclical character and is general for all types of gymnastics training. The lack of adequate feed-back in teaching and training equally destroys the control system.

An experienced coach is always an intuitive analyst, and any analysis includes procedures of division and comparison. In order to compare the goal and tasks set, the gymnast with the result of his actions relies on the coach to divide the exercise into component parts. If this is a routine, it naturally divides into series and elements. However, elements too require dividing into parts since it is very hard to compare a target of a specific element existing in the coach's and gymnast's minds with the actual performance of the movement without dividing it into constituent parts. To be able to compare movement in total is a gift of God and it is just as difficult to learn it as to learn to write talented literary or musical works. To overcome this difficulty in analysing technique we use the system-structural approach.

7.2 Technical Structure of Exercises

By technical structure of gymnastics exercises we understand a stabilised mutual contact of technical actions and the gymnast's movements in time and space. The structures of gymnastics elements that form part of a routine are a series of connected movements. In smooth connecting movements the entry and exit phases of elements intertwine and seem to be sewn together.

At the same time each element in itself is a system of movements possessing its own composition and structure, which are determined as a result of a system-structural analysis of technique. Division of elements and technical actions separating their performance into component parts is necessary to create more detailed targets and more conscious systemic perception of the actual technical actions.

To divide the element into parts we may use pedagogical, psychological, physiological, biomechanical and other criteria. As shown in Chapter 6.6, the extent of their objectivity grows in the direction from pedagogical to biomechanical. What is more, the biomechanical process is decisive in the structure of processes that characterise the sport's motor activity. Therefore, following the principle method of analysis 'from end to beginning' (see Chapter 2.1), we use biomechanical and mechanical criteria for dividing the gymnastics element into parts.

The first criterion is the athlete's *mechanical state*. This state may be supported or unsupported. The conditions of action here are principally different. In the support state there is always a support reaction. In the unsupported state there is not.

Accordingly, we may divide out *supported and unsupported periods* of movement in the technical structure of exercises. Some exercises are done exclusively in the support position (for example, giant rotations, power elements, circles). When performing others the support and unsupported periods alternate (for example, acrobatic and support jumps, fly-overs, dismounts).

The second criterion is the natural action of the force of gravity. Being always directed vertically downwards it may both accelerate and slow down the gymnast's movement. For example, with movement from above down the force of gravity accelerates the gymnast, while with movement from below up it slows him down. In the first instance the speed increases, in the second it diminishes.

We distinguish two stages according to the criterion of action of the force of gravity in the support period of elements. These are *the accumulation stages* in which there is an accumulation of kinetic energy when moving from above downwards, and the *working stage* in which kinetic energy is dispersed on work to raise the CoM of the body when moving from below upwards. At the first stage the gymnast's technical actions in support are maximal using the external forces so as to increase the speed of movement and accumulate energy, and at the second to reduce its loss and use it as fully as possible.

When executing rapid (shock-type) movements of the thrust type, the gymnast's CoM shifts from above down, and then from below up. The 'gymnast-apparatus' system initially seems to be charged with potential energy of resilient deformation, and then loses it. The potential energy turns into kinetic. The gymnast here performs short-lasting muscle work of high power. Thus, taking off includes the same two stages – accumulation and working. It should be noted that the amplitude of CoM shift is relatively small, while contact with support when performing support and acrobatic jumps is very brief (0.1-0.2 seconds).

When the force of gravity is directed perpendicularly towards the CoM movement it thereby does not influence speed, we may also distinguish the stage of accumulation in the support position (in which an accumulation of energy occurs) and the working stage (in which it is spent).

This instance occurs, for example, when performing a series of flic-flacs. The gymnast's body's CoM trajectory here resembles a horizontal segment. The vertical velocity of the CoM is close to zero, while the horizontal is practically constant. Accumulation of kinetic energy takes place while performing the run up and round off. On contact with support in the accumulation stage it transforms into energy of resilient deformation of the gymnast's support-motor apparatus, and resilient deformation of the support surface of the apparatus (acrobatic runway, vaulting board or horse). In the working stage it again becomes kinetic energy and this process is repeated cyclically.

In unsupported positions the force of gravity is applied to the gymnast's CoM and its moment is zero. It does not influence the horizontal velocity of the body CoM in flight and its rotating movement (see Chapter 6.3).

When moving in the rising branch of the flight trajectory the accumulated kinetic energy is spent on lifting the body CoM against the action of the force of gravity. This stage of movement is the working stage. The vertical velocity of CoM in this stage falls and becomes zero at the upper dead point of the flight trajectory. At this point the entire kinetic energy of movement along the vertical transforms into potential energy where it also maximal. At that moment the working stage becomes the accumulation stage. When moving from above down along the falling branch of the flight trajectory the vertical velocity of the CoM increases and reaches a maximum by the point of landing. The gymnast's kinetic energy reaches a maximum before planting his feet on the support surface.

However, since projectile movement in the flight phase takes place independent from the action of the gymnast and is wholly determined by the gymnast's mechanical state at the moment of release from support, the unsupported period of gymnastics and acrobatic exercises as a whole represents the implementation stage of flight conditions set from support phase. The goal of technical actions in flight consists in the fullest possible utilisation of these mechanical conditions.

Beginning from the moment of support (landing) after the flight phase, the gymnast's actions include the same two stages. At the first stage the CoM moves downwards, and at the second it moves upwards. However, the objective of technical actions and, correspondingly, the name of the stage depend on how the movement is to proceed. If it continues (for example, a flight over the apparatus in the middle of a routine or in a series of acrobatic jumps), the aim of the technical actions at the first stage of the support period consists in minimising the loss of accumulated kinetic energy in flight and the transformation of a certain part into energy of resilient deformation of the 'gymnast-apparatus' system. At the second stage energy is spent on work needed for performing the following element. Thus, the first stage here is this *accumulation stage*, while the next is the working.

If the preceding element ends with a landing (a dismount) or support jump, the aim of the gymnast's technical actions consists in a complete halt to movement. Here there is a rapid absorption of kinetic energy accumulated in flight of the 'gymnast-apparatus' system, where it is transformed into energy of resilient deformation and heat with subsequent dispersal.

With a precise landing this is done by the process of a squat position, when the body's CoM decelerates moving downwards. After high dismounts and jumps the gymnast's muscles during the squat phase disperse and transform enormous energy. This is the working stage of landing and it is very power intensive. At the lowest point of squat the work regime of the muscles is replaced by overcoming the previous work done. Its power depends on how much speed of movement will be extinguished at the previous stage of landing.

At the second stage of landing (the last for any gymnastics exercise), the gymnast's CoM again shifts upwards. Movement ends in a basic stance. If the speed of movement at the previous stage has been extinguished to zero, this last stage represents a purely decorative final exercise without a serious workload. It should also be noted that shifts in the body's CoM with successful landing are insignificant by contrast with the other phases of exercises. In this connection landing after jumps and dismounts should be seen as a stage of movement as a whole.

When performing strength exercises and exercises for balance there is no accumulation stage, only the working stage.

The third criterion of division of movement into parts is a comprehensive change in direction of control movements in the joints (for example, bending has ended and straightening is beginning or vice versa). Inasmuch as this does not always occur simultaneously in all joints, zones of phase transfer take shape in certain spatial-temporal intervals, in which typical *margin positions* convenient for pedagogical control may be distinguished.

According to the third designation, stages of movement are divided into phases separated by margin positions which are characterised by place and orientation of the gymnast's body in space, as well as by his pose. At each stage there are normally two phases. In accordance with a conscious direction they may be divided into *basic and concluding* actions. Here the latter phase at each stage has a double meaning. It is concluding in relation to the given stage and preparatory in relation to the following.

For example, at the accumulation stage of the support period of a giant circle the *run-up* phase is the basic, while the swing phase is the *concluding* and at the same time preparatory in relation to the following working stage of movement. The next phase (throw/thrust) is considered as basic at this stage, while the release phase into stance is the concluding. However, simultaneously this phase performs a preparatory function as well. Its task is not only to conclude the giant circle, but also to prepare the correct conditions for performing the next element, which normally commences immediately from the basic action phase. So the second and last phase at each stage is called *concluding-preparatory*.

Each movement phase has its *leading element of coordination* which may be defined at biomechanical, physiological, psychological and pedagogical levels.

In line with our methodology (see Chapter 2.1) we use a pedagogical-biomechanical definition of the leading element.

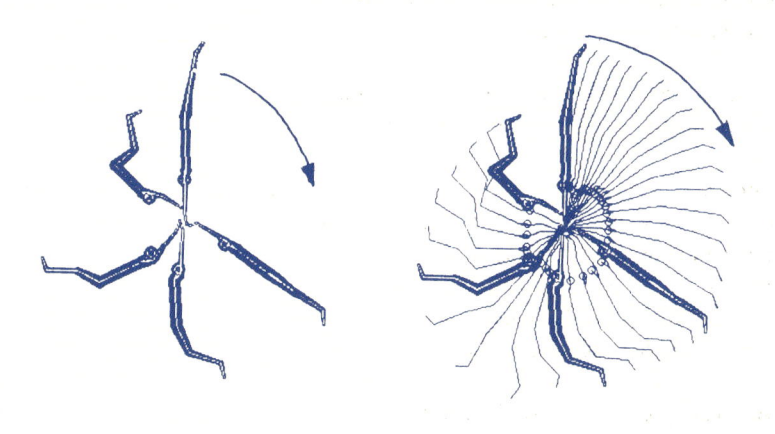

Figure 57 – *Phase structure of the support period of the Kovacs fly-over (Computer video cyclogram)*

Thus, the technical structure of elements includes three subordinate levels – *periods, stage, phase*. In phases we determine *margin positions and leading elements*, which enables us substantially to put a description of sporting technique in some order.

The phases of technical actions may include also smaller components. For example, the phase of basic actions of flight when performing double or triple tuck somersaults include sub-phases of the tuck, a tight tuck and open tuck position.

Tables 15, 16 and 17 provide an example of dividing movement into parts on the basis of the above-mentioned criteria; they show the technical structure of a giant circle, a triple somersault dismount and a Tkatchev fly-over on the horizontal bar. Figure 57 shows the margin positions in the technical structure of the support period of a Kovacs fly-over.

Table 15

Structural-phase model of a classical giant back rotation on the horizontal bar

Period		Support				
Stage		Accumulation			Working	
Phase		Start position	Run up	Swing	Thrust	Final
Nature of technical actions		Preparatory	Basic	Conclude-preparatory	Basic	Concluding
Margin Position of the moment of changing	Posture	Body straight, arms up (straight line)	Body straight, arms up (straight line)	Body bent (convex line)	Body bent (concave line)	Body straight, arms up (straight line)
	Body orientation	Vertical, head down	45° down from horizontal	Vertical, head up	Horizontal, face up	Vertical, head down
Leading element of coordination		Straightening body into handstand	Stretching from support	Hanging in shoulders	Leg thrust pressing hands on support	Straightening body into handstand

NB:

- ■ the first phase may be replaced if the giant rotation is completed after the element ends with a handstand position. In that case the final phase of this element plays a concluding-preparatory role (concluding in relation to the element and preparatory in relation to the basic phase of the accumulation stage of the giant circle). Then the giant circle begins immediately from the phase of basic actions – the lead up;

- ■ if after the giant circle the gymnast performs the next element, the final phase of the giant circle by its nature is the concluding-preparatory (concluding in relation to the working stage of the giant circle and preparatory in relation to the basic phase of the accumulation stage of the next element).

GYMNASTICS EXERCISES

Table 16

Structural-phase model of back triple somersault dismount from horizontal bar (classical technique)

Period	Support				Unsupported			Support (Landing)	
Stage	Accumulation	Pre-swing	Working	Release	Realisation		Preparation for landing	Amortisation	
Phase	Acceleration	Pre-swing	Swing	Release	Flight		Preparation for landing	Absorbing	Standing up
Nature of Technical actions	Basic	Conclude preparatory	Basic	Conclude preparatory	Basic		Conclude preparatory	Basic	Concluding
Margin Position — Posture	Body straight, arms up	Body arched, shoulders close to the ears	Body bent at the hips joints (ap.35°)	Body bent at shoulders (ap.35°), hips and knee joints (ap.90°)	Body tightly tucked.		Body in concave position, straight legs extended ankles, arms diagonally forward		
Body Orientation	15-30° below from support horizontal line (2nd quadrant)	30-15° backwards from support vertical line (2nd quadrant)	30-45° forward from support vertical line (3rd quadrant)	Trunk in horizontal position (3rd quadrant)	Body situated on the level of the support horizontal, head down		Body longitudinal Axes slightly leaning forward	Body longitudinal Axes almost vertical	Body longitudinal axes in vertical position
Leading element of co-ordination	Full extension from support	Hanging; fully extended in the shoulder	Swing legs up pressing on the bar	Quick slight tucked position	Quick bending of the hip joints and holding the tuck position		Extending the hips while stretching the legs	Bending in hip and knee joints	Stretching of the body

Table 17
Structural phase model of Tkatchev straight in giant circle (contemporary techniques)

Period	Support			Unsupported		Support (Landing)	
Stage	Accumulation			Realisation		Amortisation	
Phase	Acceleration	Pre-swing	Working	Release	Flight	Preparation for landing	Standing up
Nature of Technical actions	Basic	Conclude preparatory	Swing	Conclude preparatory	Basic	Conclude preparatory	Concluding Preparatory to the following element
Margin Position — Posture	Body bent in shoulder and hips joints (45-60°)	Body strongly arched, shoulders pressing down; Shoulders close to years	Body strongly bent at shoulder and hips joints (ap.45-60°)	Body strongly arched; elevate shoulders and strongly pressing backwards with the arms (30-45°)	Body stretched; arms down.	Body bent at shoulder and hips joints (30-45°); arms forward	Body bent in shoulder and hips joints.
Margin Position — Body Orientation	Body is in horizontal position (1st quadrant)	45-60° below from the supported vertical axes (2nd quadrant)	Body is in horizontal position (3rd quadrant)	45° above from the supported horizontal axes.	Body situated close to horizontal position (4th quadrant)	Body longitudinal axes almost vertical (2nd quadrant)	Body arched
							Trunk positioned horizontally. (3rd quadrant)
Leading element of co-ordination	Stretching the body	Hanging; fully extended in the shoulders	Swing legs up with pressing on the bar	Strong and quick backward pull (jerk chest).	Stretching the body	Bending the shoulders joints (30-45°)	Extension of the shoulder joints
							Swing legs up with pressing on the bar

Note: See the Note referring to Tables 15 and 16.

Regression analysis has shown that the phase of working actions most influences evaluation and basic parameters of movement when performing swing exercises. The starting position is secondary in value [63].

7.3 Structure of Technical Faults

Before talking about faults, it is necessary to determine what specifically we understand by them. By fault or error we understand unacceptable deviation from the target of movement.

Generally the concept of a fault is a broad concept. The gymnast's error is considered differently according to the coaches, gymnasts, experts, administrators, judges, audience, press and, finally, the performing gymnast. They may each have different criteria for errors and each could be wrong in their assessment. A gymnast's error may be technical, tactical, psychological, theoretical. It may depend on biomechanical, physiological, psychological or pedagogical levels.

We should note that in the final analysis all faults in gymnastics derive from technical faults. Therefore here we look mainly at technical faults from the point of view of the coach, the gymnast himself and, partly, the judges. These faults are first defined qualitatively on the basis of our methods of pedagogical biomechanics, and then quantitatively. The qualitative level of diagnosing technical faults presupposes the use of the language of disparity as an analogue of mathematical formalism. Definitions of the type 'less-more', 'earlier-later', 'shorter-longer', weaker-stronger', 'worse-better' are the basic operators.

A precise definition of a technical fault and its clear unambiguous treatise enables us to set the limit beyond which individual peculiarities and permitted deviations from the ideal stop being a technical fault.

The essence of a technical fault stems from the gymnast making an error using the correct technique or performing an incorrect action for that skill. In the latter case the required technical detail disappears or an extra one is added. Faults of the first type are connected with deterioration of the characteristics as a whole of the correct (in composition) technical structure of movement, while faults of the second type are associated with its distortion and deformation.

In the process of learning we strive for some ideal target model of movement that exists in our consciousness. However, in mastering an exercise we normally come up against deviations from the ideal of a general or partial nature. How do we distinguish them from faults? It is proposed that this is governed by three criteria. Deviations from the standard are permissible individual peculiarities of technique if the following three conditions are met:

1. deductions for executing an element according to the competition rules are not made by the judges;
2. the technique being used enables the gymnast to master more complex exercises (ie in the opinion of experts it is forward-looking/promising);
3. the movements are beautiful.

If just one of these demands is not met then deviations from the ideal are a technical fault.

Small deviations in themselves do not exert a substantial influence on the basic parameters of movement and its technical structure. Normally here the geometry of movement suffers, worsening its overall picture. However, if they are multiple, the style of performance as a whole acquires a negative connotation that the judges will penalise. Practice demonstrates that if small deviations are disregarded, they have a tendency to grow into faults which become rooted in the technical structure of movement and become conserved. A small error, if it is not removed in time, may develop into a major error.

In their nature technical faults may be subdivided into *systematic, chance and typical*. Systematic mistakes are made constantly, the gymnast becomes accustomed to them and they are not noticed by either the gymnast or the coach. However, the judges see them well enough and penalise the gymnast for them. Chance errors arise suddenly in disadvantageous conditions (distracting factors, stressful situations). Typical mistakes are made by most gymnasts (for example, they part their knees when doing a Kovacs fly-over, they do not let the shoulders forward enough when departing into a double somersault on the parallel bars, they begin to tuck early when pushing off from the body of the horse, etc.).

When analysing technical faults we should establish *what* sort of mistake it is, *where* and *when* it happened (in what period, stage or phase), its *calibre* and *character*. The following step is associated with elucidating how the mistake occurred and *why* it happened. Here we need to establish whether it was a consequence of previous deviations. A search in that direction should end with defining the first link in the chain of deviations from the standard, leading to the apparent fault. When the mistake is not corrected, one should remove all previous deviations from the target.

All faults may be divided into *parametric* and *structural*. In the first instance the basic parameters of movement worsen (for example, the height and length of flight diminish, rotation slows down). In the second, the quality of performing the movement as a whole or its individual details suffer.

The calibre of fault (degree of its expression) should be determined by judging criteria, as well as by the scale of variation of movement characteristics. When they change within the bounds of the optimal scale there are no technical faults, there are only acceptable individual deviations. If the characteristics vary within the bounds of the permissible scale, they are classed as minor mistakes. If the gymnast exceeds these limits this is a sign of a large error.

When we analyse the technique of exercises in the flight phase, besides evaluating the quality of technical actions we need to characterise the basic parameters of flight (starting speed and main kinetic moment). The distance of flight is a function of the starting velocity of CoM. Horizontal shift is defined by the words 'far-close' (in the middle of the norm), while vertical is defined by the words 'high-low'. We can only give a qualitative description to the main kinetic moment given from support indirectly according to the speed of rotation in flight. This is done using the words 'fast-slow'.

Parametric faults are caused by preceding structural errors with which they are closely associated. In structural mistakes we distinguish *mistakes within the margin positions and mistakes in leading elements of coordination*. These mistakes are also inter-connected and mutually conditioned. They may have a local or total character. In the first case they have deviations from the ideal of a general character (for instance, insufficient general bend or straightening of the body as a whole), and in the second they have local (for example, bending the arms or legs if this is forbidden by competition rules).

When performing elements on the apparatus the gymnast normally fixes the place of grip. So to define critical positions in the phase structure in these cases it is enough to define the body's orientation in the critical positions sufficiently to use the words 'early-late' in the spatial and temporal aspect. Errors of position are defined by the words 'insufficient-excessive' by contrast with the geometrical target of a given critical positions.

The *leading element of coordination* is characterised by the place of applying major effort, its duration and degree of development and, therefore, it is determined with the help of spatial-temporal and force parameters. Technical actions linked with performing the leading element of coordination in a given phase can begin earlier or later, continue longer or shorter and be stronger or weaker than necessary. Hence to define faults in the leading element it is enough to use three pairs of words: 'early-late', 'long-short' and 'strong-weak'. When joined together these elementary definitions form more general definitions. For example, we often use in the coaching lexicon the word *sharply* to mean short or powerful, while the word 'slack' we take to mean long and weak.

Figure 58 shows the structure of technical faults reflecting the above-mentioned approach.

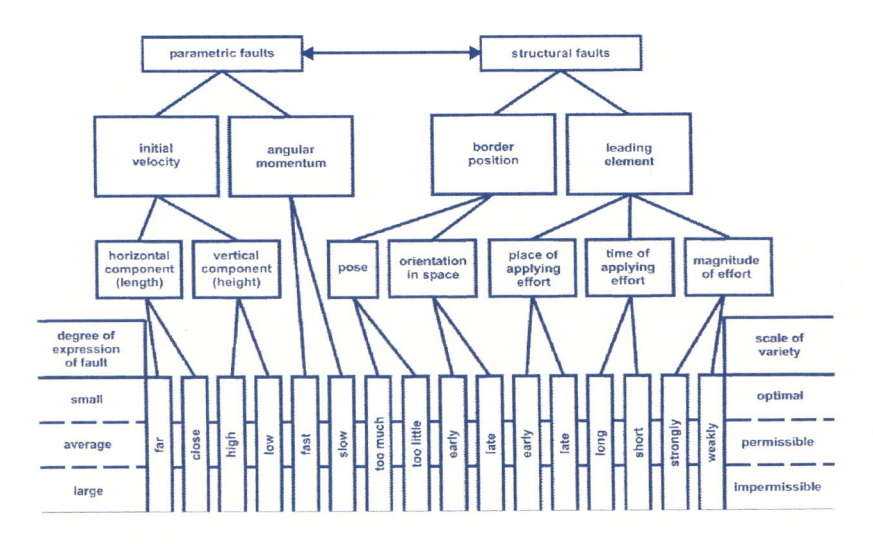

Figure 58 – *Structure of technical errors*

GYMNASTICS EXERCISES

If the diagnosis is made and the fault defined, the way to remove it is obvious: it is counterindicated to the diagnosis. For example, if the gymnast performs some control movement early, the coach will have to recommend him to do it later, and if it is long and weak, he has to be told 'do it shorter and stronger'.

Faults in critical positions worsen the geometrical design of movement and hamper a correct performance of the following technical actions. Faults in the leading elements, in turn, provoke errors in the next critical position, etc. However, the rule here is not strict. The gymnast may break the chain of faults.

The analysis we have made shows that the following causes of technical faults are the most typical:

- the gymnast does not have the right picture of technique in performing the given element (he lacks an adequate target of technical structure);
- in the preceding phases there are multiple deviations from the standard or minor mistakes which are not corrected in time;
- the gymnast cannot perform the required movement or action because he is not prepared for it technically, physically or psychologically;
- the gymnast does not exactly know where his fault lies and (or) what he has to do through lack of information, an inadequate feed-back or incomprehensible instructions from the coach;
- the gymnast does not want to perform what the coach requires of him because he thinks it incorrect or inconsequential;
- the gymnast is scared of doing the required technical action;
- the gymnast wrongly assesses his technical actions as a result of incorrect self-evaluation and (or) inadequate self-control.

Thus, a gymnast's technical faults are caused mainly by an insufficient level of preparation (technical, physical, functional, psychological, theoretical), by inferior information, inadequate feed-back and the coach's mistakes. More often insufficient level of special physical training is the cause of technical faults when performing complex exercises.

After a qualitative analysis of technique if necessary we conduct a quantitative analysis using measuring techniques, film or video analysis (see Chapter 10.2.12). For a quality analysis of technique the coach normally only has to use his eyes, ears, memory, brain and respective video apparatus. He must also have corresponding experience and professional knowledge; this Chapter and the book is intended to deepen that knowledge.

7.4 Control and Evaluation of Technique

The level of technical readiness of a world-class gymnasts is normally determined on the basis of indicators of too high a degree of generality. These are the results of competitions and control training sessions, the dynamics, the difficulty of the competitive programme, base marks, the sum total of deductions for errors committed, number of falls and precise landings, etc. However, this is not enough for an adequate analysis of the technique of performing elements from which consist routines, timely diagnosis of faults and elaboration of their causes on one of the most important levels of controlling movement – the structural-phase.

Our experiments and practice have shown that the effectiveness of learning complex exercises and the tempo of improvement of technical skill will rise if we control the phase structure of elements in the process of technical training. Here the object of control and evaluation is the technique of performing elements as a whole and their basic biomechanical parameters, then by their periods, stages and finally, the critical positions and leading elements in the movement phases. In controlling the latter and the influences directly made on them, we 'overtake' movement into a more narrow, well-controlled stream. Thereby we can define its development and facilitate the forming of the required attributes and qualities.

The essence of our method of control and evaluating of technique of executing strategic elements is explained by the example of dismounts. Let us stress that here we assess technique of performing the dismount (element) irrespective of its difficulty. Our approach is based on comprehensive use of quantitative and qualitative indicators within the framework of our methodology of pedagogical biomechanics (see Chapter 2.1).

An experienced coach-expert (preferably three) makes an assessment of the technique of performing the dismount by a specific gymnast immediately after a control approach by completing special reports. First he completes a technical report No. 1 (Table 18) where he determines the total of deductions for faults when dismounting generally. The deductions range in value and rank, with each rank having a mark in points according to the five-point system shown in Table 18.

Table 18
Technique assessment in points

Deduction Total	Rank	Mark in Points
0.0	1	5 (excellent)
up to 0.1	2	4 (good)
up to 0.2	3	3 (satisfactory)
up to 0.3	4	2 (unsatisfactory)
from 0.4 and higher	5	1 (poor)

These and the following points are filled in with the corresponding graphs in Report No. 1. Next comes assessment of the basic parameters of flight (length, height and rotation) in points. The point depends on what scale of variation the given parameter is. For that we use Table 19.

If, for example, the length of flight corresponds to the model characteristic, then in the respective graph of report No. 1 we put 5 points ('excellent'). If it varies within the bounds of the optimal scale, we put 4 points ('good'). If this parameter lies within the permissible scale, we put 3 points ('satisfactory'), and if impermissible it gets 2 points ('unsatisfactory'), etc. Similarly we assess height and rotation in flight.

To determine the length of flight on landing mats or foam rubber pits we draw a clearly divided white line with a pace of 10cm. The height of flight is evaluated on a video recording of the dismount against the background of a grid.

Table 19

Assessment of basic flight parameters

Type	Basic Flight Parameters	Model Characteristics (5 points)	Optimal Scale (4 points)	Permissible Scale (3 points)	Impermissible Scale (2 points)
Acro	Length, m	2.2	2.0-2.5	1.7-2.8	< 1.7 & > 2.8
	Height (above carpet), m	2.6	2.4-2.6	2.2-2.0	< 2.0
	Time, s	1.15	1.0-1.1	0.9-1.1	< 0.9
Rings	Length, m	0.0	0.3	0.3-0.5	> 0.5
	Height (above lower edge of rings), m	0.5	0.3-0.5	0.1-0.3	< 0.1
	Time, s	1.1	1.0-1.09	0.99-0.9	< 0.9
Vault/ Jump	Length, m	M: 0.3 W:2.5	M: 2.5-3.5	M: 2.0-4.0	< 2 & > 4
	Height (above horse), m	1.4	1.25-1.35	1.15-1.25	< 1.25
	Time, s	1.1	0.9-1.05	0.8-0.9	< 0.8
Parallel Bars	Length, m	0.0	0.3	0.3-0.5	> 0.5
	Height (above bars), m	0.8	1.25-1.39	1.1-1.24	< 1.1
	Time, s	1.05	0.9-1.0	0.9-0.8	< 0.8
Horizontal Bar	Length, m	1.8	1.7-2.4	1.4-1.69; 2.25-2.8	< 1.4 > 2.6
	Height (above bar), m	1.4	1.25-1.39	1.1-1.24	< 1.1
	Time, s	1.3	1.2-1.29	1.1-1.19	< 1.1

Height and speed of rotation in flight may be assessed visually with subsequent precision of evaluation through looking at a video recording of the dismount on a monitor with a grid. An experienced coach can do this well enough by sight. To determine the speed of rotation we use the following qualitative definitions: *swift rotation* (5 points), *rapid* (4 points), *moderate* (3 points), *slow* (2 points).

Since the time of flight is functionally associated with its height, instead of determining it by sight we may register the flight time by instruments. After a certain training the time of flight may be determined by a hand stopwatch. But the accuracy of this is not high enough (up to ± 0.05secs, and this is ± 13cm of height of CoM lift in flight). Therefore it is better to use a construction that automatically registers time of flight or a section of time in the frame of a video recorder screen.

After assessing the basic parameters of flight we assess all four stages of the dismount (*accumulation, working, implementation and landing*) using the same scale of marks. To evaluate the two last stages we should familiarise ourselves with special indicators.

Straightening the body in flight at the phase of preparing for landing is the principal indicator of improving technique at the implementation stage. This is assessed as follows: *early or full straightening (5 points), sufficient (4 points), insufficient (3 points), lacking altogether (2 points).*

Deduction for quality of landing is the major indicator at the stage of landing. Here we use the following gradation: *landing with hop without deduction (5 points, deduction 0.1 (4 points), deduction 0.2 (3 points), deduction 0.4 and more (2 points).* Experts must be able to distinguish faults committed directly in the process of landing, from faults resulting from technical errors in the previous stages of the dismount.

After filling in all the graphs of report No. 1 the assessments are added up and the sum total of points put in the last graph of this report against the surname of each gymnast tested. This mark is an integrated indicator of the technique of the performed dismount. After that the total of marks are ranked and the gymnast's place in the team is determined according to the technique of performing a working dismount. As an example Table 20 shows the report of assessing the technique of performing dismounts.

Table 20

Report No. 1: Assessing technique of performing dismounts on the horizontal bar

Surname	Name of dismount	Deduction	Assessment	Basic parameters of flight Distance	Height	Rotation	Dismount stages Acceleration	Working	Realisation	Landing	Sum Total	Rank
		0.2	3	4	3	5	4	5	4	4	32	II
		0.3	2	3	3	4	5	3	4	3	27	III
		0.0	5	5	5	5	5	5	5	5	35	I

If the technical actions at some stage are performed unsatisfactorily, we need to analyse the phase composition of the dismount. For that we need to assess the phases first as a whole, then in detail, filling in reports Nos. 2 and 3 (Tables 21 and 22). In the last case we assess the critical positions and leading elements.

Table 21

Report No. 2: Assessing the phase composition of the dismount

Name	Phases							
	Acceleration	Pre-Swing	Swing	Release	Flight	Prepare for Landing	Landing	Standing errect
1. Smith	5	3	5	3	4	3	4	4
2. Jones	5	2	3	3	4	3	2	2
3. Adams	5	4	5	4	5	4	5	

Table 22

Report No. 3: Detailed assessment of movement phase

		Name of Phase				
		Critical Position || 	Leading Element		
	Orientation	Posture	Start	Duration	Effort
Faults	Early	Excessive	Late	Long	Weak

We may test and assess the prospects of technique using the following test exercise. The gymnast is asked to perform his working dismount with a turn into the foam rubber pit in a pose when the magnitude of moment of inertia relative to the transverse axis in flight is close to the maximum. For example, he is asked to do a dismount with fully straightened body in flight if his working dismount is a version of a double piked somersault, or in a pose with open half-tuck if its modification is a Tsukahara. If the gymnast performs the dismount with an obvious over-turn and lands on his back, the gymnast's technique is promising, and if he obviously hangs in flight, then no. The prospects for technique demonstrates that the gymnast is technically ready to master more complex modifications of his working dismount.

Elements performed only in support position are considerably simpler in structure. They have only one support period which normally includes two stages (accumulation and working) and 4-5 phases. The technique of their execution is evaluated similarly, except for the flight parameters owing to the lack of them.

The technique of strategic elements on each apparatus, as well as the technique of base elements of a higher level is assessed as shown above. Such elements on each apparatus are usually from three to five. To retain, elaborate and utilise such a manner of results for assessing technique and investigating the competitive activity of national team gymnasts we need to create a computer database.

7.5 Methods of Pedagogical-biomechanical Analysis of Technique

On the basis of the theoretical prerequisites elaborated in previous sections of this Chapter, we have worked out and implemented methods of comparative qualitative pedagogical-biomechanical analysis of the technique of gymnastics exercises through the Russian 'Kinex' programme-apparatus complex [64] (see Chapter 10.2.12).

The methodology consists in the following. We record by video camera the gymnastics exercises that interest us as performed by various gymnasts. The optimal axis of the video camera here is set in the perpendicular plane of gymnast's movement and as much as possible coinciding with the centre of rotation. A video recording by frame is reproduced on the monitor screen of the video-analysis system. Each frame is marked by an experienced operator with an ordinary mouse. Comparative analysis is done as follows. Two marked files of the same gymnastics element as performed by different gymnasts is brought up by programmed methods on the computer's monitor screen. These files containing stick figures of the technical structures of two gymnasts may be put in various parts of the screen (for example one under the other, or one to the right and one to the left), combined or laid underneath each other.

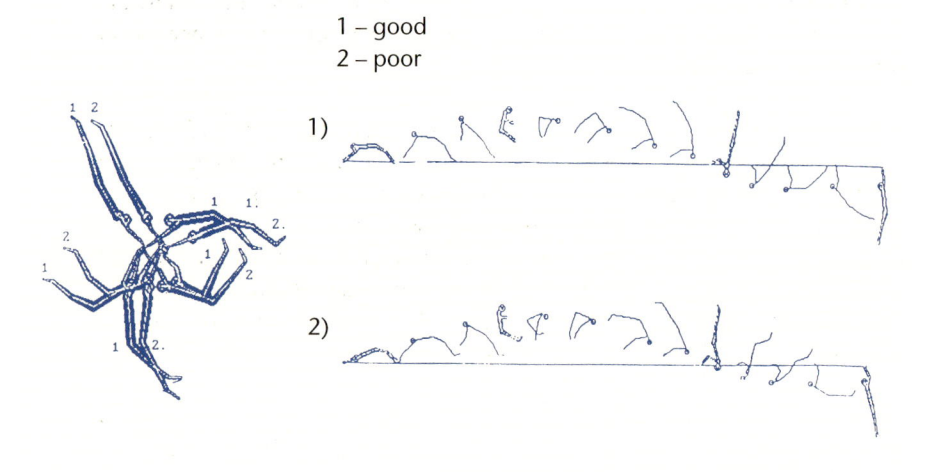

1 – good
2 – poor

Figure 59 – *The method of comparative pedagogy – biomechanical analysis of technique*

In our case (Figure 59) we used the Xio Ruizhi on the horizontal bar as performed by two members of the Russian national team – a good and one with a profound technical fault. The files are synchronised according to the moment of release from the apparatus. The support period here is placed one on top of the other with a small spread, while the unsupported period is shown so that the good performance is above and the poor below.

If we begin our comparative analysis from the start, from the first frames, we see notable differences in performance technique. But we cannot say with certainty whether they are good or bad until we follow both movements to the end and see the result of the technical actions of the gymnasts. Therefore, following through our method of analysis 'from end to start' we begin from the moment of the second gymnast making a major error – stopping below the horizontal bar after making the re-catch. A deduction of 0.5 of a point is made by competition rules for this fault. Evidently, this deduction is not the result of poor control in movement after arrival on the apparatus. It is caused by actions in the preceding phases.

Having separated out by programmed means the critical positions in the phase structure and moving in the direction from end to beginning, we subsequently determine the differences in technique of performing a given element between the two gymnasts, using the qualitative definitions shown in the previous section. They are obvious through visual comparative analysis of the two video-cyclograms.

When comparing the technical actions in the unsupported period of the two gymnasts, we can see that with a similar programme of control movements in flight the first gymnast (good performance) rotates faster. In the same time of flight he rotates about the transverse axis with an obtuse angle. Without measuring the basic flight parameters we are correct to conclude that the first gymnast produced great kinetic momentum from support (the second basic flight parameter). With the second gymnast, during the implementation stage we observe a clearly insufficient parameter in flight: the gymnast rotates too slowly.

Consequently, the technical actions of the first gymnast in the support period of the element, all things equal, are preferable since he can finish the required form of movement in flight earlier and has more time to prepare to re-grip the horizontal bar. This is more spectacular and gives him the advantage in the judges' assessment over the second gymnast.

After that, in comparing the position of the gymnasts when they release of the support, we find that with the second gymnast (performing with a large technical error) the angle in the shoulder joints is considerable less than with the first who accentuates unbending in these joints on departure. The second gymnast accentuates the opening of the hip angle.

Continuing our analysis from the end to the beginning and moving back from the unsupported period to the support, we can compare the positions of both gymnasts at the moment of release. We call them the starting positions of flight. Here we see that the first gymnast leaves the bar earlier than the second. His position is lower than the first.

Comparing straight afterwards the critical positions of the gymnasts between phases of thrust and anti-courbette we find that with the second gymnast the angle in the hips is less at the end of the thrust. With account for the fact that he began the thrust phase earlier (compare the initial critical positions of both gymnasts in the swing phase), we may conclude that the second gymnast performs the thrust longer and weaker than the first, who does both the thrust and the anti-courbette with the same timings but with stronger and greater amplitude.

Moving further in the reverse direction we see that there are no differences with the gymnasts in the starting position.

When we analyse the technique of the Xiao Ruizhi fly-over as performed by two gymnasts, we have found the primary reason in the chain of technical errors with the second gymnast and we have made our diagnosis. The reason for a major technical error leading to considerable deduction of marks lies in the following. An early and weak swing has caused a long and weak thrust. In turn it has caused a weak anti-courbette in the phase of pre-start actions of the support period without sufficient opening of the shoulder angle and an early start. All this together has led to an insufficient kinetic moment given from support. As a consequence, there has been a relatively slow rotation and a low flight, halting the movement downwards after re-griping the horizontal bar.

Recommendations to the second gymnast here are obvious and consist in the following. If the large technical error (halting or falling from the bar) is not chance and is repeated, we need to correct the source cause in the shown chain of deviations from the correct technical execution. We need to begin and end the swing phase later, and the swing itself should be performed more sharply – ie more strongly and shorter. This will enable the gymnast more energetically to perform the thrust and the anti-courbette and give a greater kinetic moment from support. Other things being equal, this will ensure more speed of rotation in flight and will increase its height (see Chapter 6.2).

Stubborn attempts to perform a successful re-grip of the bar or to correct technical shortcomings in other phases of movement will cause a significant loss of time, effort, nerves and rarely lead to success. We need to correct the source and not the consequence of errors.

After a qualitative analysis we make a comparative quantitative analysis by defining the kinematic characteristics of successful and erroneous technical actions in the phases of movement by use of computer programming. As a result we find an answer to the question not only how but to what extent one technique of performance differs from another quantitatively.

7.6 Structure of Self-control

The tempo of improvement of technical skill of world-class gymnasts and its reliability depend on the degree of development of the self-control system. A highly developed self-control system is based on objectively thought-out images and sensations affecting the objectives and results of the gymnast's actions.

A crucial component of self-control is the target programme of technical actions in the form of an ideo-motor scheme which is created on the basis of the target of the technical structure of movement. An adequate motor image of what is required in the future enables the gymnast to gain a detailed insight into what has to happen as a result of his actions. This image-model is formed through knowledge and understanding of the principal requirements made on a given exercise, technique of performance, knowledge of its particular features, as well as through personal motor experience. The more this occurs the more finely tuned and the more richer the target programmes of technical actions, and the more expansive the bank of these programmes become stored in the gymnast's motor memory.

An ideo-motor programme is a complex dynamic formation. Like the actual technical action, it has several features: spatial, temporal, rhythm-tempo, kinematic, dynamic and informational, which exist in complex interconnection.

The following component of self-control is self-assessment, being the result of comparing a performed technical action with its target programme. Self-assessment relies on an accurate analysis of the performed action being accurately compared with the result of the action and understanding of the performance. In line with the theory of functional systems a valuable result of activity is a system-building factor [37] (see Chapter 2.1).

Through self-assessment of technical actions a world-class gymnast takes a decision about their correction in the following approach. This process is repeated again and again. Thus, self-control has a circular character and is carried out by the scheme: *perception – collation with the target programme – self-assessment – decision – correction, etc., etc.*

At the early stages of learning complex gymnastics exercises self-control is usually an actively present and internalised characteristic. As skill level develops the process becomes automatic. Internalised elements of self-control come together in increasingly compact blocks. The form of self-control in learning changes in form, passing consecutively through phases of logical, sensory-logical and sensory control against the background of an increasingly adequate ideo-motor programme of technical actions.

Lack of such a programme in the learning phase will seriously impede the effective and flexible system of self-control. The formed structure represents a blockage at a level of stages (at best) comprising discrete, logically and sensorally poorly connected disparate elements of self-control.

Inasmuch as objective self-assessment of critical positions and leading elements of coordination practically fall out of one's field of vision, a return to the normal state after making a mistake presents considerable difficulty. Such a self-control system in such situations is insufficiently flexible and effective because it rests on inadequate internalised premises which skirt one of the vital levels of controlling movement – the structural-phase.

GYMNASTICS EXERCISES

For an adequate self-assessment of technical actions we need to define the parameters on which a gymnast should concentrate his attention. Practice demonstrates that in many cases even a reasonably well-experienced gymnast (for example, member of the junior national team) may fail to select, as object of self-control, the key and preceding action leading to the secondary action. It is an important scientific task at the core of pedagogical biomechanics and psychology of gymnastics to reveal the basic elements of self-control while learning and improving technique of exercises.

In investigating the structure of self-control we have separated out four types of parameters:

- parameters which the gymnast establishes control over consciously;
- parameters that are recognised only in the event of deviations;
- parameters that the control over are fully automated (though they may have been controlled consciously before);
- non-existent parameters which have never before been recognised.

Moreover, we have distinguished also levels of differentiation – ie signs by which the gymnasts recognise and distinguish elements of self-control – within elements of self-control always recognised, and elements recognised only in the event of deviations. These are according to time, space or force parameters, and even all these combined together.

Our research has shown that gymnasts base comprehensive self-control on control over their sensations. Moreover, the higher the class of athlete, the greater the degree that his system of self-control rests on sensation and how finely tuned it is. This circumstance naturally presents certain demands on the starting point of self-control and its platform – programme of action. With world-class gymnasts it acquires a marked ideo-motor character in the form of sensor or sensor-logical motor images.

With the growth in skill the structure of self-control changes form. There is an increase in number of elements being controlled automatically and a decrease in the number of elements being controlled consciously. The accent on conscious self-control shifts to the entry phases of movement. Its object becomes actions of a starting nature corresponding to a deliberate structure of movement. For example, when performing dismounts and fly-overs top-class gymnasts normally train their attention on the moment of start of the swing phase.

So we see that growth in technical skill is accompanied by a minimisation of deliberately controlled elements of self-control with transfer of emphasis on attention to the moment of starting and the main working actions become performed automatically. Technical actions here may be transformed into operations performed through automatic, unconscious self-control. The existence of gymnasts with a conscious system of self-control is one of the crucial factors in attaining a high level of technical-performing skill and its reliable implementation in circumstances of acute competitive struggle.

We studied the nature of various images of the structure of technical actions on the model of dismounts from the parallel bars of progressive complexity, and we worked out the parameters of conscious self-control with world-class gymnasts. We revealed that in the support period self-control mainly bears a complex character and to a large extent is emphasized in the spatial-power aspect. In flight self-control is done exclusively by sensation of time.

The number of consciously controlled elements of self-control varied within the bounds of 1 to 5. Young gymnasts paid special attention to correctly performing a swing and the moment of release of the support (the starting position). Analysis of the data showed that with members of the national junior team ideas about the technical structure of dismounts from the parallel bars were no lower than the stages of movement. They had no adequate idea about phase structure.

This mosaic character of self-control emphases was caused also by a lack of adequate guiding core of technical actions, as well as by conservative errors which the gymnasts committed when doing dismounts. Our analysis demonstrated that the cause of these faults lay in the incorrect methods of learning dismounts, as well as in an early 'storming' of the heights of complexity without a sufficient basic preparation.

We worked out an optimised target of the structure of self-control of technical actions when performing dismounts which was tested in training the junior national team and which provided good practical results. In this model we separated out hierarchically subordinate emphases of self-control at the level of periods, stages and phases. As a result of its introduction we developed algorithms and substantially accelerated the process of minimising the bulk of consciously controlled elements of self-control and target transferred them to an automatic level while at the same time, improving technical skill.

Experiments conducted during ideo-motor training of many generations of members of the Soviet and Russian men's and women's teams have shown that the time of actual performance of exercises on the apparatus and the time of their ideo-motor reproduction almost fully coincide. For example, Dmitri Bilozerchev even broke out into a sweat over this. The difference between the time of actual and ideo-motor performance of his routines in all items of the multi-events comprised only ±1-2 seconds [47]. This evidences the need for exceedingly fine sensation of time and space, a highly-developed ability to make an adequate ideo-motor modelling of technical actions, and the adequacy of these ideo-motor programmes themselves when it comes to world-class men and women gymnasts.

Our research and practical experience give grounds to maintain that ideo-motor training is one of the most effective means of additional training of world-class gymnasts. Unfortunately, coaches and gymnasts frequently ignore it.

How to Create Champions   8

CHAPTER EIGHT

Basic and Strategic High Level Elements

8.1 Universal Basic Habits of General Designation

Top-class gymnasts must be able to do the following:

- perfectly possess the habit of holding the correct static and dynamic carriage (posture) in a variable power field with any orientation of the body in space and at high accelerations;
- hang for a long time, correctly, comfortably and aesthetically in all basic hangs (grip from above, below, reverse, from behind, on one hand);
- remain in all basic supports on the apparatus for a long time, correctly, comfortably and aesthetically;
- stand and move with turns in handstand for a long time, correctly, comfortably and aesthetically;
- possess correct and aesthetic body lines in all basic working positions;
- perfectly possess optimal technical execution of swings, rotations, courbettes (snap-down) and anti-courbettes (counter-rotation);
- possess a good basic technical, physical and choreographic training.

8.2 General Premises

Gymnasts with claims to join the world elite and take prizes at major international competitions must perfectly possess the correct technical execution of several basic elements and connecting phases at a high level, in each event of the competition, as indicated below.

For a routine in each event to be of full value and competitive, it must have complex elements that we call strategic and target. Without such elements a successful outcome to the competitive struggle at the topmost level will be problematic.

In this Chapter we list the strategic target elements recommended for inclusion in competition routines in all events of the men's and women's multi-event programme.

Where necessary we show the number of repetitions of elements and connecting movements in a single attempt that ensures a high training effect and optimal surplus at the stage of combined technical-physical perfection of these elements. The list is accompanied by technical demands and commentaries for groups of similar elements, where we consider it necessary.

The recommended strategic elements of high complexity are not compulsory for mastering in full volume (i.e. not all together). Coaches and gymnasts may choose those which to a great extent correspond to their individual abilities, given the condition that this enables them to compose full value competitive routines necessary for successful competition at the top level.

According to the FIG 2000 competition rules, in each event all the elements are divided into several groups (five for men and up to nine for women). In the difficulty tables attached to the rules they are all given a name, numbered and represented in graphic form with corresponding squares bearing a certain group of difficulty. In the Russian Rules we use difficulty tables from the FIG Rules.

So there is no need for a detailed description of elements recommended in this Chapter. But it should be noted that classification signs when dividing elements into groups in the international rules are, in our view, not shown clearly enough.

In cases where the recommended elements carry a name (the surname of the first performer of it at international competition), in the text they are put with a capital letter and mostly equipped with numbers showing the group of difficulty according to the tables of difficulty from the FIG 2000 Rules.

8 HIGH LEVEL ELEMENTS

General technical requirements and commentary

- all power element must be done fairly slowly and evenly, without using a swing;

- all swing elements must be done fairly quickly, without using force;

- the optimal stretching of muscles before the start of basic working actions increases their power;

- when performing all elements with a large forward swing the gymnast should actively 'hang' in the shoulders;

- when performing elements the gymnast must clearly show the starting and finishing position with geometrically correct, aesthetic lines of the body. These positions must be each time designated or fixed if this is specially stipulated;

- all poses, positions, actions and posture must be technically correct, bio- mechanically targeted, aesthetic and comfortable for the gymnast when performing elements and connecting movements;

- gymnasts must be able to hold all static positions and elements with a time excess of 2-3 times that which is demanded in the Competition Rules;

- everywhere where this is specially stipulated, gymnasts must be able to repeat basic and profile elements 5-6 times (including 3-5 times in a row), profile connecting movements 3-4 times, and complex strategic elements 2-3 times in a single attempt;

- the instruction 'repeat so many times' means repeating the element with a minimal number of auxiliary elements and preparatory assisting movements;

- the instruction 'repeat in succession' means repeating the element without mixing it with others.

8.3 Men

8.3.1 Floor Exercise

Group 1. Balance, strength and flexibility elements:

- press to Japanese handstand (Japanese stand, No. 18, C) (hold 4 seconds, repeat 3 times);
- planche (Support lever, No. 22, B) (hold 5 seconds);
- from horizontal support lever legs apart or together, press handstand (nos. 27 or 28, B and C respectively) (repeat 3 times);
- Manna, with legs parallel to the floor, and press handstand (Manna, No. 9, D) (repeat twice);

Technical requirements and commentary:
the geometry of body lines must be aesthetic and faultless.

Group 2. Leaps, jumps, turns and leg circle elements:

- circles with legs together and flairs exiting into handstand (No. 32, B);
- from handstand lower into circles legs together or flairs (No. 37, B);
- Russian wendeswing with turn of 1080° (Fedorchenko, No. 54, D);
- 1/1 spindle with legs together into handstand and lowering into circles (No. 50, E);
- flair or circle to handstand and continue to flair or circle (Gogladze, No. 34, D) (repeat 3 times in a row).

Technical requirements and commentary:
all circle movements must be done together, without loss of tempo, the legs and hips must be at a sufficient height from the floor.

Group 3. Acrobatic elements forwards:

- handspring from one leg to two in tempo (no fewer than 5);
- flyspring from two on to two in tempo with mounting speed (no fewer than 5);
- tempo forward straight somersault + high forward somersault with straight body;
- forward somersault with turn of 720° (two twists forward No. 49, D);
- double tuck forward somersault (No. 29, D).

Group 4. Acrobatic elements backwards:

- round off jump with half turn, round off jump with half turn in tempo (no fewer than 5);
- back handsprings (flic flacs) in tempo with mounting speed from the spot and from a round off (no fewer than 4);
- tempo back somersault (No. 17, B) in tempo with mounting speed from the spot and from a round off (no fewer than 4);
- round off, flic flac back somersault with straight body (22B);
- three tempo back somersaults + high straight somersault;
- straight back somersault with turn of 1080° (three twists, No. 34,D);
- double back tuck somersault (No. 8, C);
- round off, flic flac, double back somersault opening and closing the tuck;
- double back straight somersault with turns of 360°, 540°, 720°, 900° and 1080° (Nos. 25 and 40, E, super-E);
- triple tuck back somersault (Ljukin, No. 5, SE).

Connecting movements with combined rotations from three somersaults 'C' and 'D':

round off, tempo, back somersault with turn of 540° forward somersault with turn of 360°, double forward somersault.

Group 5. Acrobatic elements sidewards, or backward jumps with half turn to salto forwards:

- round off, flic flac, jump with turn of 180° into forward tuck somersault or piked somersault (No. 7, B);
- round off, flic flac, double pike or with 1/2 twist (nos. 9 and 10, D and E);
- side tuck somersault from the spot (No. 22, B) (no fewer than 3 in a row after 1-2 steps).

Technical requirements and commentary:

- all exercises are done initially on the acrobatics runway, and then along a carpet diagonal for the free exercises. The diagonal length determines the number of repetitions of basic elements in the long connecting movements;
- all round offs and revolutions are done together, without loss of tempo and with a soft roll through the forward leg ('stumbling' must not occur);

- one should avoid a high braking skip step because this reduces the horizontal speed accumulated in the run-up;
- all take-offs after the round offs are done on the basis of an active courbette. In a series of round offs, one should do a jump upwards after each round off, then a half turn and only then enter into the following round off;
- one must not turn the head towards the round off and let the shoulders 'sag' to the side in the skipstep. It is also wrong to lower the arms too much. Here the round off becomes short, the gymnast 'splutters' and the direction of movement inclines away from a straight line;
- all preparatory exercises (round offs, flic flacs, tempo saltos) are done together without loss of tempo in a 'rolling' regime without significant height loss. The CoM trajectory comes close to a straight line; the CoM horizontal velocity is even or evenly accelerated, the vertical is close to zero;
- all take-offs and landings when doing preparatory exercises must be performed upright, with straight body;
- all take-offs into somersault must be done upright with straightened body after developing maximum effort while actively thrusting off from support;
- all somersaults must be high and with sufficient rotation;
- when performing all somersaults the rotation in flight must be fast without significant bending of the body;
- all straight somersaults must be done straightening the body to the maximum, raising the arms at the moment of take off (no lower than shoulder level);
- strong bending of the body in flight and (or) bending before landing is a sign of insufficiency either of height of flight, or of the main kinetic moment given from support, or both together;
- when doing jumps backwards with 1/2 turn into a forward somersault (7B) after take-off the gymnast must perform the 1/2 turn and only then a forward somersault with rotation around the shoulders;
- when doing all somersaults with twists from support it is incorrect to turn the body earlier around the longitudinal axis in the process of take-off and early entry into twist. This reduces the effectiveness of the take-off into somersault and its height and speed of rotation in twists. At the moment of take-off what is important is not the magnitude of angle of turn of links around the longitudinal axis, but the speed of turn. So all entries into twists from support must be done late, fast and sharply;

8 HIGH LEVEL ELEMENTS

- it is incorrect to continue twisting after landing: this causes injury and is a technical fault;
- all landings must have a clear dismount phase straightening the body before landing;
- when landing into a foam rubber-pit the gymnast should over-rotate onto the back;
- the absolute height of CoM lift in flight when doing a somersault may vary within the range 1.25-1.4m. The total height of all somersaults over the carpet is 2.4-2.6m;
- the height of flight when doing a double straight somersault may be lower than in other jumps, but it must be sufficient;
- the length of flight is 1.7-2.8m;
- the total time of flight when doing a somersault is 1.05-1.15 seconds for men and 0.95 seconds for women.

8.3.2   Pommel Horse

Group 1. Single-leg swings:

- high forward straight scissors (no fewer than five);
- high straight scissors backwards (no fewer than five);
- high scissors with turn in circle;
- high scissors into handstand and subsequent lowering into support (no fewer than 3).

Technical requirements and commentary:

- when doing scissors the pelvis must come to the level of the centre of the shoulder axis;
- scissors must be done without loss of tempo, extending at the topmost point (template – the Nemov straight scissor).

Group 2. Circles in side and cross support with or without spindles and handstands:

- circles with legs together on handles in side support (no fewer than 50);
- circles with legs apart on handles in side support (no fewer than 30);
- circles in cross support (no fewer than 30);
- circles in cross support facing outwards (no fewer than 30);
- circles on the body without handles in side support (no fewer than 30);
- circles in support along the handles and between the handles (no fewer than 10);

- circles on one handle in side support (no fewer than 10);
- circles on one handle in cross support (no fewer than 15);
- all spindles in side support in two circles (No. 28,C) (no fewer than 10);
- spindle in a single circle with legs apart in side support(No. 29, D);
- spindle in one circle with legs together in side support (No. 30, E);
- spindle in one circle in side support or cross support hands between handles (Nos. 25 and 35, E);
- spindle in one circle in cross support front ways (Magyar, No. 40, E);
- circle with legs together or in flair through handstand (with or without 1/2 turn), lowering into flairs or circles (No. 38, C);
- flair or circle through handstand, with 360o turn and lower to flair or circle. (No. 39, D).

Group 3. Travels in side support and cross- support:

- travel forward in cross support to other end of horse (3/3) (Magyar, No. 39, D);
- travel backward in back support to other end of horse (3/3) (Sivado, No. 49, D);
- from cross support on end of horse travel forward in two circles to first pommel, to second pommel and with 1/4 turn to side support on other end of the horse (3/3) (Bilozerchev, No. 43, C).

Group 4. Kehr swings and Wende swings:

- Czechkehr circle (No. 37,B) (no fewer than 10);
- Czechkehr circle with hands outside the handles (Pinheiro, No. 34,D);
- Schwabenflank (No. 36, A);
- double Swiss circle (No. 32,B) (no fewer than 6);
- direct Stöckli B on one handle (No. 17, B) (no fewer than 8);
- reverse Stöckli (No. 22, B) (no fewer than 6);
- Russian wendeswing in cross support on handles with turn of 360° or 540° (No. 42, B), 720° or 900° (No. 43,C), 1080° or more (No. 44, D);
- also in cross support on the leather (Nos. 47,B, 48,C and 49,D);
- Russian wendeswing in cross support on one handle with turn of 180o, 270° (No. 52,B), 360° or 540° (No. 53,C), 720° or 900° (No. 54, D), 1080° and more (No. 55,E);
- Russian wendeswing with turn of 720° and 3/3 travel (Wu Guonian, No. 40,E) or 1080°;

8 HIGH LEVEL ELEMENTS

- from side support on end Russian wendeswing forward to other end without support on or between handles (Tong-fei, No. 29, D);
- from side support on end, kehr around first pommel, reverse Stöckli around second pommel to side support (rear) on other end (Moguilny, No. 4, D);
- from side support on end, reverse Stöckli around first pommel, kehr around second pommel to side support (rear) on other end (Belenki, No. 14, D);
- Magyar with spindle;
- various routines of the 'flop' system.

Group 5. Dismounts:

- flairs (Thomas) into handstand with turn of 360° into dismount;
- straight Stöckli A or reverse Stöckli into handstand with turn of 540° and with or without travel into dismount.

Technical requirements and commentary:

- all circular movements and single leg swings must be done cleanly, together, without stopping and losing tempo, with good amplitude;
- the circles must be fairly wide and high, they must be done from the shoulders as much as possible;
- in support from the front and back there should not be a big angle in the hips;
- the shoulders and legs should work as two pendulums in counter-phase; here the amplitude of rotation of the centre of the shoulder axis should not be significantly less than of the legs;
- the hands should be taken from the support late and be put on it early and firmly;
- in all circular movements in side support at all parts of the horse, the arms must be parallel to each other;
- two-handed support positions must be geometrically precise in the sense of parallel arms;
- circles in cross support in number and passes must be done on the Pommel Horse training apparatus (see 10.2.3).

8.3.3 Rings

Group 1. Kip and swing elements:

- forward up-rise into support half lever, lay away into hang (repeat 5 times in a row, the last support half lever hold for 5 seconds);
- front up-rise, swing back over head into rear hang and with forward swing lift into support (Li Ning 2, No. 18) (repeat 3 times);
- Li Ning 2 into high V-sit (without holding) + Li Ning (Czech rotation on rings, repeat twice);
- from hang tucked double felge backwards to hang (Guzcoghy, No. 23, C) (repeat 4 times in a row);
- Guzcoghy piked (No. 24, D);
- Guzcoghy straight (O'Neil, No. 25, E);

With back swing:

- from hang upstart (hold), fall backwards into inverted hang (repeat 5 times);
- backward swing to forward straight salto into support (Honma, No. 38, C) (repeat twice);
- from hang double tucked somersault forwards to hang (Yamawaki, 42, B) (repeat 3 times);
- double piked somersault forwards to hang (Jonasson, No. 43, C) (repeat 3 times);
- double straight somersault to hang (No. 44, D) (repeat twice).

Technical requirements and commentary:

- when doing the Li Ning swing over the head, the gymnast should perform it from support without any significant backward lean of the shoulders; and the Czech hang from the rear must be shown;
- when performing the Guzcohy and Yamawaki the tension of the rings should be slackened to a free state at the upper point of the lift, with the body rising higher than the upper level of the rings. In essence these elements represent a double somersault into hang;
- the Honma represents a forward somersault into support with back swing from hang;
- all final positions must be precisely indicated.

Group 2. Swing elements performed into handstand (hold for 2 seconds) with forward swing:

- high dislocation with increasing amplitude (five times in tempo);
- felge into handstand from swinging in hang;
- long swings backward (5 times in a row)

With back swing:

- connecting movements: high in- locations with increasing amplitude (5 times in a row);
- back up-rise into a handstand from swinging in hang;
- long swings forward (5 times in a row);
- Honma piked into support, to handstand with back swing (No. 13, C) (hold 3 seconds, repeat no fewer than 4 times);
- straight Honma into support, to handstand with back swing (No. 14, D) (hold for 3 seconds, repeat no fewer than 2 times).

Connecting movements:

- giant back rotation, giant back rotation, giant forward rotation, giant forward rotation, Honma, handstand with back swing, Honma, handstand with back swing, giant forward rotation, giant back rotation, giant forward rotation, giant back rotation, Honma, handstand with back swing, giant back rotation.

Technical requirements and commentary:
- the amplitude of dislocations should increase and reach handstands in the second-third swing. After that "penetration", giant rotations are easily performed;
- rotations and lifts into handstand must be done from hang by clean swing without a marked application of force;
- giant rotations must be done without use of force with straightened body and parallel arms on the thrust-offs, lifts and rotations;
- it is incorrect to spread the arms sideways which creates loss of speed when performing giant rotations;
- handstand when doing giant rotations must be designated in each repetition and fixed every other time (3 seconds);

- when doing the Honma the load on the rings must fall to a minimum. This is actually a forward somersault into support performed with a back swing;
- in the upward swing of the long swing the hands must always be the first supporting phase.

Group 3. Swing elements ending with complex strength static elements:

- upstarts, uprises (backwards and forwards) and Felges into swallow planche or inverted cross.

Technical requirements and commentary:
- the amplitude of the swing part of the exercise must be at a maximum;
- transfer from swing to strength static position must be short, sharp and precise in time, strength and geometry of lines;
- the movement must stop very quickly;
- the gymnast must immediately fall into a geometrically perfect static position and fix it without any additional correcting movements;
- he should hold the strength static position without fluctuations no less than two times longer than this is required in the FIG competition rules.

Group 4. Power and static elements (hold):

- planche with straight arms (3 times in a row);
- horizontal support (hold no less than 5 seconds);
- horizontal support (hold 2 seconds), press into stand (2 times in a row);
- 'cross' (hold 5 seconds);
- 'cross' (hold 3 seconds), press into support;
- Azarian beginning into 'cross' (hold 3 seconds);
- 'inverted cross' (5 seconds);
- 'inverted cross' (hold 3 seconds); press into handstand;
- "Maltese" (hold 5 seconds);
- "Maltese" (hold 3 seconds, press into horizontal support (hold 2 seconds));
- from horizontal hang press into "Maltese" (hold 2 seconds);
- all dynamic strength elements must be done slowly demonstrating surplus strength and precise holding of the starting and final positions;
- the gymnast must immediately take up a geometrically faultless static position without additional correcting movements;

8 HIGH LEVEL ELEMENTS

- the geometry of body lines during all strength movements and holds must be correct and aesthetic;
- all strength elements must be held freely without deviations from the ideal body position, without shaking;
- a deep grip during entry into the element and holding it is a mistake and should be eliminated;
- to ensure immediate feed-back and adequate self-control of the geometrically correct body lines before the rings (for pumping) one should set oneself facing the big mirror so that the gymnast can easily see himself in total while he is performing strength exercises.

Group 5. Dismounts

With big forward swing:
- double back somersault with straight body;
- double back straight somersault with turn of 360°;
- double back straight somersault with turn of 720°;
- triple back tuck somersault;
- triple back piked somersault.

Dismounts done with big back swing:
- double forward piked somersault with turn in circle;
- double forward straight somersault;
- double forward straight or piked somersault with turn of 540°;
- triple forward somersault with turn of 180°.

Technical requirements and commentary:
- a precise take-off from the rings must be shown in all dismounts;
- when performing all dismounts the gymnast's body must rise to the level of the upper end of the ropes to which the rings are attached;
- rotation in flight must be fast and well-coordinated;
- it is wrong to make an early twisting of twists;
- the turn around the longitudinal axis in flight should be done in time during flight;
- it is a serious and dangerous error to carry on twisting while landing;
- the phase of preparing for landing expressed in straightening the body must be clearly shown before planting the feet on support;
- landing must be done into dismount under the rings;
- the total height of flight is 0.5m above the lower edge of the rings;

- the total time of flight is 1.1 seconds;
- the total length of flight is 0.0m.

8.3.4 Vault

Basic exercises for vaulting (without vaulting table):
- run up increasing speed;
- forward somersault with straight body from vaulting board;
- round off somersault with straight body after the standard run up from the vaulting board (without throwing the trunk forward and the head back).

Technical requirements and commentary:
- the run up must be done so as to attain highest speed in the last 5 m of the run up;
- the forward somersault and round off somersault must be done from the vaulting board after a standard run up with speed needed for doing complex support vaults;
- the trunk must be slightly inclined forward in the run up (and especially in its last part);
- when doing the back somersault on take off from the vaulting board the gymnast must not let the head and (or) trunk come forward;
- the somersault must be done with straight body, arms up and to the side;
- the somersault must be high and turned enough;
- the somersault is initially done in normal conditions with landing on foam rubber mats, then over a pile of mats equal to the height of the horse and higher, and after that over the horse without touching its body with the hands;
- landing initially may be done into a foam rubber pit.

Group 3. Forward revolutions:
- handspring forward and forward straight somersault (No. 16);
- handspring forward and double forward tuck somersault (Roche, No. 27);
- handspring forward and double forward piked somersault;
- handspring forward and double forward tuck somersault with turn of 180° (Dragalescu, No. 28).

HIGH LEVEL ELEMENTS

Group 4. Jumps with turn of 90° or 180° in the first phase of flight (Tsukhahara sub-group):

- Kasamatsu straight with turn of 720° (Lopez, No. 37);
- Tsukahara – double back tuck somersault (Yeo, No. 28);
- Tsukahara – double back piked somersault (Lu Yu Fu, No. 34);
- Tsukahara and double back somersault with turn of 360°.

Group 5. Jumps from round off:

- round off-revolution back and back straight somersault with turn of 720° (No. 20);
- round off-revolution back and two and a half back somersaults with turn of 360°.

Technical requirements and commentary:

- there must not be any quickening of paces and diminishing of speed of run up, especially in the last 5m;
- the total speed in the last 5 m of run up is 8.2 m/s;
- the jump on to the vaulting board must be low and firm;
- the total height of flight is 0.15-0.2m, the length is 2.2-2.3m, and the time of flight is 0.3-0.35 seconds, the horizontal speed of jump is 8 m/s;
- when jumping on to the vaulting board the body must be straightened, with no substantial bending at the hips at the moment of planting the feet on the vaulting board;
- the feet should be planted practically in the centre of the vaulting board, somewhat closer to the forward part where its spring will be at the maximum;
- the gymnast should actively meet the vaulting board with his feet, beginning to straighten the legs before touching the vaulting board;
- thrust off from the vaulting board is done briefly and energetically, with interaction with the vaulting board taking 0.1-0.2 seconds;
- orientation of the body should be close to the vertical at the moment of take off;
- when leaving the vaulting board the shoulders should not be allowed to move forward, nor the arms be in contact with the horse too long;
- the gymnast should, as it were, describe a parabolic trajectory of flight in unsupported somersault;

- when doing jumps with forward rotation and super-rotations on leaving the vaulting board it is useful to perform a dynamic heel drive backward;
- the total length of jump on to the horse is 0.7-0.8m, the height is 1.2m, the flight time is 0.15-0.2 seconds;
- in Tsukahara-type vaults the time from the moment of leaving the vaulting board to planting the first hand on the body of the horse is shorter -0.1-0.15 seconds;
- the hands must be put on the body of the horse at the rising part of the flight trajectory;
- when planting the hands on the body of the horse there should not be any significant angles in the shoulders and hips. The gymnast should begin to unwind in these joints in the direction of body rotation in flight before planting hands on the body of the horse;
- the hands should thrust off of the body of the horse sharply and quickly;
- the total time of thrust off when performing vaults with revolutions is 0.15-0.25 seconds, the Tsukahara – 0.25-0.35 seconds;
- in thrusting off the body links (arms, trunk, legs) must turn in the direction of body rotation in flight;
- the gymnast's body at moment of departure must be straightened out, while the support reaction at that moment must be close to the vertical;
- it is incorrect to make an early tucking in thrust off from the body of the horse;
- the gymnast must quickly and smoothly tuck in flight immediately after letting go of the support, but not before;
- if this leads to an early tucking on support, the gymnast should be given instructions for a later tucking in flight;
- after pushing off from the body of the horse, the gymnast should markedly fly up while retaining a good horizontal speed of flight;
- the total absolute height of lift of the gymnast's body CoM in flight is 0.3-0.4m, the height over the horse is 1.3-1.4m, the height over the mats is 2.6-2.7m, the time of flight is 1.0-1.1 seconds, and the length of flight is 3-3.5m;
- rotation in flight, both around the transverse, and around the longitudinal axes, must be fast, with legs together, without loss of tempo;

- when performing various modifications of the straight somersault, the body in flight must be straight; it is a technical deficiency to make additional straightening, bending or unbending;
- the form of movement defining the name of the vault, including all the twists, must be precisely and timely completed in flight;
- at the end of flight the phase of preparation for landing, connected with slowing the rotation in somersault, must be displayed (and in vaults with super-rotations this is particularly important);
- when preparing for landing in flight there should be an overall straightening of the body;
- straightening of the legs at the knees while retaining an angle in the hips with subsequent removal before planting feet on support is a technical mistake (straightening the legs into the wall and lowering them);
- it is wrong to continue making twists in support while landing: this is likely to lead to injury;
- 5 out of 10 landings must be perfect!

8.3.5   Parallel Bars

Group 1. Elements done with swing from support on both bars:

Forward swing:
- back somersault over the bars into handstand (5 times in a row);
- back somersault over the bars into handstand on one bar with transfer on to two (Peters, No. 44,B) (2-3 times in a row);
- back somersault over the bars with 1/2 turn to upper arm support, to handstand with back swing (Toumilovtich, No. 33 into support) (repeat twice);
- stutzkehre into handstand (both hands) and its modification (into handstand on one bar Bilozerchev, No. 9 and so on) (3-5 times in a row, with pirouettes forward or backward after each handstand);
- Diamidov (5 times in a row) and its modifications (with turn of 180°, 450° and 540° Nos. 18, 14, 19, 20);
- Diamidov + 3/4 Healy into support (Makuts, No. 24,D) (three times in a row);
- double back somersault over the bars in tuck and piked into upper arm hang (Morisue, No. 34, D and No. 35, E) (repeat 2-3 times);

Back swing:
- forward piked somersault into support (No. 78, C) (5 times between swings, 3 times in a row);
- forward straight somersault into support (2 times in a row);
- swing backward with 1/2 turn hop to handstand (No. 57, B) (repeat 5 times with a free swing between the elements);
- swing backward with turns of 270°, 360° (Gatson No. 59), 450° and 540° (Nos 58 and 59);
- healy into support (No. 48, D) (five times in a row) and its modifications from handstand on one bar;
- double forward somersault over the bars in tuck and piked into upper arm hang (Nos. 83, C and 84, D) (repeat 2-3 times);
- forward straight somersault with turn of 360° into upper arm hang (Urzika, No. 89, D).

Technical requirements and commentary:
- when performing elements and connecting movements in support on both bars the coach and gymnast must pay particular attention to the correct technique of shifting the shoulders and to do the swing 'from the shoulders' with maximum amplitude and as freely as possible;
- when performing any swing in support the gymnast must at all times try to hold the shoulders above the support point;
- with the right technique of elements being performed by forward swing, the objective picture of movement looks as follows:
- when doing elements with forward swing on leaving handstand, the shoulders should be pushed slightly forward;
- in the horizontal position this reaches its maximum (up to 30° forward from the vertical) and at that moment the shoulders start to shift back;
- when passing the vertical position the arms are vertical, their longitudinal axis coincides with the trunk's longitudinal axis, although the shoulder movement continues backward;
- the shoulders lean back to the maximum (up to 30° back from the vertical) in the body's horizontal position;
- at that moment the shoulders are pushed forward, and the gymnast energetically presses from the bars in the shoulder joints, accelerating the swing and ensuring a free and large forward swing from the shoulder with maximum possible amplitude;
- here the body's CoM shifts strictly upwards along the vertical (see Chapter 6.2);

- when performing elements with back swing the described picture of movement is reproduced as in a mirror and repeated in the reverse direction, but (let us stress once more) subjectively the gymnasts in all instances must try all the time to hold their shoulders above the support;
- gymnasts usually drive their shoulders back in forward swings after passing the horizontal position in support. This will bring a lessening of the speed of swing, a considerable shifting of the body back along the horizontal, and a loss of height of forward swing and flight. Therefore, just before reaching this position the gymnast should consciously start to set the shoulders forward so that the horizontal hip shift forward or backward is practically absent, and there is only a vertical shift upwards;
- the reverse picture is observed in the back swing: when passing the horizontal position gymnasts normally set the shoulders forward. To avert this, after the horizontal the gymnast should set his shoulders back so as to obviate the same effect as in the previous case;
- when performing a salto backwards into handstand (28 C), the gymnast on release should arch his chest and immediately make an energetic circle with his arms forward and up in the direction of the body's rotation in flight, hands gripping the bars before the body is vertical;
- at the end of the phase of main working actions there must always be an accent on an energetic pushing away from the bars in the direction forwards and upwards, especially when performing elements from the flight phase;
- all turns from swings must be done without loss of rhythm and quickly.

Group 2. Elements performed from upper arm support on both bars:

Forward swing:
- from handstand lower to upper arms and uprise to Manna, from Manna lower to support half lever and lift with straight arms and bent body to handstand (repeat three times, each time holding the angle for 3 seconds).

Back swing:
- back uprise to handstand (5 times) and its modifications (with turn of 180° and 360° with jump).

Technical requirements and commentary:
- when swinging in upper arm support the swing should be performed around the shoulder axis with slight bending in the hips and knees;
- when moving from "below, up" the gymnast hangs at the shoulders; when moving from "above, down" the shoulders sinks relative to the trunk. Here the gymnast actively presses his hands on the bars. Pressing of the bars in this phase must develop with equal acceleration putting the accent on the final part;
- we should remember that hanging in the shoulders is not an aim in itself, but a preparatory movement. Its task is to gather energy of a resilient deformation of the upper-ligament apparatus of the upper shoulders and prepare it for active work in the next phase of basic working actions (see 'stretch-reflex' in Chapter 6.1). Hanging in the shoulders is controlled individually. Its amplitude depends on the level of the gymnast's strength and speed-and-strength preparedness;
- if hanging in the shoulders is too much (the head, as it were, drowns in the shoulders) in the next phase the shoulders will rise up at too great a distance. Here the gymnast, pressing his hands on the bars, must do too much work whose power with active counter-action of the force of gravity may be insufficient for gaining the required additional CoM acceleration directed upward;
- if the gymnast does not manage hanging in the shoulders, the amplitude will be reduced;
- if hanging in the shoulders is missing ('hard shoulders'), this also has an adverse effect on the power of the following working actions because in the previous phase the working muscles were not being stretched to the optimally aroused state;
- hanging in the shoulders must be moderate and, what is most important, comfortable for performing the following upward swing;
- when performing swing elements from upper arm support it is important to ensure an optimally high starting position;
- often when displaying a high initial position, gymnasts let their pelvis down to the level of the bars and more (which significantly reduces the initial supply of potential energy) and from there try to perform a good swing. However, this requires a significantly greater impulse of strength in the phase of basic working actions.

HIGH LEVEL ELEMENTS

Group 3. Elements performed with swing through hang on both bars:

Forward swing movements:
- giant swing backward to handstand (Kenmotsu, No. 18, C) (repeat 4 times in a row);
- with long swing backwards with simultaneous change of grip into handstand (No. 43, C) (repeat 4 times, preferably through straight transfer into handstand);
- with long swing backwards with turn of 360° (Diamidov) into handstand (No. 44, D) (repeat 3 times);
- with long swing backwards with turn of 450° into handstand on one bar (No. 49,D);
- with long swing backwards double back tuck somersault to upper arm hang (Belle, No. 60, E) (repeat 2-3 times);
- with long swing backwards double back piked somersault to upper arm hang (Belle, No. 55, Super-E);
- with long swing backwards with 1/2 twist and one and a half forward tuck somersaults (Tanaka, No. 65, E) and piked to upper arms (repeat 2 times);
- Moy piked (No. 8) with straddle backwards to handstand (Tippelt, 9, D) (repeat 3 times in a row through straight transfer in handstand);
- Tippelt with forward somersault to upper arm hang (No. 10, E) (repeat 2 times);
- Tippelt without pause thrust with a turn of 180o or 360o into handstand (new elements).

Back swing:
- basket to handstand (No. 93,C) (repeat 4 times in a row);
- basket with tucked backward somersault to upper arm (Tajeda, No. 99,D);
- basket with 1/2 turn from handstand to handstand (No. 90, E);
- basket with 1/1 turn to handstand (Tichonkich, No. 95, super-E).

Technical requirements and commentary:
- when doing elements of this group it is important to ensure maximum extension before active swing;
- the active part of the swing (phase of main part of working actions) begins from under the lower vertical through straightening the legs

and bending them at the hips with downward pressure on the bars with the hands;
- when doing piked elements (Moy piked and so on), the gymnast passes the lower vertical with an angle in the hips;
- all the elements must be done with a marked flight phase, when the gymnast is not forced by gravitation to the bars, he continues to be pulled upwards;
- when performing elements of the Tippelt type it is necessary to begin active extending at the shoulders and hips after the thrust forward and lowering of the arms. What is important here is not the magnitude of overall extension of the body at the moment of letting the arms go, but the speed at which this arching takes place;
- all Felges should begin in time and be done during the raising of the centre of gravity of the body. Against a background of a large free swing upwards the gymnast must 'screw into' the turn, beginning from the distal links. This is ensured through evenly directed interaction of the hands with the bars, as a result of which a moment of force is created in relation to the longitudinal axis;
- it is wrong to start the turn too early because this noticeably reduces the power of the swing;
- it is also wrong to begin the turn too late because the gymnast begins to be pressed to the bars and it makes it more difficult to perform the turn.

Group 4. Power and static elements, leg swings and elements performed sideways on one bar:

- from hang upstart squatting the legs between the hands into Manna lower to support half lever on two or one bar (hold for 2 seconds), 'lower to support half lever and lift to handstand with straight arms and bent body (repeat 3 times);
- upstart with legs straddled to support half lever on one bar lift or swing to handstand (repeat 3 times).

Technical requirements and commentary:
- for perfect execution of the upstart to handstand, at the end of the forward swing extend the body and immediately afterwards quickly move the legs to the bars and strongly press with the hands on the bars.

Group 5. Dismounts:

Forward swing:
- back straight somersault;
- double back tuck somersault;
- double back piked somersault;
- double back somersault with turn of 360°.

Back swing:
- forward straight somersault;
- double forward piked somersault;
- double forward tuck or piked somersault with turn of 180°.

Technical requirements and commentary:
- the shoulder movement must be coordinated since this is described in the technical requirements for elements of the 1st group;
- in the support period of dismounts the gymnast should all the time try to hold the shoulders above the support. This will ensure a free descent with a swing of maximum amplitude forward or back with pull upwards at the final point of the swing;
- the start (letting go of the support or the release) must take place after the trunk passes the horizontal position of the 4th quadrant;
- it is wrong to let the shoulders sag back (when performing all back somersaults) and to let them forward (when performing all forward somersaults) before and at the moment of release;
- at the moment of passing the horizontal position the gymnast must allow his shoulders to move forward while pressing the bars away from himself (when performing dismounts with forward swing) or back (when performing dismounts with back swing). In the extreme case this must be done at the moment of release;
- it is wrong to make an early or late release. It must take place when the gymnast has a sufficient vertical speed upwards;
- after departure in the unsupported position the phase of movement upwards must be clearly expressed with flight above head level at the moment of releasing the support;
- the length of flight in the ideal is zero, ie there is no progression in flight along the horizontal;
- rotation in flight must be smooth and fast;
- the phase of preparing for landing must be clearly marked.

Connecting movements (series):
- handstand, overgrasp pirouette, forward swing, back swing, with undergrasp pirouette into handstand (repeat 3 times);
- stutzkehre, overgrasp pirouette, two salto backwards into handstand, Diamidov, long swing with half turn into handstand, long swing to handstand (repeat 2 times);
- long swing backwards, overgrasp pirouette, two salto backwards into handstand, Diamidov, stutzkehre, overgrasp pirouette, double back somersault piked dismount;
- salto backwards into handstand, under somersault into handstand, salto backwards into handstand, longswing backwards into handstand, under somersault into handstand, stutzkehre, overgrasp pirouette, double back piked somersault dismount.

Technical requirements and commentary:
- all swing connecting movements must be done in rhythm, without loss of tempo and use of strength with precise designation of starting and ending position when performing each element;
- requirements made on the technique of performing elements of various structural groups shown above must be observed for each element;
- the gymnast must not correct the final position of the element in order to take a more convenient or optimum starting position for doing the next; he must develop the habit of performing each connecting element from any starting position.

8.3.6 Horizontal Bar

Group 1. Elements performed with long hang swings and turns:
- forward swing in overgrasp with half turn increasing the swings with half turn until handstand is achieved (repeat 3-5 times in a row);
- with swing in undergrasp, swing backwards and half turn into undergrasp increasing the height of the swing each time (repeat 3-5 times in a row).

Technical requirements and commentary:
- swings with half turn in overgrasp and undergrasp must be done with simultaneous change of hand grip of increasing amplitude. The magnitude and precision of the turn must be controlled through the thrust, and not through letting go and planting hands at different

times. It is wrong for top-class gymnasts to change grip at different times; if they do, the exercise loses its basic essence;
- the swings with half turn are done from swinging in hang with moderate amplitude, which grows through correct control of thrusts by the moment of their starting, the continuity and intensity of effort. At the second or third swings with half turn the amplitude of swing should reach the maximum (final position is handstand with lift);
- when performing swings with half turn the gymnast should 'twist into' the turn at the end of the thrust and enter into it exceeding the leading shoulder (forward when performing a straight swing with half turn, and back when doing a reverse);
- the final position must be closed with straightened body, head slightly raised, eyes looking at the horizontal bar, shoulders pressing against the ears;
- a series of swings with half turns represent a basic profile routine for all support elements with long swing turns, Gienger somersaults, and Tkatchevs and dismounts;
- long swings forward and back (simple and with turns of 360°-540°) on two and one hand.

Technical requirements and commentary:
- long swings can be done with little effort and a very smooth action only in the shoulders. They can also be done in an accelerated manner, the latter enables the gymnast to gather up great speed, so before performing complex elements from the flight phase, including dismounts, this technique is preferable;
- top-class gymnasts should perfectly possess a technique for both speeding up giant rotations and slowing the speed of movement right up to a complete standstill in handstand;
- in the classical version of the long swing backwards rotation the gymnast straightens out after thrust in the fourth quadrant and intersects the upper vertical in a position close to the handstand;
- in this instance the active swing is done in the second quadrant. When doing the active swing it is necessary to stretch away from the horizontal bar with overall arching of the body and brief relaxation of the knees. At the end of the pre-swing the gymnast must actively sag at the shoulders;
- the thrust begins after intersecting the lower vertical in the third quadrant and continues partially in the fourth. The gymnast must actively send his legs forward and up in a circle through actively

bending in the hips and shoulders (in the order of 45°) while pressing the hands on the bar and bending at the wrist;
- after that in the fourth quadrant the gymnast must straighten up at the hips to a straight body position, leaving an angle in the shoulders and only then removing it through active extension in the wrists;
- he should then make an active straightening in the wrist joints (turning his hands round) so that he provides a good sense of support when passing through handstand;
- it is sensible to use an exaggerated active swing technique ensuring a big pre-swing when performing giant back rotations before fly-overs and dismounts;
- in this case after the active swing the gymnast does not straighten out. He passes through a high vertical position with large angles in the hips, shoulders and wrist joints. He straightens his body, immediately transferring to pre-swing in the zone of passing through the horizontal position;
- an exaggerated pre-swing and active swing are done here more sharply and powerfully, with quite a large amplitude. The bar and gymnast's body here are to a large extent deformed, which on doing the pre-swing enables the gymnast to gather a lot of energy from the resilient deformation. While performing the active swing, this energy transfers into kinetic energy. This enables him to increase the power of movement and at the end of the long swing rotation to develop a lot of speed and, correspondingly, kinetic energy;
- when performing accelerated longswings in the given modification the wrists are rotated later after intersecting the CoM of the upper vertical;
- when doing giant turns with pirouettes one should use the classical technique;
- gymnasts should possess a technique for both normal smooth turns through a single-support position and for turns with a jump. The basic exercise for them is the giant rotation letting both hands release the bar with a marked vertical lift above the bar (Quast). It is done through a powerful thrust coordinated with pushing off the bar upwards in the final phase;
- the technique of executing longswings with one hand is close to that of classical giant rotations forward and back;
- when performing a longswing forward on one hand with turn of 720° (Zou Li Min, No. 24, C) the first turn of 360° on one hand should be

done after the longswing forward and a top pirouette. Then the gymnast does a longswing forward on one hand in reverse grasp and, on exit into handstand, performs a turn of 360° on one hand, shoulders back into handstand in undergrasp.

Series I:

Longswing in undergrasp, half turn to handstand, immediate longswing backwards half turn into undergrasp, (repeat 3 times in a row).

Technical requirements and commentary:
- direct and Keller (over turn) turns are basic for mastering all complex turns performed through a single-support position. Performing connecting elements mixed with intermediate giant rotations deprives the exercise of its basic essence;
- turns must be done in the release phase into handstand when the gymnast is pulled upwards, with affected demonstration of a firm single-support position with a wide outstretched free hand to the side and a clear completion of the turn. This final position of the element must be convenient for doing the following elements.

Series II:

Longswing forwards, hop change to overgrasp, short clear circle to handstand, longswing and "back away" dismount.

Technical requirements and commentary:
- change of grip must be done with simultaneous lowering and placing of the hands with clear demonstration of the unsupported position during flight;
- the first series of change of grip may be done not in handstand;
- the second and third series may be done with clear designation of handstand and change of direction of movement in that position;
- for this when changing grip in forward swing the gymnast at the end of the active swing must straighten out with an active straightening in the shoulders when pushing away from the bar;
- in the back swing after securing movement with the heels backward he must sharply arch his body with a brief pressing of the hands on the bar away from himself through straightening in the shoulders and a light push away from the bar;

- an early straightening of the body, which is normally the result of an early thrust and (or) swing up, leads to falling short of the handstand; while a later straightening leads to overshooting it without stopping.

Group 2. Elements from the flight phase:

Elements in this group have a strategic designation. They may be done with both forward swing or backward swing, both with flight over the bar, or without. Here they may be done rotating the body in flight, both in the same direction (mono-rotation) and in support, as well as in the opposite direction (counter-rotation).

Movements performed with forward swing:

1. with flight over the horizontal bar

   a) with mono-rotation

   Kovacs sub-group
   - double back tuck somersault into hang (Kovacs, No. 69, D) (repeat 3 times with intermediate longswings and then twice in a row without);
   - piked Kovacs (No. 70, E) (2-3 times with intermediate longswings);
   - straight Kovacs (No. 75, E) (2 times with intermediate longswings);
   - Kovacs with turn of 360° (Kolman, No. 80, Super-E) (2-3 times with intermediate longswings).

   Gienger sub-group over the horizontal bar
   - straight Gienger over the bar (Gaylord-2, No. 64, D) (2-3 times with longswing forward followed by half turn into handstand);
   - Gienger with 1/2 twist over the bar (Pineda, No. 65, Super-E) (2 times through the giant back rotation).

   b) with counter-rotation in flight

   The Tkatchev sub-group
   - Tkatchev (swing forward and vault backward with straddle to hang) with legs apart (No. 13, C) (4-5 times through the giant rotation and three times in a row;
   - Tkatchev stretched (No. 14, D) (3-4 times through the giant rotation and 2-3 times in a row);

- Tkatchev with turn of 360° (Ljukin, No. 15, E) (3 times through the giant rotation and 2 in a row);
- Tkatchev and forward tuck somersault into hang (element is not valued).

2. without flight over the bar

   a) by anti-courbette

   - with longswing forward and forward tuck or piked somersault into hang with undergrasp from above (Xiao Ruizhi, No. 43, C) (repeat 3 times after upstart to handstand);
   - Xiao Ruizhi with 180° turn into hang (element is not valued) (2 times through giant back rotation).

   b) without anti-courbette

   Gienger sub-group
   - Gienger (swing forwards and pike somersault backwards with 1/2 twist to hang, No. 58, C) (3-4 times in a row after upstart to handstand);
   - back straight somersault with turn of 540° (Deff or Gienger with one and a half twists above the bar, No. 60, E) (2 times through the giant rotation).

Movements done with back swing:

1. with flight over the bar

   a) with anti-courbette (counter-rotation)

   Hecht group
   - back uprise and straddle hecht with 1/2 twist to hang (Markelov, No. 8, C) (3-4 times in a tow through giant back rotation with Keller turn);
   - fly with turn in circle into hang (Markelov with legs together or Yamawaki, No. 9,D) (2-3 times in a row through giant back rotation with Keller turn);
   - Markelov with legs together and with turn of 540° (Walstrom, No. 10, E) (twice in a single approach).

b) without the anti-courbette

Gaylord group
- forward somersault over the bar piked or legs apart into hang with under grasp (Gaylord, No. 44, D) (3-4 times through giant forward rotation or 2 times in a row);
- Gaylord with turn in circle into hang with over grasp (Pegan, No. 45, D) (repeat twice after giant back rotation with Keller turn).

2. without flight over the bar

   a) with anti-courbette

   - with back swing back tuck and piked somersault into hang (element is not valued) (2-3 times in a single approach);
   - same with turn of 360° (the element is not valued).

   b) without anti-courbette

   - swing backward and somersault forwards piked or in straddle to hang (Jaeger, No. 33, C) (3-4 times in a single approach);
   - forward straight somersault (grip from below – Balabanov, No. 34, D and in reverse grip – No. 39,D) (2-3 times in a single approach);
   - forward straight somersault with turn of 360° (under grasp – Winkler, No. 35, E; in reverse grip – Pogorolev, No. 40, E) (repeat twice in a single approach).

Technical requirements and commentary:
- top-class gymnasts should possess, as a minimum, three different elements from the flight phase of the top groups of difficulty;
- they should be able to perform a cascade of elements with the flight phase consisting, as a minimum, of three different elements performed in a row, without dilution and loss of height on the third element;
- elements with a flight phase should be performed at training sessions several times in a row in a single attempt, and with intermediate giant swings because this helps create the necessary technical-physical surplus;
- simple modification of elements with the flight phase may be executed after classical giant rotations, while more complex may be done after modern accelerated longswings with exaggerated active swing technique;

HIGH LEVEL ELEMENTS

- when performing elements with flight over the bar without anti-courbette in release (Kovacs, Gaylord, Gaylord-2, Pinedu, etc.) the swing up and thrust in all instances should be done later by comparison with such elements which do not cross the bar (Gienger, Jaeger, Balabanov, Deff). This equally applies to elements performed with forward swing and backward swing;
- when doing elements with counter-rotation after the anti-courbette (Tkatchev, Ljukin, Markelov, Yamawaki, Wolstrom) the pre-swing and active swing must be done earlier, by comparison with flight elements without changing the direction of rotation;
- the spatial and temporal characteristics of the swing up and thrust of fly-overs with counter-rotation are similar to elements of the fly-overs with mono-rotation (Gienger, Deff, Jaeger, Balabanov, Winkler, Pogorolev);
- the difference between them is that in the first case the gymnast after the active part of the swing does an anti-courbette and the release comes in the middle of the fourth quadrant, while in the second case there is no anti-courbette and the release comes at the beginning of this quadrant and earlier;
- when performing elements with mono-rotation without flight over the bar, the pre-swing begins after intersecting the horizontal in the second quadrant, while the active part of the swing is from under the vertical. It ends when the feet intersect the front support horizontal in the third quadrant. After that the gymnast does a brief phase of release (0.1-0.2 seconds);
- the pre-swing and active swing in this instance are done earlier than when performing the classical longswing (see above the technical requirements and commentary for the longswings on the horizontal bar);
- when doing elements with counter-rotation, both with flight over the horizontal bar, and without it, the pre-swing and active swing are done earlier by comparison to those elements with mono-rotation, while the release phase itself in the first case is more powerful and energetic;
- if when doing any flight over the bar the gymnast arrives on bent arms with a loss of tempo (too short a flight), most frequently this is a consequence of a too early active swing and a drawn-out phase of release. An early active swing is usually a result of an early pre-swing;
- if when doing this release and recatch the gymnast misses his grip on the bar (too long a flight), normally this is the result of a late pushing

- from the bar and (or) late active swing, while the latter is a result of a pre-swing (the gymnast has missed the optimal moment to begin it);
- if when doing any element without flight over the bar the gymnast arrives at the bar with bent arms with loss of tempo (too short a flight), normally this is a consequence of a late active swing, while the latter is a result of a late or long pre-swing (the gymnast either misses the optimal moment for pre-swing or draws it out too much);
- if when doing this element the gymnast does not reach the bar (too long a flight), usually this is the result of an early release and active swing, while the latter is the result of an early or too short a pre-swing;
- if when doing any element with the flight phase the gymnast slowly rotates in flight, most often this is the result of an insufficient angular momentum;
- if these are elements with mono-rotation, the power of the active swing in support was not enough, or the gymnast made a mistake in the release, having performed something like a counter-cycle (unnecessary anti-courbette – when performing movements with forward swing or courbette – when performing movements with back swing);
- if these are elements with counter-rotation in flight, either the power of the counter-cycle (courbette or anti-courbette) and its speed at the moment of release were not enough, or the power of the active swing was too small, or both together (usually a weak active swing causes a weak anti-courbette);
- if the height of flight is not enough, this is usually the consequence of a too weak active swing;
- in all cases the gymnast's actions in the support period (acceleration, pre-swing, active swing, release) must be done in time, energetically and powerfully;
- what is important in the phase of release of elements with counter-rotation in flight is not the magnitude of counter-tempo that determines the degree of deformation of the body (generally straightening or bending), but its speed at the moment of letting go of the support;
- in the phase of release of elements with mono-rotation even a small counter-tempo is harmful because it reduces the angular momentum given from support, which, other things being equal, diminishes rotation in flight;
- the height of CoM lift in flight when doing elements without fly-over must be in the order of 0.8-1.0m, and flight time must be 0.8-1.0 seconds;

- when doing flighted elements the gymnast starts in a higher position (0.6-0.8m above the bar), so (other things being equal) the absolute height of flight must be higher than when doing elements without fly-over the bar. However, vertical velocity of flight (other things being equal) is usually greater. So the height of flight in both cases is approximately the same;
- rotation in flight and its length must be enough to grasp the bar in the highest possible position, ensuring a smooth contact during arrival and taking a comfortable starting position for performing the following element.

Group 3. Elements performed close to the bar (in bar elements) (elements in this group without letting go of both hands repeated several times in a single approach may be done in loaps, while elements involving letting go of one hand may be done in a single loop):

- clear circle from handstand to handstand;
- longswing backwards to handstand, and clear circle to handstand;
- clear circle to handstand, hop change, immediate top change, immediate Stalder (5-6 times in a row);
- Stalder piked with turns of 360° and 540°, with jump and without (3-4 times);
- Stalder piked and back somersault into hang (courbette);
- Stalder piked and forward somersault into hang (anti-courbette);
- Endo legs apart and together (5-6 times in a row);
- Endo piked with turns of 360° and 540° with jump and without (3-4 times);
- Endo piked legs together and forward somersault with turn in circle into hang (anti-courbette).

Technical requirements and commentary:
- when doing clear circles into hang from handstand or support in the first phase, one should not let the shoulders come forward;
- ditto when doing elements of Stalder, Endo and their modifications;
- in all cases there must be a sharp increase in speed of rotation in the first phase. For this all squat in movements must be done against the background of the beginning of the fall (movements downwards from handstands), holding the angle in the shoulders;

- in the final phase of the Stalder piked or legs apart, the feet must not come over the horizontal bar, in the shoulders there must be a minimal angle, while the pelvis must be in the maximally high position;
- the feet come over the bar only in the process of falling, but no earlier and not immediately. This occurs automatically and the gymnast must not consciously perform this movement;
- after squatting in the gymnast must exit with the pelvis back (Stalder) or forward (Endo) with maximum amplitude, bringing the legs close to the shoulders. In no circumstances must he let them down towards the bar. The gymnast must try, as it were, to place the legs on the shoulders (if he has done a fly-over with legs apart) or press them to his nose (if he has done a fly-over piked);
- in the process of falling the gymnast should do a spring-like movement with his legs towards the trunk. In striving to stretch away as must as possible from the bar in the shoulders the gymnast, as it were, covers his trunk with his legs. The maximum fold occurs at the lowest point of the swing. The legs here must be parallel with the floor, while an angle of plus or minus 90° forms between maximally stretched arms and trunk at that moment;
- this spring movement in pressing attains its maximum downwards by accumulating a considerable supply of energy of resilient deformation of the bar and gymnast's body. This energy is spent when moving upwards, transferring to kinetic energy of movement;
- immediately after the maximum fold in all cases the gymnast should begin simultaneous energetic straightening of the body in the shoulders and hips up to handstand with rotating the hands in the final phase of movement;
- this movement must ensure sufficiently high vertical velocity of CoM when exiting into handstand, accompanied by a sense of upflight from the bar. Only in this case during the final phase can complex turns be successfully performed;
- if at the moment of maximum fold downwards the legs are not parallel to the floor, as a rule the gymnast either does not reach the handstand, or he misses it. Thus, if at this moment the hips are higher than the feet, the gymnast passes over the handstand when doing the Stalder and does not reach it in the Endo. If the hips are lower then vice versa: the gymnast does not reach the handstand when doing Stalders and misses them altogether when doing the Endo;

8. HIGH LEVEL ELEMENTS

- in all cases of doing turns with hops the end of straightening the body coincides with the thrust off the bar. In other cases the turns begin through a marked single-support position on exiting into handstand and in no case after it.

Group 4. Elements done in reverse grip and back hang:

- stoop circle rearward and forward to at least 45° and through handstand (Adler, Nos. 2 and 3) (repeat 4-5 times);
- Adler with turn of 180° and 360° into handstand.

Technical requirements and commentary:

- when doing an Adler element and its modifications the squat in should be done at the start of downward movement from handstand, slightly letting the shoulders forward;
- *warning:* don't let the shoulders lean forward too much;
- when doing the squat in the gymnast should actively hold up in the shoulders, counteracting bending in the shoulders under the action of the force of gravity;
- after the squat in piked the gymnast, pressing his legs to his nose, should aim to exit forward with maximum amplitude, making a spring-like movement with his legs towards his trunk (this part of the movement is similar to the Endo piked). The fold attains its maximum under the bar;
- immediately after this the gymnast should perform an energetic press off the bar backwards while straightening the shoulders and hips in the direction of handstand.
- New Elements:
    - longswing forward in L grip (4-5 rotations), changing grip to undergrasp into handstand and various turns of 180° and 360°;
    - longswing forward in half-hang from the back (Russian rotations) (4-5 times) with change of grip and various turns;
    - back lift, swing over the head, giant back rotations in rear hang (Czech rotations);
    - after Russian longswing lift with back swing and turn in circle into Czech back rotations (turn from Russian into Czech).

Technical requirements and commentary:

- when doing Russian longswings, hold the chin at all times close to the chest;

- for falling into a good semi-hang the grip on the bar should be wider than the shoulders, but not very wide. Here the angles of the shoulder blades should be maximally to the sides, while the shoulder joints should come close to the head through lifting the collar bone and shoulder blades up;
- the gymnast can feel the correct position of the semi-hang under static conditions if he begins slowly to dislocate the shoulders in back hang on the bar while relaxing his muscles under the force of gravity;
- after passing the lower vertical the gymnast should perform a securing swing with his heels backwards with subsequent substitution of the shoulders. Here he should slightly inlocate in the shoulders while bending at the hips;
- when passing the upper vertical position the legs should be parallel to the floor, with head on the chest;
- after this he does a relatively smooth but active straightening of the shoulders and hips with a sense of good support on the bar;
- when doing the swing over the head he should not strongly let the shoulders back (sagging at the shoulders). He should perform a swing away so that the hips are in the maximally high position with a strong sense of support;
- when doing Czech longswings the gymnast should make a maximum delay from the bar in rear hang;
- after passing the lower vertical the gymnast should perform a raking swing with his legs forward and up, while bending at the hips, trying to retain maximum delay in the shoulders;
- the topmost position is similar to the analogous position when doing Russian longswings. This position is rather like the Manna;
- back uprise with back turn into Manna on the parallel bars may serve as a model for the turn from Russian to Czech longswings.

Group 5. Dismounts:

With forward swing:
- double back straight somersault (No. 33, C);
- double back straight somersault with turn of 360°, 720° (Watanabe, No. 35, E) and 1080° (Fedorchenko, No. 25, Super-E);
- triple back tuck somersault (Andrianov No. 40, E);
- triple back piked somersault (Fardan, No. 45, Super-E);

8 HIGH LEVEL ELEMENTS

- triple back tuck somersault with turn of 360° (Belle, No. 50, Super-E) and 720°;
- quadruple back tuck somersault.

With back swing:
- double forward straight somersault with turn of 180° (No. 14, D);
- double forward straight somersault with turn of 540° and 900° (No. 15, E);
- triple forward tuck somersault with turn of 180° (Rumbutis, No. 5 Super-E);
- triple forward tuck somersault with turn of 540°.

Technical requirements and commentary:
- dismounts with forward swing may be done both after a classical backward longswings, and after a backward longswings with accelerated active swing technique;
- dismounts can be also done after other elements (for example, an accelerated forward longswing half turn into overgrasp and dismount with forward swing or an accelerated longswing backwards with half turn into undergrasp and a dismount on the backwards swing, also Stalder's and Endo's with turns and without can be used prior to dismounts);
- straight double back somersault and their modifications are usually done after a longswing with exaggerated active swing technique, while the triple somersault is done after the classical longswing backwards. However, there are no hard and fast rules here. An individual choice depends on taste. The main thing is to ensure high speed in the starting position;
- the acceleration phase in the support period of the dismount after the classical longswing is done in the first quadrant. When performing an accelerated longswing it merges with its next phase, and the pre-swing is done earlier – at the moment of intersecting the support horizontal. Here the amplitude of the joint movements and their power in the process of pre-swing and active swing are expressed to a significantly greater extent;
- the pre-swing is characterised by general straightening (when performing dismounts with forward swing) or bending of the body (dismounts with back swing) stretching away from the support and

hanging in the shoulders before the start of the active swing. Here the head, as it were, drowns in the shoulders. The task of the pre-swing is optimal stretching of the muscles of the working surface of the body whose contraction ensures performance of the next active part of swing;

- the active part (throw) begins when the gymnast attempts the lower support vertical while straightening his legs at the knees pressing on the bar (dismounts with forward swing) or straightening the body (dismounts with back swing). The active swing is performed through a powerful pre-stretch of the muscles of the body's working surface. The leading element of the active swing is an energetic movement of the legs forward and up while pressing on the bar. Here the wave of contraction quickly flies from the distal links to the proximal links with following-parallel switching in of the hip, vertebrae, shoulder and wrist joints;
- the active swing transfers to the phase of release, in which the gymnast performs actions determining the shape of the dismount (tuck, straight or piked body);
- when performing the triple somersault against the background of continuing active swing, the gymnast fairly early begins to tuck. The release must occur before the moment when the CoM intersects the horizontal. Here the orientation of the trunk is close to the horizontal, while the angles in the knees and hips are close to right angle. The angle in the shoulders is 30-45°;
- in flight the gymnast must quickly and compactly tuck and manage to turn 2.5 somersaults above the level of the bar;
- when doing double back straight somersaults the gymnast releases at the same moment in the piked position. At the moment of release the shoulders and hips should have angles in the order of 30-45°. The gymnast should straighten out in flight and press his arms to his trunk with a vigorous downward action which is opposite to the direction of rotation;
- the technique of dismounts done with forward swing is reflected in the technique of dismounts with back swing in reverse order. Where in the first instance it is performed bending (piked), in the second there is a straightening and vice versa;
- after completing forms of movement in flight that determine the shape of the dismount, the gymnast should have time to straighten out his

HIGH LEVEL ELEMENTS

body in the phase of preparing for landing and take a pose convenient for muffling the shock at the moment of placing his feet on the mat (see Chapter 6.4);
- with maximum time of flight (1.3 seconds) the height of CoM lift may reach 1.5m above the bar. When doing double straights the height of flight is normally somewhat less than when doing double and triple tuck somersaults (see Chapter 6.3);
- the optimum length of flight is 1.8m from the bar (see Table 14).

8.4 Women

8.4.1 Support Vault

Handsprings
- handsprings – front somersault straight;
- handsprings – forward piked somersault with a turn of 540°;
- handsprings – double forward somersault tucked;

Tsukahara
- Tsukahara straight with turn of 540° and 720°;
- Tsukahara – double back somersault.

Round off-back rotation (Yurchenko):
- round off-back rotation – one and a half back somersaults with turn of 720° and 900°;
- round off-back rotation – two and a half back somersaults.

8.4.2 Asymmetric Bars

Movements done with forward swing:
- longswing backwards with half turn into undergrasp;
- longswing backwards with a turn of 360°;
- with large swing, tucked and piked backwards somersault with half turn into hang (Deltchev, Gienger);
- with large swing backwards straight somersault with turn of 540° into hang (Deff);
- Stalder with turn of 180°;
- Stalder with turn of 360°;
- Stalder –tucked forward somersault into hang;
- Stalder – straddle forward somersault into hang;
- Stalder – piked forward somersault into hang.

Movements done with forward swing:
- longswing forward with half turn into handstand;
- longswing forward with turn of 540°;
- tucked, piked and straddle forward somersault into hang (Xiao Ruizhi);

HIGH LEVEL ELEMENTS

- forward somersault with turn of 180°;
- Endo with half turn into handstand;
- Endo with full turn into handstand.

Somersault between bars:
- from support on lower bar facing outwards swing away and forward somersault into hang on top bar;
- from support on lower bar facing outwards swing away and forward somersault with turn of 360° into hang on top bar;
- from support on top bar facing outwards swing away and forward somersault into hang on lower bar;
- from support on upper bar facing out swing away and forward somersault with turn of 360° into hang on lower bar;
- from lower bar, clear circle backwards with half turn to catch the upper bar (Khorkina).

Dismounts:
- double back straight somersault;
- double back straight somersault with turn of 360°;
- back straight somersault with turn of 720°;
- triple back somersault;
- double forward tuck somersault;
- double forward piked somersault with turn of 180°;
- double forward somersault with turn of 540°.

8.4.3   Beam

Flic flacs and back somersault:
- five flic flacs in tempo;
- three flic flacs (two to one leg, the third arriving on two feet);
- flic flac with turn of 360°;
- Kolpinsky somersault;
- flic flac half turn onto one leg into handspring;
- flic flac and straight back somersault arriving on two feet;
- flic flac, straight back somersault and Kolpinsky in tempo;
- flic flac and jump with half twist into somersault;
- back somersault, flic flac, back somersault, flic flac, back somersault.

Handspring and forward somersault:
- three handsprings arriving on one foot in tempo;
- forward tuck somersault;
- forward piked somersault;
- forward piked somersault with turn of 180°;
- handspring and tucked forward somersault;
- handspring and piked forward somersault.

Free walkovers:
- free walkover to one leg forward somersault to land on two feet;
- free walkover into forward somersault to land on two feet and forward somersault.

Sideways somersault:
- two side somersaults in tempo.

Turns:
- turn on one foot of 540°;
- turn on one foot of 720°.

8.4.4 Floor Exercises

Acrobatic jumps rotating backward:
- tempo back somersault – five times in tempo;
- two tempo somersaults and back straight somersault;
- back straight somersault with turn of 900°;
- back straight somersault with turn of 1080°;
- double back somersault in semi-tuck;
- double back somersault with turn of 360° in the first somersault;
- double back straight somersault;
- double back straight somersault with turn of 720°;
- jump with half turn, double forward somersault.

Acrobatic jumps with forward rotation:
- forward straight somersault;
- forward straight somersault with turn of 360°;
- forward somersault with turn of 720°;
- double forward somersault in tuck.

HIGH LEVEL ELEMENTS

Technical requirements and commentary:
- there is no such thing as a separate men's and women's technique;
- there is no such thing as a national technique;
- there is a correct and an incorrect technique;
- in women's gymnastics the women should take as their basis the optimal men's technique of performing the same elements and jumps;
- the parameters of the women's apparatus (vault, parallel bars, beam) lay certain boundaries on the technique of executing elements, but they do not distort their technical foundation;
- the level of strength and strength-and-speed physical readiness of top-class male gymnasts is higher than that of women. So the basic parameters of similar type movements is usually lower with women than it is with men;
- with top-class women gymnasts the speed of run up, including in the last five metres and at the moment of jump on to the board is usually lower on average. So the height of the apparatus is lower too. Correspondingly the height of flight is lower. This applies to elements from the flight phase in all forms of women's multi-events;
- these differences are smaller with women who have a high level of force – velocity qualities (for example, Yelena Zamolodchikova);
- the technique of exercises on the women's asymmetric bars is practically identical to that of executing analogous exercises on the horizontal bar apart from longswings for mature women gymnasts;
- when performing backward longswings facing outwards mature women gymnasts are obliged to bend at the hips or spread their legs in order to avoid contact with the lower bar;
- this leads to a later pre-swing and later short active swing which even top-class women gymnasts often miss. In that case the dismounts and releases and recatches are done without the necessary actions of counter rotation;
- avoiding the lower bar through spreading the legs is preferable because it is deformed to a lesser extent. A timely active swing in this case is easier to perform. Khorkina's technique here may serve as standard.

More detailed information on the performance technique and methods of teaching the above-mentioned elements may be found in the specialist literature [59, 56, 83, 21, 87, 89, et al]. See also Competition Rules [19,20,82].

How to Create Champions

9

CHAPTER NINE

Sports-Science and Sports-Medicine Back-up to Training

In preparing this Chapter we have used the technology employed by the USSR and Russian national teams over the last few decades.

Gaining good results at elite level nowadays requires well constructed training regimens, involving sports science (SM), sports medicine (MB), technical (MT), personnel (PR), financial (F), and information (IS). The main aim of Sports Science and Sports Medicine is to ensure, within the rules, the appropriate health, fitness and readiness of Squad and Team members for top competitions in the current Olympiad. [73]

9.1 Basic Principles and Tasks

The medical and scientific preparation should be:

- applied practically; all Sports Science and Sports Medicine is provided according to an informed assessment of the training and competition needs of the teams in given regions, working closely with coaches, team doctors and gymnasts;
- comprehensive; with complete control over preparation for training and coaching, involving specialists as required and appropriate technical methods;
- co-ordinated; training should not be random, but be appropriately progressive and systematic over a yearly macrocycle;
- problem-solving; any medical or scientific investigations into a problem should be carried out and reported as quickly as possible);

- approached on a group basis (the science back-up team should keep up with latest appropriate research, and relay this to the coaches and the team where appropriate);
- pro-active; (new modes of coaching and techniques should be continuously developed and applied) [73].

A scientific-medical group (CSG), comprising physical educators, doctors, physiologists, biomechanists, biochemists, and technical and conditioning experts has been the basic guarantee behind the success of the national teams of the former USSR and the present Russia. Chairing the Scientific-Medical group is a sports scientist, highly experienced in the preparation of top-class gymnasts, who works very closely with the chief coach of the National Team.

The main aim of the Scientific-Medical Group is to ensure overall control of all aspects of competitive preparedness, including general health and basic fitness. Its key task is to very thoroughly monitor the team members, and to be able to provide data on them accompanied by specific training or technical advice to modify their training, where necessary. The objects of this are to closely monitor:

- the gymnasts' general health;
- their cardio-vascular and musculo-skeletal fitness (see Chapter 3.3.7);
- their general metabolism (see Chapter 3.3.7);
- their state of physical preparedness, i.e. their overall fitness (see Chapter 3.3.6);
- their level of technical preparedness (see Chapter 3.3.5);
- their training programme (see Chapter 5);
- their competition programme (see Chapter 3.3.11).

9.2 Comprehensive Control System

This includes four basic medical and physiological screening components:

- thorough general assessment (DCI), together, usually, with thorough medical research (DCI-TMR);
- stage-by-stage comprehensive research (SCR);
- current research (CR);
- research (study) into competition activity (RCA).

This thorough General + Medical Assessment is done twice a year, at the start of each six-month macro-cycle, in January and July. The results of the first one are taken into account when working out the annual individual training schedules for National Squad and Team members.

The second Thorough General + Medical Assessment, and the SCR (which is carried out two or three times a year), are to assess all-round preparedness in terms of health and fitness, as well as the specific physical, technical and psychological preparedness of the National Team gymnasts.

The SCR involves muscle measures, pulse, heart rate, blood pressure, ECG, blood pH, blood glucose, lactate and urea. Also noted are training loads (number of elements and combinations), and other relevant data.

Current status evaluations are done at all training camps, according to the centralised training programme for the national team. Their main function is the control and evaluation of the training effect of the weekly micro-cycles and the individual training sessions. This information helps to individualise the training of National Squad and Team members. Also, immediate corrections may be made to the training programmes where necessary.

Competition Status Information (RCA) is gained at major home and international competitions, in line with the competition training model (see Chapter 3.3.11). Main contenders for the National Team will have seven to nine RCA evaluations per year.

The health of the National Squad and Team members is assessed by a full medical examination during the 'Comprehensive Investigation' (DCI-DMR), done by specialists such as orthopaedic surgeons, physiotherapists, cardiologists, ophthalmologists, radiologists, endocrinologists, urologists, gynaecologists, neurologists, dentists, etc.

During that investigation (DCI), blood pressure and ECG are assessed, as are resting heart rates, and exercise and recovery heart rates (from fixed work rates). Blood biochemistry is assessed, especially: – pH, and levels of haemoglobin, cholesterol, free fatty acids, glucose, lactate, pyruvate, urea, inorganic phosphate, etc. If necessary, functional and stress tests are carried out.

To assess the specific fitness of gymnasts, we use a specialised 'load test' – a repeat performance of free exercises with a rest interval of three minutes; when ECG, pulse, blood pressure, and heart rate are recorded. Heart rate is noted:- at rest; during warm-up; when performing free exercises; immediately on stopping; and on recovery.

From the DCI investigation we can detect any illness, in addition to well-compensated pathological and pre-pathological states. We are able to determine medical and physiological factors which limit carrying through the training and competition programme. These medical results enable us to assess the physiolgial and functional potential of National Squad and Team members, and to initiate appropriate therapy.

In addition, during the DCI investigation, we register height, weight and muscle-fibre composition, and muscle force, as well as simple and complex reaction times, together with indicators of specific physical and technical preparedness. After analysing all the data, we can assess the specific training state of the gymnasts, and can make recommendations about future training loads and regimens with a view to optimising the progressive overload.

9.3 Assessing Level of Preparation

9.3.1 Assessing Specific Physical Fitness (SPP)

After many years of studying and observing gymnasts we know that the level of specific (gymnastic) fitness is a crucial marker for the whole training programme.

Assessing this specific fitness is done by means of a set of reliable tests, built up over many years of experience. These include: running time over 20m from a standing start; speed (in m/s) in the final run-up for vaults; height of vault (in cm); ascent time of an arms-only rope climb of 4m for men, 3m for women; times of holding and releasing when doing static exercises on rings (cross; inverted cross; horizontal support); maximum number of circles on pommel (men); number of power piked handstands with legs together on handstands for women; number of upstarts and swings into handstand on the asymmetric bars for women; while hanging from wall bars, the number of straight leg raises up to touching the arms in 10 seconds (for women); with averaged deduction for measures of active and passive flexibility (see Chapter 3.3.6).

9.2.3   Assessing Technical Preparedness

Assessing technical preparedness is also a vital indicator of overall readiness. This assessment is done following competition rules. The bases are the competition exercises on all the apparatus, in which we evaluate difficulty, content, performance technique, and reliability. In line with the current FIG competition rules from 2001, the basic technical indicators are:

- initial assessment is based on the minimal level of difficulty, with deductions for the non-execution of specific requirements, and additions for elements and combinations of high-difficulty groups. The initial mark characterises the difficulty, content and composition of a combination, as well as the structural variety of its elements. The total of initial marks in the various all around (the initial base) gives a numerical account of the gymnast's technical state;

- the total of deductions for systematic and accidental technical faults (small, intermediate and large) is determined through collating the competition and training assessments of the gymnasts during the control-model training sessions. This item indicates the standard of the techniques and their execution, as well as the errors which interfere with technique;

- the final mark is the difference between the first two scores in the multi-events. The total gives a numerical indicator of technical/execution skill;

- the level of reliability is determined by the stability of performing competition combinations, expressed as a percentage, on watching competition and training activity during control-model sessions and weekly micro-cycles. The more such observations there are, the more accurate is the reliability assessment.

9.4   Observing Competition Activity

Observation of competition activity (OCA) is one of the most important items in the comprehensive control system. Its major aims are:

- assessing the level of technical preparedness and of technical skills of members of the National Team and of their strongest rivals from other countries;

- noting the main deficiencies and mistakes committed by these gymnasts at competition in the all around;

- suggesting appropriate corrections to the training programme.

Here the main indicator is the standard to which the gymnast can utilise his full motor-skill potential in competition. This level is assessed by comparing the results of particular competitions with the results shown by the gymnast during the previous control-model micro-cycles and training sessions.

In competitions, it is reckoned that a gymnast has reached nearly 100% of his motor-skill potential if these above two results, the training and the competition, are close. If the competition results are worse, then less than 100% of potential has been realised. The percentage by which the competition results are lower than the control-model sessions indicates the amount by which the gymnast is not realising his/her potential. On the other hand, if the gymnast performs better in competition than training, the indicator will be above 100%.

An important section of OCA is the determining and analysing technical shortcomings and errors made by gymnasts in multi-events. The use of video-recording during competition enables biomechanical analysis of technique (see Chapter 7.4), or a simpler qualitative assessment. Causes of errors may be found by expert analysis, and they may be put right at the next training stage.

During OCA, besides noting faults and falls (as separate items), one must note the number of precise landings, the performance of special requirements (according to competition rules), and the basic indicators of load, including timing. Volume and intensity of load may be noted from the elements and combinations performed. This should be done both directly during competition (including general and specific warm-up), and also at training sessions on days of competition (and days between competition) over the whole competition micro-cycle. One should also note and classify the main aspects of the gymnast's behaviour before competition and at warm-ups and training sessions. One should note indications of altered behaviour patterns.

This information is not only important for assessing the gymnast's competition behaviour; it is necessary for modelling future behaviour, as well as being a useful marker for the effectiveness of the training. Such effectiveness is monitored by comparing OCA data with assessments of the gymnast's state of health and general fitness, and their level of specific physical, technical and psychological readiness.

9.5 Pharmacological Preparation

In preparing the Russian National Team we have not used, and do not use, anabolic and cortico-steroids, as well as other drugs and banned substances. That is the principled position of the leadership of the Russian Federation of Gymnastics.

The strategy of winning medals for the Russian team consists in perfecting the methods and technology of training, and, above all, in its educational component, using legitimate means. Apart from the moral-ethical aspects, this is encouraged by the humane spirit of current optimism that permeates Russian gymnastics, as well as the National Russian gymnastic traditions.

Our sport requires a level of development, and a simultaneous display of all the basic physical attributes: static and dynamic strength; power; speed; skill; dexterity; and specific endurance, all together in a single competition exercise. This is demanded on each apparatus of the all-round competition, with its vividly expressed specific elements. However, an increase in muscle mass gained, for example, by taking anabolic steroids, will lead to an increase in absolute strength – but will be accompanied by a decrease in relative strength. This reduction in power/weight ratio is a negative factor in gymnastics.

Gymnastic techniques are very complex. A very tightly-controlled effort in time and space is necessary for some elements, while others need efforts close to the physical limit. Still others may require smaller efforts, but with extremely finely differentiated kinetic and dynamic movements. Finally, gymnastic exercises have to have all their elements in balance.

Apart from the run up in a Vault, and in the very short run-ups in the Floor exercise, there is very little repetition on the different apparatus – i.e. there are no monotonously repeated movement cycles, as in the repetitive endurance sports.

For example, to perform a triple somersault on Floor, or a double somersault in a Vault, the gymnast needs a powerful 'muscle explosion' on take-off similar to the instant power in the high-level strength-and-speed sports. In addition, the gymnast has to follow that with a complicated and dangerous multi-rotation movement in flight – ending with a high-precision landing. This demands an extremely fine orientation in time and space which is absent from most other power sports.

But this is by no means all. On Floor, for example, the gymnast has to balance perfectly, perform powerful static exercises, and do several series of acrobatic jumps where less explosive muscular effort is needed. This effort is delivered in 'even doses', or spread in time and space in movements such as; forward revolution, forward straight somersault, forward somersault with 360° turn and forward somersault with 540° turn.

It would be extremely difficult to perform such complex and varied technical actions precisely, with the acute lack of time, on six pieces of apparatus for men and four for women – if the competitors were doped up with anabolic steroids or other drugs. This, quite apart from moral-ethical factors, is yet another objective argument against using strong drugs and doping agents in gymnastics – and in other sports with complex coordination.

In summary, there is no objective place for doping in high-coordination sports in general nor in gymnastics in particular, due to the sheer complexity of the sport, quite apart from ethics.

Nevertheless there is, of course, a place for the use of permitted drugs and medicines in training, and the principle objectives of pharmacological help to the Russian National Gymnastics Team are as follows:

- activation of restorative processes after heavy work;
- acceleration of rehabilitation procedures after injury;
- guarding against over-training, injury and illness;
- creating additional energy reserves;
- activation of full muscle power.

Of medicines for top-class gymnasts, we recommend natural agents, mainly of plant origin. These consist of amino-acid preparations, ginseng, tonics, vitamin complexes, riboxin and food supplements such as Ammivit, Pantohaematogen, Rus-Olympic, Inozi-F, Elton, Panangin, Mildronate, Adfapton, Levzeya, Araxis and formulae for increasing muscle mass and energy.

The intensity of pharmacological preparation for top-class gymnasts changes depending on the composition of the micro-cycles. It increases during and after large training loads and sudden intense micro-cycles.

To aid recovery after physical loads and training injuries , we use physical and environmental factors. It is useful to use massage, hydro-massage, pneumo-massage, contrasting baths, steam bath, sauna, swimming, physiotherapy, ultra-violet light, and sea baths, etc, for the best relaxation and restoration back to full function.

9.6 Diet

The diet of top-class gymnasts is a vital part of restoration. Noting that 'man is what he eats', the dietary emphasis should be on ensuring a full choice of all essential amino acids and the maximum variety of fresh products. The daily energy content during centralised training is between 4500 and 5000 calories.

We should especially mention that a specialist should be in direct charge of the dietary and pharmacological provision for the gymnasts, as well as the planning and organisation. In the former USSR, and now in Russia, this was the responsibility of the doctor in charge of the national team.

How to Create Champions

10

CHAPTER TEN

Material-technical Provision of Training

10.1 Basic Equipment

The basic designation of equipping gymnastics halls and apparatus consists in ensuring conditions necessary and sufficient for full value and safe training and competition. The safety of top-class gymnasts is ensured by a set of organisational technical and pedagogical measures which are oriented on saving them from injuries and over-loading.

Ensuring the safety of gymnasts includes the use of reliable and safe apparatus, mats, gymnastics equipment and inventory, adequate methods of teaching exercises and technology of training, reasonable training and competitive loads, means for recovery and rehabilitation, as well as insurance and self-insurance.

The use of foam rubber mats and pits, training harnesses and other additional technical devices significantly facilitate the tackling of pedagogical tasks in training and enhance the safety of instruction and the motor activity of top-class gymnasts.

At the present time a number of firms are making top quality gymnastics equipment. The Russian National Team have used Spieth gymnastics equipment (Germany) for many years. The placement of gymnastics equipment and apparatus in gymnastics halls has been described many times and is in no need of commentary here [43, 89].

10.2 Additional Equipment

Implementation of the principles of 'outstripping development and optimal surplus' requires a targeted change in teaching conditions and the construction of a control situation with the aim of minimising mistakes and intensifying the training of top-class gymnasts [52]. Accordingly, besides standard gymnastics equipment and apparatus, the Russian national team uses a set of training devices and auxiliary technical means. Below we briefly describe those we recommend as additional technical means and devices.

10.2.1 Mechanical Training Devices for Developing Strength

We should note the undoubted value of well-known mechanical devices of the 'Minigym' type for a targeted development of certain muscle groups when training gymnasts. The standard set of mechanical devices of this type has been actively employed and is still employed in training the men's and women's national teams (See Chapter 5.7.1).

10.2.2 Training Aid for Warm up and Strengthening Muscle-ligament Leg Apparatus

This aid is extremely simple in construction and manufacture. It has a large undulating wavy surface covered by felt with a strong cover (Figure 60). Several gymnasts may work on it at once. They stand on the aid with right leg forward, left leg back, changing leg position by jumps in tempo at a coach-set regime – for example, in a given time or until warmed up or tired. This training aid is used by the Russian team in its first morning training session as a matter of course (see Chapter 5.7.1), as well as in routine group sessions and individually.

Figure 60 – *Training aid for the strengthening and warm up of the muscle ligament apparatus of the legs*

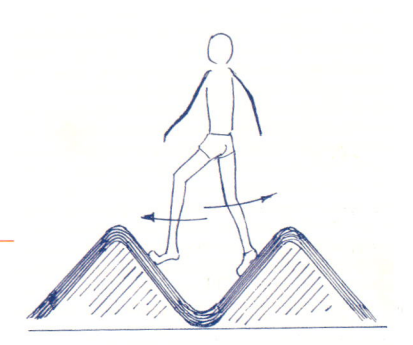

10.2.3 The 'Wave' Training Aid

This aid is a rope-pulley construction fastened to the ceiling or rings. The gymnast puts on a wide belt, fastens arm and leg straps and lies on the aid looking upwards, as shown in Figure 61. He tenses the appropriate muscles of the body's back surface and fixes this position without his back touching the floor. Then he changes into a position bending his stomach upwards (Figure 61a). After that he repeats the process.

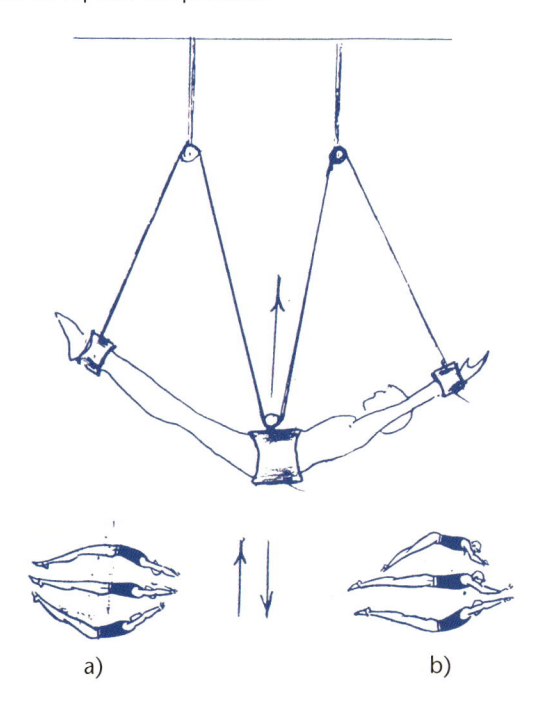

Figure 61 – *Training aid "wave" and work scheme a) and b)*

To develop the muscles of the opposite surface of the body in the starting position the gymnast takes a position on the training aid facing downwards (Figure 61b). While contracting the muscles of the back surface of the body, he transfers to a position of an 'overturned boat' and fixes this position or immediately lowers himself, depending on the method used.

Work in side positions is done in the same regime. In all cases the work can be done both by holding the pose or in a cyclical regime.

If a twisting belt is used, the gymnast is able to turn around the longitudinal axis, warming up, in turn the muscles of the front, back and both sides of the body surface in a single approach.

Justification for the expediency of this training aid and methods of its use are shown in Chapter 4.8.3 (see basic combined physical-technical training).

10.2.4   Training Aid for Twisting and Turning

The construction scheme of this aid is shown in Figure 62. In greater details justification for its utilisation and methods of use are shown in Chapter 4.8.3 (see base combined functional-rotational training).

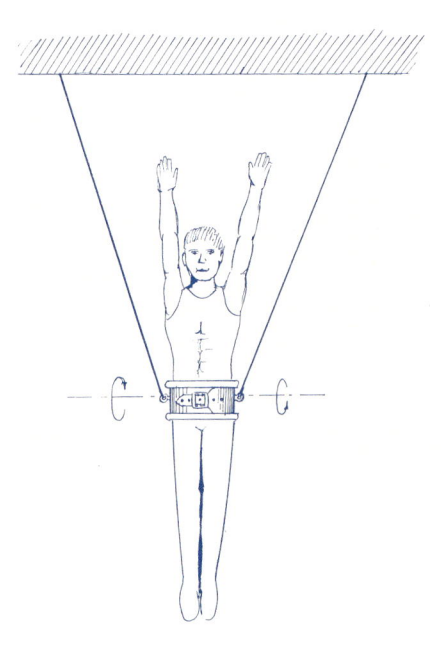

Figure 62 – *Training aid for somersaulting*

10.2.5 Parallel Bars Training Aid

(the idea of the 'Parallel Bars' 'Horse' and 'Support Vault' training devices belongs to L. Arkaev.)

The 'Parallel Bars' training device (Figure 63) is designated for improving technique of swing movements in hand support on the given apparatus. The device's construction includes the possibility of creating control moments of muscle force relative to the front-back axes of the radial joints which can help the gymnast correct deficiencies in the technique of performing swings in support on standard parallel bars. Support with open hand on a wide (by contrast with standard bars) surface of the bars with this device automatically puts the gymnast in a situation when the technique of shifting the shoulders must be perfect. Otherwise the gymnast simply falls.

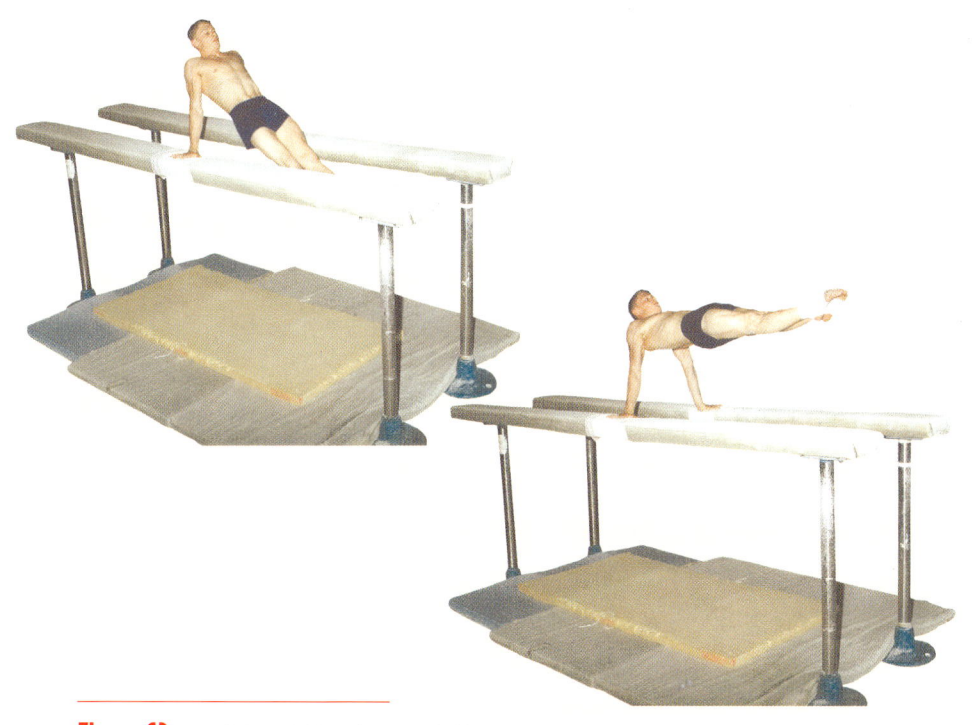

Figure 63 – *Training aid for the parallel bars*

The 'Parallel Bars' training device has been used for many years by the men's team as an obligatory auxiliary technical device for basic training of a higher level, especially in the morning training session (see Chapter 5.7.1). The gymnast is able to do swings in support with turns in handstand, somersaults, circles straight with turns of 180° and more, etc. After work on this device even top-class gymnasts feel much more confident on the standard bars. The technique of swings improves considerably.

10.2.6 The 'Horse' Training Device

Another very useful training device used by the Russian national team is the handle-less horse (Figure 64). The small attachment on the ordinary horse automatically puts the gymnast in a situation where he physically is bound to put his hands on the body of the horse properly (in parallel).

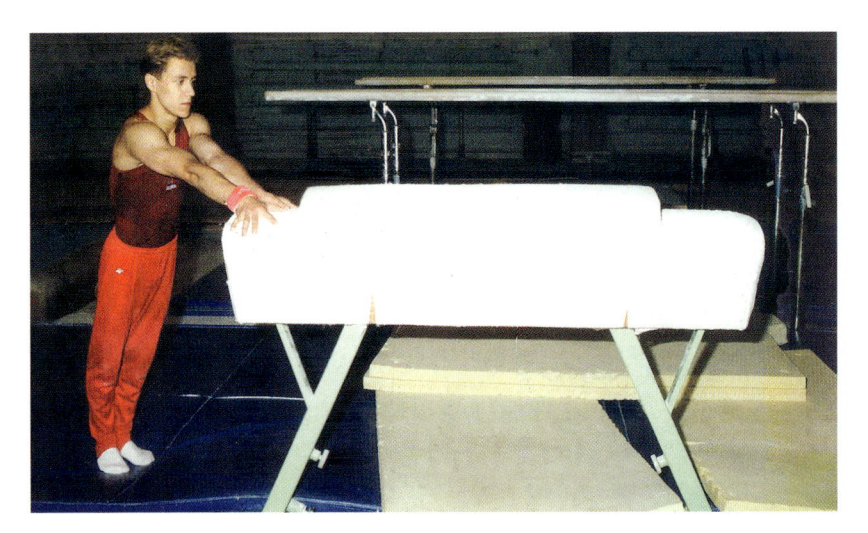

Figure 64 – *Training aid for the pommel horse*

On this device he performs circles in crosswise support facing inwards and outwards, and a number of Magyar and Sivado passes. This, along with the previous device, represents an effective technical means of implementing the concept of an artificial controlled environment and of our principle of 'exceeding development'.

10.2.7 The 'Vault' Device

An increase in the volume and intensity of jump/vault loads with powerful interaction with support of a 'shock' nature often leads to over-loading and injury to the support-motor apparatus. There arise contradictions between the need to increase the vault load for enhancing the training effect and the limited motor possibilities of gymnasts, the impossibility of fully using their motor potential in a situation of the standard gymnastics equipment.

To resolve these contradictions in training the national team we have used the support vault training device. It is a modified system of the 'trampoline-foam rubber pit' and includes a normal trampoline set into the floor and the body of the horse fixed to it with a pile of mats placed on it and an ordinary foam rubber pit with foam rubber mats piled on top of it for landing (Figure 65). A hung harness is placed above the body of the horse.

Figure 65 – *Training aid for the vault*

After several jumps on the trampoline the gymnasts accumulate the necessary horizontal speed, jump on to the pile of mats, thrust off the mats, perform in flight the required form of movement (for instance, 2.5 forward somersaults, as shown in the photograph) and land in safe conditions. They thereby reproduce the structure of simple and complex support vaults in simplified conditions.

This device is an effective auxiliary means of improving the technique of both basic and more complex support vaults. The conditions of performing complex forms of movement in flight, adequate for support vaults of top complexity, are here substantially facilitated by excluding a hard shock interaction with the standard supports (board, horse) and the possibility of gaining external assistance from the harness. What is equally important is that gymnasts do not lose any power on the run up. This enables them significantly to increase the number of attempts, and thereby the volume and intensity of technical training in support vaults and to carry out more targeted work on technique of support vaults without overloading their support-motor apparatus and substantial energy expenditure.

10.2.8 Pneumatic Training Apparatus

To resolve the same contradictions indicated in the previous section, it is useful to use as additional training means the various pneumatic training aid apparatus with regulated resilience (PTA) [26]. Pneumatic training aids are an additional cover for the apparatus on which the compressed air is used as the working body.

We have justified in our various works [61, 90, 63, 91] the effectiveness of using a PTA complex for training top-class gymnasts; it covers pneumatic cover for the acrobatic runway, a pneumatic springboard, pneumatic horse and pneumatic mats (Figure 66).

Research has demonstrated that the coefficient of PTA hardness can be greater, less or equal in relation to standard apparatus. With fixed air pressure in PTA working boxes the magnitude of the coefficient of hardness does not depend on the place of application of effort. By contrast with standard equipment the effort of interaction with support in PTA conditions is spread more evenly over the surface of parts of the gymnast's body (soles of the feed, palms of the hands), which ensures an optimal regime of thrusting off the support.

The resilient qualities of the PTA can be regulated practically at any step by changing the air pressure in the working boxes. The PTA enables the gymnast to determine and create optimal conditions for learning and improving technique of jump exercises and develop physical qualities. For each specific gymnast we may determine the optimal pressure in the PTA working boxes with the aid of special tests.

MATERIAL-TECHNICAL PROVISION

a) Pneumatic track

b) Pneumatic springboard

c) Pneumatic vault

d) Pneumatic bar

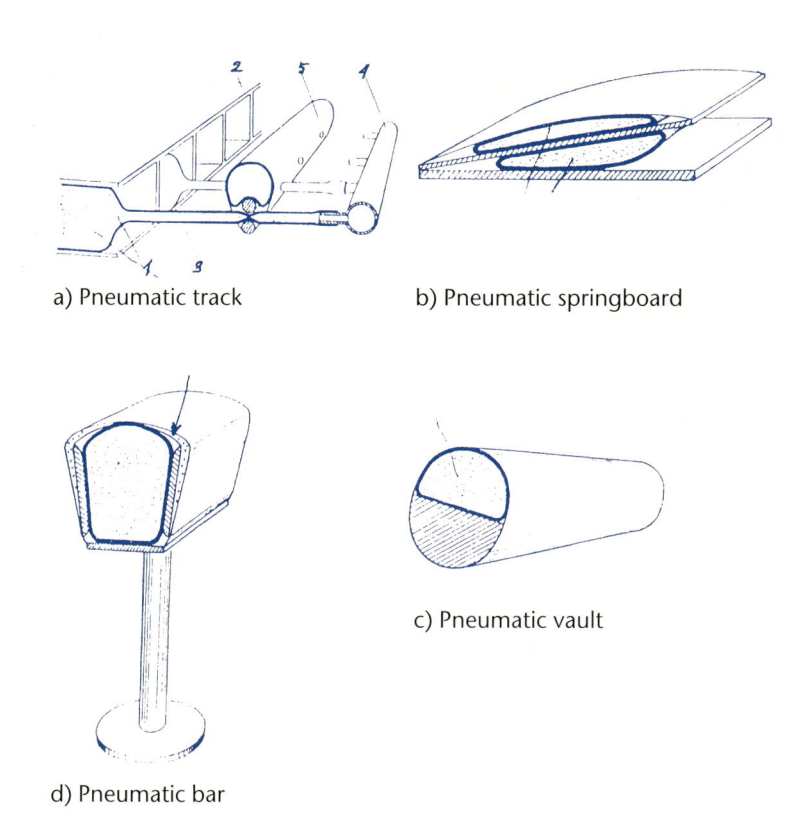

Figure 66 – *Pneumatic training aid with adjustable elasticity boxes; 1) air camera, 2) cover, 3) air inlets, 4) main pipe, 5) pressure structure*

After attaining the required effect the apparatus's resilience can be gradually brought up to competition standard, then hardened even more and, after that, returned to standard conditions. This enables us to use the classical didactic sequence of 'from simple to complex', using alternating transfers that 'pump up' the process of learning which acquires a certain stagnation when constantly using the standard equipment and apparatus. Here we create optimal surplus, when the conditions of competitive standard no longer represent the most complex for gymnasts.

10.2.9 Biomechanical Mount

For stretching and relaxing the muscles after loads we recommend biomechanical stimulation as elaborated by V.T.Nazarov [47]. This device works with the help of a biomechanical mount of the author's construction (Figure 67). We have used it for many years in the training of the national team. It consists in the following. The gymnast puts his foot on the vibrating working area of the mount and it gives him active springing movements normally used when stretching. The book written on the mount gives far more detail of its construction, methods of application and the mechanism of the effect of accelerating the stretching and restoring of working muscles after loads [47].

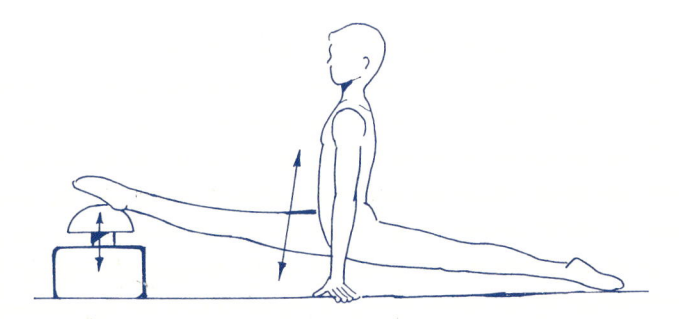

Figure 67 – *Training aid for stretching*

10.2.10 Electro-stimulation of the Muscles

It is useful to use a device for artificially activating the working muscles (I.P.Ratov) as a technical means of learning and correcting direct faults while doing exercises of varying complexity [52].

In a series of experiments we carried out at training camps we tested the effectiveness of this device, using a special construction for electro-stimulation training [62, 63]. The method consists in the following. A stimulating electro-signal (MMS impulse) is given at the moment needed and, under the action of this signal the muscles contract independent of the gymnast. The EMS impulse may be given through wires or by radio-signal. In that case the gymnast wears a light belt to which a miniature radio transmitter is fitted (Figure 68).

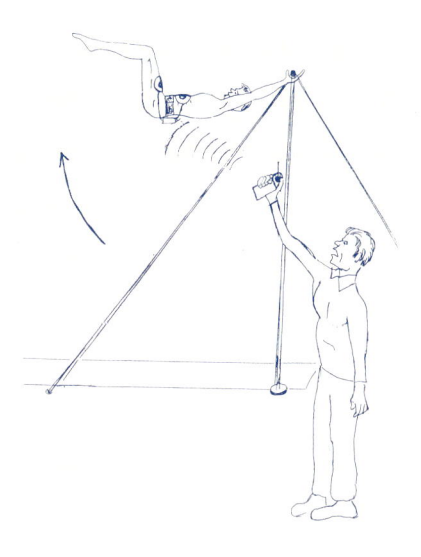

Figure 68 – *Electro-stimulator for working muscles in movement (Patov)*

We have used this method in various motor regimes for averting and removing direct faults, as well as for increasing the contracting effect of the muscles when performing complex technical actions. In our experiments we held single and multiple sessions of electro-stimulation using both wires and the radio-telemetric systems that provided stimulation EMS impulses on various muscles groups simultaneously and consecutively.

We found that the use of this method enables us to improve the biomechanical and technical characteristics, as well as assessing performance of target exercises. We established that the most positive effect occurs not at the moment of communicating EMS impulses, but when executing target exercises immediately after holding the EMS session. Evaluation of the movement as a whole increases on average by 12.8%, and flight time by 4.3%. We successfully tested the effectiveness of using this device as a means of obviating and removing conservative technical mistakes, as well as a technical means of programmed learning of exercises of varying complexity through linear teaching programmes. We justified the neuro-physiological mechanism from the established effect [63].

This electro-stimulation method may also be used to develop strength in the required muscle groups (Y.M.Kots) [35]. The method is similar to that described above, but by contrast with it the electro-stimulation training of the muscles is done in rest. Under the effect of EMS impulses the gymnast's muscles automatically contract without deliberate effort by the gymnast himself (without his direct will). In experiments done with the USSR men's national team we detected a significant growth in muscular strength when learning and improving static strength exercises, such as the cross, horizontal support, front hanging lever, etc. The method and its mechanism are described in detail in the literature (in Russian) [10].

10.2.11 Biomechanical Massage

In the Russian team we use a biomechanical recovery programme of wave pneumatic massage for recovery after training loads and treating injuries of the support-motor apparatus. This programme has been worked out and manufactured by the Biomechanical firm (Samara). It is a logical development of the direction associated with pneumatic apparatus-training devices with regulated resilience.

The programme is an automated biomechanical system in which all the parameters of running wave (speed, impulse frequency, amplitude and time) are set and controlled by a micro-processor. It is intended for general and local wave massage (therapeutic and sporting) for various zones of the body (spine, chest, stomach, hips, shins, feet, circular massage of the upper and lower extremities, the collar zone). It reproduces four major forms of hand massage (vibration, pressing, kneading, stroking). The routine of a pneumo-wire and programme control enables the programme substantially to extend the possibilities of classical hand massage.

In constructing the programme it was based on biomechanical resonance discovered by F.K.Agashin [1], where there is a sharp growth in nerve-muscle activity under the impact of elastic wave fluctuations of a non-linear structure. Wave massage exerts an effect within the range of frequencies of biomechanical resonance of the muscles (mainly from 7 to 20 Hertz).

Wave massage intensifies peripheral blood circulation, lightens the work of the heart, activates digestion, accelerates the healing of fibres and reduces the time of the rehabilitation period after injury.

MATERIAL-TECHNICAL PROVISION

The principle of action of the stimulator is based on transformation of pulsation of electric pressure into pulsation of compressed air consistently driven by a compressor into the system of elastic pneumo-boxes, which creates fluctuating movements of the elastic surface.

A micro-compressor provides the control signal with set parameters. The signal is a programmed succession of electrical impulses which turn into a running wave with the help of rapid-acting electrical pneumo-valves.

The programme consists of an electronic pneumo-dispersing block with a micro-processor, compressor, set of pneumatic cuffs for circular massage of the extremities, pneumo-covers for massaging the front and back surface of the trunk (we use a massage chair in standard modification) (Figure 69).

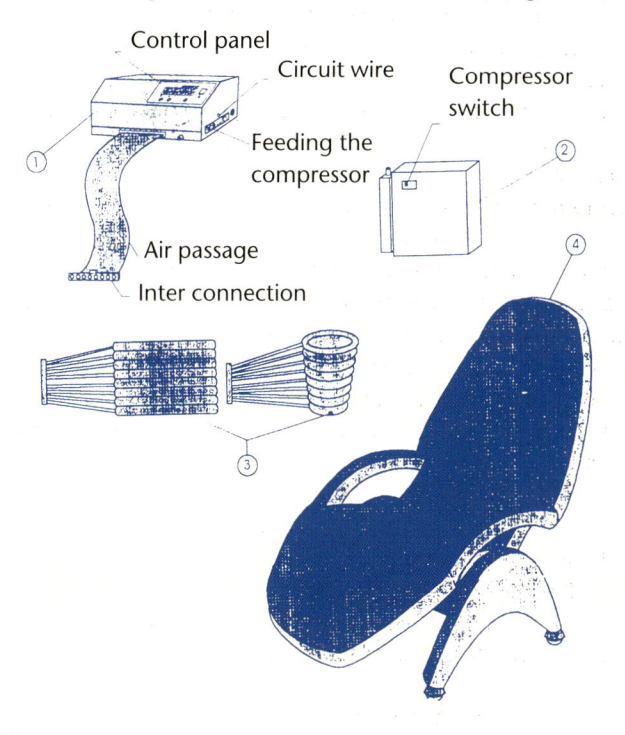

Figure 69 – *Equipment for wave biomechanical massage; 1) electro-pneumo distribution block, 2) compressor, 3) massage straps, 4) massage chair*

The programme works as follows. Compressed air with a pressure of up to 1 atmosphere comes from the compressor on to the electronic block in which it is redistributed. Then the air is let into the system of elastic pneumo-boxes fitted into the cuffs, covers or chair. Successively filled with compressed air these elastic boxes create the effect of a running wave. Its parameters (frequency, amplitude, speed) are programmed in a strictly set order. It depends on the chosen type and method of wave massage selected through pressing a button on the electronic block control panel.

The whole procedure of wave pneumo-massage is controlled by a micro-processor (micro-computer) into which programme 16 wave massage options are set. The length of a single standard session is 15 minutes, after which the programme automatically switches off.

Technical characteristics of the programme:
- supply from alternating current 220V source;
- power required 250 Watts;
- speed of wave dispersal 0.01-0.05m/s;
- length of resilient wave 0.03-0.5 m/s;
- frequency of mechanical impulses 1.0-30 Hertz;
- session time 15 minutes;
- technical pause between sessions 2 minutes;
- programme mass with all elements – no more than 20 kg.

The programme is safe, convenient and simple to deal with. It is approved in clinical and sports practice, as well as in the Centre for training cosmonauts at Zvezdny. It is recommended for use by the Ministry of Health of the Russian Federation.

10.2.12 Video-analysis

For analysing and pedagogically modelling the technique of exercises it is necessary to use video-analysis systems which are today manufactured by many firms. From 1992 the Russian national team has used the Russian-made 'Kinex' computerised programme [65]. The programme consists of a video-recorder, a video-monitor, personal computer with standard design (system block, monitor, keyboard, mouse, printer). Interface is done through a video-card mounted in the computer's system block (Figure 70).

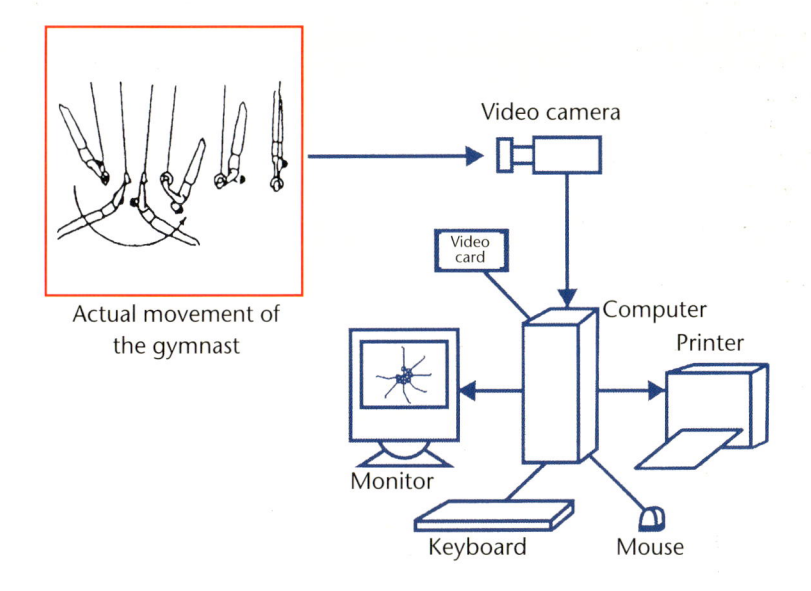

Figure 70 – *Scheme of a video analysis system*

The program works as follows. An exercise performed by a particular gymnast is recorded on a video-recorder. The video recording is reproduced on the video-monitor frame by frame using a stop frame. Each frame is numbered by an operator using the mouse. This is done by running the mouse cursor over the projection of joint centres of rotation of the selected model of the gymnast's body (see, for example, Figure 15). By pressing the mouse button two coordinates of points are put into the computer's memory. Altogether up to 23 points can be numbered in each frame. Then we use the program provision which enables us to:

- examine the stick figures of the element (in straight and reverse directions, by frame, in slowed and accelerated reproduction, as well in the actual time scale, in the form of drawn countourograms of the gymnast's movement, countourograms with the skeleton or finger schemes) generated by the computer through the given video-numeration;

- detect and record the margin and control positions in the phase structure of movement;
- draw in and colour the backgrounds and edit necessary frames and the videogram as a whole;
- call up the trajectories of any of the 18 basic points of the gymnast's body model;
- consider the kinematic characteristics of movement of any of the 18 points, any lines passing through those points, and the angles formed by them;
- compose a statistical model of the kinematic and technical structure of the element;
- make an automated comparison of the parameters of technique of the actual gymnast with the statistical model.

The 'Kinex' program is sufficiently reliable and relatively simple to deal with. Its possibilities enable us to make an applied pedagogical-biomechanical analysis of the technique of most gymnastic exercises (see Chapter 7.5). More detailed information about modern video-analysis systems may be obtained from the literature (in Russian).

10.2.13   Teaching Machine

One of the contradictions of the process of teaching and perfecting the technique of gymnastic exercises (especially basic) is the need to minimise technical errors, their precise and immediate diagnosis with swift correction – on the one hand, and the impossibility of ensuring adequate feed-back in the 'coach-gymnast' system in normal circumstances – on the other.

To resolve these contradictions when learning and perfecting the technique of basic exercises it is expedient to use a teaching machine which may teach by itself without the coach's involvement [17].

The optimum general programme of a target exercise comes from a teaching machine in the shape of a metallic 'copier' (simulator) with which the base point of the gymnast's body is strongly fastened. We insert into the machine's memory the model values of joint angles within the limit positions of the phase structure of the exercise. Information about their current actual values is fed into the control mechanism of the teaching machine from goniometers fixed to the axes of joints in which the gymnast performs principal control movements (Figures 71 and 72).

MATERIAL-TECHNICAL PROVISION

The information offered to the gymnast is his compulsory movement to the general programme of movement with the help of the teaching machine motor. Here a compulsory change in body orientation relative to the axis of rotation of the apparatus occurs independent of the will and effort of the gymnast. The gymnast's movement serves as his motor response to this – ie the programme he is performing of changing body position.

Within the limit positions the control mechanism of the teaching machine compares the actual values of the joint angles with the model (target). If they coincide, the movement continues; if not, it automatically stops. The movement to the general programme is restored only after these values coincide as a result of active searching movements in the control joints – ie after the gymnast himself removes the mistake committed.

From the point of view of biomechanics, psychology and education what is important here is that the gymnast stops automatically immediately after committing an error and must himself eliminate it. Otherwise the compulsory movement to the general programme is not renewed.

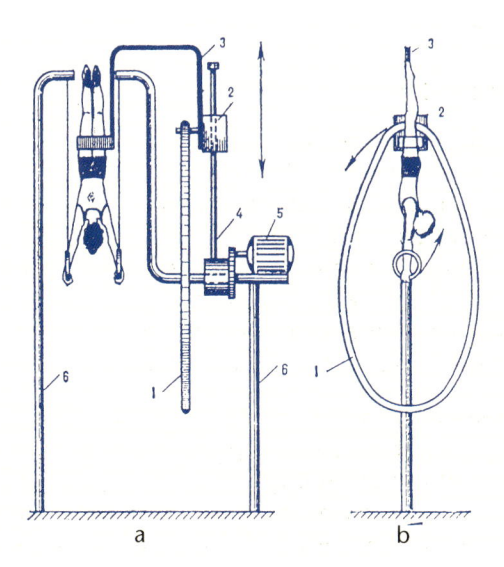

Figure 71 – *Principle scheme of a training aid; 1 – general action programme; 2 – carriage; 3 – bolt; 4 – directing bar; 5 – electromotor; 6 – support stands*

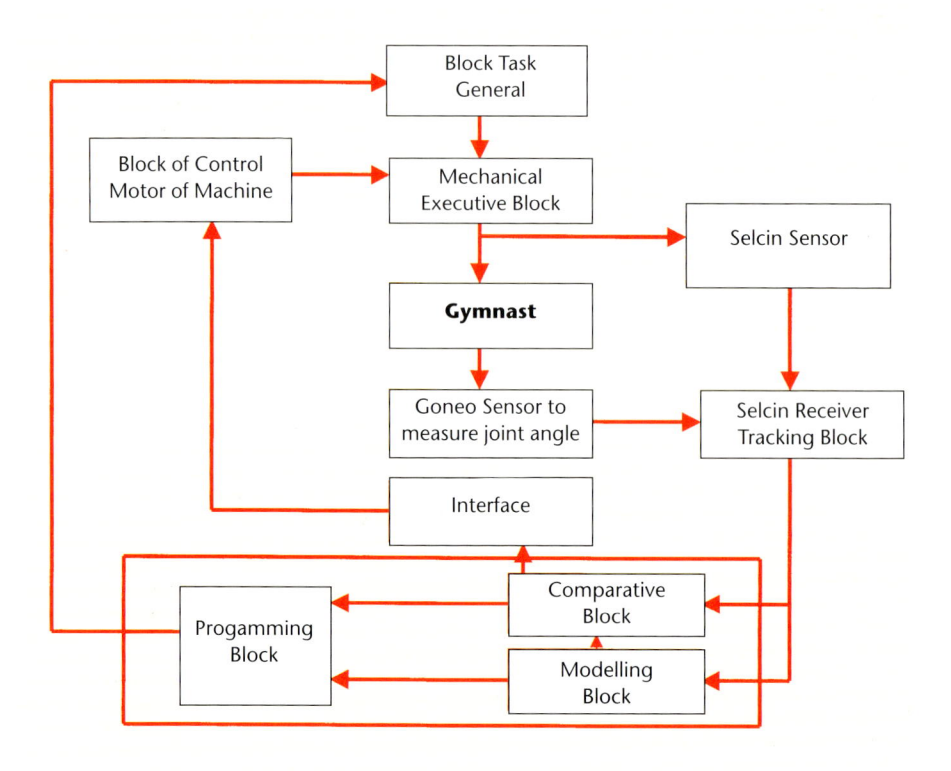

Figure 72 – *Flowchart explaining the functions of the teaching machine*

The pedagogical experiments we have done demonstrated a high pedagogical effectiveness of this teaching machine when learning simple and complex exercises on various apparatus. The number of sessions and of attempts spent on teaching basic exercises when using this machine are shortened several times, while evaluation for performance increases on average by 1.5 times.

Other auxiliary equipment is used in training the Russian national team. All the devices are known, described in detail in the specialist literature and therefore need no further commentary.

Conclusion

In conclusion we would note that in the twenty first century we expect a further growth in the complexity of competitive programmes and a leap forward in ensuring the safety of gymnastics training. We expect the emergence of new constructions of apparatus and effective additional training methods, safety, training devices and recovery programmes.

We are confident of a merger of teaching machines and video-analysis programmes. These new systems will be able to operate in the 'donor-recipient' regime. Gymnasts whose technique will be assessed by experts as standard will be filmed by video-camera, and their movements will automatically be enumerated and entered into the computer's memory as an integrated model in an actual time scale.

At the same time, the gymnast 'loaded' into a teaching machine will have to perform a general programme of movement of a standard gymnast and be tuned into the technical standard by his control movements, controlled by the machine. Compulsory movements in a general programme of movement, will be done with the help of a teaching machine, motor controlled by computer. It will correct the individual integrated model depending on the gymnast's individual peculiarities (mass-inertia characteristics, SPP level, psycho-physiological characteristics) and control the course of mastery of movement in an automatic regime without the coach's interference.

Single construction will give way in the new generations of teaching machines to massive copiers simulating the general programme of movement for each specific gymnastics element. This will ensure the reproduction of the general programme of movement of any gymnastics exercise. For this initially, it will be enough to simultaneously control just two parameters – distance from the axis of rotation to the base point, and the angle of turn of the gymnast's body [63]. We have already worked out such a construction. It remains to put it into practice. For that we need serious sponsors who love gymnastics and are ready to invest in it.

The authors express the hope bordering on confidence that the theory, methodology and technology of training top-class Russian gymnasts as set out in this book will be used not only by gymnasts, but that it will find application in other sports as well.

Bibliography

1. Agashin F.K. Biomechanics of shock movements. – M.: FiS, 1977

2. Anochin P.K. Forestall reflection of reality//Questions of philosophy – 162, N 7. C.31-36

3. Anochin P.K. Main questions of the functional systems theory. – M.: Science, 1980. 196p

4. Arkaev L.Y., Alexandrov A.S., Suchilin N.G., Tcheburaev V.S. Experience in the preparation of the All-around World Champion Dmitry Belozertchev.// Sports-Science Newspaper – 1984 N 4

5. Arkaev L.Y., Kachaev V.I. Morning training in the preparation of the gymnasts prior to competitions.// Sports-Science Newspaper – 185. N2. P17-18

6. Arkaev L.Y., Kachaev V.I., Tcheburaev V.S. Specifics of the gymnasts' competitive regime// Sports-Science Newspaper – 1985. N5. P-8 -11

7. Arkaev L.Y., Kachaev V.I., Tcheburaev V.S. Building the pre-competition stage of the preparation for major competitions in gymnastics// Sports-Science Newspaper – 1985. N 6. P.15-20

8. Arkaev L.Y. Integrated preparation of the gymnasts (National team) – Autoref. Dis. Cand. Ped. science – S.Pb., 1994-25p.

9. Arkaev L.Y., Suchilin N.G., Methodological bases of the contemporary systems of the preparation of top level gymnasts.//Theory and practice of physical culture. 1997. N11. P. 17-25

10. Belov E.V. Electro-simulative training of muscle system for top class gymnasts – Autoref. Dis. Cand. Ped. Science – M.:1974. – 25p.

11. Bernshtein N.A. Essays on physiology of movements and physiology of activity. – M.: Medicine, 1966. – 349p.

12. Bertalanfi L. History and state of general theory of systems//Systematic research: Annual. – M. Science, 1973. P.20-37

13. Big Soviet Encyclopaedia. V.XXII. M.: Soviet Encyclopaedia, 1976-639 p.

14. Verhoshanskii U.B. Basics of the special preparation for strength in sport. – M.: PhyS,1970. – 158p.

15. Gaverdovskii U.K. Complicated gymnastics movements and learning them. Dis. Dr. Ped. Science. – M., 1986-689 p.

16. Gaverdovskii U.K. "…and sails the ship"// Theory and practice of physical culture. 1997. N11. P. 47-54

17. Gostev E.B., Suchilin N.G. Training machines of adaptive type applied during technical preparation of the gymnasts// Gymnastics: Annual. – M., 1981, Issue 1. P. 47-54

18. Artistic Gymnastics. Men's Code of Points. FIG, 1996

19. Artistic Gymnastics. Men's Code of Points. FIG, 2000

20. Artistic Gymnastics. Women's Code of Points. FIG, 2000

21. Gymnastics All-around./Under general order. U.K. Gaverdovskii. – M.: PhS, 1997

22. Donskoi D.D., Zaciorskii V.M., Biomechanics: Textbook for Physical Education Institutes. – M.: PhS, 1979. 263 p.

23. Diatchkov V.M. Reliability Basics of the technical mastery of the sportsmen. – M.: PhS, 1974.

24. Evseev S.P. Theory and Methodology of creating active motion with set target: Dis. Dr. Ped. Science in the form of scientific report – M., 1995

25. Epishin N.D. Motion and state of the body of the gymnast//Special Technical means in the education and training of the sportsmen: Collection Scientific training. – Malahovka, MOGIFK, 1986. C.30-39

26. Zainkin V.G., Saveliev V.C., Suchilin N.G. Attention: pneumatic apparatus! // Gymnastics: Collection. – M., 1982, Issue 2. P. 50-52

27. Zemskov E.A. Management of the training loads in the weekly cycle of preparation of highly qualified gymnasts. – Textbook for students, specialising in Gymnastics. – M.,1982. – 60 p.

28. Zinkovskii V.S. Research of the dynamics of the human movements with the help of computer//Biophysics, 1979, T.XXIV.-Issue 2. P. 312-317

29. Yordanskaya F.A. Regularity of long-term adaptation of the body of top-level sportsmen to tensed muscular activity and evaluation of the special capacity for work, in various sports: Collection Scientific Training. – M., 1993. P.6-27

30. Ipolitov U.A. Training with gymnastics movements based on their models//Theory and Practice of Physical Education – 1987, Number 11.C.41-43

31. Kalinin E.A. Niklopets M.N. Palyi V.I., Schkola S.I., Kaduirov V.A., Kuznetsova E.N., Gladuisheva E.S. System of psychological control in individual sports//Metodical recommendations. – M., BNIIFK, 1985.-14p.

32. Kachaev V.I. Building of the pre-competition stage in the preparation of top level gymnasts, taking into account the specifics of the competition specifics. – Autoref. Diss.cand. Ped. Science. – M., 1986

33. Korenberg V.B. Quality Kinaesiological analyses as pedagogical mean in sport: Dis. Dr.Ped. Science. – M., 1986

34. Korenev G.V. Introduction into human mechanics. – M.: Science, 1977. – 204p.

35. Kots. Y.M. Electro-stimulating training of the muscular system // Materials scientific-methodical conference on the problem "Medico-biological ground of the system of physical education of high school students". Kaunas, 1975. P. 82-85

36. Krauder N. About the difference between linear and branching

programming //Programmed training abroad: Collection articles/ Edited by Tichonov I.I. – Hig School, 1968. P.58-68

37. Kuznetsov V.V., Novykov A.A. Basic direction of theoretical and experimental research in contemporary system of the preparation of sportsmen//Theory and Practice of Physical Culture – 1971, N 1.

38. Kuhn T. The Structure of Scientific Revolutions / Translation from English. – M., 1975

39. Kurierov N.A. Phases in the actions of the gymnasts. – M.: PhS, 1961. – 121p.

40. Leontiev A.N. Activities of the consciousness, personality. – M.: Politizdat, 1977. – 303 p.

41. Mac-Callock U. Reliability of biological systems. In the book: Self-organisation of systems /Translation from English. – M.: World, 1964

42. Matveev L.P. Basics of Sports Training : Text book for Students in Physical Education. – M.: PhS, 1977.- 271p.

43. Menchin U.V. Gymnastics apparatus and equipment of gyms: Methodical recommendation. – Malachovka: MOGIPK, 1988

44. Menchin U.V. Physical preparation aimed at top achievements in sports of complicated co-ordination : Dissertation, Dr. Ped. Science. – M., 1992

45. Micheev B.V., Suchilin N.G. Regularity of difficulty scale in the exercises on Rings, containing big swings//Gymnastics: Annual. – M., 1980, Issue 2. P. 38-41

46. Nazarov V.T. Biomechanical basis of the training aimed at learning non cyclic exercises (as in Artistic Gymnastics): Dis. Dr.Ped. Science. – M., 1974

47. Nazarov V.T. Bio-mechanical stimulation: reality and dreams. – Minsk, 1986. – 95 p.

48. Pask. G. Training as a process of creating managing systems//Cybernetics and problems of Education: Collection Translations / Edited by Berg A.M. – M.: Progress, 1970. P.25-85

49. Pershin V.B., Levando V.A., Susdalnitskii R.S., Kuzmin S.N. Phenomenon of the disappearing of the immune-globulin from the plasma of the periphery blood and biological secretion following sun-maximal physical load. – Diploma Opening of the USSR State Committee for Invention and Discovery, 1987. N. 345

50. Psychology Dictionary. M., Pedagogy- Press, 1966. – 439p.

51. Rapoport A. Principe Mathematical isomorphism in the common theory of systems// Systematic research: Collection. – M., Science, 1973. P. 158-172.

52. Raitov I.P. Methodology of the concept "Artificial Managing System" and possibilities for its realisation in the process of preparation of the sportsmen// Methodological problems in improving the system of sports preparation of highly qualified sportsmen/ Collection scientific works VNIIPK, M, 1984. P. 127-146

53. Rozin E.U. Some theoretical – methodical aspects of the pedagogical control of the physical state and level of preparation of sportsmen//Theory and Practice of Physical Culture. – 1997. N 11. P.41-43

54. Sechenov I.M., Selected works in Philosophy and Pedagogy/ Edited by Kaganov V.M. – M.: Gospolizdat, 1947. – 645p.

55. Skinner B. Science of Education and Art of Education/ Translation from English. – M.: High School, 1968. – 83p.

56. Artistic Gymnastics: Text Book for Institute for Physical Culture / Edited by Gaverdovsky U.K. and Smolevsky V.M. – M.: PhS, 1979. – 328p.

57. Suslov F.P., Gippenreiter E.B. Preparation of sportsmen in mountainous conditions. – M.: Olimpia- Press, 2000. – 173p.

58. Suchilin N.G. Research of gymnastics exercises with increasing difficulty and ways of managing its creation and development (based on examples from High Bar dismounts). – Dis. Cand. Ped. Science. – M., 1972 – 150p.

59. Suchilin N.G. Gymnast in the air. – M.: PhS, 1978. – 120p.

60. Suchilin N.G. Bases of perspective-prognostic planning of the process of improving technical mastery of the gymnasts// Gymnastics: Collection. – M., 1980, Issue 2. – p.42-48

61. Suchilin N.G. Saveliev V.S., Zaikin V.G., Andrianov N.E. Efficiency of the methods of using pneumatic apparatus- training aids in the education-training process// Scientific bases of management of the preparation of top class sportsmen : thesis's report Russian Scientific Conference. – M., 1986. P. 231-232.

62. Suchilin N.G., Usatyi V.G., Selivanova T.G., Electro stimulation of movements//Gymnastics: Annual – M., 1986. Issue 1. Page 42-48

63. Suchilin N.G. Creation and improvement of technical mastery in exercises of progressive difficulty.-Dis. Dr. Ped. Science . – M.,1989. – 799p.

64. Suchilin N.G. Arkaev L.Y., Saveliev V.S. Pedagogy-biochemical analyses of techniques of sports movements based on programme-apparatrus video-complex.//Theory and Practice Physical culture. – 1996, N4. Page 12-20

65. Suchilin N.G., Saveliev V.S., Popov G.I. Optical-electronic methods of measuring human movements. – M.:FON, 2000. – 127 page.

66. Talyisina N.F. Theoretical problems of programmed training. – M: MGU, 1969.-132 page.

67. Theory and Methodology of Physical Education: Text book for Institutes of Physical Education./Editing of Matveeva L.P., Novikova A.D. – M.:PhiS 1976, Volume II. – page 302

68. Theory of Sport: Text Book for Institutes for Physical Culture./ Edited by Paltoniva V.N. – Kiev, High School, 1987. – page 422

69. Ukran M. Methodology of training gymnasts. – M.: PhS, 1971

70. Philosophical Encyclopaedic Dictionary- M. Progress, 1983.-page 840.

71. Hasin L.A., Burian S.B., Minkov S.B., Rafalovich A.B. IT of the Physical Culture and Sport and expertise technologies// Theory and Practise of the Physical Culture. – 1996, n 4 Page 7-11

72. Hasin L.A. co-authorship. Mathematical modelling of human movements- Report on scientific and research work – Malahovka NIITMGAFK, 1996 N of State reg. 0194 ccc7381

73. Cheburaev B.S. Scientific-methodical back-up of the preparation of National Artistic Gymnastics Teams//Theory and Practice of Physical Culture. – 1997, N 11. P. 44-46

74. Cheburaev B.S., Kalachev O.K., Muravieva L.F. Mechanisms of functional adaptation to extreme conditions, created in the process of preparation of top level gymnasts//Evaluation of specific work-capacity of the sportsmen in various sports: N. beg. Tr. – M.,1993. C. 158-165.

Foreign Literature

75. Age Group Development Program. FIG, CD Rom.

76. Arampatzis, A, Bruggemen, G.P., (2000) Storage and Return of Elastic Energy by Gymnastic Apparatus. In: Proceedings of the FIG Medico Technical Symposium Apparatus and Injuries. Tianjin (CHN) 15-16. 10.199, 17-28

77. Biesterfeld H.J., Jr (1974) Twisting Mechanics I, II. In: Gymnast No 16 (4), p 28-31, No. 16 (6/7), p. 46-47.

78. Brewin, M., Kerwin, D., (2000) Elastic Elements in Gymnastic Apparatus and their Relation to Mechanical Loading and Performance. In: Proceedings of the FIG Medico Technical Symposium Apparatus and Injuries. Tianjin (CHN) 15-16.10.199, 39-46

79. Bruggeman G.P. (1983) Cinematic and Kinetics of the Backward Somersault Take-off from the Floor. In: Biomechanics. YIII-B, p.793-800

80. Bruggeman G.P. (2000) Mechanical Load in Artistic Gymnstics and its Relation to Apparatus and Performance. In.: Proceedings of the FIG Medicao Technical Symposium Apparatus and Injuries. Tianjin (CHN), 15-16.10.1999, 29-38

81. Code de Pointage FIG Artistic Gymnastics – FIG, 1996

82. Code de Pointage FIG Artistic Gymnastics – FIG, 2000

83. George G.S. (1980) Biomechanics of Women's Gymnastics. Englewoof Cliffs: Prentice Hall.

84. Gluck M. (1979) So You Want to Twist: Part I. Ontario Gymnast No. 31. 3.14-20

85. Hay J.G. (1978) The Biomechanics of Sport Techniques 2nd ed. Englewood Cliffs: Prentice Hall. P. 156-161

86. Hoffman D. (2000) The Use of Methodical Training Equipment ("Aids") for the Development of the Prerequisites and the Limitation of the Loads on the Support and Motor System. In: Proceedings of the FIG Medico Technical Symposium Apparatus and Injuries. Tianjin (CHN) 15-16. 10.1999, 89-92

87. Karacsony I., Cuk I (1998) Pommel Horse Exercises – Methods, Ideas, Curiosities, History. 134p.

88. Schweizer L. (2000) Recent Results Concerning the Testing Procedures of Competition Gymnastics Equipment In.: Proceedings of the FIG Medico Technical Symposium Apparatus and Injuries. Tianjin (CHN) 15-16. 10.1999, 67-76

89. Smolevskiy V. Gaverdovskiy I. Tratado General de Gimnasia Artistica Deportiva. Deporte & Entrenamiento. Editorial Paidotribo, Barcelona 385 p.

90. Suchilin N.G., Zaikin V.G., Saveliev V.S. (1988) Pneumatic Training Apparatus with Adjustable Elasticity. In: Abstracts of 6th International Symposium in Biomechanics in Sport – Montana State University P.16

91. Suchilin N.G. (2000) The Pneumatic Training Apparatus with Adjustable Elasticity and their Using in Gymnastics. In: Proceedings of the FIG Medico Technical Symposium Apparatus and Injuries Tianjin. (CHN) 15-16.10.1999, 77-86

92. Yeadon M.R. The Mechanics of Twisting Somersaults (1984) Ph.D. Dissertation Loughborough University of Technology 553.p

93. Zadeh L.A. Fuzzy Sets (1965) In: Information and Control – Vol 8 No 3 P. 338-353

Photo & Illustration Credits

Cover design: Jens Vogelsang
Cover photo: Volker Minkus
Technical Translation: Vera Atkinson

Photo Credits: Eileen Langsley and the Russian Gymnastics Federation

Acknowledgements

The authors wish to acknowledge the contribution made in funding, editing and creating this English version by the United Kingdom Sports Institute and British Gymnastics.

They wish to especially thank the following individuals: Professor Craig Sharp, Professor Lew Hardy, Dr. Mike Hiley, Dr. Jo Prescott, Bob Currier, Matthew Greenwood, Steve Green, Ngaire Plowman, Mark Young, Martin Reddin, Neil Burton, Paul Hall and Nikolai Liskovich.